Technology Tools in the Social Studies Curriculum

Joseph A. Braun, Jr.
Illinois State University

Phyllis Fernlund
Sonoma State University

Charles S. White
Boston University

Franklin, Beedle & Associates, Incorporated
8536 SW St. Helens Drive, Suite D
Wilsonville, Oregon 97070
http://www.fbeedle.com

President and Publisher	Jim Leisy (jimleisy@fbeedle.com)
Manuscript Editor	Karen Foley
Interior Design and Production	Susan Skarzynski
Cover Design	Tom Sumner
Proofreader	Stephanie Welch
Marketing Group	Victor Kaiser
	Cary Crossland
	Carrie Widman
	Jason Smith
Order Processing	Chris Alarid
	Ann Leisy

Printed in the U.S.A.

Names of all products herein are used for identification purposes only and are trademarks and/or registered trademarks of their respective owners. Franklin, Beedle & Associates, Inc., makes no claim of ownership or corporate association with the products or companies that own them.

Rights and Permissions
Franklin, Beedle & Associates, Inc.
8536 SW St. Helens Drive, Suite D
Wilsonville, Oregon 97070
http://www.fbeedle.com

Library of Congress Cataloging-in-Publication Data

Braun, Joseph A.
　　　Technology tools in the social studies curriculum / Joseph Braun, Jr., Phyllis Fernlund, Charles White.
　　　　　　p.　cm.
　　　Includes bibliographical references.
　　　ISBN 1–887902–06–6
　　　1. Social sciences--Study and teaching (Elementary)--United States--Computer-assisted instruction.　2. Social sciences--Study and teaching (Elementary)--United States--Computer programs.
　　　I. Fernlund, Phyllis M.　II. White, Charles S.　III. Title.
　　　LB1584.B66　1997
　　　372.83'078'5--dc21　　　　　　　　　　　　　　　　　　97–40537
　　　　　　　　　　　　　　　　　　　　　　　　　　　　　　　CIP

Contents

chapter 5 Optical Technologies and Hypermedia · 213

chapter 6 Building Community in the Computer Age — 289

A s fields within education, both social studies and instructional technology can be described with one word: changing. The very nature of social studies is to help students understand that history, geography, civics, and the other social sciences are ways of recording and organizing the changes humans make as civilizations develop. The changes that have occurred in instructional technology over the past twenty-five years are truly stunning. Since the introduction of the microcomputer into classrooms in the early 1980s, we have seen more powerful and speedier hardware produced; software that can make a difference in how and what students learn developed; and, most importantly, millions of computers all over the globe hooked together by the Internet exchange information via multimedia formats.

It is the changing nature of social studies and instructional technology that makes writing a book such as the one you are about to read such a frustrating experience. What seems current and cutting edge today is replaced tomorrow by hardware and software that processes information more effectively, and the day after that something even newer and better comes along. Similarly—although not occurring at as rapid a pace as the development of technology—federal, state, and local mandates to improve social studies curriculum and instruction are constantly being revised and refined. Nonetheless, we have tried to describe some key elements of technology as a tool to support achievement of enduring social studies goals—to help students acquire information from history and the social sciences and build the knowledge necessary to become effective and thoughtful citizens. Specific examples of software that we have described were selected because they are considered classics in social studies education. The descriptions of tools and applications such as databases or multimedia were kept generic enough to be relatively unaffected by revisions in software. The final chapter on the Internet was made as current as possible, but the rapidly changing nature of the Internet makes currency a particularly difficult, if not impossible, issue in authoring a printed text. It could well be that within 10 years all books will be available online on your computer. But for now, we invite you to explore the text to suit your own needs as a social studies educator.

The first two chapters of the text deal with the evolving relationship between computer technology and the social studies curriculum. Changes in the field of social studies are considered along with questions teachers should ask in making decisions about using technology in the social studies curriculum. Chapter 3 takes a look at application software designed for education tasks that have relevance for social studies education. Chapters 4 and 5 are intended to convey a conceptual understanding of the nature and use of the more generic tools of our trade: databases, spreadsheets, and hypermedia. Chapter 6 provides a theoretical and practical look at civic-moral development and the computer. The history of the Internet's development and ways of using the vast resources available through the Internet, also known as the Net, are found in Chapter 7. The final chapter of the book contains lists of resources, including publishers of software products, from which the reader can draw ideas for future use in the classroom.

In an environment of changing social studies mandates and the dynamic nature of technology, we hope the reader will be able to take from this book a basic understanding of the use of technology as a tool for teaching social studies. The teacher who can embrace and accommodate change while still incorporating the best of past practices will profit the most from this book.

Acknowledgments

A work such as this is not the work of just the authors; a number of people played roles behind the scenes and we would like to acknowledge their contributions. First of all we would like to acknowledge the encouragement and contributions of Larry Hannah, Terry Cannings, and Jim Leisy in initiating this publication. During development of the manuscript, research assistance was provided by David Braxton of California State University, San Bernardino. Assistance with identifying software evaluation criteria was contributed by Stephen Rose of the University of Wisconsin. David Dockterman of Tom Snyder Productions provided products for field testing. Walter Parker of the University of Washington shared helpful comments and suggestions, as did Ken Fansler and David Williams of Illinois State University. Tim Dugan of Princeton High School in Cincinnati supplied excellent examples of student-produced, social studies-related newspapers. A special note of appreciation goes to Mary Graham Buxton, a graduate assistant in the College of Education at Illinois State University, for assisting in the identification of the resources listed in the final chapter. We would especially like to add a special note of thanks to our families:

To Anne, with profound appreciation
for all you've shared with me about how
technology can enhance learning and, more importantly,
how my life is enhanced by you and our daughter, Sage Elizabeth.

—J.A.B.

To my children, John and Elisabeth Fernlund.

—P.F.

To my wife, Debbie, and our children,
Alysun and William, with love and gratitude.

—C.S.W.

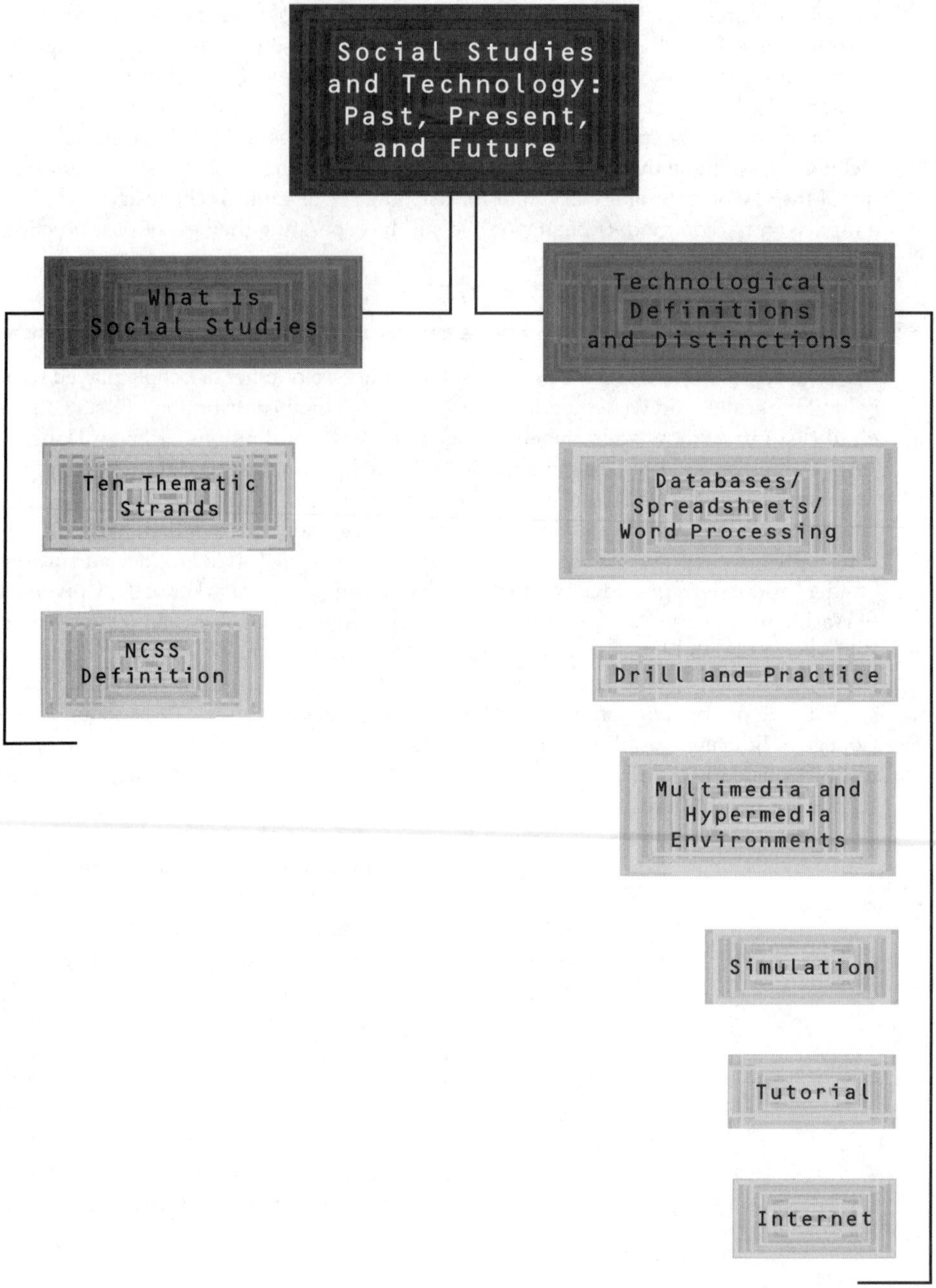

Social Studies
and Technology:
Past, Present,
and Future

What Is
Social Studies

Technological
Definitions
and Distinctions

Ten Thematic
Strands

NCSS
Definition

Databases/
Spreadsheets/
Word Processing

Drill and Practice

Multimedia and
Hypermedia
Environments

Simulation

Tutorial

Internet

chapter 1

Social Studies and Technology

Past, Present, and Future

Today we live in an information-rich society, a society in which the school is one of the many places to learn new skills, locate needed information, and communicate with others. Technology plays a critical role in such a society; it is the driving force behind the Information Age. It is now commonplace for schools in the United States to have computers and videocassette recorders. In some schools, with the help of fiber optics, telephone lines, and satellite technology, students can work with classes in other countries and states, conduct research in libraries thousands of miles away, or read newspapers from around the world. With the arrival of computers, students have access to a tool that is used by most of the business world; a computer can help students communicate, write papers, record data, analyze patterns, prepare budgets, and graphically display their work. Videodiscs and CD-ROMs combine text with photos, music, and narration: animated maps that show population development over time, historic footage from major events and speeches, and 20 encyclopedia volumes on one small disc. The Internet is a development in technology that gives schools easy access to libraries around the world including a wealth of primary source documents from depositories such as the Library of Congress.

As a tool in social studies, technology brings the world to the classroom in more powerful ways than a filmstrip projector or dated textbooks, maps, and encyclopedias can. Technology offers rich content for the social studies as well as a tool for student writing. It also can be used to develop such student skills as analysis, inquiry, and reasoned decision making. The best of social studies technology encourages teamwork and student interaction, two important goals of social studies instruction. But how is a teacher to integrate technology into the curriculum? Research studies reveal that one-third of elementary and secondary school teachers have only 10 hours of computer training. Without instruction in how to use technology, teachers will not be able to successfully use computers as a tool to transform teaching and learning.

Overview

This book is designed to help educators understand different types of technological resources for teaching social studies, plan and evaluate these resources in the curriculum, and examine potential future trends. Chapter 1 provides an overview of past, present, and potential future trends in social studies and introduces resources for further exploration of changing technologies. Chapter 2 provides guidance on how technology and computer software for social studies can place learners in an active role as they pursue social education goals. Chapter 3 focuses on computer software applications for teachers and students to create timelines, design tests and reviews, and prepare graphs or other visual displays. Chapter 4 examines software that functions as a tool—such as programs for word processing, creating and analyzing databases, and generating spreadsheets—and the importance of these particular tools in social studies. Chapter 5 explores multimedia in social studies—the use of optical technologies and hypertext as promoting social studies learning. Chapter 6 considers how technology helps achieve the social studies goals of examining values and making civic-moral decisions in an increasingly diverse classroom, society, and world. Chapter 7 is a look at the history of the Internet, some of the tools that currently can be found on it, and potential future trends in social studies and technology. Chapter 8 concludes the book with a list of resources for using technology as a teaching and learning tool in a social studies classroom.

Social Studies—A Definition

Michael Hartoonian has argued that the American republic "is built upon the principle that the people occupy an important position in government—the office of citizen; thus it is necessary that attention be paid to the education of those who assume this office" (1994). Citizenship education has been an important goal of schools and of the field of social studies for a long time. In the recent curriculum standards from the National Council for the Social Studies (NCSS 1994, 3), the following definition reinforces the emphasis on civic competence:

> Social studies is the integrated study of the social sciences and humanities to promote civic competence.... The primary purpose of social studies is to help young people develop the ability to make informed and reasoned decisions for the public good as citizens of a culturally diverse, democratic society in an interdependent world.

Social studies is an integrative field, drawing knowledge from many disciplines. NCSS has outlined 10 themes with accompanying student performance expectations to provide a framework for the curriculum:

1. culture

2. time, continuity, and change

3. people, places, and environments

4. individual development and identity

5. individuals, groups, and institutions

6. power, authority, and governance

7. production, distribution, and consumption

8. science, technology, and society

9. global connections

10. civic ideals and practices

As you will see when we examine social studies software, societal issues are multidisciplinary and they require students, voters, policy makers, and scholars to draw on knowledge from several fields when searching for solutions. The question "What caused the Civil War in the United States?" can be answered by using information from economics, sociology, political science, and geography as well as history. The same is true for current societal concerns such as the environment, health care, crime, and the criminal justice system. *Charting a Course,* a report by the National Commission on the Social Studies in the Schools, recommends extending these multidisciplinary studies to assist students in seeing the relationships among branches of knowledge: "Social studies provides the obvious connection between the humanities and the natural and physical sciences" (1989, 3). At the state level, California's *History/Social Science Framework* (1988) began a trend to use history, integrated with the humanities and social sciences, as a basis for social studies teaching. The framework states that "video programs, laserdiscs, computer software, and newly emerging forms of educational technology can provide invaluable resources for the teaching of history, geography, economics, and other disciplines" (8). Many states have followed this trend and their curriculum guides reflect a focus on history and geography as well as increased expectations for the use of computer technology to teach social studies. Although debate continues over which disciplines should be emphasized in the social studies, it is truly an interdisciplinary field—a field with many technological resources for the classroom teacher (Brophy and Alleman 1996).

Computer Use in Social Studies Classrooms

When the computer received *Time* magazine's "Machine of the Year" award in 1983, schools quickly began to acquire computers. Hassett found that by 1984, 86 percent of high schools, 81 percent of junior high schools, and 62 percent of elementary schools were using computers. But little of this computer use was affecting the social studies

classroom. Becker's survey (1986) showed only 1 percent of computer use was for social studies; Ehman and Glenn (1987) found that there was little use among social studies teachers because of low levels in teacher training and software availability.

Teachers experienced in using technology help their students reap powerful benefits. Karen Sheingold of the Educational Testing Service found that teachers with technical experience are able to present "more complex material to their students, that they
are acting more as coaches and less as information providers, and that student work
can proceed more independently and in ways that are better tailored to meet individual
needs" (Olson 1992).

Northup and Rooze (1990) conducted a study of 405 teachers who were members
of NCSS. Eighty-four percent of the teachers had access to computers, usually in a computer lab, but only 15 percent had a computer in their classrooms. Of those who had
access to computers, 54.7 percent actually used the computers. Since then, there has
been a substantial increase in the use of technology in social studies teaching. A powerful argument has been made that this trend will only continue to accelerate (Mehlinger
1995). This trend reflects the developmental nature of the integration of computer-based
technology into the schools. In the beginning phase, a school is often concerned with the
acquisition of hardware, and only some of the teachers are involved in learning how to
use the new technology. As the school moves toward a more mature phase, the importance of curriculum-based integration and district-level coordination becomes the focus.

All of the research studies point to the importance of staff development and training in making technology an important part of the social studies classroom. Becker's
recent research (1993) emphasizes the importance of top-down planning for technology. When district level administrators and full-time technology coordinators are involved, the amount of training, the extent of the use of technology, and the way in
which technology is used are all maximized. Becker's study reveals five characteristics
of the teaching environment that help teachers become exemplary users of computers
in their classrooms (1993, 7):

1. The existence of a social network of computer-using teachers at the same school.

2. Sustained use of computers for writing and publishing, industrial arts, or business
   applications.

3. Organized support for staff development, including a full-time computer coordinator.

4. School leadership concerned with equity of access to computers across all categories
   of students rather than mamixmum access for some students and minimum access
   for others.

5. Smaller class sizes and a more favorable student-to-computer ratio.

■ Technological Definitions and Distinctions

The reason the computer is such an exciting educational device is because it is adaptable to a number of instructional purposes. With the explosive expansion of the Internet
and the advent of the latest software developments such as hypermedia, the computer

becomes a tool for teachers and students. To introduce the various instructional software formats, the following provides brief definitions of the most frequently encountered educational software.

Drill and Practice

These programs rely heavily on a question-and-answer format and are intended for reinforcement of specific skills and facts. A game-like format may be employed. Based on behaviorist principles of stimulus and response as defined by the late psychologist B. F. Skinner, drill-and-practice activities promote the acquisition of knowledge or a skill through repeated opportunities to practice whatever it is being learned. Effective drill-and-practice exercises will present material randomly rather than sequentially so the material will not be repeated in the same order the next time the learner uses the software. The use of graphics, color, and sound enhance the attractiveness of a drill-and-practice program. Clear directions and appropriate, positive feedback are other features to consider in judging the worth of drill-and-practice software.

Tutorial

One of the earliest forms of educational social studies software, tutorials allow for a dialogue between the computer and the student; tutorials are particularly effective in engaging the student in new content. Textbook publishing companies are beginning to market tutorials to accompany their traditional social studies textbooks and programs. To be effective, a tutorial should sequentially arrange material into modules that recognize the attention span of the learner, which may be 15 to 20 minutes. (The younger the child, the shorter the attention span.) Branching is characteristic of tutorials where a student's correct response to an objective question will trigger the computer to proceed to new material, or in the case of an incorrect answer, the computer will continue to provide additional work on the material until the student demonstrates he or she has mastered the information.

Simulations

A potent way to make history and geography come alive for students is through simulations. As an instructional strategy, simulations predate computers in social studies education. Whether contrived by a teacher or driven by a computer, a simulation is a controllable world that is particularly motivating for students because of the inherent level of involvement in the experience. In other words, students are engaged in situations based on constructs and representations of reality that are designed to replicate real-life phenomena. Scenarios can range from being a voyager exploring and trapping in the Northwest a century ago who must decide what supplies to bring and how to deal with hardships such as inclement weather or hostile Native Americans, to being a mayor of an environmentally-conscious community who must decide whether to attract an industry that would promote rapid growth but could destroy the quality of life. The software creator presents a simulated world environment that allows students to enter the scenario and make decisions without suffering the repercussions encountered in reality.

Databases/Spreadsheets/Word Processing

These are all examples of tool applications that make possible the generation, manipulation, or communication of vast amounts of data with amazing speed and ease. An electronic database is an organized collection of information not unlike a library's card catalog, many of which are now computerized. Searches can be conducted for either a singular variable or strings of variables with the computer tracking down all requested information. An electronic spreadsheet is a program that divides the computer screen into rows and columns, called cells. Just as with an accountant's worksheet, a spreadsheet program stores numerical and textual information and formulas in these cells. A spreadsheet can be used to predict outcomes based on formulas and perform calculations on the rows and columns of numeric data. Word processing is another important tool; it permits the author to check spelling and compose and revise by electronically cutting and pasting words or phrases without ever lifting a pencil. Sometimes all three of these tools will be combined into a powerful integrated package that includes a graphics program.

Hypermedia Environments

The origin of the word hypermedia finds its antecedent in the term "hypertext," coined by Ted Nelson in the early 1960s (Paske 1990). Originally it meant nonsequential writing or text that branches and allows the reader choices. Nelson later refined his thinking and began using the word hypermedia to describe a unified system of delivering information that allows users to interactively navigate through audio, video, and text. To get a better handle on the connotations of this term, we might look at subsets of the term hypermedia. One subset harkens back to Nelson's original term of hypertext and includes software programs such as *HyperCard*, *LinkWay*, and *HyperStudio*. Another subset consists of Netscape Navigator and Microsoft Internet Explorer and other hypermedia software for use on the Internet.

Hypertext software serves as a tool for constructing, managing, accessing, and communicating information in nonsequential form. In other words, hypertext programs are somewhat like a stack of index cards that can be cross-referenced when the user pushes buttons located on a card. In addition to allowing users to cross-reference other cards in the stack, buttons open windows that provide more detailed information or activate audio-visual equipment such as a videodisc or CD-ROM. Thus, the combination of a hypertext program with audio-visual information becomes a hypermedia environment, which is also known as an interactive multimedia environment.

Interactive multimedia environments can be used in a social studies classroom in three ways: as research tools, as authoring tools for creating individualized learning modules, and as presentation tools. Before considering specific software titles and outcomes, let's complete the picture of hypermedia by examining two of its mediums.

Laser Videodiscs and CD-ROMs

Laser videodiscs and CD-ROMs refer to a special type of software that presents information in an audio-visual format. Essentially, these types of software digitally store information on a flat disc that requires separate equipment to allow the user to access data. Three reasons make this medium an attractive alternative to a book or VCR or cassette tape: 1. large amounts of information can be quickly located and accessed in any sequence; 2. all of this information is found on a small, portable disc; and 3. this software is an amazingly durable medium. This is a social studies teacher's dream—instantaneous access to massive amounts of data that is electronically archived and in a medium capable of withstanding many students handling it time and again. The only limitation of this software is that information cannot be added or changed on CD-ROM or laser videodiscs. They are both "read-only memory."

CD-ROM is an acronym for compact disc read-only memory; a CD-ROM is a disc that is 12 centimeters (about 4¾ inches) across and about 1 millimeter thick. A CD-ROM can contain 550 megabytes (or 550 million characters) of alphanumeric data and digitized images. CD-ROMs that are electronic encyclopedias, such as *Grolier's Electronic Encyclopedia*, are particularly noteworthy for social studies instruction because students can quickly search and analyze information. CD-ROMs store music in larger amounts than their technological relative, the compact audiodisc.

A laser videodisc is a larger platter than the CD-ROM disc, the former being approximately the size of a 33-rpm record, an item quickly disappearing from our culture. While a CD-ROM is used for storing alphanumeric information and individual visual images, a laser videodisc digitally stores continuous video or film footage. These discs are called CLV (constant linear velocity) discs. One format of laser videodiscs, called CAV (constant angular velocity) discs, permits continuous video in combination with individual photographs that can be accessed and arranged any way the user desires. Thus, with CAV, photographs might be interspersed with video footage.

The Internet

The information superhighway is another name for a network of computers that can be conceived of as a spider's web. Hence, the name World Wide Web (WWW) is used to refer to the most interesting area of Internet technology. The Web is intriguing because it is a seemingly vast hypermedia environment. In addition to transmitting graphics, text, and audio data across the Web through fiber-optic cable, satellite transmission, or telephone lines, the Internet supports other uses. Most of the early uses of the Internet, such as e-mail and newsgroups, can now be accessed through Web browser software such as Netscape Navigator or Microsoft Internet Explorer. The Internet is becoming a seamless web of information, and the software to access it is becoming easier to use.

Access to Technology

Equal access to technology is an important policy issue at the district, state, and national levels. Teachers encounter different workplaces in the schools. Some teach in schools that spend far less money per pupil than most industrialized countries in the world. Their textbooks are too few and too old, their rooms have only desks and a chalkboard, and supplies are minimal. These teachers are using the same technology that teachers of earlier centuries used. Compare that workplace to a model technology school (Laskey 1991) with student workstations that include a Macintosh computer, a laserdisc player, a VCR, and a TV monitor. Such a school might use *Compton's Multimedia Encyclopedia* as well as the 40-disc *Encyclopedia of the 20th Century* (CEL Educational Resources), and videodiscs and CDs would be available in a variety of subject areas for student use. Students would be able to engage in science and social studies research projects with students in classrooms in other states and other nations. These two different environments have important consequences for teachers, students, and society.

The information gap and differences in student access to computer technology is growing. Kozol (1991) found that the wealthiest elementary schools have 100 computers available for students. Half of all schools have fewer than 10 computers, and 4,000 public schools have none. Students trying to prepare for life in the twenty-first century may enter the workforce without computer skills such as word processing, database management, and numerical analysis.

When we consider the use of technology in social studies, these issues are of vital importance. As students graduate and participate more fully in political and economic life, will all students be able to use the computer as an effective tool for learning and communicating?

The way that technology is used by a teacher can also limit the type of thinking and interpersonal interaction encouraged in the classroom. Oakes (1988) and other researchers have found that the drill approach is common in lower-track classes and poorer schools. Cuban (1986, 89) argues that such narrow uses of technology may destroy the complexity of classroom life:

> Classrooms are steeped in emotions. In the fervent quest for precise rationality and technical efficiency, introducing to each classroom enough computers to tutor and drill children can dry up that emotional life, resulting in withered and uncertain relationships [between teacher and students].

Cuban sees a narrowing of life in classrooms if computer use is limited to repetitive, linear thinking. There are many drill-and-practice and tutorial programs about government, law, and economics that limit the learner to memorization. Legal, political, and economic issues are value-laden and engage the whole person; thus technology in social studies needs to present the learner with the complexity of the data, trends, values, and beliefs that are used to make decisions and develop public policy.

Educational Resources for Technology in the Social Studies

One of the certainties about technology is that it will keep changing. Finding out about the newest products and getting the training you need are tasks for continuing professional development. The social studies field and the more general field of instructional technology have a variety of rich resources.

Journals

Several general publications feature articles and research on social studies and technology: *Learning and Leading with Technology, Computer-Using Educators (CUE) Newsletter, Computers and Education, Educational Technology, Electronic Learning, Journal of Educational Computing Research, T.H.E. Journal,* and others. In the field of social studies many journals have a regular section or column on technology: *Social Education* (which has a special section on technology and also one on Internet resources), *The Social Studies, Social Studies and the Young Learner,* as well as journals from the American Historical Association, the Joint Council on Economic Education, National Council for Geographic Education, and other disciplinary organizations. Articles by teachers about classroom practice and incorporation of technology, product reviews, research studies, software evaluation, and uses of the Internet are helpful to educators making purchasing decisions, looking for new ideas, or trying to solve problems. Magazines and newspapers that specialize in a particular brand of computer or a particular type of technology are readily available at newsstands and bookstores. There are some publications that focus on the Internet. Some journals can be read or downloaded from the Internet. As Chapter 8 describes, additional resources can be found on many WWW sites and through a listserv maintained by the NCSS.

Software Evaluation

Teachers and school districts face many costly decisions about what software to purchase. There are excellent resources to assist in making these important decisions, and most evaluation formats provide a technical and an educational perspective on the products. Typical categories in software evaluation may include technical quality, instructional quality, content, curricular match, and assessment.

Technical quality refers to the reliability of the program; it needs to run smoothly without errors and delays. Teachers can now expect significant publisher support, including free previews of software, technical assistance through a toll-free telephone number, network licensing or laboratory packs for multiple workstations, inexpensive updates as newer versions are produced, and an adequate warranty.

Instructional quality focuses on the design of the program, including the presentation of content and appropriate assessment of student learning. Given the national standards for social studies, the instruction should emphasize higher-order thinking, active involvement of the learner, and deeper understanding of the content. Fernlund and

Rose (1993) have suggested evaluating instructional design not only in terms of the characteristics of the program, but also its impact on the learner and the teacher. Software programs might be judged in terms of the added value to instruction gained when the technology is incorporated.

Content is a category in software evaluation in which accuracy in grammar and spelling as well as program content is assessed. National standards would demand meaningful and current content that promotes interdisciplinary learning. Curricular match is concerned with the correlation between state, district, and/or teacher objectives and the software program. Assessment refers to the ability of the program to store and print performance records and offer a variety of ways to measure student achievement.

National Resources

National software reviews are conducted by several organizations. Educational Products Information Exchange (EPIE) provides teachers with information on the hardware configuration and requirements, the intended users, and the curriculum role. An overall rating on a scale from 1 to 10 is given for instructional design and software design, as well as an analyst's summary of strengths and weaknesses and recommendations to the producer for program improvement. The Education News Service and Facts on File are examples of other national groups that provide software reviews. Available on the WWW are sites devoted to evaluating the educational worth of other WWW sites.

State Resources

Several states have their own software reviews available. For example, Wisconsin has mandated the integration of computer literacy into K–12 curriculum plans. To assist districts and teachers, the Wisconsin Educational Media Association and the Instructional Computing Consortium were formed in the early 1980s. The California Video and Software Clearinghouse recommends products and features group buy programs in which selected commercial software is offered at a 20–60 percent discount to California schools. The evaluative criteria used by the clearinghouse are organized into three categories: essential, desirable, and exemplary criteria. In order to achieve exemplary status for interactive videodisc programs in the area of technical quality, the clearinghouse reviews programs to determine if:

1. users can separate audio segments from the video images when creating presentations or projects.

2. multiple points of view are provided for the same visual.

3. original images have been created specifically for the interactive medium.

4. program uses state-of-the-art computer graphics.

5. computer software accompanying the videodisc is available for a variety of computers and videodisc players.

6. the producer has done the best possible job considering the limitations of the hardware.

This kind of careful and thorough review is invaluable to teachers. A teacher can then focus on a few excellent programs, try them out with students, and then decide on a recommendation for purchase. Published reviews also provide incentives to publishers to improve their products.

State-based software evaluations offer teachers the advantage of a review of the technology in conjunction with state curriculum standards, scope, and sequence. At the national level, the NCSS has established 10 themes and standards for program excellence. In an evaluation of software content, reviewers may determine the contribution the programs make in achieving these national standards for program excellence. The next chapter will provide guidance for social studies teachers in selecting social studies software.

◼ Summary

This chapter provides an overview of the rest of this text as well as past, present, and potential future trends in the use of technology in social studies. Social studies is an integrative field designed to build civic competence in young people. The national standards for the field of social studies offer many opportunities to use technology in achieving these guidelines for excellence. It is essential that teachers are aware of the resources that will keep them current in this ever-changing field. Professional conferences, journals, and national and state organizations offer teachers access to product evaluation, training, and guidance. In addition to providing guidance in selecting software and hardware, the next chapter will also examine some overarching questions regarding technology and the social studies curriculum.

◼ References

▬ Articles

Becker, Henry J. "Instructional Computer Use: Findings from a National Survey of School and Teacher Practices." *The Computing Teacher* 7 (April 1993): 6–7.

Kozol, J. "Rich Child, Poor Child." *Electronic Learning* 10 (February 1991): 56.

Laskey, S. "Hats." *Social Studies Review* 30, no. 3 (1991): 45–50.

Mehlinger, Howard D. "School Reform in the Information Age." *Phi Delta Kappan* 77 (February 1996): 400–407.

Northup, Terry, and Gene E. Rooze. "Are Social Studies Teachers Using Computers? A National Survey." *Social Education* 54, no. 4 (1990): 212–14.

Olson, Lynn. "Contrary to Predictions, Use of Technology in Schools Elusive." *Education Week* (January 8, 1992): 8.

Paske, Richard. "Hypermedia: A Brief History and Progress Report." *T.H.E. Journal* 18 (March 1990): 53–55.

Books

Brophy, Jere, and Janet Alleman. *Powerful Social Studies Ideas for Elementary Students.* Fort Worth: Harcourt Brace College Publishers, 1996.

California State Department of Education. *History/Social Science Framework for California Public Schools Kindergarten through Grade Twelve.* Sacramento: California State Department of Education, 1988.

Cuban, Larry. *Teachers and Machines: The Classroom Use of Technology since 1920.* New York: Teachers College Press, 1986.

Ehman, Lee H., and Allen D. Glenn. *Computer-based Education in the Social Studies.* Bloomington, IN: Social Studies Development Center, 1987.

National Council for the Social Studies. *Expectations of Excellence: Curriculum Standards for the Social Studies.* Washington, DC: National Council for the Social Studies, 1994.

Oakes, J. *Keeping Track: How Schools Structure Inequality.* New Haven: Yale University Press, 1985.

Other Resources

Becker, Henry J. *Instructional Use of School Computers: Reports from the 1985 National Survey.* Issue 2. Baltimore: Johns Hopkins University, 1986.

Fernlund, Phyllis, and S. Rose. "Draft of Guidelines for the Evaluation of Educational Software in the Social Studies." Paper presented to the National Council for the Social Studies, Nashville, TN, 1993.

Hartoonian, Michael. Preface to *Curriculum Standards for the Social Studies.* Washington, DC: National Council for the Social Studies, 1994.

National Commission on the Social Studies in the Schools. *Charting a Course: Social Studies for the 21st Century.* National Commission on the Social Studies in the Schools, 1989.

Discussion Questions

1. What is the central goal of teaching social studies, and in what ways can the teacher use the computer to enhance the social studies?

2. As a school matures in its use of technology, how does the focus change from when the technology was first introduced? Why does the focus change?

3. What is hypermedia and what are the three ways it can be put to use in the social studies classroom?

4. How does a teacher find good software and technology-based curriculum materials? What criteria should be considered in evaluating products?

— Additional Readings and Questions ————

Harp, Lonnie. "The History Wars." *Electronic Learning* 16, no. 2 (October 1996): 32–39.

1. How does technology connect to multiculturalism in the social studies curriculum, and what is their relationship to generative learning?

2. How does technology increase the influence of primary source documents, and what mistaken beliefs do teachers sometimes hold about the power of technology?

Hope, Warren C. "It's Time to Transform Social Studies Teaching." *The Social Studies* (July/August 1996): 149–51.

1. In what ways is the teacher the pivotal personality in the social studies classroom?

2. How can technology impact the transformation of social studies from a dry, boring "collection of dates, deeds, … and boredom" into something that invigorates and stimulates students?

Means, Barbara, and Kerry Olson. "The Link between Technology and Authentic Learning." *Educational Leadership* 51, no. 7 (April 1994): 15–18.

1. What two classes of software had little impact on most teachers' daily activities in the classroom?

2. How is the educational reform effort changing the way teachers see technology's contribution to their efforts to improve classroom learning?

National Council for the Social Studies. *Expectations of Excellence: Curriculum Standards for Social Studies*. Washington, DC: National Council for the Social Studies, 1994.

1. Why is social studies "naturally integrative"?

2. In what ways can technology support the powerful teaching and learning described in the article?

Willis, Elizabeth M. "Where in the World? Technology in Social Studies Learning." *Learning and Leading with Technology* 23, no. 5 (February 1996): 7–9.

1. What does the research in the use of technology in social studies reveal in terms of instructional practices in the 1980s and 1990s?

2. What were the results of using the computer simulation, *ICONS*, with high school and college students?

The History Wars

Lonnie Harp

Sixty-six days crossing the ocean leaves plenty of time for reflection.

For 42-year-old John Winthrop, a mild-mannered, learned man, the trip aboard the Arbella offered an opportunity to start a journal and compose a sermon. When he and his fellow passengers landed in Salem, Mass., early in the summer of 1630, his essay "Christian Charitie: A Modell Hereof" explained the group's reason for leaving England and its priorities for life in Massachusetts.

Brotherly affection would be the society's chief aim; justice and mercy its calling cards. By the time the Puritan settlers finished their springtime voyage, their vision of their history and what they wanted for the new society was clear.

While some are still fighting hard for a set, traditional curriculum—with standards to match—technology has opened the history classroom door to a dizzying array of data, artifacts, and perspectives. Helping teachers and students to make sense of it all is more than half the battle.

It's not so simple now in Massachusetts—or anyplace else in America. As schools have become a battleground in what some observers describe as a culture war—a spirited fight over values and norms and fundamental truths—the story line of history has become a central issue. Math and science, after all, are guarded by cold physical laws and proven theorems. English has its known roots and references. History, on the other hand, is as much art as it is science. Less like calculus and more like beauty, it springs from the eye of the beholder.

Whose History?

In a diverse society questioning old abuses and examining its recent scars, what begins as a party for Christopher Columbus can quickly turn into a trial. Nat Love, an ex-slave who became a cowboy in the late 1800s, rises from obscurity. The legacies of industrialists like John D. Rockefeller come under scrutiny.

"In 1630, we knew who we were," says Patrick Levens, director of secondary instruction for the Capistrano (CA) Unified School District. "When John Winthrop got up and delivered his sermon on Christian charity, those people knew who they were and what they wanted to do. And for a long time, people felt like they still had the answers to those questions. But over the last 30 years, the questions have plagued us and become more and more controversial."

The battle that reached full boil in 1995 over the proposed national standards for teaching both world and American history (see sidebar) crystallized that struggle. But it is not only in standards-setting committees that social studies and history are undergoing change. They are changing in the classroom as well. Technology is quickly pushing teachers beyond the traditional "textbook" view of American exploration and conquests launched by fearless European explorers, honed by daring Industrial Revolution entrepreneurs, and sealed by brave 20th-century military commanders.

Battle by Battle: A Standards Timeline

Mid-1980s

The move toward a more inclusive history curriculum gains momentum as states such as California begin early versions of content standards. In California, controversy accompanies the adoption of textbooks that take a more critical view of traditional American heroes and begin paying more homage to African-Americans and other ethnic groups.

September 1987

New York State officials draw up a new social studies curriculum stressing more multicultural themes and encouraging critical perspectives. But Kenneth T. Jackson, a history professor at Columbia University and an original member of the curriculum group, opposes the final product. "Within any single country, one culture must be accepted as the standard," he says.

February 1992

The new national history standards group meets for the first time. Funded and supervised by the U.S. Department of Education and the National Endowment for the Humanities (NEH), the standards will be drafted by a who's who of interested parties, from the National Association for Asian and Pacific American Education to the National Alliance of Black School Educators to the National Catholic Education Association.

October 1994

After 6,000 drafts, the standards are almost ready. Just before their release, Lynne Cheney, former head of the NEH, writes a scathing *Wall Street Journal* article ripping the standards for shortchanging American icons. After tallying mentions in the 2,500 teaching examples attached to the 31 standards, Cheney asks how Harriet Tubman could rate more attention than Ulysses S. Grant. More pundits lined up to take their shots. Where was Paul Revere? Thomas Edison? Why so much about the Ku Klux Klan?

Gary B. Nash, a history professor at the University of California at Los Angeles (UCLA) and codirector of the standards project, watches in frustration as the rising criticism nearly eclipses the document's content. "The standards provide a corrective for an enormous amount of historical amnesia about different groups who were very much a part of the making of American society," Nash says.

January 1995

The U.S. Senate votes 99 to 1 to disavow the work of the standards group, which begins revising the standards for a more balanced approach.

1996

As the firestorm over the national history standards fades, standards setting shifts to the states. Some states, like Illinois, begin moving from generalized goals to explicit content standards—from requiring that students know the dates of the Great Depression to asking them to explain how federalism was affected by the New Deal, for example.

Summer 1996

The American Federation of Teachers (AFT) issues its second annual report on states' standards. The union is pushing for standards that are "detailed and comprehensive" and "firmly rooted in the content of a subject." Only 20 states earn a passing grade in social studies. "In some cases,

$\Rightarrow$

Technology Changes the Equation

On the Internet alone, even the most misbegotten searches can lead to detailed information about any number of historical figures and events, from the life of Martha Washington to the christening of the USS Arizona to the 1942 Lee Street riots of Alexandria, LA. Four different sources on the life of Napoléon may yield four distinctly different views of the French general.

"The connection between technology and multiculturalism makes sure that other voices are heard," says Brian Nelligan, a longtime social studies and history teacher in Essex Junction, VT. "We should want to teach as many points of view as possible because we want student learning to be generative—for students to generate their own meaning and know how to work with others to generate further meaning."

Where technology has taken hold, history classes have become more like paper-trail investigations than multiple choice quizzes on dates and rulers and battles.

Nelligan says his tenth-grade global studies class at Essex High School has changed more because of technology than any trend toward rewriting the curriculum in a particular direction. Through the Internet, his students this fall will be linked to students in Asia to discuss a variety of cultural and political issues. He is even hoping to link his class with high schoolers in Japan to collaborate on class projects—a step he prepared for over the summer at the TeachAsia Institute, organized by the Asia Society in New York City.

Nelligan uses technology to stretch his teaching in other ways. With an online encyclopedia like *Encarta*, students can go beyond surface learning by actually hearing Winston Churchill deliver speeches. And in addition to textbooks and supplementary reading material, he and his fellow teachers use CD-ROM simulation games like *Civilization* and *SimCity* to help students grapple with political and geographical issues affecting a society. Simulations lead students to ask tougher questions, says Nelligan. Why did ancient people settle in a certain river bend? Who gained power in society and why? How did ensuing turf battle evolve into warfare?

Smart Use of Tools

Yet online resources are only some of the many tools used by Nelligan, a 31-year veteran of the classroom. "We are careful about the use of technology—students could sit and play on a computer forever," says Nelligan, the chairman of the 1,200-student school's social studies department. "We try to be smart about the ways it can be used to meet the goals of this class.

"If computers are seen as a means to an end, they become a way of making passive students active learners," Nelligan says. "I'm sure that in 1453, when Guttenburg came out with movable type, people saw books as a means to themselves. But they quickly became a means to an end. That's our job as teachers—to become more sophisticated information managers."

periods of history are simply listed, with no elaboration as to which themes, events, or issues are more important for students to study within each period," the report states. "In other cases, history is treated more as a skill to be developed (e.g., 'historical inquiry') than knowledge to be acquired." The AFT hails California, the District of Columbia, Florida, and Virginia for producing model standards that will guide teachers' work. Other states winning mention are Alabama, Colorado, Delaware, Georgia, Idaho, Indiana, Mississippi, New Hampshire, Tennessee, Texas, and Utah. The report chides Alaska, Connecticut, and Pennsylvania for adopting social studies standards that were vague and for having no expectations for what students should know at various grade levels. Officials in Louisiana, New Mexico, Nevada, and West Virginia are still developing their social studies standards, and no social studies standards exist or are in the works in Iowa and Rhode Island.

Copies of the AFT's standards report card, "Making Standards Matter 1996," are $10 each from the American Federation of Teachers, 555 New Jersey Ave. NW, Washington, DC 20001–2079. Ask for item No. 265.

The revised national history standards document is available for $15.95 plus $5 shipping and handling from the UCLA Store, (310) 206–0788, bookorder@asucla.ucla.edu.

Advances in technology can enable students to dig deeper in their investigations and—as they draw from more and more sources and make better links around the world—into conflicting versions of historical events. Already, Nelligan's students have used Internet sites and other computer references to look at the Vietnam War and to appreciate the British perspective on the Revolutionary War.

Analyzing Bias and Objectivity

Nelligan is aware that moving past the one-textbook version of history sometimes puts his students in deep water, trying to figure out which perspective they can trust to be a more accurate portrayal of what happened, and which is less reliable. "Listen," says Nelligan, "bias is going to be there with anybody—it's there with teachers. When students go through all these new sources for information, we encourage them to find those biases and look for their own. Knowing that, knowing about the choices that people have had to make, and knowing what those choices lead to, is how students start to search for their own meaning, which is what social studies is all about."

For Nelligan, all of this is connected to the very essence of democratic ideals. "An enlightened citizenry is a lot more valuable than one that knows a lot of meaningless facts," he says. "We're not going to paint a picture that Americans are always right. There is nothing wrong with understanding the point of view of the other guy."

Indeed, educators who are actively weaving new technology into social studies courses say that some teachers can't get enough of it.

Patrick Levens of the Capistrano district offers as evidence the presentation he and a district art teacher made at a statewide technology conference. After they announced that they had limited handouts of a 22-page bibliography of software, addresses on the World Wide Web, and other technology resources, many of the 250 teachers who showed up at the session rushed to get a copy and in the process knocked Levens's fellow presenter to the floor.

"A feeding frenzy," Levens recalls. "That's what happens when you only bring handouts for 25."

The Power of Primary Sources

In the sprawling Capistrano district, "large-scale investigatory learning" is the code phrase for history and social studies teaching. Teachers now tap the diaries of laborers, old government statistics, and personal correspondence that usually doesn't adhere to anybody's party line.

"We've always thought that was what we needed, but teaching has been compromised by the four walls of a classroom," Levens says. "We get a lot of different answers now when we ask why the Haymarket riot occurred."

Donald J. Mabry, a professor of history and associate dean at Mississippi State University in Starkville, is familiar with the expanding interpretations of history. The historical text archive he manages on the World Wide Web—**http://www.msstate.edu/Archives/History**—now gets 100,000 inquiries annually. The site includes a dizzying maze of links to historical sites and documents. He has gotten e-mail from a fifth grader in Philadelphia who asked where to look for good background on cowboys. He has spoken to a Hungarian nationalist in Canada wanting to promote his own spin on Hungarian history.

"It takes a lot of time and effort to find out what's going on and about everything that's out there," Mabry says. "A lot of times there is the mistaken belief that anything and everything is available, which is not true. There is also a belief, as there is with textbooks, that if it's in print, it's got to be right—

which is also not true. With all this information sprouting up, and a lot of it very political, it's even more important for teachers and students to do some critical thinking and ask why it's there in the first place."

Changing How Teachers Teach

At San Clemente High School in the Capistrano district in California, Kathleen Sigafoos and other social studies teachers are redesigning their courses to devote more time to helping students hone the skills they need to thoroughly investigate and debate primary source documents such as diaries, letters, newspapers, and memoirs. In her tenth-grade world history course, Sigafoos uses the Internet and software to find journals, old newspaper articles, and other primary source documents for her students to analyze to help them understand the Holocaust, the detonation of the atomic bomb, and other major events.

"It's what teacher training here and the California curriculum frameworks are both stressing: bringing in primary source documents and helping students understand what people are saying and why they are saying it," says Sigafoos. "When we look at historical documents, we ask what agenda a person might have had when he or she wrote something. Then we ask students to figure out what is valid and how to weigh what is being said. The students soon realize that even newspapers, which are supposed to be more objective than personal opinion, choose what goes in that day's edition as they shape the events of the day.

"With all these new sources, teaching is about a lot more than having students read chapter 10, do the questions at the end, and then take the test," she says.

Checks and Balances

While they have watched the wave of digital information wash in, school officials are the first to admit that they still have to mobilize their curriculum leaders into quality management. Despite the reputation of local school boards for long and heated debates over textbooks, reading lists, and other curriculum materials that are sanctioned for students, many districts have yet to address questions about how to mix software and Internet resources that espouse highly political or biased opinions. Teachers say that, for now, schools are trusting the judgment of teachers to come up with a mix of resources that is appropriate and that moves toward instructional goals.

The flood of electronic information has come so fast that most school districts are still at the stage of drafting policy statements to make sure that new hookups to the Internet don't invite pornographic or otherwise inappropriate material into schools. They have yet to tackle, for example, how to deal with touchy questions like whether an Internet site espousing racist views is a worthwhile classroom tool.

Now that the Internet and a broad range of technologies have opened the floodgates on content, at least one state—Vermont—is trying to create guidelines to help teachers connect their classroom lesson plans and student projects to a broad-yet-balanced social studies curriculum. In this endeavor they are being assisted by an animated, Java-scripted compact disc that provides targeted lessons and builds tests of its own while advising teachers whether their planned activities are in sync with the state's expectations. The program also allows teachers to measure their instruction against any national or international standards they might be striving to meet.

Different Standards

Under Vermont's new standards framework, history and social science courses beginning in kindergarten and extending through high school are expected to work toward improving students' competency in the knowledge of history, geography, citizenship, and economics, as well as their understanding of issues such as diversity, criticism, conflict, and interdependence.

While the old system divided the study of the Civil War into battle experiences, military causes, and the writings of Walt Whitman, the new frameworks push for exploring more personal accounts of people involved in both sides of the conflict, an examination of how differences between the North and South caused and shaped the war, and a look at the war's long-term and short-term societal effects throughout the nation.

Unlike the proposed national standards, the Vermont version does not provide a laundry list of specific people or places that should be emphasized. In-stead, the Vermont standards concentrate on themes to be stressed and attributes like communication, reasoning, personal development, and civic responsibility that should be instilled by 12 years of schooling.

Chuck Knisley, the state education department's information technologist and a professor of education at the University of Vermont, says that when the department's CD-ROM software is launched in a year, it could help teachers begin to make better sense of the myriad influences bombarding their history and social studies classrooms.

"People have been waiting a very long time for a tool like this," Knisley says.

The Vermont standards, and the technology tool that helps to make them immediately accessible and connectable to specific lessons plans, may not by themselves provide the teachers with the clear vision of history provided by John Winthrop's sermon. But the combination of the two will help educators like Brian Nelligan, who are trying to strike a balance in their own social studies classrooms. "Schools have a tough mission, because the older generation would like to replicate what was happening when they were in school," Nelligan says. "But this is a new age, and we have a lot more information. Is there a set body of knowledge we teach from? The answer is no. Are there some set ideas that need to be taught? Of course."   ❖

L onnie Harp is an editor at Education Week.

It's Time to Transform Social Studies Teaching

Warren C. Hope

Some years ago when I was a seventh-grade social studies teacher, I came across words in the geography textbook that have remained with me to this day. While conducting a textbook inventory, that routine and dreaded procedure, I read on the front inside cover of one book the words "absolutely 100 percent junk." At first, I found the message humorous and smiled. Later, I pondered the expression, which I surmised represented a student's feelings about geography in particular and social studies in general. In the end, I considered the words an affront to me and to the subject in which I had invested much time to acquire teaching expertise and which I had grown to love.

From my perspective, I wondered how it was possible for anyone not to enjoy social studies. Why, I thought, would a student, who could learn so much about a world of people, places, and things, dismiss such an important subject as geography? The subject presented students with an opportunity to see the world vicariously. They could travel to the great capital cities, gaze at countries' natural wonders, immerse themselves in the culture, and meet the people, all of this right in the classroom. How could anyone not be excited about taking this trip around the globe?

The Social Studies, July/August 1996, 149–151. Reprinted with permission of the Helen Dwight Reid Educational Foundation. Published by Heldref Publications, 1319 Eighteenth Street, NW, Washington, DC 20036–1802. Copyright © 1996.

Lounsbury (1988) submitted that the reason for the students' lack of respect for social studies was the teacher's failure to articulate meaningful and relevant objectives. Hence, this trip around the globe really held no meaning for students who were growing up in a rural community and happened to be enrolled in a geography class. How could such study be relevant to their lives?

More than a decade has passed since the day I discovered those acrid words in the geography textbook, and since that time, thousands of students have entered and exited social studies classrooms across the nation. I wonder today how much of the "absolutely 100 percent junk" sentiment of one student years ago lies dormant in the minds of other students who have passed through social studies classes.

Today I am haunted by the statements made by my college students as they reflect on their K–12 social studies experiences. The students invariably speak of their dislike for social studies, commenting that the teacher did not make it interesting, what was taught was irrelevant, it was taught by a coach who had other things on his mind, or the teacher sat behind the desk and told the students to read the chapter and answer the questions at the end. Being bombarded with these highly distressing comments on occasion after occasion is very upsetting to a teacher. If, however, that is the pedagogy those students experienced, it is no wonder that social studies is so routinely and soundly criticized.

For decades social studies has been rated as one of the least liked subjects in the curriculum (Shaughnessy and Haladyna 1985). It is the subject students love to hate. Only one other core subject, English (Lounsbury 1988) receives more negative reviews about the teaching of its content.

To what can we attribute the characterization of social studies as a boring subject to be avoided? Who is to blame for social studies being perceived as lacking meaning and concerning unimportant talk of the past? The most important question to be asked is what can be done to energize social studies and restore respect for so important a field.

Every so often some new strategy intended to revitalize the social studies has come along. Recent movements, such as the New Social Studies, Charting a Course: Social Studies for the 21st Century, and Curriculum Standards for Social Studies, have emerged as rudders for this troubled field. The most recent, Curriculum Standards, has attempted to define the social studies and encapsulate its essence into strands. In those strands is the important content for social studies teaching. This sequencing of content is meaningful and outlines the important areas to be taught in the social studies. To what extent will social studies teachers embrace this latest effort to enhance the subject and project its great importance? Will social studies teaching, based on the content of the strands, be revitalized? Will this effort produce the tide of social studies reform that other disciplines have been engaged in for years?

The burden of implementing the latest approach will fall to the teachers themselves. What are the prospects of social studies teachers changing the way in which they teach? Has the advent of television, videotapes, audiotapes, slides, and technology significantly influenced social studies teaching? Moreover, have these changes produced exciting and stimulating classroom sessions in which students desire to acquire social studies skills? Have these changes helped students enjoy learning social studies skills?

The answer is yes and no. Although some social studies teachers have made efforts to invigorate their students through experiential learning, add real-world relevance to their teaching, and infuse their course work with stimulating assignments, too many are yoked to the textbook, captive to chalk and talk, unable or unwilling to connect objectives with the real world, which results in the perpetuation of students' derogatory comments.

The teacher is the pivotal personality in the classroom, the one who can make things happen. How a teacher projects the content of a subject in the classroom is a determining factor in the subject's being liked or disliked by students and in students' diligent efforts to acquire the skills deemed important by the teacher.

Risinger and Garcia (1995) reported that criticism of the social studies gains momentum from the results of national tests that magnify students' failure to achieve at expected levels. National test results along with negative commentary by students have caused social studies teachers to reconsider their teaching of social studies.

Hootstein (1995) identified motivational history teaching strategies for eighth-grade students from teachers' observations of what prompted students' interest in class. High on the teachers' list

of successful strategies were role-playing characters, projects, and review games, almost the same as those indicated by the students. Viewing historical videos or films was also among the students' choices. These activities, according to Hootstein (1995), are not anchored in the usual social studies instruction, which consists primarily of lecture, recitation, and textbook learning. More disturbing, however, is Hootstein's report of the findings of Brophy and Merrick (1987), noting that even when social studies teachers were introduced to new teaching strategies, they remained attached to their own ways of teaching.

When assigning blame for the sad state of social studies, we must ask if the teacher is at fault for the subject's lack of appeal to students and their criticisms of the subject. Is the teachers' failure to incorporate motivational teaching strategies, to make relevant to students the objectives being taught, and to enliven the social studies by linking students to the community and the world the cause of past and present criticisms?

Some researchers contend that social studies is characterized as a field of confusion (Risinger and Garcia 1995), others recognize that social studies exists but wonder whether it is worth saving (Barth 1993), and some are even calling for its abolition (Roldao and Egan 1992). These challenges are too great to ignore. They should move social studies teachers to indignation and foster a zeal for the field that would manifest itself in transformed teaching.

That social studies education needs reforming is easily understood (White 1991). By what means and in what time frame will the reformation take place?

The means to transform social studies teaching is within reach. Meeting the challenge through transformed teaching is especially important now when the swirl of debate is becoming so acrimonious. I believe social studies teachers ought to take personally the attack by critics and move deliberately to force themselves out of obsolete methods and the drudgery of following the same routine day after day. There is no better time than now to revitalize social studies.

Teachers can make any subject interesting, motivating, and worth a student's time. Because of their respect for the social studies and its importance in teaching students how to live when they leave school, teachers need to recognize that their teaching of social studies must be transformed into a relevant discourse that encourages students to create meaning in their own lives from the diversity and dynamism of social studies.

Although other core subjects, such as English and mathematics, are moving toward student-centered, experiential, hands-on learning and constructivist learning strategies, the social studies remains subject-centered. Social studies, perhaps more than any other subject, needs to offer experiential learning to students. A constructivist approach that empowers students to ask their own questions and seek their own answers (Brooks and Brooks 1993) fits well into the social studies curriculum. The constructivist approach to teaching social studies allows students to deal from their viewpoint with the facets of citizenship: What is my responsibility? What are my values? What is the right thing to do? Which side should I support?

Technology is a promise waiting to be fulfilled by teachers bold enough to realize its potential and seize the opportunity to bring the world into the classroom. The Internet and other telecommunications options are resources that can contribute directly to transforming social studies teaching. The Internet is a great resource for making students aware that they are intertwined in the global community (Peha 1995). State of the art software and CD-ROMs to engage students are available to the social studies teacher. Regrettably, however, researchers have found that there is no widespread use of technology in the social studies (Ehman and Glenn 1987; White 1991; Ross 1991). Social studies teachers need to invest time in understanding the possibilities and potential of technology in the classroom and use technology to create a dynamic classroom, demonstrating for their students that the social studies classroom is an exciting place to be. The extent to which social studies teachers integrate technology into their classrooms will be the answer to the critics who decry social studies as "dates, deeds, dullness, battles, biographies, and boredom" (Lounsbury 1988, 116), as the memorization of contextless information (Ruenzel 1993), or as mimetic (Brooks and Brooks 1993).

Teachers using technology in their classrooms to motivate students to learn and change their minds about social studies can make the content of social studies relevant and connect with the needs, objectives, and goals of the students (Hootstein 1995). They will be creating a different and better learning environment in which to teach social studies by using technology to provide experiential learning. Social studies teachers need to integrate technology into their repertoire of skills so that they can bring an end to boring lessons, stimulate creativity, and exploit the need to be able to locate, identify, and use information in the new century. As part of their transformation process, social studies teachers will see the need for change to meet the challenges of a curriculum for the twenty-first century.

In *A Vision of Powerful Teaching and Learning in the Social Studies: Building Social Understanding and Civic Efficacy* (National Council of the Social Studies 1994), five features of ideal social studies teaching and learning are identified. The authors of the report maintain that social studies teaching and learning are powerful when they are meaningful, integrative, value-based, challenging, and active. When teachers use these features in their social studies teaching, they eliminate the process of presenting facts and ideas taught in isolation, connect events of the past with the present, build an appreciation for the diversity of people, require their students' thoughtful examination of ideas and events, and involve students in constructing learning from the content presented by the teacher (National Council of the Social Studies 1994).

To transform social studies teaching, teachers need to implement experiential learning in classrooms. The new focus of instruction will permit students to become active, rather than passive, learners. In the process of better preparing students for the twenty-first century,

social studies teachers must concentrate on preparing their students for adulthood. Service learning is a great way to achieve that goal. Change is always easier to talk about than to accomplish, yet it is essential that social studies teachers undergo this metamorphosis for the sake of their professional responsibility and love of teaching social studies.

When the transformation has taken place, the critics of social studies will become like dinosaurs, and students will speak enthusiastically about their social studies course of study with comments such as, "I had the greatest social studies teacher ever. My social studies classroom was an exciting place. I learned things that I will never forget, and I apply them to my life even now."   ❖

References

Barth, J. "Social Studies: There Is a History, There Is a Body, but Is It Worth Saving?" *Social Education* 57, no. 2 (1993): 56–57.

Brooks, J., and G. Brooks. *In Search of Understanding: The Case for Constructivist Classrooms*. Alexandria, VA: Association for Supervision and Curriculum Development, 1993.

Ehman, L., and A. Glenn. *Computer-based Education in the Studies*. Bloomington, IN: Social Studies Development Center, 1987.

Hootstein, E. "Motivational Strategies of Middle School Social Studies Teachers." *Social Education* 59, no. 1 (1995): 23–26.

Lounsbury, J. "Middle Level Social Studies: Points to Ponder." *Social Education* 52, no. 2 (1988): 116–18.

National Council for the Social Studies. *Expectations of Excellence: Curriculum Standards for Social Studies*. Washington, DC, 1994.

Peha, J. "How K–12 Teachers Are Using Computer Networks." *Educational Leadership* 53, no. 2 (1995): 18–25.

Risinger, C., and J. Garcia. "National Assessment and the Social Studies." *The Clearing House* 68, no. 4 (1995): 225–28.

Roldao, M., and K. Egan. "The Social Studies Curriculum: The Case for Its Abolition." 1992. ERIC, ED 350208.

Ross, E. "Microcomputer Use in Secondary Social Studies Classrooms." *Journal of Educational Research* 85, no. 1 (1991): 39–46.

Ruenzel, D. "A Course of Action." *Teacher Magazine* 4, no. 4 (1993): 14–18.

Shaughnessy, J. M., and T. M. Haladyna. "Research on Student Attitude toward Social Studies." *Social Education* 49, no. 8 (1985): 692–95.

White, C. "Technology and Social Studies Education: Potentials and a Prognosis." *NASSP* 75, no. 531 (1991): 3–41.

W*arren C. Hope is an assistant professor of middle-grades education at Georgia Southwestern College in Americus, Georgia.*

The Link between
Technology
and
Authentic
Learning

Barbara Means
and Kerry Olson

Television in the 1960s, computers in the 1970s, videodiscs and artificial intelligence in the 1980s—all were predicted to transform America's classrooms. As we know, they did not.

Certain technologies have definitely found niches in education, but the technology of the last two decades has changed schools far less than it has the worlds of work, entertainment, and communication. On the whole, teachers have simply closed their classroom doors and gone right on teaching just as they were taught (Smith and O'Day 1990).

A new climate in school reform welcomes technology as never before. Case studies show that as a tool for complex, authentic tasks, technology will be a powerful performer.

Why Earlier Efforts Failed

Despite its disappointing record, technology now has the potential to exert a much stronger impact on learning in schools. The greater potential is not due solely to technological advances per se— the exciting new capabilities like multimedia and wireless communication, the increasing accessibility of technology, and the beginnings of a national infor-

Means, B., and K. Olson. (April 1994). "The Link between Technology and Authentic Learning." *Educational Leadership* 51, no. 7: 15–18. Reprinted with permission of the Association for Supervision and Curriculum Development. Copyright © 1994 by ASCD. All rights reserved.

mation infrastructure. A more important basis for optimism is progress in *education reform*.

In our view, early efforts to introduce technology in schools failed to have profound effects because the attempts were based on the wrong model of teaching with technology. Product developers believed in their content knowledge, pedagogical techniques, and in the power of technology to transmit knowledge to students. With satisfaction, the developers touted the so-called "teacher-proof" instructional programs.

How surprised they must have been that most of their applications were never used for very long. The applications had, as it turned out, a primary problem. They were an imperfect and incomplete match with the bulk of the core curriculum.

Two types of software were common. The dominator of the software market, computer-assisted instruction, tended to focus narrowly on drill-and-practice activities in very basic skills. Thus, CAI was used extensively among students with disadvantaged backgrounds. At the other end of the software spectrum, instructional games, simulations, and intelligent tutoring systems generally conveyed more challenging material, but only covered a very narrow slice of a subject domain and were often a poor match with state curriculum guidelines or teacher preferences. This genre of software, too, was commonly reserved for limited populations: gifted students, those who finished their work early, or students in innovative schools serving affluent neighborhoods.

Because of their narrow applicability, these two classes of software had little effect on what most teachers did with the bulk of their students for the majority of the school day (Cohen 1988). In contrast, today's applications software is likely to fare much better because of a new climate in school reform.

In the 1980s, reform efforts tried to improve student performance by increasing course requirements. Reformers did not, however, examine the way that teaching and learning unfold. Today's reform efforts, in contrast, strive to change the education system by fostering a different style of learning (David and Shields 1991). The efforts seek to move classrooms away from conventional didactic instructional approaches, in which teachers do most of the talking and students listen and complete short exercises on well-defined, subject-area-specific material. Instead, students are challenged with complex, authentic tasks, and reformers are pushing for lengthy multidisciplinary projects, cooperative learning groups, flexible scheduling, and authentic assessments.

In such a setting, technology is a valuable tool. It has the power to support students and teachers in obtaining, organizing, manipulating, and displaying information. These uses of technology will, we believe, become an integral feature of schooling.

When technology is used as a tool for accomplishing complex tasks, the issue of mismatch between technology content and curriculum disappears altogether. Technological tools can be used to organize and present any kind of information. Moreover, it is not necessary for the teacher to know everything about the tools that students use; students and teachers can acquire whatever technology skills they need for specific projects. In fact, one of the best things that teachers can do with respect to technology is to model what to do when one doesn't know what to do.

Technology in the Hands of a Skilled Teacher

As part of an ongoing project[1] funded by the Office of Educational Research and Improvement, we are conducting case studies[2] in schools that are using technology as part of a concentrated program of school reform. On one of our initial site visits to a school in our study, we found a fifth-grade classroom that illustrated how a skilled teacher can use technology to help orchestrate a project.

Frank Paul Elementary School is located in an agricultural area of California, which is troubled by poverty, crime, drugs, and gangs. The student population is 86 percent Hispanic, seven percent African-American, four percent Anglo, and three percent Asian American. A third of the students qualify for migrant education. Nearly two-thirds are limited-English-proficient.

One of the school's goals is to produce students who are literate in both English and Spanish, so some students do their content reading in English, while others use comparable materials in Spanish. The school's philosophy shows up in three other concrete ways as well: an ethic of respect for everyone's contributions; the extensive use of collaborative learning and small-group work; and an attempt to provide a homelike atmosphere (lighting is soft, and in classroom reading corners, kids can lounge on pillows as they read).

The fifth-grade teacher, Cliff Gilkey, has 12 years of teaching experience, nine of them at his current school. In his prior teaching experience, Gilkey used computers with primary school students. Accordingly, when the opportunity arose to obtain four computers for his 31 current students, Gilkey welcomed it. He shared the school's commitment to thematic instruction and collaborative learning, so he did not necessarily need enough computers for the whole class to use at once.

At first, the class used computers primarily for word processing and telecommunications with distant classrooms through the National Geographic Society *Kids' Network*. At the time of our visit, the students were involved in a long-term project employing technology to develop curriculum materials on local minority leaders. The particulars of the project illustrate five features of reformed classrooms:

1. *An authentic, challenging task is the starting point.* Authentic tasks are completed for reasons beyond earning a grade. Students also see the activity as worthwhile in its own right.

---

1. This article is based on work conducted as part of the Studies of Education Reform program, which is supported by the U.S. Department of Education, Office of Educational Research and Improvement, Office of Research, under contract RR 91–1720–2010. The opinions expressed in this article do not necessarily reflect the position or policy of the U.S. Department of Education, and no official endorsement should be inferred.

2. Several of these cases are described more fully in Barbara Means and Kerry Olson, "Tomorrow's Schools: Technology and Reform in Partnership," in *Technology and Education Reform: The Reality behind the Promise*, ed. Barbara Means (San Francisco: Jossey-Bass, 1994).

The Local Heroes Project grew out of two genuine needs. In the past, students had participated in a popular, week-long science camp during their sixth-grade year. In 1992–93, funding cuts led to suspension of the camp activity, and the fifth graders did not expect it to be funded in the next year either. The trip was important to them, so they were interested in raising money.

The second need was for appropriate curriculum materials about contemporary Hispanic leaders. Materials in textbooks and libraries were limited, and when the material did exist, the reading level was too high for students just learning to read English. Furthermore, the Hispanic leaders featured were generally entertainers or people who are no longer well known.

The class not only wanted to find better materials for its own use, but also became convinced that there was a market for such materials in other schools. The students got an idea, a multimedia project on local heroes. The project would involve:

◆ identifying local Hispanic, African-American, and Vietnamese leaders (including politicians, businessmen, researchers, and educators);

◆ conducting and videotaping interviews; and

◆ composing written highlights from the interviews.

In this undertaking, technology would be important. Students needed it to assemble their materials and produce many copies of salable quality.

2. *All students practice advanced skills.* Complex tasks involve both basic and advanced skills. In this regard, the heroes project was typical. It involved students in a wide range of tasks, some of which called for high-level thinking.

For example, the students prepared to conduct their interviews by analyzing interviews with famous people. From these, they developed a set of questions that would elicit certain information and generate interesting responses.

Through this process, students learned concepts (such as the difference between open- and close-ended questions) and presentation techniques (like maintaining eye contact during an interview). Further, as the class organized its activities, selected appropriate local leaders, and carried out the videorecording and editing, the students learned and practiced complex skills in a variety of domains (cognitive, social, and technical).

3. *Work takes place in heterogeneous, collaborative groups.* Initial practice convinced students that it is hard to conduct a good interview and take notes at the same time, so three-student teams went out to conduct each interview. One student asked the questions, a second videotaped, and a third recorded notes.

After completing the fieldwork, each team of students reviewed and critiqued its videotaped interviews. In their groups, students discussed ways to improve their technique and considered additional questions that should have been asked. Students also prepared a written transcript and summary of the key points in the videotape and recorder's notes. While entering text onto the computer for later editing and formatting, the individuals on a team each took responsibility for aspects of the task (such as typing, spelling, or remembering and repeating what was said on the videotape).

4. *The teacher is a coach.* Coaching, as Cliff Gilkey practices it, does not mean fading into the background. It means providing structure and actively supporting students' performances and reflections.

As we observed the classroom, small groups of students were working on a range of project activities—creating a large mural of famous minority leaders, telephoning local leaders to schedule interviews, transcribing videotapes, and practicing interviewing skills. Gilkey moved from group to group, checking on progress, monitoring students' practice, and suggesting questions to explore.

At the video monitor, Gilkey helped a group improve its interviewing technique. He asked, "What could you have asked when she mentioned that she had dropped out of school? What will the listener want to know?" Moving on to another group, Gilkey sat on the floor with students as they practiced opening an interview with a simulated microphone and camera (for fifth graders, simply introducing themselves and asking the first question brings on waves of self-consciousness). Gilkey had students work on maintaining eye contact and posing the initial question without looking down at the prompt sheet.

5. *Work occurs over extended blocks of time.* Serious intellectual activity doesn't usually fall neatly into 50-minute periods for a set number of days. Thus, complex tasks put pressure on the conventional small blocks of instructional time.

Gilkey's project began in January 1993 and was expected to continue through the rest of the school year. In fact, at the time of our visit, Gilkey was contemplating extending the project into the next year by teaching a mixed fifth- and sixth-grade class, allowing him to continue working with a core of students from the first year of the project.

The Contributions of Technology

In the Local Heroes Project, technology itself is not the driving force behind the learning. Nevertheless, our observations in settings that couple technology with education reform suggest that the technology certainly amplifies what teachers are able to do and what they expect from students.

One reason that technology has this positive effect is that teachers see complex assignments as feasible. For example, in some case-study schools, the availability of database programs and graphing capacities is leading teachers to think in terms of extensive data collection and analysis projects.

Technology also appears to provide an entry point to content areas and inquiries that might otherwise be inaccessible until much later in an academic career. For instance, when we start assuming that first graders will have access to word-processing programs, it becomes much more sensible to think about asking them to write before they are fluent readers.

A third benefit from technology is that it can extend and enhance what students are able to produce, whether the task at hand is writing a report or graphing data. The selection and manipulation of appropriate tools for such purposes also appear to stimulate problem-solving and other thinking skills.

In addition, technology lends authenticity to school tasks. Because the products of student efforts are more polished, schoolwork seems real and important. Students take great pride in using the same tools as practicing professionals. At one school we visited, a student informed us with glee that "I know musicians who would die for the technology we have in our music class." Technology also supports collaborative efforts (like Gilkey's interview teams).

Finally, in many of the classrooms we visited, the introduction of technology has given teachers the opportunity to become learners again. The challenge of planning and implementing technology-supported activities has provided a context in which an initial lack of knowledge is not regarded as cause for embarrassment. As a result, teachers are eager to share their developing expertise and to learn from one another. As they search out the links among their instructional goals, the curriculum, and technology's possibilities, they collaborate more, reflect more, and engage in more dialogue.

What technology will not do is make the teacher's life simple. The kind of teaching and learning that we have described requires teachers with multiple skills. The subject matter is inherently challenging, and because it is evolving and open-ended, it can never be totally mastered. Especially at first, the technology itself poses challenges, like learning to set up equipment, remembering software commands, and troubleshooting system problems. New roles pose many challenges, too. The teacher must be able to launch and orchestrate multiple groups of students, intervene at critical points, diagnose individual learning problems, and provide feedback.

Nevertheless, in classrooms where teachers have risen to this challenge, a profound change is occurring in the learning environment. Technology plays an important role, but it is a supporting role. The students are the stars. The playwright and director—and the power behind the scene—is, as always, the teacher. ❖

References

Cohen, D. K. "Educational Technology and School Organization." In *Technology in Education: Looking toward 2020.* Hillsdale, NJ: Erlbaum, 1988.

David, J. K., and P. M. Shields. *From Effective Schools to Restructuring: A Literature Review.* Menlo Park, CA: SRI International, 1991.

Means, B., and K. Olson. "Tomorrow's Schools: Technology and Reform in Partnership." In *Technology and Education Reform: The Reality behind the Promise,* edited by B. Means. San Francisco: Jossey-Bass, 1994.

Smith, M. S., and J. O'Day. "Systemic School Reform." In *Politics of Education Association Yearbook,* edited by R. S. Nickerson and P. P. Zodhiates. London: Taylor and Francis, 1990.

B arbara Means heads the Learning and Technology Program at SRI International, 333 Ravenswood Ave., Menlo Park, CA 94025.

K erry Olson is a Research Social Scientist with the Learning and Technology Program.

Task Force:

Donald Schneider, Chair

Susan A. Adler; R. Beery; Gloria Ladson-Billings; William R. Fernekes; Michael Hartoonian; Mary A. McFarland; Gerald Marker; Marjorie A. Montgomery; Pat Nickell; Corrinne Tevis

Social Studies Teaching and Learning Are Powerful When They Are Meaningful

Powerful social studies teaching and learning are meaningful to both teachers and students. The content selected for emphasis is worth learning because it promotes progress toward important social understanding and civic efficacy goals, and teaching methods are designed to enable students to appreciate how the content relates to those goals. Rather than memorizing disconnected bits of information or practicing skills in isolation, students learn connected networks of knowledge, skills, beliefs, and attitudes that they will find useful both in and outside of school. This worthwhile content is taught in ways that relate to each student's culture and assists the student in recognizing its value. As a result, students' learning efforts are motivated by appreciation and interest, not just by accountability and grading systems. Students become disposed to care about what is happening in the world around them and to use the thinking frameworks and research skills of social science professionals to gather and interpret information. As a result, social learning becomes a lifelong interest and a basis for informed social action.

Thoughtfully planned to accomplish significant goals, meaningful social studies teaching embodies several other key features. Instruction emphasizes depth of development of important ideas within appropriate breadth of topic coverage and focuses on teaching these important ideas for understanding, appreciation, and life application. A great many facts, definitions, and generalizations are taught because understanding often-used information and ideas enhances communication within and between cultures. The most effective teachers, however, do not diffuse their efforts by covering too many topics superficially. Instead, they select for emphasis the most useful landmark locations, the most representative case studies, the most inspiring models, the truly precedent-setting events, and the concepts and principles that their students must know and be able to apply in their lives outside of school. Furthermore, teachers inform students of when and how this content will be useful to them in realistic contexts, and they follow through with activities that engage students in applying the content in simulated or real situations.

Facts and ideas are not taught in isolation from other content, nor are skills. Instead, they are embedded in networks of knowledge, skills, beliefs, and attitudes that are structured around important ideas and taught emphasizing their connections and potential applications.

The significance and meaningfulness of the content is emphasized both in how it is presented to students and how it is developed through activities. New topics are framed with reference to where they fit within the big picture, and students are alerted to their citizen education implications. The new content is developed in ways that help students see how its elements relate to one another (e.g., using diagrams of concept networks or causal chains, lists of key steps in narrative sequences, or other graphic learning aids or illustrations). Students are encouraged to process what they learn on several levels simultaneously, rather than always starting with low-level factual information and only later engaging in higher-order thinking. From the very beginning, students may be asked to relate new learning to knowledge, think critically about it, or to use it to construct arguments or make informed decisions.

Teachers' questions are designed to promote understanding of important ideas and to stimulate thinking about their potential implications. As a result, classroom interaction focuses on sustained examination of a few important topics rather than superficial coverage of many. Teacher-student interactions emphasize thoughtful discussion of connected major themes, not rapid-fire recitation of miscellaneous bits of information.

Meaningful learning activities and assessment strategies focus students' attention on the most important ideas embedded in what they are learning. They encourage students to connect these ideas to their previous knowledge and experience, to think critically and creatively about them, and to consider their social implications. Thus, meaningful social studies teaching emphasizes authentic activities and assessment tasks—opportunities for students to engage in the sorts of applications of content that justify the inclusion of that content in the curriculum in the first place. For example, instead of labeling a map, students might plan a travel route and sketch landscapes that a traveler might see on the route. Instead of listing the amendments in the Bill of Rights, students might discuss or write about the implications of the Bill of Rights for a defendant in a selection of court cases. Instead of filling in a blank to complete the definition of a principle, students might use the principle to make predictions about a related situation or to guide their strategies in a simulation game.

This vision of meaningful social studies teaching and learning implies that the teacher is reflective in planning, implementing, and assessing instruction. Reflective teachers are well informed about the nature and purposes of social studies, and they remain current with developments in the field. They construct well-articulated ideas about their students' citizen education needs, plan their social studies teaching accordingly, and continue to adjust their practices in response to classroom feedback and growth in their own professional knowledge. They work within state and district guidelines, but adapt and supplement these guidelines and their adopted curriculum materials in ways that support their students' social studies education.

In particular, reflective teachers select and present content to students in ways that connect it with the students' interests and with local history, cultures, and issues. Local history and geography receive special attention, as do local examples of social, economic, political, or cultural topics studied at each grade level. There exists a systematic effort to increase awareness and validate the diversity found in the community by involving family members or local ethnic or cultural groups, encouraging students to share their cultural knowledge and experiences, and involving students in the community.

Social Studies Teaching and Learning Are Powerful When They Are Integrative

Social studies is naturally integrative because it addresses a broad range of content using varied instructional resources and learning activities. But powerful social studies is both integrated and integrative in other respects as well.

First, powerful social studies teaching is integrative in its treatment of topics. It crosses disciplinary boundaries to address topics in ways that promote students' social understanding and civic efficacy. Its content is anchored by themes, generalizations, and concepts drawn from the social studies foundational disciplines, supplemented by ideas drawn from the arts, sciences, and humanities, from current events, and from local examples and students' experiences. Powerfully integrated social studies teaching builds a working knowledge of the evolution of the human condition through time, its current variations across locations and cultures, and an appreciation of the potential implications of this knowledge for social and civic decision-making.

Powerful social studies teaching is integrative across time and space, connecting with past experiences and looking ahead to the future. It helps students appreciate how aspects of the social world function, not only in their local community and in the contemporary United States but also in the past and in other cultures. It puts what is familiar to students into historical, geographical, and cultural perspectives, thus expanding their limited purviews on social phenomena that they may have taken for granted.

Powerful social studies teaching integrates knowledge, skills, beliefs, values, and attitudes to action. In particular, it teaches skills within the context of applying knowledge. Skills are included when they are necessary for applying content in natural ways. They are taught directly when opportunities for practice are embedded in authentic application activities. Content flow is not interrupted for practice of related skills.

Integrated social studies teaching and learning include effective use of technology that can add important dimensions to students' learning. Teachers can provide students with information through films, videotapes, videodiscs, and other electronic media, and they can teach students to use computers to compose, edit, and illustrate social studies research reports. Computer-based learning, especially games and simulations, can allow students to apply important ideas in authentic problem-tackling or decision-making contexts. If students have access to computerized databases, they can search these resources for relevant research information. If they can communicate with peers in other states or nations, they can engage in personalized cultural exchanges or compare parallel data collected in geographically or culturally diverse locations.

Finally, powerful social studies teaching integrates across the curriculum. It provides opportunities for students to read and study text materials, appreciate art and literature, communicate orally and in writing, observe and take measurements, develop and display data, and in various other ways to conduct inquiry and synthesize findings using knowledge and skills taught in all school subjects. Because it addresses such a broad range of content and does so in

an integrative fashion that includes attention to ethical and social policy implications, social studies is a natural bridging subject across the curriculum. Particularly in elementary and middle schools, instruction can feature social studies as the core around which the rest of the curriculum is built.

These integrative aspects have the potential for enhancing the scope and power of social studies. They also, however, have the potential for undermining its coherence and thrust as a curriculum component that addresses unique citizen education goals. Citizen literary selection, writing assignment, cooperative learning activity, or computerized simulation cannot be considered curriculum simply because it features social studies combined with some other subject or see of skills. Nor can such activities be substituted for genuine social studies activities. To qualify as worthwhile elements of social studies curricula, activities must engage students in using important ideas in ways that promote progress toward social understanding and civic efficacy goals. Consequently, programs that feature a great deal of integration of social studies with other school subjects—even programs ostensibly built around social studies as the core of the curriculum—do not necessarily create powerful social studies learning. Unless they are developed as plans for accomplishing major social studies goals, such programs may focus on trivial or disconnected information.

Social Studies Teaching and Learning Are Powerful When They Are Value-based

Powerful social studies teaching considers the ethical dimensions of topics and addresses controversial issues providing an arena for reflective development of concern for the common good and application of social values. Students learn to be respectful of the dignity and rights of others when interacting socially, and to emphasize basic democratic concepts and principles when making personal policy decisions or participating in civic affairs.

Topics are created comprehensively and realistically, with attention to their disturbing or controversial aspects. Students are made aware of potential social policy implications and taught to think critically and make value-based decisions about related social issues. They learn to gather and analyze relevant information, assess the merits of competing arguments, and make reasoned decisions that include consideration of the values within alternative policy recommendations. Through discussions, debates, simulations, research, and other occasions for critical thinking and decision-making, students learn to apply value-based reasoning when addressing social problems.

The best social studies teachers develop awareness of their own values and how those values influence their selection of content, materials, questions, activities, and assessment methods. They assess their teaching from multiple perspectives and, where appropriate, adjust it to achieve a better balance.

Rather than promulgating personal, sectarian, or political views, these teachers make sure these students: 1. become aware of the values, complexities, and dilemmas involved in an issue; 2. consider the costs and benefits to various groups that are embedded in potential courses of action; and 3. develop well-reasoned positions consistent with basic democratic social and political values. The teacher provides guidance to such

value-based reasoning especially when it is difficult to discern the connections between core democratic values and the issues at hand, when various core values suggest conflicting policies, or when there is conflict between these core values and students' personal or family values. When this is done most effectively, students may remain unsure about the teachers personal views on an issue, at least until after it has been discussed thoroughly. Students become more aware of the complexities involved in addressing the issue in ways that serve the common good, and are more articulate about their own and others' policy recommendations and supporting rationales.

Powerful social studies teaching encourages recognition of opposing points of view, respect for well-supported positions, sensitivity to cultural similarities and differences, and a commitment to social responsibility and action. It recognizes the reality and persistence of tensions but promotes positive human relationships built on understanding, commitment to the common good, and willingness to compromise and search for common good.

Social Studies Teaching and Learning Are Powerful When They Are Challenging

Students are expected to strive to accomplish instructional goals both as individuals and as group members through thoughtful participation in lessons and activities and careful work on assignments. To establish a context that will support productively challenging teaching and learning, the teacher encourages the class to function as a learning community. Students learn that the purpose of reflective discussion is to work collaboratively to deepen understanding of the meanings and implications of content. Consequently, they are expected to listen carefully and respond thoughtfully to one another's ideas.

In advancing their own ideas and in responding critically to others, students are expected to build a case based on relevant evidence and arguments and to avoid derisive and other inappropriate behavior. They are challenged to come to grips with controversial issues, to participate assertively but respectfully in group discussions, and to work productively with partners or groups of peers in cooperative learning activities. Such experiences foster the development of competencies essential to civic efficacy.

Making social studies teaching challenging should not be construed as merely articulating high standards and then leaving it to students to try to meet them. Rather, the teacher models seriousness of purpose and a thoughtful approach to inquiry and uses instructional strategies designed to elicit and support similar qualities from students. The teacher paves the way for successful learning experiences by making sure that the content is suited to the students' developmental levels and cultural backgrounds and by providing assistance that enables students to handle challenging activities. The teacher also makes it clear, however, that students are expected to connect thoughtfully what they are learning to their prior knowledge and experience, to offer comments, and to raise questions.

To stimulate and challenge students' thinking, teachers should expose them to many information sources that include varying perspectives on topics and offer conflicting opinions on controversial issues. Questions call for thoughtful examination of the content, not just retrieval of information from memory. After posing such questions, the teacher allows sufficient time for students to think and formulate responses and to elaborate on their peers' responses.

Many of the questions call for critical or creative thinking, suggested solutions to problems, or reasoned positions on policy issues. Such questions often produce numerous and conflicting responses. When this occurs, the teacher withholds evaluation and instead invites the students to engage in sustained dialogue and debate. This shifts some of the authority for evaluating the validity of knowledge from teacher to students.

Challenge is also communicated in the teacher's reactions to students' ideas. The teacher shows interest in and respect for students' thinking, but demands well-reasoned arguments rather than opinions voiced without adequate thought or commitment. Routinely, students are asked to explain and defend their ideas using content-based arguments. Instead of always accepting students' views or asking the class to discuss them, the teacher sometimes challenges students' assumptions or responds with comments or questions that help students identify misconceptions, flaws in the argument, or unrecognized complications. The teacher must act with sensitivity, because some students become anxious or embarrassed when someone questions their ideas in this way. The teacher makes it clear that the purpose of such a challenge is not to put students on the spot but to help them construct new understanding through engagement in thoughtful dialogue.

Social Studies Teaching and Learning Are Powerful When They Are Active

Powerful social studies teaching and learning are rewarding, but they demand a great deal from both teachers and students. Thoughtful preparation and instruction by the teacher and sustained effort by students are required for students to make sense of and apply what they are learning.

Powerful social studies teaching demands that the teacher actively make curricular plans and adjustments. Rather than mechanically following the instructions in a manual, an exemplary teacher is prepared to: 1. acquire and update continuously the subject-matter knowledge and related pedagogical knowledge needed to teach the content effectively; 2. adjust goals and content to the students' needs; 3. participate as a partner in learning with students, modeling the joy of both discovering new knowledge and increasing understanding of familiar topics; 4. use a variety of instructional materials such as physical examples, photographs, maps, illustrations, films, videos, textbooks, literary selections, and computerized databases; 5. plan field trips, visits to the class by resource people, and other experiences that will help students relate what they are learning to their lives outside the classroom; 6. plan lessons and activities that introduce content to students, and encourage them to process it actively, think about it critically and creatively, and explore its implications; 7. develop current or local examples that relate the content to students' lives; 8. plan sequences of questions that allow for numerous responses and stimulate reflective discussion; 9. provide students with guidance and assistance as needed, yet encourage them to assume increasing responsibility for managing their own learning; 10. structure learning environments and activities in ways that encourage students to behave as a community of learners; 11. use accountability and grading systems that are compatible with instructional methods and that focus on accomplishment of major social understanding and civic efficacy goals; and 12. monitor reflectively and adjust as necessary.

Besides advance planning and preparation, active social studies teaching requires reflective thinking and decision-making as events unfold during instruction. Teachers must adjust plans to developing circumstances such as teachable moments that arise when students ask questions, make comments, or offer challenges worth pursuing. The teacher decides whether to persist with a topic or conclude it and move on to a new topic, whether to try to elicit an insight from students or to supply it directly, and how thoroughly the students will need to be prepared for an activity before they can begin work on it independently.

After the teacher launches an activity and students are working on their own or in collaboration with their peers, the teacher remains active by monitoring individual or group progress and providing assistance. Interventions are designed to clear up confusion, while enabling students to cope with task demands productively; students should be allowed to handle as much of the task as they can at the moment while at the same time making progress toward fully independent and successful performance. The teacher does not perform the tasks for students or simplify them to the point that they no longer engage the students in the cognitive processes required to accomplish the activity's goals.

Students develop new understanding through a process of active construction. They do not passively receive or copy curriculum content; rather, they actively process it by relating it to what they already know (or think they know) about the topic. Instead of relying on rote learning methods, they strive to make sense of what they are learning by developing a network of connections that link the new content to preexisting knowledge and beliefs anchored in their prior experience. Sometimes the learning involves conceptual change in which students discover that some of their beliefs are inaccurate and need to be modified.

The construction of meaning required to develop important social understanding takes time and is facilitated by interactive discourse. Clear explanation and modeling from the teacher are important, as are opportunities to answer questions about content, discuss or debate the meanings and implications of content, or use the content in activities that call for tackling problems or making decisions. These activities allow students to process content actively and make it their own by paraphrasing it into their own words, exploring its relationship to other knowledge and to past experience, appreciating the insights it provides, or identifying its implications for social or civic decision-making.

Teacher and student roles shift as learning progresses. Early in a unit of study, the teacher may need to provide considerable guidance by modeling, explaining, or supplying information that builds on students' existing knowledge while also assuming much of the responsibility for structuring and managing learning activities. As students develop expertise, however, they can begin to assume responsibility for regulating their learning by asking questions and by working on increasingly complex applications with increasing degrees of autonomy. The teacher still assists students with challenges they are not yet ready to handle by themselves but such assistance is gradually reduced in response to increases in students' readiness to engage in independent and self-regulating learning.

Because what one learns is intimately linked to how one learns it, powerful social studies programs feature learning that is both social and active. The learning is social because it occurs in a group setting and includes substantial student-student interaction during discussions and collaborative work on activities. The learning is active because the curriculum emphasizes hands-on (and minds-on) activities that call for students to react to what they are learning and use it for some authentic purpose.

Effective activities encourage students to think about and apply what they are learning. Teachers may provide opportunities for students to apply their existing knowledge to questions about new content, to understand new content, to synthesize and communicate what they have learned, to generate new knowledge or make creative applications, or to think critically about the content and make decisions or take actions that relate to it.

Powerful social studies teaching emphasizes authentic activities that call for using content for accomplishing life applications. For example, critical-thinking attitudes and abilities are developed through policy debates or assignments calling for critique of currently or historically important policy arguments or decisions, not through artificial exercises in identifying logical or rhetorical flaws. Similarly, in addition to more traditional assignments, students frequently engage in cooperative learning, construction of models or plans, dramatic recreations of historical events that shaped democratic values or civic policies, role-play, and simulation activities (e.g., mock trials or simulated legislative activities, interviewing family members, and collecting data in the local community). They also participate in various social and civic roles (e.g., discussing home safety or energy conservation checklists with parents and planning appropriate follow-up action, participating in student government activities and local community restoration or improvement efforts, or doing volunteer work for nursing homes or political campaigns).

Through such activities, students develop social understanding that they can explain in their own words and can access and apply in appropriate situations. For example, they learn to think critically as they read newspapers and magazines, watch television, or monitor political or policy debates. They learn to recognize the problematic aspects of statements, to project the probable social consequences of advocated policies, and to take these complexities into account when forming their opinions.

The teacher's modeling, classroom management, motivational techniques, instructional methods, and assessment procedures all communicate to students that they are expected to participate in social studies classes actively and with a sense of purpose. The students learn to reflect thoughtfully on what they are learning and to ask questions, share opinions, and engage in public content-based dialogue. Through authentic application activities they develop civic efficacy by practicing it engaging in the inquiry and debate required to make informed decisions about real social issues then following up with appropriate social or civic action.   ❖

Where in the World?

Technology in Social Studies Learning

Elizabeth M. Willis

When the editor of this column invited me to review the recent research in technology and social studies, I recognized it as an opportunity to investigate the exciting learning experiences I expected students and teachers were having with new technologies (i.e., video, television, laserdisc, computers), new software, and the Internet.

To my dismay, what I found is that while social studies students may indeed be using technology in classroom activities that take advantage of its possibilities (such as the many World Wide Web sites full of lesson plans and projects), few educators are taking time to design and carry out empirical research with which to inform future practice (J. A. Braun, Jr., *Personal Communication*, 1995).

In 1984 John Goodlad reported that only five percent to 10 percent of elementary and secondary school classes were places of reasonably intense student involvement with learning, while most were dominated by teacher talk (Benenson, Braun, and Klass 1992). Studies done during the late 1980s (Ross 1988; Sabir 1986; White 1986; U.S. Congress, Office of Technology Assessment, 1988) indicated that teachers (including those in social studies) were searching for ways to improve teaching and learning, and wanted to use interactive technologies, especially computers, in their classrooms. Becker (1986) found, however, in a number of surveys that few teachers actually used technology in that way. In fact, Becker reported that in the middle school

From *Learning and Leading with Technology* 25, no. 5 (February 1996): 7–9. Reprinted with permission from the International Society for Technology in Education. All rights reserved.

social studies classroom, simple simulation games were the extent of computer use. Those same surveys also indicated that teachers believed that computer use would significantly affect student enthusiasm and personal growth, and promote additional learning for the gifted as well as learning disabled and handicapped students.

Where in the world have these findings and beliefs led us for the past 10 years? Have teachers and teacher educators in social studies incorporated the promise of technology into the classroom environment? Have cooperative learning, small-group collaborative learning, advances in the development of computer software, and the focus on critical thinking and problem-solving skills (Benenson, Braun, and Klass 1992) brought us to an emerging classroom environment in which the information technologies are recognized as an integral part of the social studies curriculum? This column examines three recent studies that investigated the potential technology holds for teaching and learning in social studies.

Project ICONS

The first study is Project ICONS—International Communication and Negotiation Simulation—a computer-assisted simulation begun by the University of Maryland in 1981. The project allows college and secondary school students from institutions in countries around the world to play the roles of diplomats and policymakers in order to find answers to real-world issues such as human rights, world health, and nuclear weapons.

Rottier, Kathleen L. "If Kids Ruled the World: ICONS." *Educational Leadership* 53, no. 2 (1995): 51–53.

The technology used in the ICONS project includes a computer, modem, telephone line, and word-processing and telecommunications software at each site. Although the project requires access to technology, it is not a curriculum about technology. Its skeletal yet robust simulation curriculum is based on the notion that students need to develop a greater awareness of the world order and alternative policy options. Students deepen their understanding of a wide range of topics in the social sciences by using this technology as a tool.

There are three phases to the simulation:

1. Country research for four to six weeks. The University of Maryland sets out the parameters of the simulation, outlining the issues of the negotiation.

2. Negotiation for the next four weeks. Participants acting as diplomats exchange e-mail, write messages, and conduct teleconferences, continually reassessing their national position as the simulation evolves.

3. Reflection and debriefing at the end of the simulation. Students reflect upon their experience and apply their learning to a new problem or activity.

Students were tested before and after the simulation scenario to determine their knowledge of vocabulary as well as pertinent global issues. At the outset, no one could define nuclear nonproliferation or deforestation—by the end of the simulation, everyone was able to expound on the significance of these issues. Not coincidentally, at the start of the semester students reported reading newspapers infrequently, with little or no interest in foreign affairs. When the simulation ended eight weeks later, they reported reading the newspaper five to seven times a week and exhibiting a particular interest in foreign affairs. They also reported becoming regular readers of weekly news magazines. In class, their discussions of current events supported these self-reports.

The researchers report that the nontraditional approach of the ICONS Project encourages the high-level communication, language skills, and reasoning capabilities required of employees in today's real-world occupations; it also enhances student motivation and learning through participation in something they perceive as important.

The Archaeotype Study

Another fascinating study was done at Teachers College of Columbia University (New York) and the Dalton School, an independent school in New York City, in which 20 Dalton School sixth graders were compared with 20 from another independent school. The Dalton School students used *Archaeotype*, a computer-simulated archaeological site, to dig up artifacts, research on their finds, and apply their knowledge in the simulation. To test learning and understanding from the simulation, the researchers compared the ability of the students using *Archaeotype* to investigate and come to conclusions with these abilities among students who did not use the program.

Black, J. B., R. McClintock, and C. Hill. "Assessing Student Understanding and Learning in Constructivist Study Environments." Proceedings of selected research and development presentations at the 1994 National Convention of the Association for Educational Communications and Technology, 1994.

Results of this study indicated that the performance of the students using *Archaeotype* was 73 percent higher than the control group in the explanation and argumentation areas, which is a statistically significant difference between groups, $t(38) = 3.34$, $p < .001$. The *Archaeotype* students displayed a high ability to create explanations for their observations as well as argue their validity by mixing concepts and terminology from the simulation with their own terms and ideas. However, the students in the experimental group scored lower in the area of data representation. They didn't use such methods as counts, means, and proportions; nor did they use visual techniques such as graphs or diagrams to represent data. The researchers concluded from these disappointing results that the simulation would seem to be a context in which to introduce innovative ways to represent data, but that students need to have experience using computer programs for manipulating data as well as practice using them meaningfully as part of their work in analyzing authentic tasks.

Decision-making Study

A third study was one in which students in two eighth-grade social studies classes received either direct instruction in decision making using a computer simulation in cooperative groups or received no instruction in decision making and small-group communication, proceeding instead with a traditional curriculum. The treatment groups practiced their decision-making skills with a computer simulation different from the *Decisions, Decisions* lesson used to measure their skills, and they also participated in a class discussion after both simulations. The control group's exposure to computer technology in class was restricted to drill-and-practice or tutorial exercises with no exposure to a computer simulation.

Benenson, W., J. A. Braun, Jr., and P. H. Klass. "Did You Ever Have to Make Up Your Mind? Decision Making in a Social Studies Classroom." *Illinois School Research and Development* 29, no. 2 (1992): 8–10.

The study focused on small-group discussion to determine whether the topics and lengths of discussions differed categorically and quantitatively between those who were taught skills in decision making and those who were not. *Colonization*, a computer simulation in the *Decisions, Decisions* program line, was played by both groups, who also were given tape recorders to record their conversations while using the simulation. The researchers found that the two classes devoted most of their discussions to topics related to technology, decisions, and procedures. Furthermore, the classes spent about 39 percent of their time both on higher order discussions and on distractions (technology and disruptions). Students using this computer simulation engaged in conversation a great deal more than the five percent to 10 percent rate in Goodlad's (1984) study. Transcripts reveal that students were intensely involved in their learning based on the amount of higher order thinking in which they engaged.

Conclusion

These three studies investigating the varied use of technology simulations in the social studies clearly show that students who use them demonstrate not only better communication and language skills, but also have discussions that involve higher order thinking. This is particularly important in social studies courses where teachers are preparing students to become citizens in a democracy. The information technologies promote meaningful and intense conversation, engaging students in learning and growth.

These studies are clear in their findings, but much more empirical research needs to be done in the field of social studies and technology. For instance, how do students' perceptions of the world change as they begin to explore other cultures via the Internet—or do they change? As students in all disciplines drown in the information coming at them from radio, television, movies, newspapers, magazines, computer applications, and books, where in the world are the researchers and studies designed to investigate the impact of the information technologies on students in social studies classes? How does this explosion of information affect a student's view of the world? The studies reviewed here appear to be isolated. Perhaps they are a beginning.   ◆

References

Becker, H. J. *Instructional Use of School Computers: Reports from the 1985 National Survey.* Issues 1–2. Baltimore: Johns Hopkins University, 1986.

Goodlad, J. I. *A Place Called School: Prospects for the Future.* New York: McGraw Hill, 1984.

Ross, E. W. "Survey of Microcomputer Use in Secondary Social Studies Classrooms." Paper presented at the meeting of the National Council of the Social Studies, Orlando, FL, 1988.

Sabir, A. B. "An Investigation of Social Studies Teachers' Definitional Orientation and Its Relationship with Teachers' Attitudes toward, Knowledge about, and Willingness to Use Computer-based Education." Ph.D. diss., Pennsylvania State University, 1986. Abstract in *Dissertation Abstracts International*, 47: 1274A.

U.S. Congress, Office of Technology Assessment. *Power On! New Tools for Teaching and Learning.* Washington, DC: Government Printing Office, 1988.

White, C. S. "Committee Surveys Teachers about Instructional Media." *Social Studies Professional* 84, no. 4 (1986a).

E lizabeth M. Willis
New Mexico State University
Curriculum & Instruction
Box 30001
Dept. 3 CUR
Las Cruces, NM 88003
e-mail beckyw@nmsu.edu

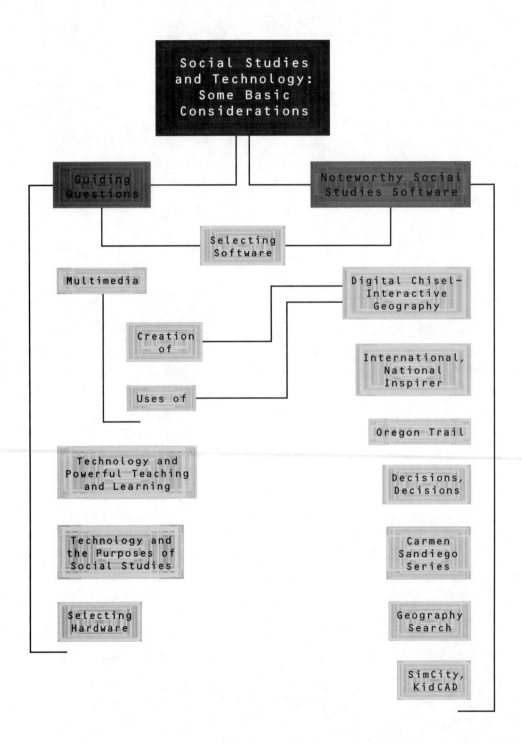

chapter 2

Promoting Social Studies Learning with Technology

Some Basic Considerations

Here is one teacher's dream for an ideal computer: Just give me "a reliable, reasonably fast box with a CD-ROM drive, 16–24 megabytes of memory, a 1-gigabyte hard drive, and built-in Ethernet for under $1000. My school will buy a ton of them," says John Darago, an elementary school teacher in Thousand Oaks, California. This is his wish today, but how will this dream change in two years? Five years? What software will be needed to fulfill Mr. Darago's dream in the future? In this era of rapidly changing technology, selecting appropriate hardware and software to promote social studies learning is a constant challenge for educators.

The purpose of this chapter is to provide guidance for social studies teachers as they decide what hardware and software will help meet the goals of the social studies curriculum as well as the needs of their students. First, however, some overarching considerations of social studies learning and technology will be examined.

General Considerations in Selecting Technology

While there is some disagreement in the profession about which academic discipline should be the center of attention in the social studies arena, social studies teachers generally agree that students should possess a certain basic knowledge and set of skills for use as citizens in a pluralistic, democratic society. The previous chapter highlights current efforts to bring coherence to the field by groups like the National Council for the Social Studies (NCSS), which published its curriculum standards in 1994. The NCSS's definition and 10 thematic strands of social studies, listed in Chapter 1, provide vital information for making decisions about using technology in the social studies.

To help us further clarify our vision regarding the purposes of using technology in social studies, the following section presents two evaluation templates, in the form of questions, that can be applied to decisions about the use of technology in the social studies classroom. If a committee of teachers were to meet to make decisions about technology and the social studies curriculum, these would be ideal questions to guide its discussion.

The first template is a set of questions focusing on whether technology can achieve social studies purposes. These are questions that can be broadly applied to any aspect of technology use in the social studies curriculum.

Does the technology/product

❖ foster the acquisition of knowledge, skills, and attitudes required of people who participate in public life?

❖ promote the development of personal perspectives that enable exploration of events and persistent issues, resulting in informed choices that reflect assessment of personal and societal consequences?

❖ develop an academic perspective that is interdisciplinary?

❖ further the construction of a pluralistic perspective that recognizes that divergent viewpoints are desirable in a democratic society?

(Rose and Fernlund 1997, 164)

Any technology product (particularly its content, organization, and activities) that does not rate an affirmative response to at least two of these questions would be only marginally useful. If a positive response for three of these questions could be substantiated, the product would be above average. Any product that fulfills all four would be exceptional (some such products will be identified towards the end of this chapter).

The principles of teaching and learning identified by NCSS as essential to social studies programs of excellence are the basis for the second template.

Does the technology/product

❖ help promote meaningful social studies?

❖ foster social studies teaching and learning that is integrative?

❖ further value-based social studies instruction?

❖ assist in planning challenging social studies instruction?

❖ actively engage the learner?

(Rose and Fernlund 1997, 165)

As with the first template, any technology product (particularly its content, organization, and activities) that does not rate an affirmative response to at least two of these questions would be only marginally useful. If a positive response for three could be substantiated, the product would be above average. Four or five affirmative responses would make it exemplary (again, some examples conclude this chapter).

Evaluating Hardware and Software

Educators need to be able to select the hardware configurations that serve the purposes of social studies education and facilitate the kind of powerful learning desired. Do you need to teach in a computer lab with multiple workstations that have access to the Internet? Do you need a large-screen projection device and a teacher workstation that includes a computer with a range of multimedia capabilities for large-group presentations? Or do you want several computers and printers arranged in six small groups with adequate space for a team of students to work together at each station? Each of these hardware configurations may be desirable depending on the curricular goals, type of learning activity, needs of the students, and software requirements.

Hardware

An evaluation template for decisions about hardware raises the issues of resources, budget, and facilities. A social studies teacher needs to work with a school or district technology coordinator and an on-site administrator. Wiring, technical support, networking, and accessibility of resources are among the issues that need to be addressed by a team of educators with an expertise for technology planning and the capacity to respond to teachers' needs.

Hardware-related questions to consider:

◆ What are the instructional tasks and the level of complexity of these tasks to be performed?

◆ Do my computers have enough memory to run the desired software application?

◆ What type of computer delivery system will be used—single computer(s), computers attached to a local area network (LAN), a wide area network (WAN), and/or the Internet?

◆ Is the speed of the network fast enough to accomplish the instructional task in an efficient and timely manner?

(Rose and Fernlund 1997, 161)

Software

Software is a term used to describe the wide variety of programs that tell computers what to do. Telecommunications software allows you to connect with the Internet, bulletin boards, and other online services. Educational software products may focus on particular content areas such as the history of the Civil War, world geography, or recent presidential elections. Other software applications are tools that allow you to do word processing, generate crossword puzzles, or develop tests.

Educational software that is used to teach content-specific knowledge or skills belongs to a genre often called computer-assisted instruction (CAI); it includes tutorials, drill-and-practice programs, and simulations. *Tutorial* software can teach social studies skills, such as interpreting map symbols or reading graphs and charts. Tutorials can also present students with new information on a part of the world, a historical era, or a topic such as United States presidents or Supreme Court cases. Tutorials offer the teacher an opportunity to provide individualized instruction for students who may need more learning time, students who have been absent and missed class activities on a subject, or special needs students who may find the tutorial a helpful way to learn.

Drill-and-practice programs are designed to reinforce previously taught content, providing students an opportunity to work on vocabulary, memorize facts, and perform other repetitive learning tasks. High-quality drill-and-practice programs offer diverse levels of difficulty, effective feedback to students, and opportunities for students to move forward or review parts of the program.

Simulations present a real-world problem, allowing students to explore a situation from their own classroom. For example, the award-winning *SimCity* series (Maxis Software) is designed to let students create their own cities, solve problems, and assess the local and global impact of their solutions. Some simulations are played on a network with teams in other classrooms within or outside of the United States.

CAI-related questions to consider:

❖ How does this computer program help achieve my objectives for this unit of study? Can I modify the program to better fit my plans?

❖ Does my computer system have the right hardware to run this program (required memory, printers, speech synthesizer, other peripherals)?

❖ Is the program easy for students to use? What preparation do students need? What preparation do I need?

❖ Does the publisher offer technical assistance, free or inexpensive updates, or network licenses?

❖ Does the program offer options for delivery? For example, can the program be used over the Internet or linked to sites on the World Wide Web?

(Rose and Fernlund 1997, 162)

The use of CAI in the social studies classroom continues to be strong because teachers have found effective programs that enhance learning. Many schools have a sizable investment in hardware and commercial software that have been integrated into the school curriculum. As CAI software becomes more available on the Internet, teachers gain a helpful tool to review products and consult online with other teachers who have used a particular program with their students.

▬ Multimedia ────────────────────────────

Multimedia is a special category of technology that will be discussed throughout this book, with particular emphasis in Chapter 5. Multimedia includes text as well as graphics, sound, images, and video, possibly all combined within one program. Multimedia products are produced on disk, CD-ROM, and videodisc. As Rose and Fernlund (1997) point out, commercially prepared multimedia products can do one of two things (sometimes both) powerfully: 1. Multimedia can present information to teachers and students interactively. 2. Multimedia can be created by teachers and students to present information to others. Each of these uses has a unique evaluation template:

Questions to consider when using multimedia:

❖ Do I have the necessary technology to use this multimedia package, including sufficient computer memory, a videodisc player/CD-ROM drive, or a large-screen monitor or projection device for whole-class viewing?

❖ What is the perspective of this commercial package? How does this viewpoint differ from other resources that I plan to have students use?

❖ Is this product to be used by teachers or students? Do I want to use the entire package or just some parts?

❖ In what ways will this use of technology enhance my students' learning? How can I assess its impact on learning?

(Rose and Fernlund 1997, 162)

Questions to consider when creating multimedia:

❖ Are my school's technology resources sufficient to produce a multimedia product? Are workstations available for the amount of time required to develop multimedia?

❖ What authoring program is best, given the previous experience of my students and the time I have allowed for this project?

❖ What do my students already know about multimedia? What technical skills do I need to teach? Are there expert students who can help teach others?

❖ How will I evaluate the multimedia projects? What are my requirements for the content of the presentations as well as the technical production?

(Rose and Fernlund 1997, 163)

As CAI for the social studies continues to improve, teachers will find many ways to incorporate this technology into opportunities for active learning, problem solving, and meaningful involvement of students. Programs that require students to manipulate data make use of inquiry skills that are important for learning social studies. Computer simulations can raise issues of vital importance to a democratic, pluralistic society; good social studies teachers can follow up on these issues with discussions like those described in Chapter 6. In addition, the computer can be a vehicle for cooperative learning and team-centered decision making. As you search for ways to achieve your instructional goals, you will find a wide range of software to enhance student achievement in the social studies. The above evaluation templates offer critical questions to consider in making these important decisions about technology. In the next section of this chapter, exemplary software for the social studies will be highlighted.

▪ Noteworthy Social Studies Software ▪▪▪▪

The proliferation of worthwhile simulations that present opportunities for historical learning is remarkable. Certainly one of the most widely acclaimed programs is Tom Snyder Productions' *Decisions, Decisions* series (Rooze and Northup 1989). *Decisions, Decisions* consists of 18 separate programs, four of which focus on historical content: *Colonization, Building a Nation, Ancient Empires,* and *Feudalism, Immigration, Urbanization, and Revolutionary Wars.* (Chapter 6 describes some of the other programs and their implications for moral development.) Any one of these can be learned quickly by instructors and students, and all are accompanied by well-written documentation in the form of a teacher's guide and student pre- and post-experience handouts.

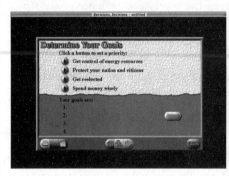

The above represent the range of choices that teachers and students enter into when using *Decisions, Decisions*.

What makes *Decisions, Decisions* unique is that it is designed for a teacher to use with an entire class and only one computer. Thus, the students can play as one large group or the teacher can divide the class into six smaller groups, with each group taking turns at the computer for input and feedback and then completing the decision making offscreen. The computer's purpose is to drive and store the students' progress in the simulation, which frees the teacher to promote thoughtful discussion about the issues and decisions that face students.

In essence, each program works similarly. The initial task for the students is to establish a list of priorities after they have read a short description of the situation in the student booklets that accompany the program. After establishing the team's priorities, the students make one of five decisions needed to complete the program. Following each decision are screens that report the consequences of the previous action, remind the team of its original goal, present a new decision to be made, and show the pictures of four advisers who represent different perspectives. Each adviser is accompanied by a booklet containing references that students consider as "pieces of advice." The pieces of advice are based on historical content, but they usually represent divergent points of view. They can provoke a good deal of discussion regarding the pros and cons of any decision. After students have completed the five decision-making loops, a score is reported, although its outcome is somewhat arbitrarily computed by the computer because the real emphasis in *Decisions, Decisions* is on promoting discussion and decision-making skills among students working in groups. The latest version of *Decisions, Decisions* includes an online feature that gives students access to a text editor with which they can enter their reasons for a decision. Students using the network at a later time can read about the basis for a previous group's decision and use this as a topic to initiate a discussion. Tom Snyder Productions also helps classrooms that are interested in playing this simulation connect with each other via e-mail over the Internet.

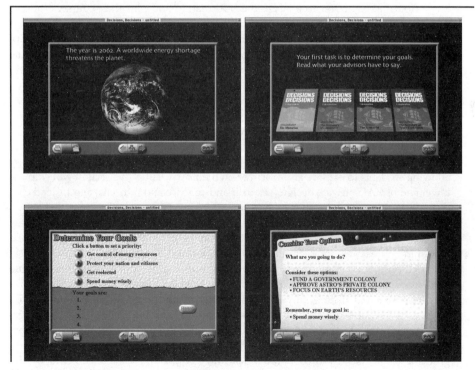

Although based on futuristic scenarios, *Decisions, Decisions* draws on historical content.

Teachers can incorporate these programs into units of study in a number of ways. For example, *Colonization* would be an ideal way to introduce or end a unit on the Age of Exploration. The individual references of the advisers could serve as springboards for further inquiry. Using database and spreadsheet programs, files could be created that contain pertinent information on the length of a journey, a host country, the countries visited, etc., for the stories of the intrepid explorers whom the students study.

Oregon Trail (and the latest CD-ROM version, *Oregon Trail II*), produced by MECC, has remained a popular program with students; it allows them to become pioneers in a wagon-train trip across the American frontier during which they face a number of calamities, including illness, attacks by hostile Native Americans and wild animals, and bad weather. There is a network version of this available and teams of students can work at individual computers to complete the simulation. This particular program, while widely acclaimed and very popular, is not without its critics. (See Reading 2 of this chapter.)

Geography Search, a simulation by Tom Snyder Productions, combines history and geography and allows up to six groups of students to be involved. The software has each group of students work as a "crew" setting sail to find the New World. The computer provides them with data relative to wind speed, weather, time of day, longitude and latitude, and provisions. Students record the data in their crew logbook and work away from the computer to analyze the information and plot their course. Students then enter their planned route into the computer and get an update on data. The quest for the New World continues until it is discovered and the crew returns. Students learn about the history of early naval exploration, such as ship building and navigational instruments, and geographic concepts, such as the earth's rotation and longitude and latitude.

Geographers are concerned with spatial patterns and data that document how human relationships with the environment vary over time and from place to place. Because of its graphic capabilities and data-retrieval functions, the computer is an ideal tool for studying the vast array of words, numbers, and spatial patterns that comprise the field of geography. Enlisting a computer as a tool for studying geography maximizes learning by allowing students to explore and discover on their own. Thus, this section will skip the lower end of CAI software design (i.e., drill-and-practice and tutorials) and instead concentrate on software that fosters higher-order thinking. Geographic software that allows students to compare and contrast regions of the earth, synthesize geographic data, seek correlations, and hypothesize and test for conclusions about the world we live in can be placed into three categories: simulations, databases, and multimedia.

Two programs in another simulation series by Tom Snyder Productions provide students with access to a wealth of information about demographics, economics, political affiliations and history, physical characteristics, and location. Like many of Tom Snyder Productions' other programs, *National Inspirer* and *International Inspirer* are designed as groupware and are for use in a classroom equipped with only one computer. Multiple-team or whole-class play, however, can be accommodated. These two programs lend themselves to cooperative learning groups and their documentation describes how teachers can orchestrate the use of these strategies in conjunction with the programs.

National Inspirer and *International Inspirer* involve students in the task of visiting 10 different states and countries, respectively. Students accumulate points by landing in locations that have one of two characteristics identified before play begins (points are maximized if a location has both characteristics). Examples of the characteristics that students seek include high dairy production, certain mineral resources, and demographic characteristics such as a high literacy rate. But for points to be awarded, the player(s) must land on the tenth move in a location with another specific characteristic. Accompanying the software are reference books that contain the necessary information to match characteristics and locations. Students must use these reference books to research their best itinerary prior to playing. Herein lies the real educational value of the programs: students work with graphs, maps, and a variety of data to plan their stops and final destination.

Above are some of the screens that prompt students to research specific characteristics in the reference booklets that they study as they plan their trip.

An enormously popular series that develops a spatial sense as well as research and deductive-reasoning skills are the *Carmen Sandiego* simulations developed by Brøderbund Software. In *Where in Time is Carmen Sandiego?*, an infamous international criminal travels back in time to countries around the world during the Middle Ages, the Renaissance, the Industrial Revolution, and Modern Times. The student's task is to track the criminal down based on clues provided by the simulation. *The New American Desktop Encyclopedia* accompanies the program to help students make sense of the clues. Other programs in this series focus on the United States, the world, and Europe. To make optimum use of programs such as these in a social studies classroom, a teacher must be ready to act as a facilitator of follow-up discussions and a resource for further learning.

Two simulations that involve students in the construction of an environment—a microworld—are *SimCity* and *KidCAD*. *SimCity* is a systems simulation where events and variables can be manipulated. Students are provided with the rules and tools that allow them to design and control a system, in this case a city. *SimCity* allows students to see the end results of their decisions without suffering real-world consequences.

KidCAD is another microworld construction kit. It comes with town, city, and farm files that are already constructed. In the Design Center, students can build, decorate, and locate structures and living things in an environment they control. There is a multitude of cross-curricular possibilities with this software as students develop geographic concepts regarding space and human use of it. Students can be encouraged to write stories about the communities they construct. (One class wrote about life in a castle that they constructed with *KidCAD* during a world history unit.) Mathematical concepts such as scale and proportion are developed with this program as the students plan and construct environments. This software is particularly adaptable to cooperative group-learning structures.

Digital Chisel from Pierian Springs Software is another good CAI program; it combines instructional lessons, application activities, and multimedia potential. Using the visual interface of a college campus (although it's appropriate for students in fourth grade and above), the designers of *Digital Chisel* have included *Interactive Geography* as one of the "buildings" on its computerized campus. This software offers a "course" centered on the five themes of geography: location, place, human-environment interactions, regions, and movement. The student enters the geography building of the campus and then selects a room that features instruction and skill lessons based on one of the themes. For example, in the room dedicated to the theme of movement there are lessons on people and products as well as lessons on movement and communication. Lessons focus on skill acquisition by timing and scoring student success as the skills are applied.

In addition to offering drill-and-practice and tutorial learning experiences through *Interactive Geography*, *Digital Chisel* is a multimedia authoring tool used in conjunction with any of the college buildings that house the courses students take; currently geography and art are available, with other areas on the campus "under construction." *Digital Chisel* allows teachers or students to combine graphics, video clips, sound, animation, and text into customized multimedia presentations. Thus, a teacher or student who would like to make a presentation on a particular facet of geography (or history) could use this tool and link it to any lesson from *Interactive Geography*. A CD-ROM included with *Interactive Geography* contains hundreds of photos and graphic images to be used in the creation of multimedia presentations. The CD-ROM can be used in conjunction with *Digital Chisel*, *HyperCard*, or any other hypermedia authoring program, as well as with word-processing programs. (See Chapter 5 for a more complete description of hypermedia.)

Summary

At the annual NCSS meeting in 1989, Harland Cleveland invoked the ancient Chinese blessing, "may you live in interesting times," to describe the use of technology in social studies education in the twenty-first century. Part of what makes our times so interesting is the vast array of choices we have regarding the use of technology.

This chapter provides some guidance for a social studies teacher making selections amid the rapidly changing field of technology. The templates and exemplary software are intended to serve as starting points from which teachers can begin to make decisions about how they will use the tools of technology in their social studies curriculum.

In upcoming chapters, the tool and problem-solving potential of software is emphasized. Specific software and strategies that promote higher-order and critical thinking will also be highlighted. Whether an elementary or secondary school teacher of social studies, you should feel properly prepared to begin using technology in your classroom when you are finished reading this book. However, as the history of computer-based technology development over the past 10 years has taught us, rapid change and improvement proceed exponentially. Once you begin using technology in teaching social studies, a process of life-long learning sets in. May you live in interesting times.

References

Articles

Betts, Frank. "On the Birth of the Communication Age: A Conversation with David Thornburg." *Educational Leadership* 51 (April 1994): 20–23.

Darago, John. Quoted in a column by Charles Pillar. *Los Angeles Times*, 5 May 1997.

Hertzberg, Lanny. "World Exploration." *Electronic Learning* 10 (November/December 1990): 42–43.

Means, Barbara, and Kerry Olson. "The Link between Technology and Authentic Learning." *Educational Leadership* 51, no. 7 (April 1994): 15–18.

Rose, Stephan A., and Phyllis Maxey Fernlund. "Using Technology for Powerful Social Studies Learning." *Social Education* 61 (March 1997): 160–66.

Books

National Council for the Social Studies. *Expectations of Excellence: Curriculum Standards for the Social Studies*. Washington, DC: National Council for the Social Studies, 1994.

Rooze, Gene, and Terry Northup. *Computers, Thinking, and Social Studies*. Englewood, CO: Teachers Idea Press, 1989.

Discussion Questions

1. Describe how the simulation *Decisions, Decisions* can be used with an entire class and only one computer. How can the students have access to the computer? What is the function of the computer in this simulation?

2. Describe one of the three frameworks for evaluating hardware, CAI, and multimedia. What are the essential questions it poses?

Additional Readings and Questions

Flake, Janice L., and Marvel Lou Sandon. "Using Maps and Computers as Integrative Tools for the Elementary Classroom." *Journal of Computing in Childhood Education* 2, no. 1 (fall 1990): 19–31.

1. What are some of the cognitive skills that can be developed when students use computers to learn about maps and map skills?

2. Pick a content area, such as science or mathematics, and describe some of the ways students apply knowledge gained from using maps and computers.

Bigelow, Bill. "On the Road to Cultural Bias: A Critique of the *Oregon Trail* CD-ROM." *Social Studies and the Young Learner* 8, no. 3 (January/February 1996): 26–29.

1. Although students encounter a significant number of women when playing *Oregon Trail II*, how is women's historical significance excluded in the simulation?

2. Why is the treatment of African-Americans in *Oregon Trail II* characterized as superficial multiculturalism?

Carroll, Terry, Cheryl Knight, and Ed Hutchinson. "*Carmen Sandiego*: Crime Can Pay When It Comes to Learning." *Social Education* 59, no. 3 (February 1995): 165–69.

1. What are some of the skills that students can develop through playing *Where in the World is Carmen Sandiego*?

2. How can *Where in the World is Carmen Sandiego?* be incorporated into other content areas of the curriculum such as mathematics or language arts?

Teague, Marianne, and Gerald Teague. "Planning with Computers: A Social Studies Simulation." *Learning and Leading with Technology* 23, no. 1 (September 1995): 20, 22.

1. How does the *SimCity* project described in the article encourage a learner-centered setting in the classroom?

2. What are the rewards and pitfalls of this teacher's experience with a computer simulation?

▬ Activities ▬

1. Reading 2, "On the Road to Cultural Bias," provides a review of a popular simulation. Take a simulation that you think would appeal to students and evaluate it based on the set of questions posed by Bigelow.

2. Review a district's educational learning outcomes for social studies (or use a set of standards recently produced by an organization such as NCSS or the National Geographic Educators Association). Using the simulation chosen in the previous activity, determine whether the program furthers these outcomes (or standards). In what ways is the content of the program consistent with the district goals?

3. Reading 3 on *Carmen Sandiego* describes how a simulation can be used as a springboard for curriculum integration by teaching a variety of skills and processes to students. Using another social studies simulation, develop an integrated curriculum plan that incorporates the simulation into lessons that meet the learning objectives from two or more disciplines.

Using Maps and Computers as Integrative Tools for the Elementary Classroom

Janice L. Flake and Marvel Lou Sandon

Maps have enormous potential for an integrative curriculum. Through the use of maps students can develop a number of cognitive processes, as well as meaningfully investigate many different content areas. Maps involve measurement and scale drawings, spatial relations and locations, geography, history, science, literature, current events, just to name a few topics. This article reports on work we have actually done with fourth graders at the Florida State University Developmental Research School.

Abstract

This article describes actual experiences from a fourth-grade classroom where students used maps as a central theme, in a theme-oriented curriculum. Their experiences included a number of computer experiences with the theme of maps. Map skills include: orientation and location and manipulating images. Cognitive skills involved include: problem solving, spatial development/visualization, and logical reasoning. Maps can be related to many subject areas. A number of relevant computer programs and other resources are listed.

Maps and Computers

Computers can be most useful in the study of maps and related map skills. Computer uses involving maps include: orientation and location, manipulating images, and simulations.

Orientation and Location

A major area that students need to learn to cope with in using maps is orientation and location. Knowing north, south, east, and west is not trivial for children. As they work on these ideas, they can learn to move up, down, left, or right on the video screen. Work with Logo can be most helpful in assisting them to develop this sense of orientation. Further, they need to learn to move to a specific location on a map or a video screen. Students can draw their own maps on a piece of paper, thermofax the drawing on a transparency, then place it on a computer screen. Experience shows that if the transparency is placed on the video screen before the monitor is turned on, static electricity will hold the transparency on the screen. Then students can tell their Logo turtle directions to go to trace out a path on the screen tracing a path on the transparency map.

Students can gain experiences working with grids and exploring the meaning of moving over X units and up Y units. Students can make more refined maps as they continue making maps.

Computer adventure games provide a good way for students to learn map skills through active learning rather than passively learning simply how to read a map. Students learn to make their own maps to help them solve the adventure games. Forsyth (1986) found that computer adventure games can provide effective and enjoyable ways for students to learn place location for both boys and girls.

Manipulating Images

Closely connected to map skills are transformation skills. Through working with maps and computer images, stu-

dents can develop transformation skills, which closely connect to imagery development. Such transformations include: zooming and/or dilating, translating, rotating, reflecting, and changing perspectives.

Zooming/Dilating

Zooming and/or dilating is a natural part of map skills. One can look at a large region, zoom in to get a closer look at a smaller part of the larger picture, or vice versa. One can relate concepts of universe, continents, countries, states, counties, precincts, and so on. Furthermore, as students examine different types of maps, scales should enter in, so that they can relate how far it is between two locations within each scale. The British journal, *Arts & Crafts*, has several articles illustrating concrete ways of working with zooming and dilation, including using pantographs (Kenneway 1987), building a sense of scale (Lack 1987), and large and small (Jones 1987).

Translating

Translations closely connect to traveling from one location to another. Students can connect the idea that if traveling from A to B and then from B to C, then how far would it be to go directly, if possible, from A to C. Students can explore under what conditions would it make a difference whether they went directly from A to C.

Rotating

Treasure maps and/or Logo can involve rotations. Degree measures are not trivial for fourth graders. But through gaming activities, rotation and/or angle measures can become fun and meaningful. Through concepts of rotation, students can concretely relate the ideas of north, south, east, west, northeast, and so on. Students also can connect the ideas of rotating with doing some desktop publishing, such as with *PrintMaster* or *Print Shop*, where they can use pictures that they can rotate. Furthermore, students can make shapes with Logo and rotate these shapes quite easily.

Reflecting

Students can relate to treasure hunts, where the map is coded so that when the directions say go left, it really means go right, when they say go north, they really mean go south, and vice versa. Logo lends itself very well for this type of reflection. Students can learn to draw a path or shape and then explore the effects of replacing rt with lt or fd with bk, and vice versa. Students could investigate artwork around the world, statues, reflecting ponds, and so on that are symmetric. A figure is symmetric if a line of symmetry exists so that when the figure is reflected about that line, an identical image appears.

Changing Perspectives

Maps can relate to changing perspectives. Students can relate, if they have flown, to looking down on their city from an airplane and how differently the region looks. Computer programs such as *Flight Simulator* (which is advanced for fourth graders) and *Perspectives* (which these fourth graders have done) relate to changing perspectives. Students can construct dioramas, three-dimensional constructions, and view them from different perspectives, as well as compare size relationships. They also can take pictures of a three-dimensional scene, then at a later time try to match the picture with where the person taking the picture was standing at the time he or she took the picture.

Simulations

Simulations work very well for students working with maps. A number of excellent computer programs that can help students include: *Where in the USA is Carmen Sandiego?*, *Where in the World is Carmen Sandiego?*, *Oregon Trail*, *In Search of the Most Amazing Thing*, and *Snoopers Troops* Cases 1 and 2.

Simulations are working analogies of real situations. Students become actively involved in simulations through making decisions, having actions occur, getting feedback, and so on. Through these processes students will learn major concepts in an active manner. The students in the fourth grade where we are working immediately went about doing their own creative writing about adventures around the world in *Where in the World is Carmen Sandiego?*, and creating stories analogous to the Carmen program.

Microzine Magazine is a disk magazine that often has adventure games, where students can make choices within a story and consequently branching occurs in the program. The story might be relating to a map and the branching may lead to students taking different paths.

Simulation Construction Kit allows teachers and/or students to construct their own simulations. People can create their own stories, graphics, and branching choices.

Cognitive Skills

Students can develop a number of cognitive skills through map and computer activities. Such cognitive skills they can develop include: problem solving, spatial development and/or visualization, and logical reasoning.

Problem Solving

As students attempt to solve problems such as in the *Carmen Sandiego* programs, they will need to develop some of the problem-solving strategies, such as brainstorming; isolating and controlling variables; decomposition and recombination; working backwards; using a model; estimating, predicting, and projecting; looking for a pattern or sequence; relating to a similar problem; and organizing and systematizing information. See Flake et al. (1987) and Flake et al. (1990) for further discussion of these problem-solving processes.

Spatial Development/ Visualization

Through working with different orientations on the screen and in the maps, students can develop concepts of spatial development and/or visualization. Students can begin to develop a good orientation through these activities. In addition to the two-dimensional monitor screen, students can get involved in working with robots and/or Lego Logo, and tell their robots or Lego Logo constructions to move about in the three-dimensional world. See Flake (1990a) and Flake (1990b) for additional discussion about these.

Furthermore, in the Lego Logo designs, students can learn to follow two-dimensional drawings or maps of three-dimensional objects which involve slices layer by layer of these designs. Also as students create their own designs, they should learn to write reports on their designs, which means that they need to learn to make depictions or maps of their figures, including a two-dimensional drawing of their three-dimensional design, as well as two-dimensional illustrations of the different layers or exploded drawings so that the next child can make the student's original creation.

Logical Reasoning

Logical reasoning can evolve out of mapping and computer activities. For example, suppose the students are working with the *Where in the USA is Carmen Sandiego?* program, and they want to go from Miami to Honolulu. There is not a direct connection between Miami and Honolulu, but if they carefully examine the program, they can find that they could go from Miami to Jackson, Mississippi; from Jackson to Minneapolis, Minnesota; and from Minneapolis to Honolulu. Another example comes from *Logo* and/or *Lego Logo*. To make designs such as the *Logo* or *Lego Logo* figures and to create relevant motions, students need to think through step for step how to get the kind of action that they want. Through such activities, students can begin to develop a sense of multiple step reasoning and chaining several ideas together.

Note that students can work in time duration connected with taking trips. For example, the times could be: in Miami headed for Jackson, Mississippi, on Thursday at 7 P.M.; in Jackson, Mississippi, headed for Minneapolis on Thursday at 10 P.M.; and in Minneapolis headed for Honolulu on Friday at 10 A.M. Do those times make sense? Other time combinations could be considered that may or may not make sense.

Themes and Maps

An elementary curriculum can be theme oriented. There are a number of themes that can tie nicely to an overall theme of maps. Bridges could be a theme. For example, Parsons (1987) uses the concept of famous bridges around the world, such as the London Bridge, the

Figure 1.   Traveling from Florida to Mississippi in Carmen Sandiego

Figure 2.   Departing Mississippi for Minnesota

Figure 3.   Reaching Hawaii, the Final Destination

Golden Gate Bridge, and the Sydney Harbour Bridge in Australia. There are old bridges in history, bridges associated with disasters, and different types of bridges—for example, suspension, covered, foot, arch, beamed, and cable. Through studying bridges students can locate the bridges on the maps or plan routes using the bridges or avoiding the bridges. In addition, they can make scale drawings or three-dimensional models of some of the bridges.

Another theme within the map theme could be transportation. Students could study a variety of types of transportation, such as trains, ships, cars, rockets. Liston (1989) illustrates ideas for studying historical ships. Mercer (1989) describes a whole-school project related to transportation. Angus (1989) describes ways of using Artstraws for construction of various models, such as a gate, trap, or drawbridge. He illustrates how students use problem solving in constructing these models and their motions. The students will need to remember to take into account the roles of weights, springs, levers, and the effect of gravity.

Relief maps are an interesting area of study. Smith (1987) suggests ways of having students make their own relief maps using simple three-dimensional figures. Students build three-dimensional maps in cardboard boxes.

Rivers could be another area of study. Students could examine the flow of water, find main rivers, find the great rivers of the world, identify towns or cities that evolved because they are on the banks of major rivers. Students can map beaches and see the relationships of the beaches with water flow.

Maps in the Content Areas

The study of maps cuts across many content areas. Such areas include: social studies, science, mathematics, language arts, reading, library reference skills, art, music, and multilingual/multicultural education.

Social Studies

Maps are often associated with social studies. Through studying different societies, seeing where they live or lived, and how they related to their neighbors is an important part of social studies. Furthermore, tying in current events, such as the downfall of communism in eastern Europe, provides many excellent opportunities for students to learn a large number of concepts, including examining the eastern European maps and seeing where these countries are and how they relate to Russia and the western world.

Science

As students examine different parts of the world, they can examine types of soil, animals, weather, and so on from that region. They might connect some history of science by studying major contributors of science from some regions of the world.

Students also study the universe, planets, and the planets' relationship with each other. This all relates to maps.

Mathematics

Measurement, spatial relationships, and visualization are critical parts of mathematics learning. These are underlying concepts related to maps. In addition students could learn to read schedules of flights and trains and learn to sequence time elapse events, such as setting up a schedule to go from A to B and from B to C so that they can minimize the amount of travel time. For example, suppose it is getting close to a holiday, and one student is planning a trip, such as going to visit his or her grandparents or other parent, turn it into a class activity. Planning a class trip is a very rich learning experience. Get some real time schedules and consider different routes and times and map out a best trip. Of course, also involved with taking trips are costs, distance traveled, efficient trips, and so on.

Language Arts

Students can learn to keep journals about their travels and things they have learned. They could either write their journals by hand, or they could use a word processor and/or a desktop publishing system. Through keeping such records, they can develop their writing skills in a meaningful way.

Reading

Students can learn to read about places and do research on such places. Through reading about places of interest, reading becomes a meaningful activity for the students. Students learn about legends, how to read them and how to use them. They can examine an atlas, world almanacs, and state handbooks to gather information. The students also enjoy reading factual stories, literature, and folklore related to geographic regions discussed in class.

Library Reference Skills

Through reading and writing about places, students can develop library reference skills. Myers (1989) makes suggestions of such reference skills. In addition students can learn to search databases and spreadsheets to get information.

Art

Many opportunities for art can evolve out of experiences with maps. Students constructing their own maps can be an art activity. One of the first maps students can develop is a map of themselves through drawing their own self portraits. They can draw maps of their classroom, their portion of the school, their school, the path from their homes to the school, and so on. Bowen (1989) suggests ways that children can add details to their pictures. Some journals make a number of suggestions of ways of connecting art and technology, for example, through design (Angus 1989), through towns and cities (Fallow 1986; Littlemore 1986; Moore 1986; Rowe 1986; Smart 1986).

Music

As students examine different parts of the world, they can explore music related to those different parts of the world, and they can begin to see patterns related to the evolution of music.

Multilingual/ Multicultural Education

Multilingual/multicultural education lends itself very well to the study of maps. As students examine a region, they can explore the culture and language of that area.

Overall

A major theme such as maps can be continued throughout the school year and throughout all subject areas. Current events, such as the flight of a space shuttle, eastern European events, and Panama events, can continually be tied into class discussions. The classroom should have a number of different types and sizes of maps displayed around the room, so that students can investigate places on their own whenever they want.   ❖

References

Angus, C. "Craft, Design, and Technology: Artstraws." *Arts & Crafts* (June 1989): 28–29.

Appleby, M. "Exploring a Church." *Arts & Crafts* (July 1986): 14.

Bowen, S. "First Art: Painting Detail," *Arts & Crafts* (September 1989): 4–5.

Fallow, E. "Towns and Cities: Road Sense." *Child Education* (September 1986): 22.

Flake, J. L. "An Exploratory Study of Lego Logo." *Journal of Computing in Childhood Education* 1, no. 3 (1990a): 15–22.

Flake, J. L. "Spatial Ability, Construction Toys, and Technology." *Journal of Computing in Childhood Education* 1, no. 3 (1990b): 45–55.

Flake, J. L., C. E. McClintock, L. Edson, K. Ellington, F. Mack, M. L. Sandon, and J. Urrita. "Mapping." In *Classroom Activities for Computer Education*. Belmont, CA: Wadsworth Publishing Co., 1987.

Flake, J. L., C. E. McClintock, and S. V. Turner. *Fundamentals of Computer Education*. 2d ed. Belmont, CA: Wadsworth Publishing Co., 1990.

Forsyth, A. S., Jr. "A Computer Adventure Game and Place Location Learning: Effects of Map Type and Player Gender (Geography, Instruction, Map Skills, Sex Differences, Social Studies)." Ph.D. diss., Utah State University, 1986. Abstract in *Dissertation Abstracts International* 47(6A): 2132.

Greenwood, M. "Old Buildings." *Arts & Crafts* (July 1986): 16–18.

Hunt, A. "Project Work: Simulations." In *Computers and the Primary Curriculum 3–13*, edited by R. Compton, 104–21. Philadelphia: The Falmer Press, 1989.

Jones, J. "Large and Small." *Arts & Crafts* (December 1987): 20–21.

Kenneway, E. "Make a Pantograph." *Arts & Crafts* (December 1987): 7.

Lack, M. "A Sense of Scale." *Arts & Crafts* (December 1987): 16–19.

Liston, A. "Historical Ships." *Arts & Crafts* (September 1989): 14–15.

Littlemore, J. "Towns and Cities: Maths on Your Doorstep." *Child Education* (September 1986): 22–23.

"Map Maker, Map Maker, Measure a Map..." *Lego Dacta Connection: A Newsletter for LEGO TC Logo Users* 1, no. 2 (fall 1989): 4–5.

Mercer, C. "A Whole-school Project." *Arts & Crafts* (September 1989): 16–23.

Moore, G. "Towns and Cities: Poster Pointers." *Child Education* (September 1986): 17.

Myers, L. "Using *Carmen Sandiego* to Teach Reference Skills." *The Computing Teacher* 17, no. 2 (October 1989): 12, 14, 43.

Parsons, J., ed. *Junior Projects No. 31: Bridges*. Warwickshire, England: Scholastic Publications Ltd., 1987.

Rowe, S. "Towns and Cities: Little Boxes." *Child Education* (September 1986): 18–21.

Smart, J. "Towns and Cities: Resources." *Child Education* (September 1986): 24.

Smith, R. "Landscapes in Relief." *Arts & Crafts* (April 1987): 12–13.

Underhay, S. "Project Work: Adventure Games." In *Computers and the Primary Curriculum 3–13*, edited by R. Crompton, 90–103. Philadelphia: The Falmer Press, 1989.

Williams, P., and D. Jinks. *Design and Technology 5–12*. Philadelphia: The Falmer Press, 1985.

J anice L. Flake
Department of Curriculum and Instruction
Florida State University, Tallahassee, FL 32306

M arvel Lou Sandon
Developmental Research School
Florida State University, Tallahassee, FL 32306

On the Road to Cultural Bias

A Critique of the Oregon Trail CD-ROM

Bill Bigelow

The critics all agree: *Oregon Trail* is one of the greatest educational computer games ever produced. *Pride's Guide to Educational Software* awards it five stars for being "a wholesome, absorbing historical simulation," and "multi-ethnic," to boot. The new 1994 version, *Oregon Trail II*, is the "best history simulation we've seen to date," according to Warren Buckleitner, editor of *Children's Software Review Newsletter*.

Because interactive CD-ROMs like *Oregon Trail* are encyclopedic in the amount of information they offer, and because they allow students a seemingly endless number of choices, the new software may appear educationally progressive. But like the walls of a maze, the choices built into interactive CD-ROMs also channel participants in very definite directions. The CD-ROMs are programmed by people—people with particular cultural biases—and children who play the new computer games encounter the biases of the programmers. Just as we would not invite a stranger into our classrooms and then leave the room, teachers need to become aware of the political perspectives of CD-ROMs, and to equip their students to "read" them critically.

Playing the Game

In both *Oregon Trail* and *Oregon Trail II*, students become members of families and wagon trains crossing the Plains in the 1840s or 1850s on the way to Oregon

Reprinted with permission from *Rethinking Schools* 10, no. 1, Rethinking Schools, 1001 E. Keefe Ave., Milwaukee, WI 53212; 414–964–9646.

Territory. A player's objective, according to the game guidebook, is to safely reach Oregon Territory with one's family, thereby "increasing one's options for economic success."

The enormous number of choices offered in any one session—what to buy for the journey; the kind of wagon to take; whether to use horses, oxen, or mules; the size of the wagon train with which to travel; whom to "talk" to along the way; when and where to hunt; when to rest; how fast to travel—is a kind of gentle seduction to students. It invites them to "try on this world view; see how it fits." In an interactive CD-ROM, you don't merely identify with a particular character, you actually adopt his or her frame of reference and act as if you were that character. In *Oregon Trail*, a player quickly bonds to the "pioneer" maneuvering through the "wilderness."

They Look Like Women, but ...

To its credit, *OT II* includes large numbers of women. Although I didn't count, women appear to make up roughly half the people students encounter as they play. But this surface equity is misleading. Women may be present, but gender is not acknowledged as an issue in *Oregon Trail*. In the opening sequences, the game requires students to select a profession, special skills they possess, the kind of wagon to take, the city they'll depart from, etc. Class is recognized as an issue—bankers begin with more money than saddlemakers, for example—but not gender or race; a player cannot choose these.

Without acknowledging it, *Oregon Trail* maneuvers students into thinking and acting as if they were all males—and, as we'll see, *white* males. The game highlights a male lifestyle and poses problems that historically fell within the male domain: whether and where to hunt, which route to take, whether and what to trade, to caulk a wagon or ford a river. However, as I began to read more feminist scholarship on the Oregon Trail, I realized that women and men experienced the Trail very differently. It's clear from reading women's diaries of the period that women played little or no role in deciding whether to embark on the trip, where to camp, which routes to take and the like. In real life, women's decisions revolved around how to maintain a semblance of community under great stress, how "to preserve the home in transit." Women decided where to look for firewood or buffalo chips, how and what to cook using rocks, how to care for the children, and how to resolve conflicts between travelers, especially the men.

Oregon Trail offers no opportunities to encounter the choices of the Trail as women of the time would have encountered them and to make decisions that might enhance community and thus "morale." It masks an essential problem: the choice-structure of the simulation privileges men's experience and virtually erases women's experience.

African-Americans as Tokens

Oregon Trail's treatment of African-Americans reflects a very superficial multiculturalism. Black people are present, but their lives aren't. Attending to matters of race requires more than including lots of black faces, or having little girls "talk Black."

Even though one's life prospects and world view in the 1840s and 1850s—as today—were dramatically shaped by one's race, this factor is invisible in *Oregon Trail*. *Oregon Trail* players know their occupations but not their racial identities, even though this knowledge is vital to decisions participants would make before leaving on the journey as well as along the way.

For example, many of the constitutions of societies that sponsored wagon trains specifically excluded Blacks from making the trip west. Nonetheless, Blacks did travel the Oregon Trail, some as slaves, some as servants, and at least some, like George Bush, as well-to-do pioneers. Race mattered a great deal to Bush: along the Trail, he confided to another emigrant that if he experienced too much prejudice in Oregon, he would travel south to California or New Mexico and seek protection from the Mexican government.

And Bush had reason to be apprehensive: African-Americans arriving in Oregon Territory during the 1840s and 1850s were greeted by laws barring Blacks from residency. Black exclusion laws were passed twice in Oregon Territory in the 1840s, and a clause in the Oregon state constitution barring Black residency was ratified in 1857 by a margin of eight to one—a clause, incidentally, not removed until 1926.

Upon completion of an episode of *OT*, Bigelow had established a successful small business and built a home—clearly he had taken on the role of a white man, because in 1850 the U.S. Congress passed the Oregon Donation Land Act granting 640 acres to free white males and their wives only.

Just Passing Through?

Oregon Trail programmers are careful not to portray Indians as the "enemy" of westward trekkers. However, the simulation's superficial sympathy for Native groups masks a profound insensitivity to Indian cultures and to the earth that sustained these cultures.

Emigrants often spread disease, according to the guidebook, which made the Indians "distrust and dislike" the emigrants. The guidebook further warns *Oregon Trail* players not to overhunt game in any one place as "few things will incur the wrath of the Indian peoples more than an overstayed welcome accompanied by the egregious waste of the natural resources upon which they depend."

Oregon Trail promotes an anthropocentric earth-as-natural-resource outlook. Nature is a *thing* to be consumed or overcome as people traverse the country in search of success in a faraway land. The simulation's structure coerces children into identifying with white settlers and dismissing nonwhite others. It contributes to the broader curricular racialization of identity students absorb—learning who constitutes the normalized "we" and who is excluded.

The Oregon Trail itself, not just contact with the so-called pioneers, devastated Indian cultures and the ecology of which those cultures were an integral part. For example, pioneers—let's begin to call them their Lakota name, *Wasi'chu*, "greedy persons"—cut down all the cottonwood trees found along the rich bottomlands of plains rivers—trees which "offered crucial protection during winter blizzards as well as concealing a village's smoke from its enemies. In lean seasons, horses fed on its bark, which was surprisingly nourishing."

The Oregon Trail created serious wood shortages, which even the *Wasi'chu* acknowledged. *Wasi'chu* rifles also killed tremendous numbers of buffalo that Plains Indians depended upon for survival. Edward Lazarus points out in *BlackHills/White Justice: The Sioux Nation Versus the United States—1775 to the Present:* "But the Oregon Trail did more than move the buffalo; it destroyed the hunting pattern of the Sioux, forcing them to follow the herds to the fringes of their domain and to expose themselves to the raids of their enemies."

Players pursue their own goals oblivious to the mayhem and misery they cause in their westward drive, ignoring the social and ecological consequences.

No Violence Here

Oregon Trail never suggests to its simulated pioneers that they should seek permission from Indian nations to travel through their territory. And from this key omission flow other omissions. The simulation doesn't inform players that because of the disruptions wrought by the daily intrusions of the westward migration, Plains Indians regularly demanded tribute from the trekkers. Travelers resented the taxation and frequently became hostile and violent. More accurate historical choices in this simulation would include harming the Indians or speaking ill of them. The origins of these conflicts are omitted.

In all my play of *Oregon Trail* I can't recall any blatant racism directed at Indians. But as John Unruh, Jr., points out, "the callous attitude of cultural and racial superiority so many overlanders

exemplified was of considerable significance in producing the volatile milieu in which more and more tragedies occurred."

The End of the Trail

In its section on the "Destination," the guidebook offers students its wisdom on how they should view life in a new land. It's a passage that underscores the messages students absorb while engaged in the simulation. These comforting words of advice and social vision are worth quoting at length:

> Once you reach the end of your journey, you should go to the nearest large town to establish your land claim. If there are no large towns in the area, simply find an unclaimed tract of land and settle down. As they say, possession is nine-tenths of the law, and if you have settled and worked land that hasn't yet been claimed by anyone else, you should have little or no trouble legally establishing your claim at a later time.
>
> As more and more Americans move into the region, more cities and towns will spring up, further increasing one's options for economic success. Rest assured in the facts that men and women who are willing to work hard will find their labors richly rewarded, and that you, by going west, are helping to spread American civilization from ocean to ocean across this great continent, building a glorious future for generations to come!

The Lakota scholar/activist Vine Deloria, Jr. in his book, *Indians of the Pacific Northwest*, offers a less sanguine perspective than that included in the CD-ROM guidebook. People coming in on the Oregon Trail "simply arrived on the scene and started building. If there were Indians or previous settlers on the spot they were promptly run off under one pretext or another. Lawlessness and thievery dominated the area." From 1850 on, using provisions of the Oregon Donation Act, thousands of "pioneers" invaded "with impunity."

As Deloria points out, there were some in Congress who were aware that they were encouraging settlers to steal Indian land, and so shortly after, Congress passed the Indian Treaty Act requiring the United States to get formal agreements from Indian tribes. Anson Dart, appointed to secure land concessions, pursued his objective in a despicable fashion. For example, he refused to have the treaties translated into the Indians' languages, instead favoring "Chinook jargon," a nonlanguage of fewer than 300 words good for trading, giving orders, and little else. Dart's mandate was to move all the Indians east of the Cascades, but he decided some tribes, like the Tillamooks and Chinooks, should keep small amounts of land as cheap labor reserves:

> Almost without exception, I have found the Indians anxious to work at employment at common labor and willing too, to work at prices much below that demanded by the whites. The Indians make all the rails used in fencing, and at this time do the boating upon the rivers: In consideration, therefore, of the usefulness as

labourers in the settlements, it was believed to be far better for the Country that they should not be removed from the settled portion [sic] of Oregon if it were possible to do so.

Meanwhile, in southwestern Oregon white vigilantes didn't wait for treaty niceties to be consummated. Between 1852 and 1856 self-proclaimed Volunteers attacked Indians for alleged misdeeds, or simply because they were Indians. In August of 1853, one Martin Angel rode into the Rogue River valley gold mining town of Jacksonville shouting, "Nits breed lice. We have been killing Indians in the valley all day," and "Exterminate the whole race." Minutes later a mob of about 800 white men hanged a seven-year-old Indian boy. In October 1855, a group of whites massacred 23 Indian men, women, and children. This incident began the Rogue Indian war, which lasted until June 1856. Recall that this is the same region and the same year in one *Oregon Trail* session where "Bill" built a home and experienced "moderate success"—but thanks to the *Oregon Trail* programmers, learned nothing of the social conflicts swirling around him.

Oregon Trail hides the nature of the Euro-American invasion in at least two ways. In the first place, the *Oregon Trail* CD-ROM simply fails to inform simulation participants what happened between settlers and Indians. To the *Oregon Trail* player, it doesn't feel like an invasion, it doesn't feel wrong. After one of my arrivals, in 1848, "Life in the new land turned out to be happy and successful for Bill, who always cherished bittersweet but proud memories of the months spent on the Oregon Trail." (This struck me as a rather odd account, given that I had lost all three of my children on the trip.) The only person that matters is the simulation player, in this case Bill. I was never told whether life turned out equally "happy and successful" for the Native American nations who occupied this land generations before the *Wasi'chu* arrived. The second way the nature of the white invasion is hidden has to do with the structure of the simulation. For a couple hours or more the player endures a substantial dose of frustration, tedium, and difficulty. By the time the Willamette or Rogue Valleys come up on the screen we, the simulated trekkers, feel that we *deserve* the land, that our labors in transit should be "richly rewarded" with the best land we can find.

Conclusions

Before choosing to use CD-ROMs that involve people and place, like *Oregon Trail*—or, for example, its newer siblings *Yukon Trail* and *Amazon Trail*—teachers can consider a series of questions. These include:

❖ Which social groups are students *not* invited to identify with in the simulation?

❖ How might these social groups frame problems differently than they are framed in the simulation?

❖ What decisions do simulation participants make that may have consequences for social groups not highlighted in the simulation? And what are these consequences?

❖ What decisions do simulation participants make that may have consequences for the earth and nonhuman life?

❖ If the simulation is time specific, as in the case of *Oregon Trail*, what were the social and environmental consequences *after* the time period covered in the simulation?

❖ Can we name the ideological orientation of a particular CD-ROM?

Oregon Trail is not necessarily more morally obnoxious than other CD-ROMs or curricular materials with similar ideological biases. My aim here is broader than to merely shake a scolding finger at MECC, producer of the *Oregon Trail* series. I've tried to demonstrate why teachers and students must develop a critical computer literacy. It's vital that we remember that coincident with the arrival of these new educational toys is a deepening social and ecological crisis. Thus, a critical computer literacy, one with a social/ecological conscience, is more than just a good idea—it's a basic skill.   ❖

*B*ill *Bigelow is on leave from teaching high school history in Portland, Oregon. He currently teaches in the Graduate Teacher Education Program at Portland State University.*

Carmen Sandiego

Crime Can Pay When It Comes to Learning

Terry Carroll, Cheryl Knight, and Ed Hutchinson

Critics of education in this country have consistently complained about weaknesses in fundamental knowledge of "the basics." Some critics have placed particular blame on ineffective teaching, saying that teachers need to bring more imagination to their classroom duties to compete with expectations aroused by their students' constant exposure to television, movies, video games, and other highly attractive and easily accessible media (Goodkind 1992).

Computer guru Alan Kay has suggested that "Computers are the antidote to television." Kay believes that computers can inspire learning and enthusiasm. And he believes that they can transport viewers beyond the passive observation of many of these new media or the mindless button-pushing that is common to many electronic games (Rogers 1990).

An excellent example of a computer application that meets Kay's prescription is the software series *Where in the World is Carmen Sandiego?* by Brøderbund Software, Inc. This "classic" is part of a series available for all platforms—ProDos, MS-DOS, and Macintosh. It offers a computer-based, "arcade approach" to provide scenarios that can be used to teach students not just about social studies, but a wide range of other subjects. It can also introduce them to important research skills and group learning processes (Bingham and Portwood 1992).

The Basic Story Line and Software

For those not already exposed to this software program, its story line consists of a series of arcade-approach, computer-based activities in which a bewitching young woman (Carmen Sandiego) and her gang (Villains' International League of Evil, or V.I.L.E.) pull off a series of audacious thefts of many of the world's great treasures (Rogers 1990). Carmen and V.I.L.E. have eluded Interpol everywhere, so students join the Acme Detective Agency to track them down.

These student-detectives must trace the steps of these culprits through cities on as many as six continents, obtain a warrant, and make an arrest within a specified time frame. Their detective work at each locale produces clues about geography and history that point to the next city in the chase, e.g., "He said he was a cobra buyer." There are also hints about the villain's identity that are needed to obtain a warrant. Success leads to promotions in rank as well as increasingly challenging scenarios. Higher-ranking sleuths must cover more cities, spend less time in each, and occasionally take calculated risks (Hurlburt 1989).

The *Carmen* software features advanced, high-resolution windowing, beautiful city scenes, and an abundance of geographical facts. Sound effects, animated sequences, and a comprehensive manual round out the package. Both *The World Almanac and Book of Facts* and the software user's manual are included in the software package.

Motivation, Social Skills, and Learning Linked

This software program motivates students to learn and introduces them to a variety of cultures, people, places, and events that may have been foreign or unknown to them before. While educational, it is absorbing and thoroughly entertaining. The series combines real information with a humorous format that is suitable for students from the fourth through the 12th grades, and can be played by individual students, small groups of students, or entire classes (Miller and Caley 1987).

Carmen is useful because of the opportunities it offers to teach students a wide range of skills. Teachers can use it not only to guide their students' development of their data gathering, organizational, and research skills, but to foster their abilities in group learning, group problem-solving, and group decision-making exercises (Goodkind 1992). Moreover, *Carmen* can be used together with a *Carmen* database taken from *The World Almanac and Book of Facts* to stimulate in-depth investigations into geography as either a separate subject or as an integral part of instruction in mathematics, language arts, science, music, and fine art.

This article focuses on how teachers can use *Carmen* together with *The World Almanac and Book of Facts* to enhance students' critical thinking and problem-solving skills.

Playing Carmen in Class: Getting Acquainted

When playing *Carmen* in class for the first time, be sure to give students enough time to become acquainted with the program. If the classroom is like most and doesn't have enough computers, use a large-screen monitor for displays. Allow the entire class to work together to solve several cases. Let students or groups of students take turns suggesting how to solve the case. Provide instruction on the game logistics and the group dynamics required to track the criminals. At the end of the session, lead a discussion that focuses on concepts learned and skills attempted, incorporating instruction on the vocabulary used, locations "visited," and the components of the dossier and the database.

Once the class fully understands the game, divide them into cooperative learning groups to work on a computer together. The team members should rotate the task of typing at the keyboard, compiling clues, tracing routes on maps, consulting reference materials, and working with the computer database (Miller and Caley 1987).

Now tell your students to pretend they are working on a case. The actual investigation begins at the Acme Detective Agency. After entering their names into the "Crime Computer," the students see that the display shows their current detective rank and briefs them on the details of the assignment. These include what

Supporting Educational Materials

The Teacher's Manual

The teacher's manual (Miller and Caley 1987) provides all the information needed to use *Carmen* with students. The guide includes:

- Suggestions for introducing *Where in the World is Carmen Sandiego?* to your class.

- Suggestions for using the program in various areas of your curriculum.

- Reproducible blackline masters for use with the program. These are designed to help students succeed at playing the game and to extend the program's instructional value.

The Masters and Their Uses

The Police Dossiers include valuable information that students can use to identify and track down suspects. Each student should be provided with a set of these dossiers and be instructed to ready them before a game begins. The dossiers require students to apply a wide range of reading, vocabulary, and comprehension skills.

The Summary of Police Dossiers provides a list of categories of clues identical to those listed in the "Crime Computer" for each suspect.

Students should use the Clues Checklist to keep track of information gathered about the suspects in each case. This list asks students to match what they have learned about suspects in the dossiers with clues presented in the case.

The Database blackline master provides a list of cities and currencies for each country. This information can be useful because many clues require students to know the name of a currency or city that matches a particular country.

⟹

The glossary blackline master lists words from the game and the dossiers along with brief definitions.

Masters for two crossword puzzles and a Word Power Worksheet are provided to help students master the vocabulary in the glossary.

Teachers can reproduce masters for three separate map activities to help students identify countries and match them with their capitals or major cities; identify countries, continents, and interesting geographic facts; and trace the routes followed during their investigations.

The Flag Sheets provided are designed to help students recognize the flags associated with each country and thereby help them solve the case.

Two masters are provided to encourage students to apply writing skills as an extension of the program. These writing activities require students to create a fictitious suspect's profile and write a report of their "investigation" (Miller and Caley 1987).

Other Resources

Other useful resources include the two latest books in Hayden's "'Carmen' Discovery" series, *Where in the World is Carmen Sandiego?* and *Where in the USA is Carmen Sandiego?* These books feature complete alphabetical lists of cross-referenced clues, game hints, descriptions of suspects, and a checklist of stolen treasures. These "Discovery" books are intended as helpful supplements, not replacements, for documentation. They help to make these exercises more enjoyable without sacrificing educational value (Hayden 1992).

A Teachers Idea and Information Exchange database is now on the market for the subjects Europe, Time, USA, and World.

treasure has been stolen, where it was stolen, the gender of the thief, and the deadline for making an arrest. Clues to the identity of the thief enable the "detectives" to pursue the villain from city to city. Log the identifying clues into the computer. When the "detectives" have identified the suspect, the computer will issue a warrant, a document necessary for completing an arrest.

The main computer screen gives the detectives' current location, current time, and day of the week. Additional descriptions provide information that will prove useful as the detectives pursue Carmen and her gang. The pictures themselves, of notable landmarks or typical scenes in a country, also provide clues. When your students think they've gathered sufficient clues to identify the criminal, they should click the "Crime Computer" icon and the "Interpol Crime Computer" will be displayed. The computer will issue a warrant if the characteristics entered fit the profile of only one suspect. If the characteristics fit more than one suspect, the computer will display the names of all possible suspects. If this is the case, your students will have to gather more clues before they can get an arrest warrant (Brøderbund 1990).

Playing Carmen in Class: Exploring the Database

To utilize this technology even further, the teacher and the class can develop a database that can be used to record clues uncovered while pursuing

Carmen and her gang. The source for the database is *The World Almanac and Book of Facts.* Here is an example of a record from that database:

City: *New York (largest city)*
Population: *7 million*
Landmark 1: *United Nations Building*
Landmark 2: *World Trade Center*
Landmark 3: *Stock Exchange*
Tourist 1: *Skyscrapers, Subways*
Tourist 2: *Grant's Tomb*
Tourist 3: *Statue of Liberty*
Country: *United States*
Leader: *President*
Type of Govt.: *Democracy*
Population: *230 million*
Size: *One-third of Russia's*
People:
Neighbors: *Canada, Mexico*
Language: *English*
Currency: *Dollar*
Mountains:
Flag: *Red, white, and blue*
Products: *Designer jeans, latest fashions*
Animals: *Copperhead snakes*

The database allows students to research clues from all over the world. Take, for example, the clue: "The bank teller reports that the suspect had his money changed to liras." The students could then look in the database under "currency" and search for all countries that use liras as the basis of their monetary systems. That should narrow the search to a point where students should be able to pick the right locale.

Another example of a clue might be: "The suspect was seen leaving in a plane flying a red and white flag." The students would search for countries with red and white flags, then match that list to the list of likely destinations and make appropriate choices.

Building Custom Carmen Databases: Excellent Opportunities for Learning

Teachers frequently draw on their students' normal, everyday interests as a standard method of teaching. The *Carmen Sandiego* story line can be incorporated into many areas of the curriculum including mathematics (working with currency exchange rates, for example), language arts, music, and art. It can be used to develop thinking skills, research skills, data gathering abilities, and group dynamics.

Many social studies teachers have found that integrating the *Carmen Sandiego* story line with instruction and practice in the development of databases can produce significant added value to the curriculum. Developing the database could, in fact, constitute a discrete project that, like the *Carmen* exercise itself, incorporates features of cooperative learning. Teachers should encourage students to find new sources for information to add to their *Carmen* databases. They might suggest that students write or call travel agencies for brochures and road maps, or invite a travel agent or international visitor to speak to their class or school. It should not be hard for students to get their hands on a map of the world or a globe upon which to plot V.I.L.E.'s travels.

Teachers could also use a *Carmen* program to launch studies of other countries while having the class build a database. One way would be to hang a large map of the world on one wall to track the criminals' flight. As students play, the teacher would instruct them to gather information about the countries through which they are tracking Carmen and her gang. This information would include such things as the name and location of the capital city, geographic features, and the national currency (Castella 1986). The students would complete a record in the database for each country studied.

In a language arts application, teachers might ask students to use the computer in teams, solve a case, then write a creative story about their adventure. The teams could write and publish a detective newsletter, mystery story, or newspaper accounts of the gang's exploits or capture, keep travel logs or diaries, or ghostwrite an autobiography of Carmen or one of her gang members.

The *Carmen Sandiego* story line can also—and perhaps best—be used to teach geography. It lends itself well to the teaching of the five themes of geography: location, place, interaction between environment and humans, movement, and regions. Units in such a curriculum might include continents and other land forms; oceans and other bodies of water; cities, countries, and political divisions; directions; hemispheres; latitude and longitude; and time zones. Students, working cooperatively, could create world maps showing latitude, longitude, geographic change, and time zones and plot the progress of Carmen and V.I.L.E. across the maps they've created. Pointedly, in view of Ms. Sandiego's flight, the teacher could ask students to discuss the effects of geography on transportation, then ask them to calculate the gang's progress in terms of time, distance, speed, and, perhaps, typical weather conditions.

In a mathematics class, groups of students could chart the investigation, analyze travel costs, compute foreign exchange rates, and record expenses in ledgers. The plotting of locations traveled could be extended to a database and spreadsheet to calculate time of day; cost of meals using currency appropriate to the given country; and speed, distance, and the time necessary for travel. Students could use these data to study currency conversion, export-import trade balances, per capita incomes, and the national debt of the countries traversed. Teachers could have students keep track of the value of a particular currency by monitoring the exchange rate through reading their community's daily newspaper. Or they could assign groups of students a fixed amount of money to exchange in ten different countries on ten different days, then compare the final amount with its equivalent in U.S. currency. This type of information-gathering could lead to the study of the economic principles at work around the world.

Students in civics classes could be led to investigate the various types of governments of the countries they traverse as they pursue Ms. Sandiego. Class projects could include researching and discussing different systems of government or engaging in role-playing exercises based on being a citizen or official under that type of government. Or students could conduct a mock trial of Carmen and her gang members.

Anthropology comes alive in the artifacts, treasures, ancient relics, and cultural icons unearthed in the tracking process. Teachers of anthropology could instruct their students to research these objects and draw pictures or make models of them.

The teacher might ask artistic students to create "mug shots" or "wanted" posters of Carmen Sandiego and her gang members. Other assignments, particularly for art students, could include drawing pictures of Carmen and her fellow criminals or illustrating a theft, chase, and arrest. Students could create comic strips about Carmen and her gang, producing new episodes as evidence is discovered, or draw and illustrate foreign-language signs and banners. As for musical instruction, teachers could present, or students could research, the folk music of the countries visited in their search for the fleeing thieves.

Students could enhance their communication skills by using a word-processing program to carry out writing assignments associated with the unfolding search for the whereabouts of Ms. Sandiego and her accomplices. Vocabulary instruction could address three categories: 1. The "standard" *Carmen Sandiego* vocabulary list (including such words as "avid," "dossier," and "fedora"); 2. jargon and its meaning (e.g., "hard-boiled," "plug-ugly," and "compulsive criminal"); and 3. word categories.

In a much larger context, teachers could consider the following exercises as they exploit their students' interest in the hunt to capture Ms. Sandiego: 1. a timeline showing the sequence of events as they unfold; 2. a class discussion of values associated with Ms. Sandiego's crimes and the search to capture her; 3. an analysis of the careers, hobbies, and other interests of both the gang members and the witnesses to their crimes; 4. preparation—and serving of—the foods from countries and regions the

Curriculum Correlation

Where in the World is Carmen Sandiego? can be used as a springboard for a variety of instructional topics. These are some of the instructional objectives that can be practiced:

Map and Globe Skills

- ❖ Locate countries and capitals.
- ❖ Identify map symbols.
- ❖ Trace routes on maps.

Thinking Skills

- ❖ Recall and use information.
- ❖ Analyze and evaluate information.
- ❖ Use information to make decisions and solve problems.

Study Skills

- ❖ Use reference materials.
- ❖ Collect information from various sources.
- ❖ Take notes.

Comprehension Skills

- ❖ Identify supporting details.
- ❖ Draw inferences and conclusions.
- ❖ Make judgments based on information read.
- ❖ Understand figurative language.
- ❖ Predict outcomes based on prior knowledge.
- ❖ Recall details.
- ❖ Skim and scan for details.

Writing Skills

- ❖ Write about information collected from various sources.
- ❖ Write creatively.

Vocabulary Skills

❖ Match words to their definitions.

❖ Use a glossary to learn new meanings of words.

❖ Develop specialized vocabulary for content areas.

Research Skills

❖ Identify and define problems and suggest ways of solving them.

❖ Determine methods of finding the most reasonable solution to a problem.

Locate and Gather Information

❖ Choose appropriate reference books and sources.

❖ Evaluate information.

❖ Determine the completeness or inconsistency of data.

❖ Organize and analyze information and draw conclusions.

❖ Decide upon a rational course of action.

❖ Participate in group activities, including group discussion and planning.

❖ Engage in group decision making.

❖ Act upon group decisions.

(Miller and Caley 1987)

students have visited in their quests; and 5. research and discussion of the unique cultures encountered during the hunt, with special emphasis on dress, customs, and religion (Robinson and Schonborn 1991).

Teachers in schools where more comprehensive databases or software programs are available might consider an even greater in-depth examination of the fanciful flight of Carmen Sandiego and the countries traversed by the students pursuing her. This would be possible if the school had, for example, the *PC Globe* series, which consists of an electronic atlas that provides instant profiles of 190 countries with detailed maps, graphics, facts, and figures all available at the touch of a key or the click of a mouse. These could be used as the basis for in-depth reports and debates in class (Goodkind 1992).

Carmen Sandiego: The Game Show

Teachers have another, easily accessible option for using the *Where in the World is Carmen Sandiego?* story line in their teaching: The *Carmen Sandiego* game show is broadcast weekdays by PBS. Aired in the late afternoon, this television program provides a good model for classroom lessons presented in a game show format. An ideal set-up might include a computer with an overhead projection panel as well as enough computers for small teams to delve into the database to answer game show questions, taking turns at the computers if there are too few of them. To build suspense and extend their students' use of the database, teachers could withhold or hide the names of some of the locales. All students could be awarded "points" for correct answers, but teachers could award higher scores for correct responses early on, when there are fewer clues, and fewer points when discovery of the villains' hideaway becomes more and more inevitable.

Carmen in Action: Where in Greensboro Is Carmen Sandiego?

This article has explored many of the creative ways that teachers can use the imaginative *Carmen Sandiego* software package and the other materials associated with it to teach a host of subjects. The authors have learned of one particularly innovative example of how a teacher and students at one school in North Carolina used *Where in the World is Carmen Sandiego?* to their best teaching advantage.

For "Computer Learning Month," the interdisciplinary facilitator at the Lincoln Middle School of Science, Math and Technology in Greensboro, North Carolina, developed a multidisciplinary format for studying North Carolina that integrated written data, sound, digitized images, and videos into the curriculum. A group of eighth graders created and then portrayed a gang of villains who joined Carmen Sandiego in a month of "goody grabbing" in Greensboro.

The group, which consisted of 20 students, created two mysteries for elementary students to solve. Twenty-five groups of pupils from nine of Greensboro's elementary schools registered to chase the conniving culprits. The local cable television presented clues videotaped at Lincoln School; media specialists at each participating school then recorded them. The broadcast provided students with two new clues each day for five days. One clue helped the student detectives deduce the villain's hideout that day. The other clue revealed some characteristic of the villain (e.g., "ebony-haired," "carrot topped," "insatiable appetite for shellfish"), thus helping the students to reduce the num-

ber of suspects. The students recorded their conclusions each day on special worksheets provided for the exercise.

By the fourth day, Greensboro's young detectives had enough information to fill out "Warrant for Arrest" certificates for Carmen and the villains who had eluded capture thus far. The solution to that week's caper was then broadcast on the fifth day. The following week, students followed the second episode.

The software used in preparing materials for this activity included *ComputerEyes* (to create "mug" shots of the villains); *MacWrite II* (word processing); *AppleWorks* (to create the database of information about Carmen and her gang); *Top Honors* (to produce the arrest warrant); and *Print Shop* (to prepare the art for the front cover of the "Police Dossier" booklet and the work sheets used in the hunt).

The equipment included a Macintosh LC II, an Apple JIGS, a monitor, a camcorder and tripod, VHS tapes, a remote microphone, a copier machine, and a printer.

The only prerequisite needed by the students was a desire to participate and a willingness to be open-minded to all suggestions.

The eighth-grade class and the facilitator used two class periods to research interesting areas in Greensboro. After they developed a list of "Prospective Places to Pillage," the students took a school day to videotape the locations. They used another day and a half to edit these tapes and add narration. They then took five class periods to develop the story line for each caper. Altogether, it took approximately 15 periods for the students to type and edit the various scripts for two capers, to create the database of villains, and to produce worksheets, certificates, and the dossier booklet. Two sessions were needed after school to copy and collate all the different materials needed to participate in the capers into individual packets for each elementary class taking part in the exercise.

This exercise provided the experience necessary to replicate the exercise in other parts of North Carolina. Each semester, eighth-grade social studies classes can create new capers dealing with other cities in the state. Like the original group of eighth graders, these students can use a variety of skills to develop the clues, scripts, costumes, and backdrops for further exercises. Skills in mathematics can be tapped—and taught—as students learn to draw maps of cities in North Carolina to scale. Scientific aspects of the state, including climate, topography, and geology, can be discussed and displayed in graphic form. Students in social studies classes can research areas of historical and geographical significance (Thanos and Tedder 1992).

This exercise shows that when teachers combine alluring story lines with today's electronic classroom technology, there are great opportunities for imaginative—and effective—instruction.   ❖

References

Bingham, D., G. Portwood, and L. Elliott. "Where in the World Is Carmen Sandiego?" *Journal of Reading* 30, no. 4 (1992): 370–71.

Brøderbund Software, Inc. *Where in the World is Carmen Sandiego? Users Manual.* San Rafael, CA: 1990.

Castella, V. "Computers-in-the-Curriculum Workshop." *Instructor* 96 (October 1986): 127.

Goodkind, T. "Interactive Geography: Some Cross-discipline Multimedia Application." *The Learning Post* (1992): 19–20.

Hurlburt, J. "In Pursuit of Jet-Setters." *A+ Magazine* (1989): 115–16.

Miller, S., and M. Caley. *Where in the World is Carmen Sandiego? Teachers Manual.* San Rafael, CA: 1987.

Robinson, M., and A. Schonborn. "Three Instructional Approaches to the *Carmen Sandiego* Software Series." *Social Education* 55 (1991): 353–54.

Rogers, M. "Crime Doesn't Pay: It Teaches." *Newsweek* 115 (March 1990): 72–73.

Thanos, L., and M. Tedder. "Where in Greensboro Is Carmen Sandiego?" Paper delivered at North Carolina Educational Technology Conference, Greensboro, NC, December 1992.

*T*erry Carroll is an Assistant Professor in the Department of Curriculum and Instruction at Appalachian State University, Boone, NC.

*C*heryl Knight is an Associate Professor in the Department of Curriculum and Instruction at Appalachian State University.

*E*d Hutchinson, who has now retired, was a professor in the Department of Learning, Reading and Exceptionalities at Appalachian State University.

Planning with Computers

A Social Studies Simulation

Marianne Teague
and Gerald Teague

Simulations are a wonderful teaching and learning tool that work especially well in the social studies curriculum. When enhanced with computer technology, simulations provide exciting and enriching instructional activity for students. This was our experience when we used a computer simulation on community planning with seventh-grade students at Northern Middle School in Calvert County, Maryland. The activity was supported by a small grant from the Washington Post Grants in Education Program. As a result of the project, students became aware of their responsibility to become informed citizens and to participate in local decision making. In addition, they

As a result of the SimCity project, students became aware of their responsibility to become informed citizens and to participate in local decision making.

learned how to work cooperatively in teams and use the computer in the planning process.

The Activity

With the cooperation of the social studies teacher, we introduced 52 students to *SimCity*, a computer simulation program allowing users to manipulate a variety of factors in the development of a community. The idea for the project originated with the reports in our local newspaper paper about the creation of a master plan for our township and the announcement of public hearings to present and discuss alternative plans. This event tied directly into the citizenship and geography components of the social studies curriculum.

As a springboard into the project, a representative from the county planning and zoning office visited the school. The representative described for the students the concept of community development and the factors considered during the community development process. A demonstration of *SimCity* then was conducted for the class.

Groups of four or five students formed teams and began their own community planning projects. Teams met weekly for one hour. All teams used the same surface area for their communities and decided as a group on the selection and placement of items such as roads, residences, and utilities. They recorded their decisions on paper before entering selections into the computer. Team members then discussed the program's feedback regarding taxes, crime rate, and public opinion, which helped them make future choices. Students maintained a log of their interactions, and group discussions and computer manipulations were videotaped.

Student Presentations

The student groups spent three months planning their communities with *SimCity*. Each group then presented its plan for consideration to the classroom teacher and the school's media specialist. Several groups that met previously announced criteria—achieving low crime rates and pollution levels with reasonable expenditures and public approval—were asked to prepare a more formal presentation.

Several members of the county planning and zoning office joined the educators as review panelists. Teams presented their community designs using the computer and computer-generated printouts. They described their final designs, explained their steps, justified their choices, and responded to questions. Although a bit overwhelmed by the review process, they experienced what it is like to develop ideas and defend the labors of one's work. Following this review, 20 team members accompanied several educators to the 1994 National Education Computer Conference in Boston to participate in a 90-minute poster session during which the students fielded many questions about their experiences. After a brief period of stage fright, the students began interacting freely with inquiring teachers, and wound up benefiting greatly from the exchange.

Some Observations

Two characteristics—realism and relevance—seem to separate simulations from outright games and make their use an excellent teaching and learning activity. Realism, as the portrayal of a real-life situation, reflects true-life experiences and better prepares students for the actual circumstances they are likely to encounter later in life. Relevance connects the material to meaningful experiences, so students are able to identify with and relate to projects that have a significant bearing on their everyday lives.

Simulations provide other benefits. Students seem to be motivated by "gaming." The problem-solving orientation challenges their creativity and allows for multiple solutions. The active, nonthreatening environment of simulations offers participation without risk-taking. Computer technology enhances simulations in a number of ways. Immediate feedback and record keeping streamlines decision making. The situation can be controlled and manipulated easily to provide various levels of difficulty and complexity. Cost and time do not become limiting factors. And, importantly, computer simulations allow the teacher to shift roles from presenter to facilitator, stimulating students to think critically while guiding their exploration through questions and comments around a relevant issue.

Several pitfalls with this computer simulation activity were experienced. Some students developed an oversimplified sense of reality with regard to factors such as construction, crime, pollution, and taxation. The solutions they posed brought adequate responses from the computer program but did not mirror the complexity of the actual process and possible consequences. Some students displayed a no-risk attitude: Why be concerned about public opinion when actual repercussions would not be experienced?

Other possible pitfalls include raising the students' expectations that other learning tasks will be equally entertaining, encouraging the sometimes false assumption among educators that active participation equals learning, and creating a situation where the teacher withdraws, despite the fact that teacher involvement is critical in computer-directed activities.

Future Activities

Now that this small-scale project has been completed and we have experienced both the rewards and pitfalls, we will embark on an expanded activity. During the coming school year, we plan to use the more sophisticated *SimCity 2000* computer simulation program. A select group of students will be involved with a more extensive community development project that integrates several subject areas around the media-center-based research and resource activity. In the mathematics area, students will engage in calculations and projections for land mass, budget, and taxation. As part of the language arts curriculum, students will record and report discussions and negotiations. They will engage in persuasive writing. The science class will focus on the impact development has on the environment. The social studies teacher will continue to link the simulation to geography and citizenship. It should be a most exciting and challenging experience.   ◆

Software

SimCity, Maxis Software, Morgana, CA.

M arianne Teague, Media Generalist
Northern Middle School
Chaneyville Road, MD 20639
e-mail: mteague@umail@umd.edu

G erald Teague
College of Education
University of Maryland
College Park, MD 20742
e-mail. gt3@umail.umd.edu

```
┌─────────────────────┐
│    Application       │
│     Software         ├──────────┐
└─────────────────────┘          │
                                 │
┌─────────────────────┐          │
│    Electronic        │          │
│   Encyclopedias      │          │
└─────────────────────┘          │
                                 │
    ┌─────────────────┐          │
    │    Timelines     │          │
    └─────────────────┘          │
                                 │
      ┌───────────────┐          │
      │    Graphs      │          │
      └───────────────┘          │
                                 │
┌─────────────────────┐          │
│    Authoring         │          │
│    Programs          │          │
└──────┬──────────────┘──────────┘
       │
┌──────┴──────────────┐
│    Desktop           │
│   Publishing         │
└─────────────────────┘

┌─────────────────────┐
│      Test            │
│   Generators         │
└──────┬──────────────┘
```

chapter 3

Application and Research

for the Software Social Studies

What would you buy if you had $1500 available to purchase software for teaching social studies? Let's say that presently your school has a few 10-year-old drill-and-practice computer programs on state capitals, the United States Constitution, and selling lemonade. Most of the floppy disks you find in the department office are representative of first-generation software, those boring drill-and-practice worksheets brought to the computer screen. What new software could you buy that would be the most useful? Considering your limited budget, is there software that teachers could use for different topics and for different purposes?

One solution to your shopping dilemma is to buy programs that are tools with which you and your students can perform a variety of tasks. Such programs are shells into which you can pour the content of your choice. When you use the computer as a tool, you are using its capability to store data, arrange it in a variety of ways, and print out results. Teachers of different grade levels and subjects can use application programs to produce custom-designed instructional materials. Such software can be used repeatedly for different units in the curriculum. A second solution to your purchasing dilemma is to buy software programs that are information-rich and can be used by teachers and students in a variety of contexts for researching information. The choices are not limited to programs that students use once and never need again.

In this chapter we will look at software that many teachers consider the most useful because it is adaptable to diverse curricular needs and stretches a limited budget. A computer can serve as a highly effective teaching assistant in social studies instruction and simplify the production of timelines, graphs, surveys, word searches, crossword puzzles, newspapers, campaign buttons, and tests. Some of the software is particularly effective with special needs students. Educational software that can be used for different tasks in different disciplines falls under the category of applications. In Chapter 4 you will examine the computer as a tool for word processing, database management, and spreadsheets. These are general-purpose applications that may be used in business, education, government organizations, or for personal use.

Electronic encyclopedias (available on CD-ROM) comprise a genre of software that can help students conduct research in much more powerful ways than was previously available with the hardbound volumes of encyclopedias found in classrooms and libraries. Not only are the research tools much more powerful with CD-ROM technology, but the amount of information that can be compactly stored on a disc is mind boggling. A more specific discussion of the technology that makes this compaction of information possible is found in Chapter 5. In the current chapter, we will examine the powerful changes in encyclopedias brought about by the combination of multimedia and computer technology and outline some criteria for evaluating electronic (also called multimedia) encyclopedias.

Educational application software programs have a special purpose. The computer is used as a tool just as it is in word processing, but the utility programs have a particular function such as making graphs, timelines, worksheets, or tests. Utility programs are valuable to teachers because they save time, can be adapted to curricular needs, and produce a valuable educational product. Let's begin by looking at some of these utility programs that are of particular interest to social studies. We will then turn our attention to electronic encyclopedias and the power of multimedia software as a research tool.

Making Timelines

Imagine a program that can print a timeline for any period of history, ranging from one to 99 pages. You could focus on local history, women's history, or world history; you could limit the timeline to various times in a single day or to a scope that includes centuries.

TimeLiner (Tom Snyder Productions) allows you to edit, save, print, and expand or compress timelines. Thus, a timeline's content can be stretched to the equivalent of 99 pages or reduced to a single page. The teacher will need to demonstrate the procedures for entering and editing data if a particular format is required. *TimeLiner* is capable of merging and printing two timelines, which simplifies comparing and contrasting events in local history with national or global events. To distinguish the two timelines, you might type one in uppercase letters and the other in lowercase letters, or you could use different-colored markers to highlight each timeline. There is also a new version of this program (for Windows and Macintosh) that allows the user to represent the timeline in multiple forms, including banners and lists. The new version of *TimeLiner* permits the user to import graphics, customized fonts, styles, and color.

Teachers can use *TimeLiner* to create a large visual display that wraps around the walls of the classroom. In primary grades, the teacher might have each student enter his or her name and birthday. This class timeline can then be printed, and a picture or drawing of each child could be attached where his or her name appears. Children could use *TimeLiner* to graphically display the order of events in a day in their lives or to order the events in a story they read. Older students can use *TimeLiner* to visually portray the chronological development of the curriculum during the school year, with student work displayed at each step. For example, if students were studying the European period of the Age of Exploration, they might begin a timeline with the Portuguese explorations of the Madeira and Azores Islands at the beginning of the fifteenth century and continue through the Pilgrims arriving at Plymouth Rock a century later. As each event and date is entered, students could be assigned the task of writing a short research summary explaining the significance of the event that can be appended above the timeline. Butcher paper can be stretched below the length of the timeline and used to create a mural highlighting various events. Thus, a living wall of history can be created, providing a visual record of any period of study.

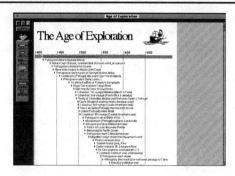

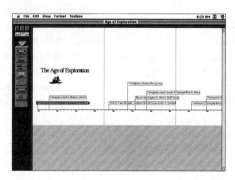

The above show the different ways that *TimeLiner* displays a chronological order of events.

This versatile program is a welcome addition to the teaching/learning resources for social studies. Although many programs claim to be appropriate for a wide age range, this program is truly adaptable for classrooms in both elementary and secondary schools.

Chronos is a similar product for creating timelines from Tom Snyder Productions, but it includes multimedia capabilities and is geared toward students in sixth grade or above. It allows for detailed timelines that incorporate text, graphics, and sound. Several timelines can be layered so that within a particular period, events in several civilizations can be displayed simultaneously. Thus, the European Age of Exploration can be viewed in conjunction with the explorations taking place at the beginning of the Ming dynasty in China or during the initial phase of empire building in Africa, all of which transpired concurrently. Keywords and a Find function allow the user to sort through multilayered timelines.

Authoring Programs and Utilities

A high-quality authoring system (often used in corporate training) allows an instructor to create course material for individualized or teacher-led instruction. It is a menu-driven program in which you can choose among several options for displaying text, graphics, sound, animation, branching and feedback, and record keeping. *HyperCard* for the Macintosh utilizes a scripting language called HyperTalk. It offers exciting multimedia possibilities for creating templates for student projects. Chapter 5 provides you with more information on hypertext.

A growing number of teacher utility programs allow you to enter your curriculum content into a predesigned game, a test generator, a puzzle, or a worksheet. These versatile programs offer an interesting format to reinforce and review content. Some teachers have successfully used a combination of programs to allow students to create their own review materials. Using a crossword puzzle, a test generator, and a word processor, high school students entered their own items and responded to each other's items, resulting in a highly participatory unit review (Sales and Goodlander 1987).

Test Generators

A computer is an excellent tool for storing test items and printing out different versions of the same test. There are many occasions when these features prove useful. Different forms of a test may be needed for different classes or for make-up exams. Perhaps this year in the social studies unit on the Middle Ages, the teacher emphasized the lives of common people far more than events connected with lords and kings. New items could be added to an item bank to reflect the new content. Items entered and saved from last year's test could be selected as appropriate. Over the years, a teacher builds an item bank that could greatly improve the evaluation process.

Most test generators allow several types of questions on the same exam: multiple choice, matching, true/false, completion, and essay. Statistical analyses available with some test generators can help identify weak items that need to be dropped or modified. If you consider purchasing a program, preview several different test generators. Programs differ in ease of editing items, formatting text, importing graphics, and other tasks that may be important to you. For example, if you have access to multiple computer stations, you may want a testing program that allows online testing. Then students can go right to a computer and enter their answers, and you can grade the results without ever printing a copy of the test. Some teachers will want a test generator with bilingual modes that support a particular language in addition to English. Others will need diagrams in their tests and want graphics support. Identify the features most important to you and your colleagues and invest in that program.

Review and Reinforcement

Drill-and-practice review is a tedious but essential part of learning. With the aid of computer graphics, animation, and record keeping, computer software can provide students with high-interest approaches to this part of learning. These programs allow a teacher to enter items or a teacher can involve the active participation of students in entering data and using it for review.

Some of the game-like programs that fall into this category are patterned after familiar television game shows. Others use sports such as baseball to organize the drill. *All Star Drill* (Tom Snyder Productions), *Jeopardy* (Gametek), and *The Game Show* (Advanced Ideas) are examples of such software. Others focus on concept formation, using clues as the critical attributes of a concept. An example is *Ten Clues* (Sunburst), a game designed for students in grades four through six. Demonstration games are provided by the program, but the primary purpose is for a teacher or student to create a game based on concept formation.

A teacher must first teach students the nature of a concept and the differences between critical and variable attributes. In social studies, each small group of students might be assigned a concept from the unit that has been studied. In the study of colonial America, concepts might include colony, plantation, Native Americans, governor, or slavery. Each group develops a list of 10 clues, including five critical attributes and five variable attributes for their concept. For example, the critical attributes for colony might include land, dependent, claimed territory, or controlled by another country; the variable attributes might include British, French, Spanish, Southern, or New England. Students arrange their clues in the desired order and enter them into the computer program. Other students then play *Ten Clues* and try to guess the concept. Each player begins a game with 80 points and one clue. When players guess the wrong answer or request an additional clue, they lose some of their points. The critical attributes are contained in clues that cost the player more points. After playing each other's games, students can discuss the importance of critical and variable attributes in narrowing down the possible answers. The documentation that comes with this program offers teachers a series of lesson plans to help introduce concept formation to their students.

Word Searches and Puzzles

A computer can take over the laborious task of creating a layout for puzzles. Teachers often need to review information with students in social studies, and computer-generated puzzles can save a great deal of time that a teacher spends formatting. The ease of using the software opens up the possibility of students working with the content while creating puzzles for each other.

Word search programs often offer teachers several options that affect the difficulty of the puzzle. Words can be hidden vertically, horizontally, diagonally, backwards, or forwards. A list of hidden words can be printed at the bottom or the puzzle or omitted from the page. In a program such as *Puzzles and Posters* (MECC) or *Crossword Magic* (Mindscape), a teacher or a student generates the words and clues, and the computer program puts it all together as a crossword puzzle. Teachers can choose the location of particular words and print out a copy of the puzzle with the answers filled in the blanks to use as an answer key.

Graphs and Polls

There are programs available that help students understand how to gather and present statistics. Students can gain hands-on experience translating statistics into a visual format, using bar, line, or pie graphs. A program that handles statistics well uses the computer's capabilities to spatially arrange and present information. Graphs and surveys can be created with a teacher utility program or with integrated software that includes word-processing, database, and spreadsheet programs. There are programs for very young children that combine mathematics and social studies. *The Graph Club* (Tom Snyder Productions) connects graphing to a story that accompanies the software, *Fizz & Martina: The Incredible, Not-for-Profit Pet Resort*. Line, bar, and pie graphs are used in connection with the story, and a marketing strategy creates a context for taking a survey.

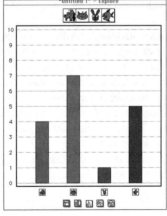

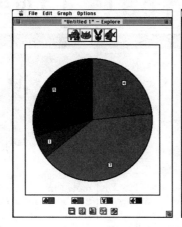 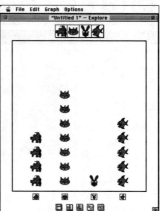

The above are the different ways that *Graph Club* displays data about four variables. Programs that help students understand and organize data from surveys and polls often include a graphing component. *Survey Taker* (Scholastic) is designed for students in grades four through eight. It simplifies the procedure of entering data and offers simple statistics, bar graphs, and tables. *Social Studies Tool Kits* (Tom Snyder Productions) offers social science data files for the United States and the world. Teachers and students can produce maps, charts, and graphs using the databases. Some graphing programs are specific to a particular subject such as *Good Graphs!*, in which students learn to accurately draw graphs for economic data. If students make an error, the program provides feedback on the type of error and supplies the correct answer.

Desktop Publishing

Classroom newspapers, newsletters, and reports have gained a polished look with the arrival of desktop publishing software. The computer assists teachers and students in word processing, page layout, and the incorporation of graphics. The following newspaper was produced by a Cincinnati high school student as part of a course in world civilzations. After studying a historical period, small groups were assigned a particular date and place from which to publish their papers. Stories were entered into the computer by teams of students. A wide range of desktop publishing programs are available to teachers. More powerful software requires more memory, but produces results that rival expensive typesetting. One of the most popular desktop publishing programs is Adobe *PageMaker*, which offers many type sizes, fonts, and layout options.

Archaeological Times

Overview of the Toltecs

New Evidence Uncovered about the Toltecs

The fall of the Teotihuacan* empire during the 8th century occurred for unknown reasons. It was replaced by the Toltec civilization that was comprised of two distinct ethnic groups: the Nonoalcas* from the region of the Gulf Coast and the Tolteca-Chichimecas* from the northwest part of the central valley region. The Toltecs settled near the city of Teotihuacan and established an empire based on tribute from the surrounding communities, which extended well beyond the Valley of Mexico.*

In the middle of the 12th century, external pressures from militaristic groups migrating into Toltec territory from the northwest and the east, combined with internal division, caused the Toltec empire to fall. After the fall of the Toltec civilization was a period of about 250 years where civil conflict and territorial wars interacted to prevent any single native group from gaining dominance. Finally, about 1400 A.D., the Actecs began their rise to power.

The Arts

The word Toltec* means "master builder," and during the time of the Spanish Conquest the Toltecs were a legendary people. One city identified with the Toltecs is Tula* in the state of Hidalgo, highland Mexico.

Map of Mexico

Tula rose to power after 600 A.D. and likely replaced Teotihuacan as the great state in central Mexico. The Toltecs of Tula are thought by some people to have invaded the Maya country and established themselves at Chichen Itza. The reason some scholars believe in a Toltec invasion is that the art of Chichen Itza shows remarkable resemblance to art at Tula in the highlands. Further, there are legends and histories from the Maya that speak directly of an invasion of Itza from the eastern coast by people who eventually settled at Chichen Itza.

The Toltecs developed a coarse form of architecture and sculpture that was used in the Classic Period. The characteristic features of the Toltec culture were columned halls, colossal statues of the Atlantes, the strange reclining figure of the Chac-mool (red jaguar), and walls of snakes and skulls. The first examples of metalworking brought from Guerrero have also been traced to the Toltec city of Tollán.

Present-day Tula has the finest displays of Toltec art, and basic Toltec design can be seen in the Yucatan at Chichen Itza,* although it has been decorated by Mayan sculptors and artists.

Chichen Itza

Chichen Itza'a history is rooted in the Mayan civilization, beginning in 600 A.D., but it was subsequently taken over by the Toltecs in approximately 1000 A.D. Many of their bloody practices are reflected in the prominent structures from this era. Dominating the center is the majestic pyramid of Kulkulkan—the plumed serpent. Named by the Spanish "El Castillo,"* it is the crowning feature in this ancient city, which was built to reflect both the Mayan and Toltec reliance upon astrological movements for agricultural predictions.

Timeline

7th century A.D.   The Toltecs move into the Valley of Mexico after the fall of the Teotihuacan Empire

10th century A.D.   Tula becomes capital and grows to over 30,000–40,000 people

10th to 12th century A.D. Toltecs dominate central Mexico

12th century A.D.   Tula is destroyed and the fall of the Toltecs

* important vocabulary terms

Created by Manish Mistry, a freshman in Tim Dugan's world civilizations class at Princeton High School in Cincinnati, Ohio.

Tom Snyder Productions has two related pieces of software that are ideal desktop publishing applications. One is *Classroom Newspaper Workshop,* which, as its name implies, is an interactive unit that takes students step-by-step through the various phases of publishing a newspaper. Skills such as interviewing, writing, editing, and design are taught in a six- to 10-week workshop format. *Research Paper Writer* is a program that helps students learn and practice the techniques of research, reading comprehension, note taking, organization, interviewing, and most importantly, writing. Desktop publishing software packages are important resources for a social studies classroom.

There are also desktop publishing programs for younger students. *The Children's Writing and Publishing Center* (Learning Company) is simple enough for primary-grade children to produce a flyer, announcement, or letterhead the first time they use the program. Screen prompts eliminate the need for a detailed reading of the manual or extended time for training. As students become more familiar with an easy-to-use desktop publishing program, they can create reports, newspapers, or stories incorporating text and graphics in a variety of page layouts. Some programs include a spelling checker and a thesaurus and support color printing. Lab packages or network licenses permit these tools to be placed on multiple computers within a classroom, school, or district.

A Powerful Combination: Language Arts and Social Studies ▬▬▬▬

Application software can help bring social studies and language arts together in meaningful and imaginative ways. Children can use a program such as *Create with Garfield* (DLM) to write their own cartoons with dialog and captions. Characters, props, and backgrounds can be changed to produce a creative student product set in a historical context. Elementary and middle school students can use utility software to create calendars, award certificates, posters, cartoons, buttons, and stickers. Students may want to create buttons that celebrate a recycling campaign, a political election, or a national holiday. *LogoWriter* (LCSI) is a tool that combines *Logo* and word processing. Although the program takes some time to learn how it is used, it enables children to use commands and write their own programs to instruct the computer to write a story, design an illustration, make an animated cartoon, or create a game.

Students may benefit from software being developed that uses graphic concept maps, webbing, and advanced organizers for reading and writing in various subject areas. This software moves beyond the language arts software that focuses on word recognition or phonics to a more holistic approach to reading and writing. *Thinking Networks* (St. John's University) includes content area selections to help learners understand the structure of knowledge presented in various texts. The program includes word-processing functions so that students can be coached in writing for various audiences. *The Semantic Mapper* (Teacher Support Software) is one of many prewriting tools that encourages students to brainstorm and cluster information, linking new information from their recent studies in history and social science with prior knowledge.

■ Electronic Encyclopedias: A Multimedia Research Tool ━━━━━━━

Volumes of hard-covered encyclopedias containing of vast amounts of information on a multitude of alphabetized subjects is an image that comes to mind easily for most teachers. The advent of the computer and the evolution of multimedia technologies available for the computer are drastically altering this image for future generations.

Electronic encyclopedias allow users to browse through the contents and conduct searches geographically using an atlas interface, chronologically using a timeline interface, or thematically using an alphabetized list of topics. Different search modes are generally accessed through icons, and the searches are relatively simple to conduct. Some of the more recent producers of electronic encyclopedias are offering built-in support for online information updates. Chapter 7 provides a description of online telecommunications via the Internet. The promise of the electronic encyclopedia as a research tool lies in its ability to motivate students to discover and learn a variety of research approaches and provide information in sound, text, motion video, and still image formats.

Electronic encyclopedias can give students easy access to materials and concepts at an earlier age than would be possible with a traditional text format. A number of criteria have been suggested for assessing electronic reference tools' potential to stimulate student research and provide informational access for students (Johnson 1996):

◈ The modes for searching can be matched to the student's level or interest and these modes should have an intuitive graphical interface (e.g., timeline mode should be clearly identified by an icon that depicts a timeline). Products from the same publisher should have consistent command structures.

◈ Boolean searches are fully supported and properly identified.

◈ There should be hypertext linkages between related references and images as well as text. In other words, by pointing and clicking the mouse over a highlighted word or image, the computer will jump to a screen that presents additional or related information.

◈ High-quality audio enhances program effectiveness. Programs that include audio clips should have a simultaneous textual presentation of the same words (via a dialogue box onscreen) and vice versa (students should have an audio option to text passages). It should be noted that currently no program consistently provides this simultaneous audio and text presentation of information.

◈ The search strategy design encourages students to use higher-order thinking, but the strategies are transparent enough to allow the learner to focus on the information as opposed to the mechanics of searching.

◈ Students are given progress of the search, and searches can be reviewed and repeated. It should be simple to backtrack a search and edit it when necessary.

A number of high-quality electronic encyclopedias are available commercially. Among the more highly regarded ones are *Encarta* (Microsoft), *Compton's Interactive Encyclopedia* (Compton's New Media), *Guinness Encyclopedia* (Wayzata Technology), and *1996 Grolier Multimedia Encyclopedia* (Grolier Interactive). Each of these has unique strengths and shortcomings, but all have demonstrated their capacities for classroom and home use as research tools for social studies and other subject areas.

Summary

The hypothetical problem of how to spend $1500 for social studies software has some interesting solutions. Educators' interest in application programs and electronic encyclopedias reflects the changing role of software in education. Rather than simply using a computer to present specific information to passive students, software enables teachers and students to absorb knowledge, to manipulate information, and to creatively show the relationships among ideas. As Kozma and Johnston (1991) point out:

> Most of the award-winning computer innovations are designed to give students a more active role in constructing knowledge, with an implicit change in the role of the teacher.

With applications and research programs, a school can purchase software that can be used by a variety of teachers from different grade levels who teach different units or courses. Those scarce dollars available for instructional materials will be stretched further and will maximize the number of teachers and students who can benefit from using the computer as a tool for learning.

The next chapter will explore particular organizational tools for which social scientists might use a computer. Databases and spreadsheets are the common means to store and retrieve data in almost all the disciplines that comprise the social studies. The fundamentals of using databases and spreadsheets and their value as tools in a social studies curriculum will be emphasized.

References

Articles

"CETAP Report." *CUE Newsletter* 9 (January/February 1992): 13.

Kozma, R. B., and J. Johnston. "The Technological Revolution Comes to the Classroom." *Change* 23 (January/February 1991): 10–23.

Pogrow, S. "A Socratic Approach to Using Computers with At-risk Students." *Educational Leadership* (February 1990): 61–66.

Sales, G. C. "Using Computers for Unit Review." *The Computing Teacher* 15 (October 1987): 16.

▬ Discussion Questions ▬

1. How are the types of application programs described in this chapter useful to a wide variety of teachers?

2. Give an example of a utility program that will help a student review content that has already been taught. How can the teacher or student modify this program?

3. What is desktop publishing? What programs are available for children? for older students? for teachers? In what ways could this type of software fit into the social studies curriculum?

4. What are some of the qualities and features that should be considered when examining an electronic encyclopedia's suitability as a research tool?

▬ Additional Readings and Questions ▬

DuPlass, James A. "Charts, Tables, Graphs, and Diagrams: An Approach for Social Studies Teachers." *The Social Studies* (January/February 1996): 32–38.

1. What are the characteristics of charts, graphs, and diagrams? Why do some students find these graphic images confusing?

2. In what ways can software programs that are capable of producing graphic images help students create and interpret information in social studies?

Armstrong, Karen, Jacquelyn Brand, Robert Glass, and Lynn Regan. "Special Software for Special Kids." *Technology and Learning* 16, no. 2 (October 1995): 56–61.

1. Which products described in this article are most appropriate for special needs students in learning social studies?

2. In reviewing social studies software, how often have you found the features for software accessibility listed in this article?

Johnson, Judi Mathis. "Software Reviews." *Learning and Leading with Technology* 23, no. 6 (March 1996): 53–58.

1. What are the advantages of CD-ROM electronic encyclopedias compared to bound volumes in print?

2. Explain the ways a social studies teacher might use an electronic encyclopedia that connects to an online network.

3. Do you think an electronic encyclopedia would be most useful in the classroom or in the library/media center? Why?

Activities

Activity 1—Constructing Tests

Objectives

Participants will be able to:

1. Describe desirable features of computerized test construction software.

2. Use software to create a social studies test.

3. Edit their computer-generated tests based on general guidelines for test construction for mainstreamed students in social studies.

Rationale

Generating tests is a difficult, time-consuming task for teachers. A computer offers assistance in this critical area by making it easier to create test item banks, generate alternate forms of the same test, and analyze test results with statistical procedures. Suggestions for testing mainstreamed students in social studies can be applied to computer-generated tests, and the testing guidelines may ultimately result in greater clarity for all students.

Materials Needed

A test generator software program.

Advance Preparation

Select software to be used for this activity. Direct students to bring test items to the next class to enter on the computer.

Procedure

Review data entry procedures with students, following the requirements of your software. Ask students to work in pairs, one entering data and the other serving as editor and assistant. Ask students to print out two versions of their tests.

If your software permits, have students take one or more of the tests online. Use the statistical analyses to evaluate item difficulty and item discrimination.

After using a test generator, you may want to compare this teacher utility program with the use of word-processing or database programs for test construction. Ask students to evaluate each based on such criteria as ease in entering test items, editing items, storage and retrieval of items, random arrangement, interactive testing, and printouts.

Activity 2—Constructing Graphs

Objectives

Participants will be able to:

1. Translate statistical data into graphs using a computer graphing program.

2. Evaluate a computer graphing program based on ease of use, clarity of graphs and labels, and variety of graphs.

Rationale

One of the most important skills in social studies is reading and interpreting graphs. The actual creation of graphs can aid in developing skills in this area.

Materials Needed

A graphing program; a handout on data to be put into graphs; a copy of "Charts, Tables, Graphs, and Diagrams: An Approach for Social Studies Teachers" by James DuPlass.

Advance Preparation

Have students read the article before the class session to review the use of bar, line, pie, and pictographs in social studies. Select graphing software.

Procedure

Review data entry procedures required by your graphing program. You may want to use one of the data sets from the handout to illustrate how to translate historical or social science data into different types of graphs.

Assign students in groups of two to translate the data on the handout into graphs.

Group pairs to make teams of four, and have the groups compare their graphs and evaluate the computer graphing program.

Discuss with the entire group any bias that might be embedded in a particular display of data and compare that bias with the message that each graph conveys.

If additional software is available, students might compare other graphing programs for a range of grade levels.

— Activity 3—Producing a Classroom Newspaper —

Objectives

Participants will be able to:

1. Use desktop publishing software to produce a historical newspaper.

2. Describe the use of cooperative learning groups that use the computer as one of the tools to accomplish a group task.

3. Evaluate computer programs that generate newspapers and newsletters.

Rationale

The combination of text and graphics can make professional-looking products with the help of a computer. Social studies teachers can apply this tool to helping their students learn history, learn to work with others, and take pride in creating an attractive historical newspaper.

Materials Needed

Specialized computer software for producing a newspaper. Word-processing programs such as *Microsoft Works* combined with clip art can also be used, although the newspaper would have to be created by cutting and pasting text. Handouts that must be provided with this activity include assignment sheets for a particular date and place in the Civil War era, an outline of cooperative learning group tasks, a written evaluation, and a guide for the software being used.

Advance Preparation

Select the publishing software to be used in this activity. Collect reference materials on the Civil War that students can use for research. This activity requires at least two 2-hour class sessions (Sessions One and Five) with the remainder of the work done by the groups outside of class. If students have no access to the desktop publishing program outside of class, they will need five class sessions to complete the group project.

Procedure

Session One   Introduce the activity by giving an overview of the steps each group will follow. Divide the class into teams of four to five students and assign each team a date and place of publication. Try to assign two groups the same date but different places so that north-south perspectives will be represented.

Enumerate the different roles members of the group will assume in creating the newspaper (editor, layout expert, etc.). Explain that both individuals and the group will be held accountable for the finished work. Allow groups time to meet to select people for each role.

Demonstration

Using a large screen monitor, introduce the desktop publishing program. Demonstrate the steps students will go through in creating their paper—designing the banner and entering, editing, and laying out the articles. Review the types of articles that will be in the newspapers and the reference material available to the students. Demonstrate how to create a panel that includes both text and graphics.

Session Two   Provide time for groups to research topics and enter their articles. Teach the program to the editors and experts.

Session Three   Check with editors about the progress of their group in writing articles. Print out banner and any completed panels for each paper.

Session Four   Discuss layout with experts and make suggestions for a professional-looking product. Provide time for teams to edit their work and design layout.

Session Five   Publish team papers and complete evaluations of team members. Provide time for teams to read each other's papers. Evaluate the advantages and the barriers to using publishing software in teaching history. If possible, compare other desktop publishing to the program you used to create the newspapers.

Handout—Group Assignments for a Historical Newspaper

Each group will publish a newspaper from a specific place and time during the Civil War era. The stories should be written as if they were just breaking, and they should reflect the perspective of the geographical region.

Group One — Lincoln's inauguration, March 4, 1861, as reported in *The Albany Ledger*, Albany, New York.

Group Two — Lincoln's inauguration, March 4, 1861, as reported in *The Columbia Telegraph*, Columbia, South Carolina.

Group Three — Union troops defeated at the Battle of Bull Run, July 21, 1861, as reported in *The Newark News*, Newark, New Jersey.

Group Four — Union troops defeated at the Battle of Bull Run, July 21, 1861, as reported in *The Jackson Times*, Jackson, Mississippi.

Group Five — Lincoln delivers the Emancipation Proclamation, January 1, 1863, as reported in *The Washington Post*, Washington, DC.

Group Six — Lincoln delivers the Emancipation Proclamation, January 1, 1863, as reported in *The Richmond Post*, Richmond, Virginia.

Group Seven — Lee surrenders to Grant, April 9, 1865, as reported in *The New Orleans Angel*, New Orleans, Louisiana.

Group Eight — Lee surrenders to Grant, April 9, 1865, as reported in *The Providence Herald*, Providence, Rhode Island.

Charts, Tables, Graphs, and Diagrams

An Approach for Social Studies Teachers

James A. DuPlass

Charts, tables, graphs, and diagrams are powerful learning devices, and yet the ability of the American public to understand such graphics is suspect (Kamm, Askov, and Klumb 1977; Kirsch and Jungeblut 1986; Piston 1992). Graphic images have particular relevance to the social studies teacher's quest to cultivate problem-solving skills and to build an informed citizenry. A cursory review of newspapers and magazines reveals that new technology in printing and software is escalating the use of graphic displays to convey information. The use of charts in the 1993 presidential election campaign by Ross Perot—and later, by his opponents—and the timeline charts used by opposing counsels on the Court TV channel demonstrate practical uses of charts in the world outside the classroom.

Studies comparing the performance of students who were presented materials with and without graphic displays provide convincing evidence that comprehension was improved for those who were taught with graphics (Arnold and Dwyer 1975; Booher 1975; Decker and Wheatly 1982; Holliday, Brunner, and Donais 1977; Rigney and Lutz 1976). And while we can conclude that graphic images will increase in number in the learning media (text, workbooks, multimedia, overheads, etc.) of schools and in the larger classroom—society—and that our understanding will be improved by them, we have not adopted a consistent method for teaching how to interpret such images.

In this article, I want to establish an effective protocol for teachers to use

The Social Studies, January/February 1996, 32–38. Reprinted with permission of the Helen Dwight Reid Educational Foundation. Published by Heldref Publications, 1319 Eighteenth Street, NW, Washington, DC 20036–1802. Copyright © 1996.

when teaching students at the elementary, middle, and secondary levels how to interpret the kinds of graphical images found in the social sciences. I present first a review of the unique qualities of graphic images and follow that with two learning episodes and two proposed models for creating and interpreting graphical images.

Graphical Images Defined

Graphic displays, graphical images, images, and *graphics* are the terms frequently used to refer to the set of images used in print and multimedia. When Gillespie (1993, 350) pointed out that "[g]raphic displays found in content area textbooks are often ignored by students and teachers," he created a classification system as follows:

1. Sequential: flow charts, timelines, organizational charts, and process charts

2. Quantitative: number lines, bar graphs, line graphs, pictographs, and pie charts

3. Maps: political, physical, and special purpose maps

4. Diagrams: crosscuttings, blueprints, and machine drawings

5. Tables/charts: row by column matrices

Bill Winn (1987), in *The Psychology of Illustration*, wrote an exhaustive examination of graphs, charts, and diagrams and how they "communicate and instruct" (152), and provided the following definitions.

Graphs are taken to be those graphic tones that illustrate relationships among variables, at least one of which is continuous. Thus, a plot of height with age (two continuous variables) or a histogram showing the Gross National Products of different countries (one continuous and one categorical variable) are both referred to as "graphs."

Charts are those graphic forms that illustrate relationships among categorical variables. Tables showing the sources and effects of vitamins or stages in insect metamorphosis are examples of charts. Neither vitamin type nor stage of metamorphosis is a continuous variable in the sense that time or temperature is.

The difference between *diagrams* and the other two graphic forms is first and foremost one of function and then also often one of complexity. While the function of graphs and charts is to illustrate simple relationships among variables, the function of diagrams is to describe whole processes and structures often at levels of great complexity (153).

The Unique Attributes of Graphics

Graphics may pose a number of unique problems for students and teachers of social studies and may even inhibit their development of the graphical literacy required to be an informed citizen in a democratic society. Charts, tables, graphs, and diagrams can be viewed as a unique fusion of numbers and text. Depending on one's quantitative inclination, when confronted with a graphic, the student, and also the teacher in preparing for a class, may experience some latent apprehensions about coping with numbers and an X and Y axis. (Handler 1990).

Moreover, issues of right-left brain processing influence deep-seated individual experience and preferences for visual and nonvisual learning media (Springer and Deutsch 1985). Whereas a text provides its readers with facts, concepts, and generalizations in a familiar, structured, and commonly practiced form, a graphic does not supply students with the verbs to connect the nouns that are the substance of charts, tables, graphs, and diagrams. The very simplicity that makes graphical images appealing to many is the source of confusion for others (Boardman 1976). To interpret graphic images, viewers must intuitively supply the verbs, and not all, or even the best, students necessarily have adequate intuition for that task (Monk 1988).

Graphical images take on the eclectic nature of art. Unlike the author who creates information by the creative use of words and phrases and their juxtaposition in the linear form of text, the artist of a graphic image expresses ideas with line, shading, and juxtaposition. Graphic displays are art, implicit with the artist's imperatives of shape, form, and context. The rules for charts, tables, graphs, and diagrams lack the consistency and continuity provided by the universally accepted grammatical rules that guide us in language arts. Unlike the author who presents information in prose form by selecting words and phrases to amplify meaning within the known and rigid structure of a language, the graphic designer can organize both the structure and content of a graphic according to his or her eclectic, egocentric eye. The type, scale, and artistic features of the graphs created for this article could have taken on entirely different forms, based on another person's sensibilities, but conveyed the same information.

Although the type and form of a graphic selected by someone to convey information is an aesthetic consideration, certain forms convey some information better than others. For example, a pie chart cannot convey a change in population over time.

As Carole Paine (1983, 38) pointed out, "No amount of careful reading and attention to detail, however, can overcome the problem of graphs that are technically incorrect, even when the figures presented are accurate." As Paine explained, a graph's scales should start at zero, and the axis interval increments should always be constant or a graph's meaning will be distorted. It is essential that the scale and proportion of a chart reflect the numerical relationships of the data for the graphic to convey the intended concept. Such a rule requires the creator of a graphic to choose the type and number of images and the data to be included in each graphic. For the reader, the simplicity of graphic images may be misleading: readers need to give images the same intense critical scrutiny they give to prose. Holliday (1975) wrote that students may not take the time to evaluate graphic images in textbooks because they assume the images are redundant to textual explanations.

To evaluate the instruction being given to preservice social studies teachers on the art of preparing students to be discriminating users of graphical images, I reviewed the coverage of the topic in textbooks used in university courses. I examined 10 textbooks on social studies methods (see the appendix) and found a variety of perspectives and treatments.

Social Studies
Methods and Content

Encouraging education majors to consider incorporating graphical images into learning episodes is one matter that deserves consideration by the authors of texts on social studies instruction. Another is the method of teaching how to evaluate graphical images. Charts, diagrams, tables, and graphs appear frequently as examples of instructional materials in the social studies content areas and range from simple groupings of candy bars for preschool students to sophisticated economic supply and demand curves. Alas, directions on how to teach the skill of interpreting graphic displays are very limited and typically tied to the content area.

Geography makes extensive use of maps, perhaps the most common form of graphical image. Map graphics have the advantage of being based on real images (a map of Africa is based on the form of the African continent), whereas the other forms of graphical displays are images of man-made abstractions (a pie may exist but not a pie chart). Map-interpreting skills, as well as the use of maps to support the subject matter, are typically treated as an integral part of a geography section of the textbooks used in teacher training.

Economics with its preponderance of graphs would appear to be particularly dependent on the use of the graphic image. Highfill and Weber (1990) indicate that understanding economics involves command of both abstract concepts and their application, and they insist, "Both levels of learning can be greatly facilitated by the judicious use of graphing" (53). The kind of extensive treatment given in textbooks to maps and map-reading skills as an essential part of geography, however, is not repeated for economics.

Unlike maps with their long-standing and fundamental kinship to geography and, to a lesser degree, graphs to economics, other forms of graphic displays are not tied to any one discipline. That may account for the absence of a universal protocol on how to teach graphic image interpretation in the social sciences. Typically, a text on teaching social studies refers to graphic image interpretation in a section on skills, competencies, decision making, or critical thinking, unless the topic is taught as part of geography or economics. The authors of the social studies texts stress that learning episodes should start with what is familiar to the learners and that students' understanding can be enhanced through doing (Anderson and Winston 1977).

Analysis of
Existing Strategies

In their text, Manhood, Biemer, and Lowe (1991) provided strategies for teaching the interpretation of graphical images. Their suggestions have some basic attributes similar to a protocol developed by Hilda Taba (1967) that has been widely accepted for teaching concept formation in social studies. Their strategies are similar also to the deductive instructional approach developed by Madeline Hunter (1985). The authors presented three lesson-plan strategies for teaching charts, graphs, and tables.

Strategies for Understanding a Graph

For the teaching of graphs, Manhood, Biemer, and Lowe (1991) recommended this three-step process:

1. Read the outside of the graph: title, date, and source. This step is intended to ensure that students evaluate a graph based on the title as an indicator of the topic or purpose; the date to determine accuracy based on the point in time the data was collected; and the source to access potential bias.

2. Read the inside of the graph: literal information and interpretive information. By reviewing the literal data contained in the graph to ensure a baseline of understanding for all students, the authors position students to identify the inferred facts, concepts, and generalizations intended by the creator of the graph.

3. Read above and beyond the graph. The graph can be more meaningful to the students if the topic of the graph relates to the life experiences of the students.

Strategies for Teaching a Chart or Table

For the teaching of charts and tables, Manhood, Biemer, and Lowe again employed a three-step strategy but introduced hypothesis testing.

1. What information is being presented? This step focuses students' attention on literal information both inside and outside the chart's cells.

2. Analyze the information being presented. Interpretive information both inside and outside the chart cells is the focus of this step.

3. Develop hypotheses from the information. A series of hypotheses are posed to determine the significance of the interpretive information.

In another model for teaching about charts and tables, the three-step process takes on a slightly different form.

1. Read the outside of the chart. (The literal level of the data is determined.)

2. Make some meaning of the chart. (The interpretive level of the data is determined.)

3. Go beyond the chart. (The understandings gained in the first two steps are applied by hypotheses and/or by the students making a connection to their lives.)

Recommended Models for Teaching Graphic Images

The preceding strategies, combined with the instructional tenets of starting with the familiar and learning by doing, offer the potential for two comprehensive models that can be used in elementary, middle, and high school social studies classes to promote the discriminating interpretation of graphical images. The two strategies presented, one to create a graphic and the other to interpret a graphic, include the graphical images, a learning episode to demonstrate the strategy, and the model to be used in future applications.

Figure 1.   Students' Average Daily Activities: ——————————
A Pie Chart Comparison

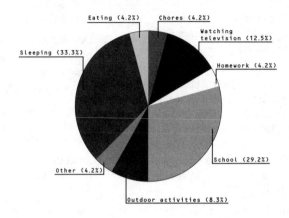

Figure 2.   Handout for Developing Bar Graph about Average ——————
Daily Activities: A Stacked Bar Chart Comparison

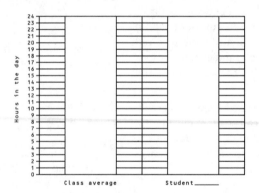

Teaching Students How to Create a Graphic

I devised the following learning episode to teach upper elementary-school students how to produce two graphics. My design involves a learning-by-doing approach and starts with something familiar, the students' daily activities. I used a pie chart (Figure 1) to show the data collected by the class. So that my students would realize that the same information can be conveyed in different forms, I gave them a handout (Figure 2) with information that they used for a bar chart, showing the data from Figure 1 in a different format.

Gathering the Data and Creating Charts

I introduced the topic by starting with a discovery focus: "Let's see how we spend our time." I listed the students' reports of their daily activities on the board so that the group could identify the categories for the charts. I explained that the class would be surveyed to collect data and gave the students a survey form with the categories we had developed. The survey form was in a columns-and-rows format (a table), with categories creating the rows, the first column for class averages, and the second column for individual student data. Each student was to record in the second column the amount of time he or she spent in each category of the table. Once the surveys were collected, teams calculated the averages for each of the categories. After the results had been posted on the chalkboard in the same form as they appeared on the survey, the surveys were redistributed to the students so that they could record the class average in the column next to their personal reports.

While at the board creating a pie chart for the class, I explained that this graphic device is one type of chart and is one of the best forms to show the ratio of categories (allocation of time) to the total (24 hours). I reviewed the chart, proceeding from left to right, top to bottom, line by line, so that the students would be aware that I was following the established pattern for reading. The components of the chart, not the content, received the emphasis: titles, type of chart, labels, percentages as averages, slice sizes as reflective of a proportionate share of a whole, and source. Each student was ready to create a personal pie chart based on his or her responses to the survey. I reviewed Figure 1 and the students' personal charts for content and discussed the literal and interpretive information in the class chart and the individual's chart and the inferences that could be drawn from the charts. The students' learning may increase if the discussion centers on homework and its relationship to success, and if the teacher

proposes that the homework slice of the pie chart be enlarged. This proposal could serve as the basis for an examination of bias in the construction of a graphic image.

Creating a Different Chart with the Same Data

I introduced Figure 2 and helped the students identify the components that were provided and those that were missing. The students received instruction about legends, scale, interval frequency, and X and Y axes. They then converted the data from the pie chart to the stacked bar chart, using Figure 2 as a fill-in-the-blank handout. To hone their writing skills, students explained in narrative form the data from the table (Figure 1) and their personal pie chart.

In a class discussion, the students can explain their preference for a particular type of chart and assess the effectiveness of the graphic as a form of communication. The teacher might ask the class to comment on this statement: An alien from outer space would conclude, after reviewing Figure 1, that humans do not take baths or attend religious services.

A Model for Creating a Graphic

The topic for the graphic should be relevant to the students' experiences or social studies content. The categories of information to be collected must be determined, and the data based on the categories must be gathered. Meaningful comparisons based on the data should be made. An effective graphic form that includes title, date, source, categories, and labels, as well as literal formation, linear connections, axis titles, data labels, and scale, should be selected. When the

Figure 3.   American Birth and Death Rates: A Line Chart————

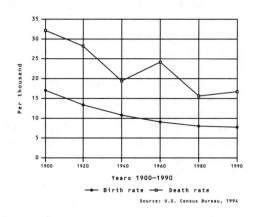

Years 1900–1990

—•— Birth rate —□— Death rate

Source: U.S. Census Bureau, 1994

Figure 4.   American Population: A Line Chart————

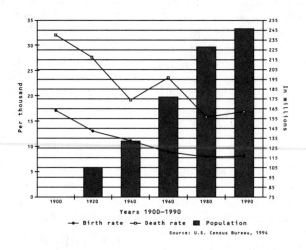

Years 1900–1990

—•— Birth rate —□— Death rate ■ Population

Source: U.S. Census Bureau, 1994

graphic is completed, the class can compare and contrast the literal and interpretive information presented. The teacher can extend the students' learning by relating the information to the students' experience or to social studies content. The group should assess the effectiveness of the graphic as a form of communication and expose possible bias (intended or unintended) by the choice of categories and chart format.

Teaching Students How to Interpret a Graphic

For this second activity, I have my class examine two graphics (Figures 3 and 4) that I developed for use with high school students. Both graphics are line charts that are used to convey the distortion possibilities of graphs when significant content is not included.

I use a series of questions to promote the active involvement of my students. Once the class has had an opportunity to view Figure 3, I ask the students these questions:

◆ What topics about what populations are being addressed in Figure 3?

◆ What type of graph is used in Figure 3?

◆ Using the information from this graph, can you develop a hypothesis about theAmerican population?

◆ Is the U.S. Census Bureau a reliable source for this kind of data? Are there any reasons why that bureau might want to provide misleading data?

◆ How might the data have been collected by the Census Bureau?

These questions help the students examine the categories of the graphic:

◆ What does "per thousand" mean?

◆ At what number does the Y axis start and end? Why?

◆ What time period is being covered?

◆ What is meant by the terms *birth rate* and *death rate*?

◆ Why are these two categories presented together?

The class should examine the literal information on the chart and cite the birth and death rates for each decade on the chart. Do the lines on the graphic indicate a trend of declining or increasing birth rate? After studying the chart, the students should be able to discern the overall pattern of the birth and death rates.

To generate interpretative information, which they should record to discover the possible inferences by hypothesis testing, the students should ask themselves these questions: What factors might have caused a decline in the birth and death rates? Does this mean there are fewer people dying and being born in America?

What caused the increase in the birth rate in 1960? What data would we need to collect to determine if your hypotheses are correct?

To extend the students' learning, the teacher should involve the class in a discussion of these questions: Based on the graph, what might we say the birth and death rates might be in the year 2000? What might be some of the good and bad consequences of this prediction for American society? To assess the value of the chart, the class should consider this question: Is there anything about the death and birth rates that should be included on the chart but is not?

With Figure 4, the teacher can introduce the second learning experience. The same process used to understand Figure 3 can help the students read the line-bar chart. The students must now deal with the task of converting the per thousand rate of births and deaths into actual numbers in the population, the issues associated with our immigration policy, and the concept of exponential growth of populations. Teachers should anticipate that because the students focused on Figure 3 to answer the preceding questions, the introduction of Figure 4 will raise issues of bias because of the absence of information in Figure 3.

Interpreting a Graphic

Teachers should present the graphic to the class and explain its type (bar, line-chart, table). The group can identify the title, make connections to the facts, concepts, and generalizations of the social studies topic, and evaluate reliability of the source and date.

The students should examine the categories of the literal information to ensure a baseline of understanding of the axis titles, headings, scale and data labels. They need to define the categories to reveal any assumptions being made by the readers of the graphic. They can explore other possible categories based on the topic. A careful examination of the literal information will ensure that the students have a baseline of understanding.

Once the students have recorded their interpretations of the information, they can endeavor to discover the possible inferences by hypothesis testing based on the literal information that they compare to the title and the social studies topic under consideration.

To promote further learning by the students, the teacher should extend the hypothesis testing by asking the group to predict future outcomes based on the literal and interpretative information. At the conclusion of the session on interpreting a graphic, the class can assess the effectiveness of the graphic as a form of communication and expose any possible bias (intended or unintended) in the choice of categories and chart format.

Conclusion

These procedures can be used to teach students at all levels of social sciences the skills needed for interpreting graphical images. For students to become informed citizens, teachers of social studies should teach a process of interpreting graphics as a skill, and they should use graphics to communicate the content of the social sciences.

Given the increasing use of graphical images in our society, I recommend that this skill be elevated to a higher priority in social studies instruction. The processes of reading and creating a graphic meet the significant learning objectives in the elementary classroom and in the middle and secondary social studies classroom. The preparation of a graphic requires an integrated approach that employs art, math, language arts, and social studies. Students creating their own graphics employ inductive and deductive reasoning skills.

The same technology that has led to increased incidences of graphical images has also made it possible for citizens to construct effective graphical images. The creation of such images and the almost painless experimentation with various forms, scales, labels, axes, and so forth are greatly facilitated by the menu-driven interface, previewing capability, and preformatted options of current softwares. The use of such software by the teacher for a classroom demonstration and by the students would facilitate the process of creating and understanding graphical images. ◆

Appendix

A Reading List for Teachers

Ellis, A. K., J. T. Fouts, and A. D. Glenn. *Teaching and Learning Secondary Social Studies.* New York: Harper Collins, 1991.

Jarolimek, J., and W. C. Parker. *Social Studies in Elementary Education.* New York: Macmillan, 1993.

Manhood, W., L. Biemer, and W. T. Lowe. *Teaching Social Studies in Middle and Senior High Schools.* New York: Merrill, 1991.

Martorella, P. *Social Studies for Elementary School Children*. New York: Merrill, 1994.

———. *Teaching Social Studies in Middle and Secondary Schools*. New York: Macmillan, 1991.

Maxim, G. W. *Social Studies and the Elementary School Child*. New York: Macmillan, 1991.

Savage, T. V., and D. G. Armstrong. *Effective Teaching in Elementary Social Studies*. New York: Macmillan, 1992.

Schuncke, G. M. *Elementary Social Studies: Knowing, Doing, Caring*. New York: Macmillan, 1988.

Stopsky, F., and L. Sharon. *Social Studies in a Global Society*. New York: Delmar, 1994.

Zevin, J. *Social Studies for the Twenty-first Century*. New York: Longman, 1992.

References

Anderson, C. C., and B. J. Winston. "Acquiring Information by Asking Questions, Using Maps and Graphs, and Making Direct Observations." In *Developing Decision-making Skills* (47th Yearbook), edited by D. Kurfman. Washington, DC: National Council for the Social Studies, 1977.

Arnold, T., and F. Dwyer. "Realism in Visualized Instruction." *Perception and Motor Skills* 40 (1975): 369–70.

Boardman, D. "Graphicy in the Curriculum." *Educational Review* 28 (1976): 118–25.

Booher, R. "Relative Comprehensibility of Pictorial Information and Printed Words in Proceduralized Instruction." *Human Factors* 17 (1975): 266–77.

Decker, W., and P. Wheatly. "Spatial Grouping, Imagery, and Free Recall." *Perceptual and Motor Skills* 55 (1982): 45–46.

Gillespie, C. S. "Reading Graphic Displays: What Teachers Should Know." *Journal of Reading* 36, no. 5 (1993): 350.

Handler, J. R. "Math Anxiety in Adult Learning." *Adult Learning* 1 (1990): 20–23.

Highfill, J. K., and W. V. Weber. "Graphing to Learn Economics: Concrete and Abstract Graphs." *The Social Studies* 81 (1990): 53–58.

Holliday, W. G. "What's in a Picture?" *The Science School Teacher* 42 (1975): 21–22.

Holliday, W. G., L. L. Brunner, and E. L. Donais. "Differential Cognitive and Affective Responses to Flow Diagrams in Science." *Journal of Research in Science Teaching* 14 (1977): 129–38.

Hunter, M. *Mastery Teaching*. El Segundo, CA: TIP Publications, 1985.

Kamm, K., E. Askov, and R. Klumb. *Study-skills Mastery among Middle and High School Students*. 1977. ERIC, ED 141780.

Kirsch, I., and A. Jungeblut. *Literacy: Profile of America's Young Adults*. 1986. ERIC, ED 275692.

Manhood, W., L. Biemer, and W. T. Lowe. *Teaching Social Studies in Middle and Senior High Schools*. New York: Merrill, 1991.

Monk, G. S. "Students' Understanding of Functions in Calculus." *Humanistic Mathematics Network Newsletter* 2 (1988): 236–41.

Paine, C. "Graphing Matters." *Learning* 11 (1983): 38–40.

Piston, C. "Supplementing the Graphing Curriculum." *Mathematics Teacher* 84, no. 6 (1992): 336.

Rigney, J. W., and K. Lutz. "Effect of Graphic Analogies of Concepts in Chemistry on Learning and Attitude." *Journal of Educational Psychology* 68 (1976): 305–11.

Springer, S. P., and G. Deutsch. *Left Brain, Right Brain*. New York: Freeman, 1985.

Taba, H. *Teachers Handbook for Elementary Social Studies*. Reading, MA: Addison-Wesley, 1967.

Willows, D. M., and H. A. Houghton. *The Psychology of Illustration*. New York: Springer-Verlag, 1987.

J ames A. DuPlass is a professor of education at the University of South Florida, where he currently teaches social studies methods at the graduate and undergraduate levels and teaches instructional technology to undergraduates.

Special Software for Special Kids

Karen Armstrong, Jacquelyn Brand, Robert Glass, and Lynn Regan

M ost articles on technology for special education focus on the hardware end of the equation. This is understandable when you consider the key role adaptive hardware, such as switches, seating devices, and alternate keyboards, plays in making technology—and learning—accessible to so many users with disabilities. This month, however, we are focusing on *software* for students with a broad range of special needs.

For recommendations, we turned to some of the most knowledgeable people in the special education field—including two classroom teachers and a national team of well-known experts. As you can see, they come from a wide range of settings.

A panel of experts recommends software for students with disabilities.

Karen Armstrong is a special education teacher at Andrew Johnson Elementary School in Oklahoma City. She teaches children in kindergarten through fifth grade whose special needs range from orthopedic impairments to speech and language dysfunctions. All of the students Armstrong works with are immersed in the total life of the school—taking part in regular education classes with age-appropriate peers and participating in such school-wide events as talent shows, assemblies, and student council meetings. For many of them, technology is the key that makes this sort of inclusion possible.

Lynn Regan, the 1990 *Technology and Learning* Teacher of the Year, works with seventh- and eighth-grade special education students at Toms River Intermediate School East in Toms River, New Jersey. Increasingly, she reports, the students she teaches are intelligent, intuitive, and street smart kids who have emotional or social difficulties that make it difficult for them to avoid confrontation with peers and authority figures and to focus on learning tasks. Motivation, she finds, is a key factor in enticing her students to remain active participants in their own education. For this reason, she is careful to select programs that coincide with the school curriculum, are of high interest, can be tailored to meet individual needs, and avoid making their users feel "different" from their peers.

Jacquelyn Brand and Robert Glass bring to us the collective wisdom of a national coalition of community-based service providers. The Alliance for Technology Access, founded by Brand in 1987, includes 44 community technology resource centers across the country. Alliance centers work with approximately 100,000 visitors each year, including families, teachers, and students of all ages. For this article, all of the ATA centers were surveyed about their all-time favorite software products for kids with disabilities. Brand warns us that asking for a short list of favorites is a lot like walking into the Library of Congress and asking for the ten most popular books. She points out that there are hundreds of important and valuable software products for people with disabilities, and the recommendations which follow represent only a small sampling of the titles with the most general appeal to the special young people with whom the authors of this article work.

Access Software

Many of the software titles our experts recommend for use by students with disabilities are the very same products that are popular with *all* students. There is, however, an important role being played by companies that design software to help students with disabilities *access* the computer and communicate effectively with others. Here, organized by company, are some outstanding examples that lend themselves well to a range of special education users.

Don Johnston, Inc., produces an array of special education products, both hardware and software. Some of the best software options include these:

❖ *Write: OutLoud* is a basic "talking" word processor which helps provide access to writing for students with learning, cognitive, and/or vision issues. It includes a spell checker and especially easy access to menu items. It can be used with scanned-in text or to create templates that have speech output.

❖ *Co:Writer* is word prediction software at its best. The user can quickly and easily create sentences that are automatically pasted into a full-functioning word processor or other application, where the text can be manipulated and arranged to the user's satisfaction. As the student begins to type, the program offers choices by displaying words from a list from which the user can choose in a variety of simple ways.

❖ *Ke:nx* is generally thought of as a hardware item, but it is the *Ke:nx Create* software that comes with this interface that makes it work so well. It is a powerful and flexible environment that enables teachers, parents, and students to create individualized tools for computer access from multiple input options including single switches, alternate keyboards, and augmentative communication devices.

Intellitools, well known in the special education world for its IntelliKeys alternate keyboard, also produces some powerful and flexible software products:

- *Overlay Maker* allows teachers, parents, and students to create individualized "keyboards" for IntelliKeys, geared to the needs of their own students and the lessons or concepts being taught.

- *Click It!* is a powerful tool that enables teachers, parents, and students to customize any Macintosh software program for students who best access a computer using a switch—by creating rotating hot spots on the screen.

- *IntelliPics* enables teachers, parents, and students to create unique, individualized learning activities, using pictures, colors, numbers, and speech output. It can be used for anything from teaching basic concepts to providing step-by-step directions for students who need such help.

- *IntelliTalk* is a "talking" word processor that helps provide access to writing for students with learning, cognitive, and / or vision issues who might benefit from speech output. It works simply and makes it very easy for the user to correct the sound of words that are not pronounced correctly.

Software Accessibility Features to Consider

The following features, incorporated into some software programs, can be very helpful for users with disabilities.

Easy-to-Read Screens

Screens which are easy to read and understand can make a critical difference for many users. Typical features to consider are text that is simple and legible and menu items that are represented in both graphics and text.

Consistency

Consistent placement of menus and objects on the screen makes using the program more intuitive and predictable. Consistency also supports the use of "markers" that can identify fixed locations on the screen for access by users who use switches.

Intuitive Characteristics

An intuitive program makes the user feel able to navigate a program's features at first try. Clear and obvious options presented as they are needed make a user feel more comfortable right from the beginning.

Logical Labels

Programs that present choices in lists or menus should be labeled with logical, easily understandable names that give a reasonable sense of what will happen when a choice is made.

Instructional Choices

Instructional software should allow control of lesson and content presentation, difficulty level, vocabulary, sound, timing, speed, and the amounts of text and/or graphics presented. The potential to record or track progress is also very helpful.

Growth Potential

For classroom use, you'll generally want software that can be used by more than one level of student and that focuses on more than one learning task.

Graphics

Graphics can encourage interaction or convey information in interesting and motivating ways. They can also play a supporting role for non-readers or beginning readers.

Support for Inclusion

Software that is usable by and appeals to both special needs and non-disabled students is ideal for promoting inclusion.

Friendly Documentation

Easy-to-understand software instructions are important, and may be available to buyers in large print, Braille, electronic text, or recorded form.

Onscreen Instructions

Onscreen instructions in the form of help lines, help balloons, or windows and instructional prompts can guide the user through a program. User control over these prompts is also important.

Audio/Visual Cues

Synthesized or digitized prompts or feedback can keep students on the right track. Icons, pointers, and various signals can provide important visual support. In some cases software will allow

→

Teacher support software offers a number of software titles for at-risk students and those with learning disabilities. Particularly recommended is *Language Experience Recorder*, a talking word processor that allows students to have their writing read back to them by a non-judgmental source. The program can also import and export from other teacher support applications in order to enhance vocabulary and comprehension.

Across-the-Board Favorites that Work Well for Students with Disabilities

The software below plays many roles. Some of it is particularly good at fostering independence—a quality that is of great importance to children with special needs. Other programs encourage interactive and cooperative learning—always a bonus during inclusion activities. Most of them score well on several of the criteria outlined in the sidebar "Software Accessibility Features to Consider." Here, then, are our experts' recommendations of "general" software that provides motivation, success, and educational discovery for all learners, including learners with disabilities.

Productivity Tools

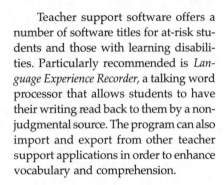 *KidDesk* (Edmark) is an excellent desktop shell that enables young children with or without special needs to work independently using picture icons. At the same time, adults keep control over hard-disk and system security and are able to customize software selections for each student. Special ed features include built-in single switch scanning and TouchWindow compatibility.

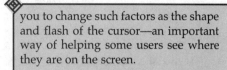

❧ *ClarisWorks* (Claris), the easy-to-use integrated package including word processor, spreadsheet, database, painting, drawing, and communications programs, is a great all-around tool for kids and teachers. It is especially helpful for students with learning issues because the same set of commands is used across all the applications.

❧ *Creative Writer* (Microsoft) is another good word processor that works well with all sorts of children. It combines creativity-sparking ideas, lots of noises and comments, colorful graphics, and all the basic word-processing tools.

❧ *KidPix* (Brøderbund) has become an almost universal tool in the ATA centers for both kids and adults to learn how Macintosh and DOS computers function and how to be creative with them. Its stimulating and motivating graphics capture the imagination of children and adults as it easily taps into "multiple intelligences." It can also be used with scanned-in pictures to modify the curriculum.

❧ *KidWorks 2* (Davidson), a talking word processor and graphics program all in one, works well with primary-level students and other beginning readers. A particularly appealing feature is its rebus writing tool, which lets pictures represent words and enhances meaning for students learning what reading is all about.

❧ *Storybook Weaver* (MECC) is an outstanding multimedia product which can be used across curriculum and age levels. It encourages creative writing and has many objects from

you to change such factors as the shape and flash of the cursor—an important way of helping some users see where they are on the screen.

Built-in Access Methods

Some programs have built-in alternative access methods which allow users to select options such as a joystick or touch screen in lieu of a keyboard or mouse. In some cases, it's helpful simply to be able to operate the program through the keyboard instead of the mouse.

which to construct pictures. The ability to display a picture by highlighting its name or to insert the picture label into a story is very helpful for children who find reading, spelling, or typing challenging.

❧ *Student Writing Center* (The Learning Company), like the older titles in the Learning Company's publishing series, is a very easy-to-use tool that incorporates graphics, encourages choices, and makes it easy for users to produce documents ranging from reports to newspapers. Students can grow into this program as their skills develop—making it an excellent vehicle for inclusion and multi-level cooperation.

❧ *Print Shop Deluxe* (Brøderbund) is another software favorite that works very well for children with special needs. It has high interest, produces quick results, and can be used independently or cooperatively. Karen Armstrong finds this is a great program for promoting inclusion activities, such as a class project requiring a poster or invitation to a school event.

◈ *Linkway Live!* (IBM), *HyperCard* (Claris), and *HyperStudio* (Roger Wagner) are authoring programs that can play two important roles in special education. First, they can be used by teachers to build tutorials, communication boards, instructional aids, and other customized software for students. In addition, they offer special needs students a vehicle to tailor "reports" that best suit their learning styles. Research and reporting need not be limited to text, and multimedia elements add high motivation level.

Educational and Recreational Software

◈ The *Carmen Sandiego* series (Brøderbund) teaches history, science, and social studies in fun and exciting ways. In addition to gaining knowledge in these particular subject areas, students are also able to develop information search skills in an intuitive, easy-to-follow format.

◈ The *Living Books* series (Brøderbund/Living Books) is loved by many younger users for its tremendous graphics, sound, animation, and playful appeal. It's a wonderful series to use for early reading instruction and language development.

◈ *Math Blaster* (Davidson) is a real favorite with Lynn Regan's second- through eighth-grade students and at many of the ATA centers. With a variety of skill levels and problem types in an entertaining format, the mathematics programs in the *Blaster* series have lasting

value, provide fun challenges, and generally hold the interest of students who have attention deficit disorders. Like many other Davidson products, they can also be tailored by teachers to meet the needs of their students.

◈ The *Early Learning Neighborhood* titles (Edmark), which include *Millie's Math House*, *Bailey's Book House*, and *Sammy's Science House*, are fun with lots of growth potential for young users. With appealing speech, graphics, animation, and humor, plus lots of opportunities for student exploration and discovery, these programs receive high marks for the way they facilitate interaction between kids. The software is accessible to both switch and TouchWindow users.

◈ *Number Munchers* (MECC) is an old favorite that allows for customization and a practice option in which skills can be built in a nonthreatening environment. A time-out feature is available in the game mode to remove some of the pressure that can be felt in this otherwise fast-paced environment.

◈ *Oregon Trail* (MECC) is a perennial favorite in ATA centers. Aside from teaching about history, it fosters problem-solving skills and encourages reading and cooperation when used in small groups.

◈ *Thinkin' Things* (Edmark) teaches thinking skills to primary-grade students in a fun and creative way. This program works very well with a TouchWindow. It encourages children to explore basic concepts in a graphic format.

- *Toy Store* (Don Johnston, Inc.) is a favorite with Karen Armstrong and many of the ATA teachers. Accessible with a switch, mouse, keyboard, or TouchWindow, it provides six fun discovery activities that accommodate a wide range of abilities. A hidden bonus: This program encourages cooperative learning and communication among children.

- *Super Solvers Outnumbered* (The Learning Company) is a particular favorite with Lynn Regan's middle-school students. They like the engaging game format and she appreciates the ability to choose the facts that will appear in both the drill and word programs.

- *Cornerstone* (Skills Bank) provides straightforward drill in the basics of language and math for grades 3–8. Flexible lesson assignments and a variety of recordkeeping methods make it easy for a teacher to individualize the learning process.

- *The Great Ocean Rescue* (Tom Snyder Productions) and others in the videodisc simulation series from Tom Snyder combine the power of video with group learning and flexibility. Students can work in teams or independently, computer use is optional, and there are suggestions included to help teachers or parents in scaling up or down the activity levels.   ❖

Learning More about (and from) the Alliance for Technology Access

The Alliance for Technology Access has just published a book entitled *Computer Resources for People with Disabilities* (Alameda, CA: Hunter House, 1994). With a foreword by Stephen Hawking, the book provides the information necessary for using conventional and assistive technology at school, at work, and at home. Up-to-date and comprehensive, this book offers guidelines for developing a technology plan; explanations of the ADA, IDEA, Tech Act, and other relevant legislation; descriptions of hardware and software currently available in assistive technology; and a complete listing of helpful resources and organizations.

The book is available in paperback ($14.95) or spiral-bound ($19.95) format. To order, or to get additional information on Alliance for Technology Access resources, contact: Alliance for Technology Access, 2173 E. Francisco Blvd., Suite L, San Rafael, CA 94901; (800) 455-7970; e-mail: atafta@aol.com.

Software Reviews

Judi Mathis Johnson

One area of computer software that has shown tremendous growth and improvement since the advent of the CD-ROM is the multimedia encyclopedia. This month's column is devoted to a review of just a few of the many multimedia encyclopedias available.

The image and definition of an encyclopedia as a linear set of short articles in alphabetical order has been shattered by this group of titles. Fortunately, content can still be accessed alphabetically in most of these multimedia packages, but other methods allow much more to be accomplished, learned, and reported using any of these CD-ROMs. Content may be organized and accessed geographically (using an atlas), historically (along a timeline), or thematically (by topic).

Although some programs have 1996 in their titles and a copyright date of 1996, the content of the CD-ROM may only extend through part of 1995. But unlike their cousins, the print encyclopedias, some programs come with built-in access to online suppliers of current or updated information. Of the encyclopedias reviewed here, *Microsoft Encarta 96 Encyclopedia* has the most aggressive way of updating information.

Three products are clearly superior to the rest in providing a balanced presentation of quality material in an understandable fashion—*1996 Grolier Interactive Encyclopedia*, *Microsoft Encarta 96 Encyclopedia*, and *Compton's Interactive Encyclopedia: 1996 Family Edition*. Each of the other packages reviewed here provides insights into the

From *Learning and Leading with Technology* 23, no. 6 (March 1996): 53–58. Reprinted with permission from the International Society for Technology in Education. All rights reserved.

ways that encyclopedias can be better designed for all students.

The reviews are organized alphabetically by title. They do not focus on how many megabytes of video or how many color maps each CD-ROM contains. Instead, the goal was to identify CD-ROMs that stimulated student curiosity to learn more and easily accommodated the circuitous browsing the curiosity spawned. These CD-ROMs, for one reason or another, captivate students and can maintain their attention for hours. The minimal set of keywords, based on students' choices, used for examining and comparing the packages were *Bosnia, environment, Maya Angelou, saxophone,* and *sharks.* (I have seen enough sharks now, thank you very much.) The photographs, pictures, and videos of sharks truly make them one of the most popular topics in these encyclopedias.

The fact that a CD-ROM is motivational or captivating is not sufficient as an evaluation criterion. It is even more important that the encyclopedia be an effective learning tool. Because the goal of clarifying and enunciating criteria is central to this column, please keep in mind the evaluation criterion and its components described in the following list whenever encyclopedias are examined. The criterion applies to sophisticated, often expensive, and fairly comprehensive packages for professional libraries, as well as to CD-ROM encyclopedias designed for classroom and home use.

Evaluation Criterion

The search strategy software for electronic reference tools is designed to stimulate student research and facilitate student access to information.

- The browse, menu, and command search modes are available as needed to support program design.
- The choice of search modes matches the level or interest of the learner.
- There is a graphical interface for the search strategy.
- There are hypertext linkages between related references and images as well as text.
- Any fill-in-the-blank search-entry screens provide clear instructions.
- The manual includes sample search screens at varied levels of complexity.
- Boolean searching is fully supported.
- Boolean operations are clearly and properly identified.
- It is easy to search for multiword phrases.
- The search software makes it possible for students to access materials and concepts at earlier grades than would be possible with materials in traditional print formats.
- The search strategy design encourages learners to use higher order thinking skills.
- Search strategies are so transparent that learners can focus on the informational content or task rather than on the mechanics of searching.
- Search-entry points are varied and appropriate for the program.
- Students can search all appropriate fields.
- Feedback is given on the progress of the search.

❖ Messages appear on the screen when a search begins and when it has ended.

❖ The search path can be reviewed and repeated as needed.

❖ It is simple to backtrack one step at a time through the search.

❖ Searches can be recalled and edited when necessary.

❖ Products from the same publisher have a consistent command structure.

One additional requirement is related to technical quality—high-quality audio contributes to program effectiveness. In a minimal interpretation of this idea, most programs have sound that contributes to the program's effectiveness, but for encyclopedias the minimum acceptable level should be set higher. If during the course of using a program a voice provides instructions, then a small dialog box should simultaneously appear on the screen so that students can read the words as they hear them. If text can be read on the screen, then an option should exist for students to have that text read to them. Some programs reviewed in this column had text-to-voice features (although some were quite robotic), and a few had text accompanying voice. But none of the programs reviewed consistently provided text and voice at all times.

Complete Reference Library

Subject: Library Reference

Grade Level: 7–12 (ages 12–adult)

Cost: $79.95

Hardware: PC with *Windows*, color, sound, and a CD-ROM drive

Complete Reference Library contains *The Concise Columbia Electronic Encyclopedia*, along with nine other reference works. The contents of the encyclopedia are traditional in style and scope and heavily rely on text-based references, but accessing the additional references is simple because they are so readily available. This model of additional tools combined with an encyclopedia needs to be acknowledged and encouraged.

Description

The screen for working with the *Complete Reference Library* models a personal library. Each reference is selected by highlighting its spine on the "book" shelf. Students can choose to search among one or more reference works for each keyword or text search. In addition to the encyclopedia, the reference works include: *The American Heritage Dictionary of the English Language, Roget's II: The New Thesaurus, The National Directory of Addresses and Telephone Numbers (1995 edition), Wall Street Words, The Reader's Companion to American History, Simpson's Contemporary Quotations, The Legal Word Book (Third Edition), The 1994 Information Please® Almanac,* and *The Written Word III.*

Students can choose the Media Library and then select maps, videos, pictures, animations, audios, or music selections. When they choose a keyword, such as *shark,* the search results in two listings, but neither provides the video of a shark. Students must go to the Media Library to find any video.

Browse and Search

Being text-based, the whole environment for browsing and searching is accessed by typing in words. If a keyword search comes up empty, students can choose to search the text for the desired phrase or word.

Opportunities for serendipitous finds are reduced in this search structure. Students cannot "open" the D encyclopedia and peruse all the topics listed that begin with D. The only grouping that offers this temptation is in the Media Library where students can view videos.

Students had success with all the keywords only when additional references were available. For example, highlighting all the references before the search for *Maya Angelou* resulted in finding two of her quotes and a description of her as an outstanding person from Arkansas.

Conclusion

Complete Reference Library models how students can access more than one tool at a time. It is too text-based for use as a motivational tool but still contains a wealth of information. Multimedia aspects need to be more integrated with the text selections for it to be more effective as a learning and reference tool. Although it is more time-consuming to search all the references for each keyword, the additional information is worth it.

Compton Interactive Encyclopedia: 1996 Family Edition

Subject: Library Reference

Grade Level: 4–12 (ages 9–adult)

Cost: $129.95

Hardware: Macintosh or PC with color, sound, and a CD-ROM drive

The 1996 edition of *Compton's Interactive Encyclopedia* has been further refined, improved, and enhanced. The tools are designed for maximizing the breadth of a topic. Just describing the potential of this CD-ROM with all its tools could fill this month's column, so here are just a few key points.

Description

The screen contains three windows simultaneously. All the functions can be selected using buttons placed next to each appropriate window. The onscreen menu selections and window arrangement are a model of a simple, concise, and convenient interface.

Students type in a keyword, and the search results in a list. Each item in the list has an icon next to it. The icons represent the following items: animation, another look (for explaining a difficult concept), atlas, chart, fact, flag, map, midi, more about (more information), picture, sidebar (a table, list, or other related document), slide show, sound, table, timeline, video, and see also. Students can quickly identify specific information, such as selecting the globe icon for atlas to view a map related to a keyword.

The major windows for viewing are called Contents (alphabetical listings), Idea Search (keyword search), Infopilot (groups of related articles), Topic Tree (arranged by topic and subtopic), Atlas (locations on the globe), Timeline (in relation to world history and to United States history since 1485), Explore (six thematic settings), Editing Room (for creating electronic reports), and On-Line (for accessing *Compton's Living Encyclopedia*). The concept of the Editing Room should be included in any multimedia encyclopedia used in education. Students need reporting mediums that are commensurate with the tools they are using.

The Explore window contains Grandma's Attic, Madcap Music Store, Newsroom, Wild and Free (nature),

Kaleidescape (patterns playroom), and Space Quest. Each room is filled with objects to explore and connect visually (and aurally) to other objects and ideas. For example, in the Kaleidescape exploration, selecting "Diamonds to Spy. What am I?" may conjure a picture of the fabric craft called *hardanger*; here the pulled threads form diamond patterns. The picture is larger than the window but can be easily moved about with the cursor (a hand holding a scroll). Selecting the same object twice does not necessarily conjure the same image in the viewing window; the next picture may contain Polynesian huts embodying a diamond pattern. The pictures appear to have been chosen not only for their connection to the topic and for their complexity but also for their texture. Although students view a two-dimensional screen, there has been a conscious attempt to connect the onscreen activity to real-world, three-dimensional, multicultural objects.

The screen was somewhat complex for younger students. In a library or classroom, the largest monitor available should be used. Parents are encouraged to sit with their children as they explore the encyclopedia at home.

The current package includes an excellent bonus, a CD-ROM called *Small Blue Planet: The Real Picture World Atlas*, which runs on a Macintosh or PC. One feature students systematically examined was the map of the world organized by countries; as each country is selected students hear "Good Morning" (or another phrase from a list of 11) in the country's official language. The corresponding text is viewed on the screen in its native alphabet.

Browse and Search

Compton's Interactive Encyclopedia has the traditional linear browsing potential. Students can begin to type in a search word, and the index quickly narrows the search. This greatly assists students with limited typing skills or spelling problems. The topic may come into view well before the keyword is typed.

The program's design is also rich in connections. Students can follow a complex knowledge web of information as they learn about a topic. They can also form a complex mental web of a topic due to the many different senses stimulated by the explorations.

In using the test phrases, only one keyword, *environment*, was found to be too limited. Although there were multiple content listings for the word, they were all under the topic labeled Pollution, Environmental.

Making an exploration to one of the rooms in Explore could stimulate curiosity in students who need or want a little more encouragement. The three levels of installation for this program correspond to three speeds for conducting searches. The Slow level requires the least amount of hard drive space but takes longer to search the material. To maintain the students' enthusiasm using the Explore window, the highest level of installation on the hard drive should be used.

Conclusion

Recommending the 1996 edition of *Compton's Interactive Encyclopedia* is easy. Any student who has access to this extensive tool can have a richer education experience. The multimedia authoring tool enables students to report more easily the results of an exploration, thus facilitating assessment.

Earth Explorer

Subject: Environment

Grade Level: 5–10 (ages 10–15)

Cost: $99.00

Hardware: Macintosh with color, sound, and a CD-ROM drive

Earth Explorer specifically addresses the environment. Middle school students seem to love studying and writing about this topic. Although this CD-ROM was not a part of the original list of encyclopedias to be reviewed for this column, students felt it offered more interactivity (see Figure 1) than some of the others and modeled how an encyclopedia on a particular topic might be designed.

Description

Earth Explorer organizes the material into four groups: Articles, Explore, Hot Topics, and Data Sets. Articles and Data Sets provide necessary background information for evaluating the pros and cons of a controversial environmental issue in Hot Topics or for investigating questions about the way the natural world works in Explore. Figure 2 shows the Explore Menu and its 12 topics.

Figure 1. Interactive Screen from Earth Explorer

Figure 2. Explore Menu in Earth Explorer

Selecting a topic, such as How Much Energy?, under Explore takes students to an investigation containing three parts: an Introduction, What to Notice, and Conclusions. This exploration design lends itself to easy integration into a science curriculum. In How Much Energy?, students are asked to use as a basic unit the energy output from pedaling a bike and then learn how much pedaling it would take to accomplish various feats. For students, this basic energy unit is more personal and understandable than ergs and horsepower.

By selecting the Data Sets option, students can pick from 21 topics. The data can be extensive; however, it is rarely exhaustive. For additional offline tasks, students can print the pages of data. For example, the data set on water and sanitation fills 18 printed pages.

The interconnectedness of ideas is achieved through topic exploration and through the interactions. Students preferred the interactions, but the interactions also stimulated them to explore the articles and view the graphics and videos. Thus, they gathered more information and returned to the interactions to answer more questions correctly the next time.

The reading level of the material is suitable primarily for students in grades seven and eight. Although this level challenged some of the younger students, it stimulated reading rather than discouraged it. Some of the other material is too simplified to really challenge them. According to the documentation for *Earth Explorer*, there is a PC version of the program that can be installed under Windows 3.1 enhanced, but this was not confirmed by phone.

Browse and Search

A simple linear search can be conducted using the alphabetical listing of topics. The onscreen alphabet keys make it easier for students to hop to a letter—no high-level typing skills are necessary.

Conclusion

Earth Explorer strives in an entertaining fashion to provide information about the environment and how we can protect it—and it succeeds. This may conjure up the word edutainment, but that term is far too vacuous for the depth and breadth of this program.

Guinness Encyclopedia

Subject: Library Reference

Grade Level: 6–11 (ages 11–16)

Cost: $39.00

Hardware: Macintosh or PC (*Windows*) with color, sound, and a CD-ROM drive

Guinness Encyclopedia is not a compendium of Guinness records—that's a different product. This two-disc package presents a limited amount of knowledge in a thematic fashion. Although fewer topics are covered, each topic is treated in a more connected way.

Description

The main menu offers information via three avenues: Multimedia Gallery, Encyclopedia, or Explorer. Figure 3 shows how the encyclopedia's content has been organized into 11 categories or can be searched using Outline. Here is one example of the connected design: The student can select Encyclopedia and then use Outline Search to reach the same screen and content as reached by first selecting Explorer and then choosing

Figure 3.   Section Choices from the Guinness Encyclopedia

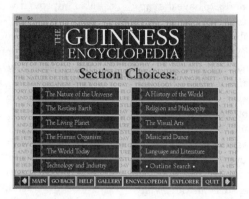

Figure 4.   Screen from the Guinness Encyclopedia

Encyclopedia Outline. The program remembers which route a student takes and backtracks accordingly.

The Multimedia Gallery is organized by photographs, illustrations, languages, movies, and animations. There are 29 languages plus two Spanish versions (Castillian and Latin American) and three English versions. Students can hear any of 13 phrases in each of the language offerings. The clear recordings in various voices can be used for learning the phrases. Unfortunately, no text on the screen corresponds to the respective languages or their alphabets. One small glitch appears under languages; if students want to hear the differences among the three English samples (American, Australian, and British), the British recordings are missing. However, Disc 2 has the same options available, and on this disc all recordings can be heard.

The screen layout is clear and easy to read. Figure 4 shows a screen with a photograph, caption, text, related information, and a location tree in the upper-left corner. This tree helps students mentally organize the information as well as navigate through the content.

By selecting Reader from a menu bar, students can choose to have the caption or text read to them. The voice is produced by a robotic speech-synthesizer, but a reader should be available on all encyclopedias.

Disc 2 contains information on countries of the world, a full text-search engine, NASA photographs in three formats for reports, and *QuickTime* movies. Students may find that Disc 2 is a useful reference for electronic reports. Unfortunately, it is not made clear in the documentation whether students can legally use the images for classroom reports.

Browse and Search

Traditional searches are difficult. If the topic a student is researching fits one of the categories or can be found via simple searches, then students can find related material and possibly gather enough information.

Conclusion

Some of the topics are covered fairly well with photographs, animations, and text. The Reader option for captions and text is a desirable feature. For classroom use, additional materials should be supplied, such as a complete listing of the organization of the topics with full annotations on connected resources.

Microsoft Encarta 96 Encyclopedia

Subject: Library Reference

Grade Level: 4–12 (ages 9–adult)

Cost: $54.95

Hardware: Macintosh, or PC with color, sound, and a CD-ROM drive

Microsoft Encarta 96 Encyclopedia has also improved with each new version. A feature that allows the encyclopedia to be updated monthly combines the power of telecommunications with the multimedia power of the computer to create an exciting new view of what an encyclopedia can be.

Description

The organizational divisions of *Microsoft Encarta 96 Encyclopedia* are fairly universal and appropriate. Students can select from Find (alphabetical listing), Look and Listen (multimedia presentations), Experiment (interactivities), Take a Tour, Explore Maps (select using a globe), Explore History (organized by a multilevel timeline), Play a Game, or Stay Current (Yearbook Builder).

Take a Tour is modeled on worldwide travel tours. Each tour has a designated number of stops and a theme. Unlike most real-world tours, if students find a topic particularly interesting they can go exploring to have a richer experience and return later to complete the tour. The Guided Tour menu contains 11 choices; each choice represents numerous tours with even more numerous stops. The tours are designed for appreciation. For example, students can focus on dangerous animals under Flora and Fauna or make the 27 stops on the tour under Role Models to meet and learn about inspirational people who have overcome adversity.

Yearbook Builder is clearly the most aggressive way to update an encyclopedia. During 1996, the trial subscription is free. The updates run from September 1995 through August 1996, and can be downloaded through December 1996.

Each month's summary (approximately 35 articles and photographs) and connections to the program are available on about the tenth of the succeeding month. Teachers and students can download the updated information from a Microsoft Network account or from the World Wide Web site. In a traditional yearbook update, the connections to the other topics are accomplished with a See Also list at the end of the article. When using Yearbook Builder, students download additional articles, and the programs are expanded to include the new information, thus providing true linking.

Browse and Search

Microsoft Encarta 96 Encyclopedia has a wealth of predesigned ways for accessing, browsing, and exploring knowledge. This makes it much easier for home use and independent work, but students will have a richer experience if they work together or with a parent.

The multilevel timeline is an excellent presentation tool for the classroom to tie together various topics and create a broader vision of a time. Cultural, military, and other events mix together to create a more balanced picture of the world through time.

Conclusion

Microsoft Encarta 96 Encyclopedia is an excellent home product. It is designed to motivate students to explore topics. If a media center is trying to maintain a current file on key events and has access to telecommunications, it should definitely consider *Encarta 96* as one more student resource.

Microsoft Explorapedia— The World of Nature; Microsoft Explorapedia— The World of People

Subject: Library Reference

Grade Level: 1–5 (ages 6–10)

Cost: $34.95

Hardware: PC (*Windows*) with color, sound, and a CD-ROM drive

Microsoft Explorapedia—The World of Nature and *Microsoft Explorapedia—The World of People* are both designed to present encyclopedic material in a playful and very organized way. Thaddeus (Tad) Pole is the host, guide, and helpful frog for both programs. From within the programs, students can "leap" to a writing or painting program already installed on their computer. A picture or text can be copied to the clipboard before "leaping."

Description

In *The World of People*, students can move about the command center and select to go to the Health Center, Classroom, Locker Room, Home, Neighborhood, City, Country, Factory, Scientists' Lab, Military Museum, Transportation Museum, Studio, or Backstage. After selecting one of these locations, two other movement choices are available from the preceding list. In each locale, students can select objects and "wander around the screen." For those wanting more direction, Tad will supply a list of topics contained in each scene.

In *The World of Nature*, a frogship can send students to visit lakes, rivers, farms, grasslands, savannas, deserts, deciduous forests, evergreen forests, mountains, oceans, polar regions, rain forests, wetlands, seashores, coral reefs, and the universe.

The screen design is somewhat too sophisticated and complex for the visual acuity of some of the younger members of the designated audience. Both programs have a Little Kids Mode, which turns off information in the exploratron. This action seems contrary to the purpose of the programs. Another toggle automatically reads all the captions to students, a useful option for younger students and those learning English.

Another option allows students to play Wise Crackers. The program will pose five queggs (question eggs). Students need only to find keyword(s), search for the word(s), read the resultant screens, and press a button when the screen with the answer is showing. However, the five questions are unrelated. No recording device is used so that students can take the knowledge away with them (other than printing each page as they come to it). With this structure, students may not learn any new content, but they will have practiced searching using keywords.

In *The World of People*, the subject *religions* is found only in the Classroom location. Some students felt that connecting religion to the Neighborhood location and having the houses of worship (one of the screens under religions) in the Neighborhood would have been more realistic.

The worlds are engaging and interesting. Much time was invested in the graphics and screen design. The material is based on the *Dorling Kindersley Children's Encyclopedia*, which is sold as the *Random House Children's Encyclopedia* in the United States.

Students can easily exit to writing and painting programs with a filled clipboard. A set of activities that would stimulate and encourage students to write about what they learn would enhance this product for both the classroom and the home.

Conclusion

Students should work with partners to get the most out of the content. This will stimulate vocabulary development, a key value of both programs. Although the programs can keep students interested, the programs are better as home products than as school products.

1996 Grolier Multimedia Encyclopedia

Subject: Library Reference

Grade Level: 5–12 (ages 10–adult)

Cost: $49.95

Hardware: Macintosh, or PC with color, sound, and a CD-ROM drive

This newest version of this encyclopedia, called the *1996 Grolier Multimedia Encyclopedia*, continues to improve and maintain high standards of quality information. The scholarly impression is still evident, and the reading level is generally higher than in other resources.

Figure 5. Text Screen from the 1996 Grolier Multimedia Encyclopedia

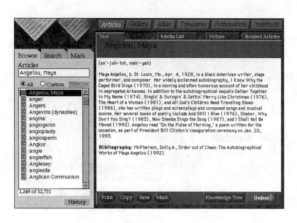

Figure 6. Screen Describing Maya Angelou's Contemporaries in the 1996 Grolier Multimedia Encyclopedia

Description

The visual connection to a text-based reference is clear (see Figure 5). The screen models a tabbed tomb or a set of files at a student's fingertips. For example, after finding the text on Maya Angelou, the student can select Picture to see a photograph of the inspirational lady. The tab marked Media List contains only her picture, so clicking on the listing produces the same picture. Some topics have multiple entries in the Media List file. The section titled Related

Articles includes information about Maya Angelou under the topics of American literature and black American literature. Figure 6 shows the portion of the text describing her contemporaries in American literature.

In the lower right corner of Figure 5 is a button labeled Online. This connects to CompuServe®; the software for an account comes with the CD-ROM. The Online button leads students to a CompuServe directory. For the example of Maya Angelou, the subset of the

Figure 7.   Searching for the "Saxophone" Entry in the
1996 Grolier Multimedia Encyclopedia

CompuServe directory lists the African-American Forum, Archive Photos Forum, Literary Forum, Music and Performing Arts Forum, People Online, Time Warner Author Forum, White House Forum, Women's Forum, and Writer's Forum. If a CompuServe account has been activated and connected, students can simply click a button to connect to the selected forum. Teachers planning to integrate the use of online searches may find this feature invaluable. Otherwise, they might want to make sure this feature is inactive until all components, including monies for the account, are in place.

The Knowledge Tree button, found at the immediate left of the Online button (see Figure 5), positions the current topic in reference to related information. This encourages connected browsing rather than the random jumps typical of a Trivial Pursuit-type game.

Grolier continues to be a leader among encyclopedias. Their presentation style is reserved but not austere or overwhelmed with entertainment. Material is timely and reliable, and has depth as well as breadth. Just one example demonstrates how Grolier's many years of experience has helped this company achieve a high level of quality. Figure 7 shows the search for the subject *saxophone*. By the time the students had typed the first three letters of the word, the Index had scrolled to the point where it was easier to just select the desired topic and not be concerned about spelling the whole word. Searching for *saxophone* resulted in a picture of a sax, the text history, and an audio clip. The audio clip begins with a simple scale that clearly demonstrates the tonal qualities of this instrument. The rest of the audio is a melodic jazz rendering of the scale; thus, the audio clip also provides an example of jazz, an original American music style.

An extra treat in this package is a Modern Art CD-ROM. Wandering around the sculpture garden and learning about modern art is like taking a refreshing walk in a real garden. The Maeght Foundation compiled this hybrid CD-ROM that runs under *Windows* or on a Macintosh.

Browse and Search

Searches can be conducted by typing a keyword, scrolling through the Index, browsing around the Gallery, wandering through the Atlas, tromping along the timelines, or reading about pathmakers. A complex search can be conducted using the three Boolean operators *and, or,* and *not.*

Material from January 1994 through June 1995 is highlighted in the section titled Yearbook. Information more current than June 1995 must be accessed from CompuServe.

Conclusion

Numerous connections to related information make the *1996 Grolier Multimedia Encyclopedia* the richest home resource among electronic encyclopedias. Earlier versions have been popular in school media centers, and this edition continues to effectively expand what a school media center can offer. Although this is a good resource, younger students may not find the motivational interaction that other CD-ROM encyclopedias offer.

An Editor's Musings

I still have the set of Grolier encyclopedias I used as a child. The dark reddish binding still conjures images of hours and hours of exploration. Only the D encyclopedia (for Dinosaur) did not survive the trip of time. I did not discover less rigorous encyclopedias until fifth grade, but by then my reading level was well above the levels they offered. Of all the childhood gifts I received, that set ranks very high. What will childhood memories be like 40 years from now? Will children keep their first CD-ROM encyclopedias? Will these tools prepare them for the future? ❖

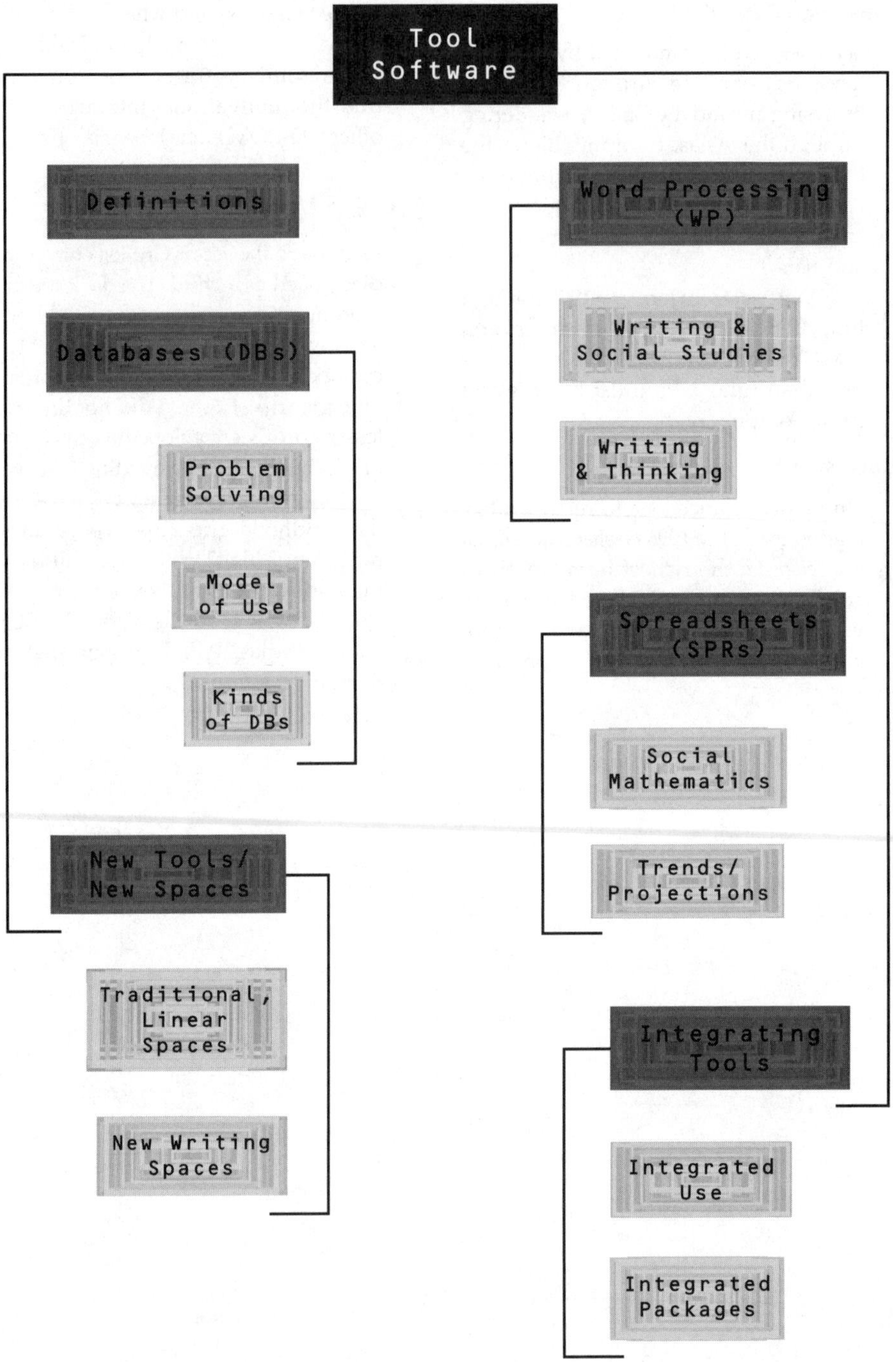

Tool Software

- **Definitions**

- **Databases (DBs)**
  - Problem Solving
  - Model of Use
  - Kinds of DBs

- **New Tools/ New Spaces**
  - Traditional, Linear Spaces
  - New Writing Spaces

- **Word Processing (WP)**
  - Writing & Social Studies
  - Writing & Thinking

- **Spreadsheets (SPRs)**
  - Social Mathematics
  - Trends/ Projections

- **Integrating Tools**
  - Integrated Use
  - Integrated Packages

chapter 4

Tool Software in the Social Studies

What do we mean by tool software? One unifying characteristic of drill-and-practice, tutorial, simulation, and problem-solving software is their relatively narrow range of uses, since each program is focused on a particular topic. Contrasted with this is what is often referred to as tool software—general-purpose applications software that supports a wide range of tasks across the curriculum. These applications include such software as database management (or database software for short), electronic spreadsheets, and word processors, along with graphics and communications programs.

Database Software

A database is a collection of data organized for searching and retrieving information to solve problems or tasks. Based on that definition, a telephone book would be an example of a database, as would a library's card catalog. To search and retrieve data electronically from these databases, you would need a database-management system or a file-management system. In common parlance, we call these applications database software or database tools. Using an index card as a metaphor, database tools and their associated databases store information as records (with each record equivalent to an individual index card) that contain fields of data. In the case of the telephone book database, fields might include last name, first name, street, city, state, zip code, and telephone number. (See the following figure of a database.) Unlike the traditional telephone book, which must be manually searched according to last name, an electronic telephone book database would allow users to reorganize the data according to any field (to search by telephone number, for example). Which data are retrieved and how the data are organized depends on the nature of the information problem or task and the capabilities of the database software.

An Example of a Telephone and Address Book Database

Spreadsheets and Word Processors

Spreadsheets and word processors help to solve other kinds of information problems or tasks. Like an accountant's ledger, a spreadsheet presents a matrix of rows and columns, where each row-by-column intersection is a cell containing textual or numerical information. (See the figure below that shows a spreadsheet.) Calculations can be performed on cells, rows, or columns of numerical data to generate sums, averages, and other statistics needed to solve problems. Word processors, perhaps the most widely used computer-based tool, allow users to compose documents and revise them electronically before printing them out. In contrast with a typewritten page, word processors encourage balanced attention to all steps of the writing process by simplifying the editing task. This increases the likelihood that the writer will achieve high levels of clarity and thoughtfulness in written communication.

A Sample Federal Budget Spreadsheet

	Federal Budget						
		1988	1989	1990	1991	1992	1993
RECEIPTS ($million)							
	Indiv. income tax	401,181	445,690	466,884	467,827		
	Corp. income tax	94,195	103,291	93,507	98,086		
	Social insurance	334,335	359,416	380,047	396,011		
	Other	78,455	82,304	90,870	91,908		
	TOTAL INCOME	908,166	990,701	1,031,308	1,053,832	0	0
OUTLAYS ($million)							
	Legislative branch	1,852	2,095	2,244	2,295		
	Judiciary branch	1,337	1,492	1,641	1,989		
	Executive office	121	124	157	193		
	President	7,262	4,257	10,086	11,724		
	Agriculture	44,003	48,316	46,012	54,119		
	Commerce	2,279	2,571	3,734	2,585		
	Census	333	557	1,575	451		
	Defense (military)	281,935	294,881	289,755	261,925		
	Defense (civil)	22,047	23,450	24,975	26,538		
	Education	18,246	21,608	23,109	25,339		
	Energy	11,166	11,387	12,023	12,459		
	HHS	158,991	172,301	193,679	217,541		
	Soc. Security	214,178	227,473	244,998	266,395		

In this chapter, we will explore how these three predominant tools—databases, spreadsheets, and word processors—can each be used to support thinking and learning in social studies. Powerful learning experiences can also be realized by combining two or more of these tools within a set of activities. Currently, the main computer-based tools are most often integrated in a single software package, allowing students to move easily among a word-processing document, spreadsheet, and database to accomplish problem-solving tasks. These integrated tool products may represent the early stages of a dramatic transformation in the nature of writing and thinking across the curriculum, made possible by emerging information technologies.

We'll first focus our attention on databases, the preeminent tool application in social studies for supporting problem-solving and thinking skills.

Databases in Social Studies

Potential of Databases in Social Studies Learning

Much of the commentary on education reform has focused on students' abilities to be independent thinkers, to learn on their own, and to solve problems (Darling-Hammond 1993). At the heart of this cluster of cognitive activities lies the ability to access and manipulate data from a variety of sources—to convert data into information by giving it meaning and to use this information to solve problems and make decisions. Students are immersed daily in an increasing deluge of information from nonprint sources, particularly television (and especially cable television). More information in the future will be accessible primarily (if not solely) in electronic form—in databases. The ability to skillfully query electronic databases to extract and give meaning to data necessary for problem solving and decision making will be crucial to effective civic participation. Moreover, crafting search strategies for electronic databases requires thoughtful consideration of one's information needs; it requires students to think about the thinking process as they work through a problem or decision. Finally, experience with databases helps students gain insights about the nature of data and information—their utility and their limitations and how individuals use data to construct understandings of social events and processes.

Modes of Student Use

Beverly Hunter outlined a useful taxonomy of database use in social studies in a 1985 issue of *The Computing Teacher*. She referred to three stages of activity to describe how students work with databases: use, build, and design. Those three stages are useful categories within which to consider the kinds of insights students might gain about information—its use, misuse, and limitations.

Using Databases

At this introductory stage of database use, students are searching existing files compiled by someone else. This stage is typical of most database use, from the electronic library catalog to encyclopedias on CD-ROM, except that curriculum databases often allow students to update the information by adding more records. Skillful teachers can help students develop understandings of information at this stage, as illustrated by the following student comments:

1. "Why is some information missing?" (For a variety of reasons, the information we seek is not always available.)

2. "Why is *this* information included?" (Each category of data says something important about the purpose for which the database was constructed.)

3. "What information do we need to answer this question/solve this problem?"

4. "The information we need isn't here." (Even computers don't store all the information we need; often, our information needs require that we look in a number of places.)

5. "How can we make a decision if we don't have all the information we need?" (In real life, we rarely have all the information we would like before making a decision or solving a problem. In decision making, we make the best decision we can based on our current understanding; in problem solving, we keep our conclusions tentative in light of future information we may obtain.)

Building Databases

When students are ready for a more challenging task, they can build a database based on a sample record prepared for them. This template is then used to guide students as they locate information sources and gather the necessary data. The resulting database file can then be used to uncover historical trends or other relationships. The following comments illustrate the understandings students can gain at this stage:

1. "Where can I find *this* kind of information?" (Knowing what kind of information is available, and where, is fundamental to the skilled use of information.)

2. "Why do these two sources disagree about the same information?" (Different sources might define the same phenomenon differently, might calculate the same economic indicator differently, or might date events based on different criteria.)

3. "Which source is most reliable?" (A fundamental critical-thinking skill.)

Designing Databases

At the most sophisticated stage of database use, students design and build their own database on a particular topic. Beyond the tasks required in building databases, as described above, the students select categories of data that are relevant to the topic and that will help them answer important questions about the topic. The kinds of questions to be considered are similarly more sophisticated:

1. "What categories of information (i.e., fields) would we need to discover historical/social trends or patterns?" (For example, what categories of information would best illustrate swings between prosperity and decline in twentieth-century America?)

2. Which information is most important/reliable/straight-forward/illustrative?

3. "What problems can we solve with these categories of information? What other information would we need?" (What questions can we answer/what patterns can we illustrate?)

Problem Solving with Databases

At their best, electronic databases can serve as an intellectual tool in service of solving problems that involve substantial volumes of data. To be used successfully, students need to be able to determine what information they need in order to test hypotheses, to express those information needs in formulating data search commands for the database, and to apply the information skillfully—to know whether the information retrieved supports or refutes their hypotheses or answers their question. Teachers can help students develop those skills by structuring inquiry around a problem-solving model that incorporates the use of electronic databases. "Problem Solving Using Databases" presents such a model adapted from recent research (White 1987; Ehman, Glenn, Johnson, and White 1992).

The problem-solving model looks very linear, but in practice, there is a lot of repetition of the same sequence of steps.

Problem Definition and Database Scanning

Which action should come first? Scanning a database is essential so that students can ask questions about the meaning of data fields or category names (for example, how is "infant mortality" defined?). If students scan the data before defining their problem, however, they run the risk of making their problem fit the data rather than the reverse. This is fine for initial exposure to problem solving using databases, but as students become more sophisticated, their problem solving ought to be guided by more realism. Real-world problems don't often conform neatly to readily available data. All of this suggests careful problem selection by teachers before embarking on inquiry using databases.

Model for Problem Solving with Electronic Databases

Problem Solving Using Databases

◈ Define the problem.

◈ Scan the database to identify available data.

◈ Formulate a hypothesis.

◈ Determine the information needed to solve the problem.

◈ Scan the database to identify relevant fields/categories of data.

◈ Identify information needs beyond the database (e.g., the library).

◈ Formulate expectations about the data. ("If my hypothesis is correct, the data should look like …")

◈ Select/arrange the data according to information needs.

◈ Test the information against the original hypothesis. ("Does the data I retrieved match my expectations?")

◈ Draw a tentative conclusion.

◈ Devise an effective presentation of the case.

Determining Information Needs

Related to the previous point, students ought to discover fairly early that not all the information they need is going to appear in an electronic database, as rich as that database might be. Other sources—print-based, visual, or human—often must be tapped.

Formulating Expectations

This vital step in the process helps students clarify the relationships between categories of data and their relevance to the problem at hand. It also provides criteria by which to judge whether the data do or do not support the hypothesis being tested.

Drawing a Tentative Conclusion

Because real social or historical problems are complex, because the available data rarely provide completely useful information, and because other (perhaps better) data may be found later, emphasis should be placed strongly on the tentative nature of conclusions.

Presenting the Results

Much can be gained by having students share the results of their research. Presentations underscore the importance of keeping social inquiry open to public scrutiny and critique and provide a context in which students develop a range of communication skills. The problem-solving effort moves toward a tangible outcome and a purpose when presentation of the results is encouraged.

— Some General Considerations for the Teacher —

To generate the maximum benefit from problem-solving efforts, teachers should generally consider the size of the problem-solving unit, ways to structure problem-solving activities, and how students will come to view data.

Cooperative Learning

Research and experience have shown that enormous benefits can be gained through group problem solving (Slavin 1990). Two to four students per group help move the effort forward—overcoming minor computer-use problems, clarifying each other's thinking, and sharing the workload (through appropriate teacher guidance).

Providing Structure

Educators have learned over the last several years that skills such as problem solving do not materialize solely through repetitive exposure to problems. Teachers must provide explicit supports, particularly among novice problem solvers and database users. One very effective approach is to model the process in a whole-group activity. Attach the computer to a large monitor or LCD projection pad with an overhead projector and have the class formulate and test a hypothesis using a database program. Debrief the activity by presenting the problem-solving model, and use that model as the basis for activity sheets that student groups will complete as they engage in their own problem solving. Those sheets could be submitted as part of the group's final presentation, or (even better) used as interim assignments. Not only will periodic checking of such assignments help maintain group accountability, but it will also help the teacher locate the steps in problem solving with which students have particular difficulty.

Whether done through activity sheets or some other mechanism, teachers must also help students keep track of their thinking—where are they in the problem-solving process? What do they need to do next? This kind of metacognitive support will increase the quality of the final outcome of the process and help students apply the process in future problem solving.

Attitudes about Data

When teachers use electronic databases in problem solving, they help students develop a view of data as raw material that can be used to construct their own understandings—just as, for example, historians use primary sources (data) to construct their understandings of history. This use of databases can help dispel the view of history and social studies as the mere memorization of disembodied facts.

Adjusting for Grade Level

Teachers have used electronic databases as early as third grade—some earlier. Of course, how databases are used with young children differ from how databases are used by older students. Hunter's stages of database use provide one guide, suggesting that elementary children spend most of their time at the "use" stage and move to successive stages in middle school and high school. Obviously, the kinds of questions asked will depend on students' existing knowledge and experience. The number of records and the number of fields per record should be reduced for younger children. Finally, the trends illustrated by the data should be more explicit and obvious for younger children, but can be more subtle and imperfect as students become more sophisticated.

Kinds of Databases for Social Studies

It is useful to consider two categories of databases (White 1990). The first category consists of databases that require only a single microcomputer workstation (what can be called "self-contained" databases). The second category of databases requires that the user connect a microcomputer or terminal to a distant computer via a telephone line (called "online" databases).

Self-contained Databases

A typical self-contained database consists of two kinds of files: files that contain the data and files that constitute the specialized database management software needed to manipulate the data. Among the latter are general-purpose database management programs like *ClarisWorks* (Apple), *FoxPro* (Microsoft), and *FileMaker Pro* (Claris), which allow the students and teacher to build their own databases or work with commercially available databases. Other self-contained databases are driven by proprietary database management software; such software is developed for one company's database(s) only.

Online Databases

In contrast to self-contained databases are online databases. The data reside in computer files located at some distant site, and the information-seeker must use a computer or terminal that can communicate over telephone lines with that distant computer. The flow chart that follows illustrates the two-way transmission of an online system. (Queries from the user to the database flow downward in the figure, while responses from the database to the user flow upward.)

The school's computer uses a modem, which facilitates the transfer of data between the two computers over a telephone line. Depending on the database of interest, the students may be connected directly to the database or to a vendor of databases—a commercial service company like America Online, CompuServe, or the Microsoft Network (MSN) that provides access to a variety (perhaps hundreds) of individual databases. Such a service generally requires a subscription fee, and users pay for online usage time.

A Graphic Representation of Online Database Access

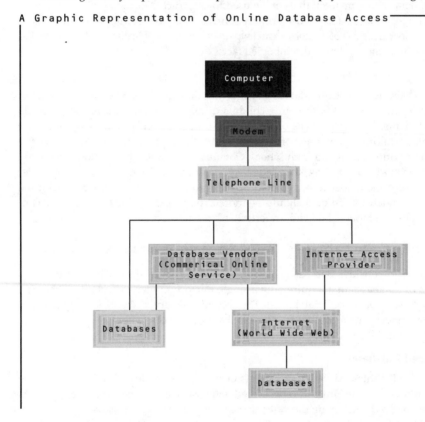

Alternately, the school's computer might be connected to the Internet, either through an online service such as America Online or through an Internet access provider. Internet access providers charge either a flat monthly fee, an hourly usage fee, or both. They serve as gateways to the Net and the World Wide Web without many of the additional services provided by commercial online services. More will be said about the Internet and the Web in a later chapter.

Using communications software in conjunction with a modem, students can send commands to retrieve the data they need for their problem solving (Hunter and Lodish 1989).

Spreadsheets in Social Studies

Our discussion of databases underscored the need for skillful manipulation and use of social data as a basis for effective problem solving and decision making. Much of the information in electronic databases is stored as words and pictures, but effective citizenship is becoming increasingly dependent on understanding numerical data as well. For manipulating numerical or "quantitative" data, an electronic spreadsheet can be a powerful tool for problem solving.

Social Mathematics

Confronted with survey results reported nightly on the evening news, along with economic indicators, voting trends, and advertising claims, citizens must become more skilled in what Hartoonian (1989) called "social mathematics." This includes

> abilities that are used when we measure or quantify social phenomena in any way and communicate these measures to others, plus those related abilities that we need when judging the information presented to us as we decide whom to vote for, what car to purchase, or what personal economic course to follow (51).

Part of the task is understanding key statistical concepts, such as ratio, percent, index number, and mean. Beyond this, students need to learn how to apply these concepts to recognize trends and make predictions based on quantitative analysis.

From Trends to Projections

Spreadsheets and databases share some capabilities when dealing with numerical information. Databases can help students identify social trends reflected in quantitative data; for example, a United States history database containing a field for birth rate could be used to discover the overall downward trend in birth rates during the twentieth century. By comparing the search results for birth rate and unemployment, a student could test the hypothesis that economic well-being has been positively related to birth rate during the same period. Here, students are exploring relationships among social variables. Since most microcomputer-based database products have graphing capabilities, students can also produce a visual display of the results of their searches. A spreadsheet program can also support all of these tasks.

While spreadsheet programs cannot match database programs' powerful manipulation of textual data, they excel in manipulating numbers. This fact allows spreadsheets to expand the scope of student problem solving. Electronic spreadsheets provide a unique environment for summarizing numerical data, analyzing trends, and pursuing "what-if" questions that arise from changes in numbers. Based on historical trends, students can create projections and make predictions. For example, based on current population growth rate, students can extend population numbers into the future to see what the population of the United States might be in the year 2093, as shown in the following figure. Countries with different growth rates can be compared, and the results serve as a basis for speculation about the social, political, and economic consequences of rapid population growth.

A Spreadsheet and Graph Showing Population Projections

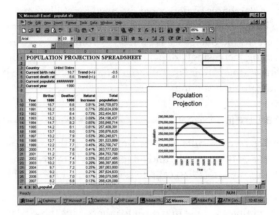

Students are not locked into a single future when they create projections. They can alter the values of variables to explore alternative futures and support decision making about those futures. Consider the following scenario and the questions that are raised: Tropical rain forests currently cover about 15.7 million square miles of the Earth. We are losing 100 acres per minute to slash-and-burn agriculture and other development activities. At this current rate of loss, when will tropical rain forests be completely lost? How much sooner would that occur if the loss rate increased 2 percent annually? If we could reduce the annual loss by 25 percent each year, how long would it take to stabilize the tropical rain forests? How much of the 15.7 million square miles would remain? Once the mathematical relationships are worked out and the formulas are entered into the spreadsheet cells, changes in one variable ripple throughout the spreadsheet as the new results are calculated almost instantaneously.

Finally, students can use spreadsheets to build quantitative models of economic and social processes and can test the impact of their decisions when elements of the model are changed. Put a simplified federal budget in a spreadsheet. See what it would take to balance the budget, and then what steps would be necessary to reduce the national debt. For each change in the budget, though, students have to determine its impact on programs and people and justify the change. Simulate a small business and keep "the books" in a spreadsheet. Explore the impact of inflation on a young couples' efforts to save for a down payment for their first home. The more complex the relationships among variables, the closer students come to understanding the basis of simulations and systems modeling.

Word Processing in Social Studies

Databases and spreadsheets allow students to explore textual and numerical problems. The challenge of thoughtfully explaining and integrating the results of these explorations is aided by another computer-based tool: the word processor. Understanding the instructional power of the word processor in social studies requires that we understand the instructional power of writing in general, and the importance of writing as a thinking tool for social studies in particular.

Writing, Thinking, and Social Studies

According to Gilstrap (1991), writing has traditionally been used in the classroom as a means of assessment; the typical research paper is a good example of this in social studies. Such "transactional writing" is quite narrow, with a limited audience (usually just the teacher), and it rarely transcends low-level writing (reporting, recording, or classifying). Students are given little guidance in preparing the paper beyond the stated expectations for the final product (Britton, Burgess, Martin, McLeod, and Rosen 1975). Over the last 25 years, an increasing number of researchers and teachers have recognized the value of writing beyond assessment—as a tool for learning. Frequent, ungraded writing helps students learn course content and helps them to think about that content. Ultimately, writing is an aspect of thinking (Vygotsky 1978).

During the 1970s, interest in writing as a thinking tool was reflected in research on the "writing process," which consists of several steps: prewriting, writing, rewriting, editing, and sharing (or "publication"). The writing process as applied to social studies was the featured topic of the March 1979 issue of *Social Education*, edited by Barry K. Beyer and Anita Brostoff. In one article, Beyer focused on two of the most challenging parts of the writing process: prewriting and rewriting (1979). At the prewriting stage, teachers must engage students with the information on which the writing assignment will be based, the goal being to focus or limit the topic and to formulate a statement that will serve as the organizing idea for the assignment. At this stage, students must identify the audience for their writing and consider the purpose for which they are writing. At the rewriting stage, students must evaluate and revise based on their own judgments and those of their peers. Beyer suggested that students at the rewriting stage might practice revising their assignments to address a different audience or to achieve a different purpose.

Word Processing and Social Studies

Many of the recommendations above have little to do with technology. What, then, can a word processor contribute to writing or thinking in social studies? It can reduce the burden of revising, serve as a metacognitive reminder, and provide a shared writing area for peer collaboration and evaluation.

Easing the Burden of the Process

"What do you mean 'a good first draft?' This is the final paper!" exclaims the astonished student in the U.S. history class. The writing process described above breaks with traditional writing practice among students in social studies. Carrying out each step of the writing process using paper-and-pen/typewriter technology is an arduous mechanical task, often distracting students from the benefits to be gained. Certainly one solution is to avoid limiting writing to the single, large research paper and to allow students to tackle more frequently assigned, smaller, and more focused writing tasks. Even in this case, though, the flexibility in manipulating text within a word processor makes the revision and editing tasks in the writing process less daunting and the concept of "first draft" less ominous. Moreover, related electronic tools, including outline processors (a tool that automatically shuffles paragraphs and sections when the underlying outline is reordered) and grammar / spelling checkers, supplement the basic word processor and provide added support for the writing process.

Templates for Thinking

Researchers agree that part of thinking skill development is the development of metacognitive skill—the ability to think about one's own thinking process. As students learn new thinking skills, they benefit from metacognitive guidance, either from the teacher or the materials and tools they use. Teachers can translate such guidance into word-processing files for students to use as templates for preparing essays and reports. Consider, for example, what Parker, Mueller, and Wendling (1989) called "dialectical reasoning"—the ability to explore "competing logics (frames of reference; points of view)" concerning civic issues (9). They found that nearly all the eleventh graders in their study were able to produce an essay that exhibited such reasoning if the students were provided with metacognitive guidance. Adapted from their study, the following template shows what a dialectical reasoning word-processing template might look like.

Task: Write a four-paragraph essay about the issue you have chosen. Each paragraph should be approximately one-fourth to two-thirds of a page long. Each paragraph has a particular purpose. When you have finished your essay, you should delete all but your text.

Paragraph 1: In this space summarize what you believe are the facts about this issue. Be careful to avoid revealing your position and reasons for your position in this paragraph. This is what the next paragraph is for.

Paragraph 2: In this space state your position on the issue and give a few reasons for your position. In other words, state your position and then support it with two or three different, good reasons.

Paragraph 3: In this space argue against each of the reasons you gave for your position in paragraph two. Be sure to think carefully about these counterarguments and present them convincingly, as one who believes them might.

Paragraph 4: In this space write a tentative conclusion. Be sure that your conclusion shows that you have considered the arguments against your position as well as the arguments that support your position.

Adapted from Parker et al. (1989)

For the Parker et al. study, students were asked to select one of two issues: Should publishers of schoolbooks use language that includes both sexes, like person and people, and avoid words like man or men when appropriate? or Should citizens be allowed to voice their opinions even if they disagree with the government? A wide range of civic issues can be addressed using this template, either teacher-assigned or selected from a list of issues. Other templates could focus on dimensions of other social studies-related thinking skills.

Providing a Shared Writing Space

Word processors can also facilitate cooperative writing and peer evaluation of writing by conceiving of an electronic document as a shared writing space. As such, teams of students can construct and refine a common piece of writing, each taking responsibility for one or more parts of the writing assignment, and the team as a whole taking responsibility for crafting a smooth-flowing product. For evaluation, teachers, student-writers, and peers can embed comments and highlight passages that identify particularly effective prose or suggest refinements for future drafts.

◾ Integrating Tools ━━━━━━━━━━━━

Thus far, we have discussed three major tool applications separately. This is an artificial arrangement, of course, since social studies problems often require problem-solving tasks that span all three tools. Following the maxim that "the whole is greater than the sum of its parts," producers of tool software have been abandoning stand-alone tools in favor of integrated packages, such as *Lotus 1-2-3*, *AppleWorks*, *Microsoft Works*, *ClarisWorks*, and numerous others. Some, like *AppleWorks*, share a common command syntax and allow users to move easily from tool to tool; but each tool creates its own files, which can be merged only in a limited way. Others, like *ClarisWorks*, have added graphics, paint, and communications tools to the mix and permit much tighter integration among applications. For example, in a word-processing document, one can open a spreadsheet window and have full access to the spreadsheet tools. Similarly, a word-processing window can be opened in a graphics document. No complex merge commands are required.

For the social studies curriculum, tool integration may refer to the use of stand-alone tools at various stages of a single lesson, activity, or project. Alternately, students might use integrated packages to pull together the results of their inquiry. The standard research project is a useful context within which to use an integrated tool package since the central task of such a project is to synthesize information to advance an argument, to defend a position, or to explain an event. We want students to consider a broad range of information—textual, numerical, pictorial, and graphical—as they engage in thinking and problem solving; we also want students to communicate effectively, using the most appropriate mode of presentation—textual, numerical, pictorial, or graphical.

◾ New Tools for New Writing Spaces ━━━━━

When new technologies are introduced, they tend to emulate the older technology they are superseding. Thus, Guttenberg's printed books tried to look like medieval manuscripts and early educational television provided "talking heads" of lecturers. The electronic tools we have described in this chapter also retain traces of prior technologies. For example, the word processor has a typewriter as a metaphor. A typewriter, in turn, reflects the nature of the writing space within print technology—the notion of pages made up of paragraphs intended to be read linearly. According to Bolter (1991), electronic technology is not bound by the printed page and its assumption of linearity. A new "electronic writing space" will emerge as current computer-based tool applications throw off their outdated metaphors. That writing space is hypertext/hypermedia (see Chapter 5), and the high school research paper may never look the same.

As a starting point, consider "Hannibal's Travels," a ninth-grade research document by Craig Hofmeister of the Cincinnati Country Day School. The map that appears in the figure below is the table of contents, to use a print-based metaphor. The reader reads the document by clicking a mouse pointer at various locations on Hannibal's route and reading the text that appears. Unlike a printed research paper, however, the reader is not bound to start at the beginning and proceed in a linear manner. Any point along the route can be accessed with the mouse. Interwoven with the text are graphs of river flow rates, which highlight one of the difficulties Hannibal faced. The author's welcome on the title screen, among other locations, includes an audio clip of elephants. This is a small sample of the new writing space.

Map that Serves as Table of Contents for Craig Hofmeister's Hannibal's Travels

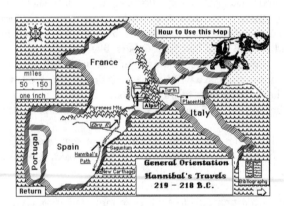

In the electronic writing space Bolter envisions, the writer will use multiple modes of representation—words, pictures, sounds, animation, and full-motion video. Spreadsheet and graphics tools will be seamlessly integrated into the writing space, along with data retrieval from local and distant databases. In fact, the space students write in may span the globe through telecommunications. That research "paper" might be read by others on a network who send along suggestions or actively participate in a collaborative writing assignment.

None of this will happen overnight, but it is likely that the tool applications described in this chapter and today's hypertext and hypermedia applications will begin to converge. If Vygotsky was correct—that writing is an aspect of thinking—then the changes ahead may not only influence the intellectual tools we use, but also the way we think.

Summary

Programs such as those for word processing, databases, and spreadsheets are general tools that have the potential to extend the intellectual reach of their users. Together, the tool and the user can become "partners in cognition" (Salomon, Perkins, and Globerson 1991), not only in social studies but across many knowledge domains. Establishing that partnership and reaping its benefits is highly dependent on the teacher's ability to foster students' mindful engagement with a challenging intellectual task for which a particular technological tool is well suited (4). This chapter outlined some of the potential productive partnerships between social studies students and three widely-used technology tools.

References

Articles/Chapters

Beyer, B. K. "Prewriting and Rewriting to Learn." *Social Education* 43, no. 3 (1979): 187–89, 197.

Darling-Hammond, L. "Reframing the School Reform Agenda." *Phi Delta Kappan* 74, no. 10 (1993): 752–61.

Ehman, L. H., and A. D. Glenn. "Interactive Technology in Social Studies." In *Handbook of Research on Social Studies Teaching and Learning*, edited by J. P. Shaver. New York: Macmillan, 1991.

Gilstap, R. L. "Writing for the Social Studies." In *Handbook of Research on Social Studies Teaching and Learning*, edited by J. P. Shaver. New York: Macmillan, 1991.

Hartoonian, H. M. "Social Mathematics." In *From Information to Decision Making: New Challenges for Effective Citizenship*, Bulletin No. 83, edited by M. A. Laughlin, H. M. Hartoonian, and N. Sanders. Washington, DC: National Council for the Social Studies, 1989.

Parker, W. C., M. Mueller, and L. Wendling. "Critical Reasoning on Civic Issues." *Theory and Research in Social Education* 17, no. 1 (1989): 7–32.

Salomon, G., D. N. Perkins, and T. Globerson. "Partners in Cognition: Extending Human Intelligence with Intelligent Technologies." *Educational Researcher* 20, no. 3 (1991): 2–9.

White, C. S. "Access to and Use of Databases in the Social Studies." *International Journal for Social Education* 5, no. 1 (1990): 61–73.

White, C. S. "Developing Information-processing Skills through Structured Activities with a Computerized File-management Program." *Journal of Educational Computing Research* 3, no. 3 (1987): 355–75.

Books

Bolter, J. D. *Writing Space: The Computer, Hypertext, and the History of Writing*. Hillsdale, NJ: Lawrence Erlbaum Associates, 1991.

Britton, J., T. Burgess, N. Martin, A. McLeod, and H. Rosen. *The Development of Writing Abilities*. London: Macmillan, 1975.

Hunter, B., and E. K. Lodish. *Online Searching in the Curriculum*. Santa Barbara, CA: ABC/Clio, 1989.

Slavin, R. E. *Cooperative Learning: Theory, Research, and Practice*. Englewood Cliffs, NJ: Prentice-Hall, 1990.

Vygotsky, L. S. *Mind in Society: The Development of Higher Psychological Processes*. Cambridge, MA: Harvard University Press, 1978.

Discussion Questions

1. What kinds of information skills are necessary for efficient and effective use of databases in social studies?

2. What examples of social mathematics can you think of that relate to the grade level and topics that you teach (or will teach), beyond those presented in the book and the readings?

3. In what ways can tool software in social studies provide metacognitive support for student thinking? In what nontechnological ways do teachers provide similar support to students?

4. What positive and negative effects do you see in the broader use of hypertext- and hypermedia-based "writing spaces"?

Additional Readings and Questions

Ehman, L. H., A. D. Glenn, V. Johnson, and C. S. White. "Using Computer Databases in Student Problem Solving: A Study of Eight Social Studies Teachers' Classrooms." *Theory and Research in Social Education* 20, no. 2 (spring 1992): 179–206.

1. According to the study, what teacher behaviors characterized effective use of databases within a problem-solving model? What teacher behaviors appeared to be ineffective?

2. What were some of the limitations the authors found in the particular database programs used in the study? What do these limitations suggest about how teachers ought to evaluate new database applications?

Elder, C. L., and C. S. White. "A World Geography Database Project: Meeting Thinking Skills Head-on." *The Computing Teacher* 17, no. 3 (November 1989): 29–32.

1. In what ways is the authors' approach to problem solving consistent with the model presented on page 145 of this chapter?

2. What distinctions do the authors make between direct and indirect instruction in their world geography materials? Why is such a distinction important?

3. What was the effect of the world geography database materials on student attitudes and performance?

Hannah, L. "Social Studies, Spreadsheets, and the Quality of Life." *The Computing Teacher* 13, no. 4 (December/January 1985–86): 13–16.

1. What are some examples of the ways the author integrated multiple tools and multiple data sources?

2. What did the author say he would do differently in the future? What connections do you see between these recommendations and the discussion of database problem solving and social mathematics in the chapter?

Paul, J. R. M., and C. Kaiser. "Do Women Live Longer Than Men? Investigating Graveyard Data with Computers." *Learning and Leading with Technology* 23, no. 8 (May 1996): 13–15.

1. In what ways is the graveyard project consistent (or inconsistent) with the recommendations for problem solving with databases summarized in the figure on page 145?

2. In what ways does this project provide students with experiences in "social mathematics," as described in the chapter?

Wheeler, Ron. "R$_x$ for Social Studies." *Social Education* 60, no. 5 (September 1996): 313–14.

1. According to Wheeler, why did the inquiry-oriented curricula developed for "the new social studies" in the 1960s and early 1970s fail to take hold in schools?

2. How has access to electronic databases made the goals of inquiry-oriented social studies more achievable, according to Wheeler? Do you agree?

▬ Activities ▬▬▬▬▬▬▬▬▬▬▬▬▬▬▬▬▬▬▬▬▬▬▬▬

▬ Activity 1—Identifying Hypotheses ▬▬▬▬▬▬

Objectives

Participants will be able to:

1. Identify social studies hypotheses that could be tested using a commercial database product.

2. Identify additional information sources that would be required to adequately test social studies hypotheses that are only partially testable using a commercial database product.

3. Propose fields the teacher or students could add to the database in order to test more social studies hypotheses.

Rationale

If you look in the teacher's materials for instructional databases, you'll find suggested questions for students to answer using the database. Unfortunately, these questions are heavily weighted toward low-level thinking activities. On the other hand, if you want students to engage in problem solving, you want to make sure the database contains sufficient data to test hypotheses of importance to our curriculum. If not, you'll need to direct students to other sources or add new fields to the database. In this activity, you'll ask yourself "If these are the data available, what hypotheses can I test?" which is just the flip side of the question "If this is my hypothesis, what data do I need to test it?"

Materials Needed

One or several commercial database(s), preferably ones that can be altered by the user (so you can add new fields if necessary).

Advance Preparation

Select database(s) to be used in the activity. For each database used, prepare a handout that lists the field names, with explanations/definitions where clarification is necessary. Make an overhead transparency of each for discussion purposes. Review the "Problem Solving Using Databases" model on page 145 of this chapter.

Procedure

Divide participants into teams of three, with each team assigned to a computer with one of the database software programs. Each team must complete three tasks:

1. After scanning the database, state as many hypotheses as you can that could be tested using the data available from the computer. For each hypothesis, record the fields you would use and how you would manipulate the data in these fields to test the hypothesis (how you would search and sort).

2. State as many hypotheses as you can that could be partially tested using the data available from the computer. For each hypothesis, record the fields you would use, and what additional information you would need to test the hypothesis more adequately.

3. For hypotheses proposed in task 2, propose one or more fields that could be added to the database to test the hypotheses. For each proposed field, state where you might find such data.

Debrief the activity by displaying the field names and descriptions of one database and asking teams who analyzed the database to present the results of tasks 1–3. So that each team can present, you might limit each to a single hypothesis for tasks 1, 2, and 3 until all teams using that database have reported. Repeat the process for teams that used different databases. Conclude the activity by asking participants to characterize the adequacy and/or completeness of instructional databases to support social studies problem solving.

Activity 2—Database Construction

Objectives

Participants will be able to:

1. Identify information sources that can provide data for database construction.

2. Use sources such as almanacs to construct a database for problem solving.

3. Construct a database and related instructional support material that supports social studies problem solving.

Rationale

The literature on database use and thinking skills is unanimous in the view that students are not likely to develop refined thinking skills if their exploration of information is aimless and unstructured. This activity provides participants with the opportunity to examine the various dimensions of structure necessary for successful database use in the social studies classroom.

Materials Needed

Articles by Elder and White and Ehman et al.; section in the text titled "Databases in Social Studies," including the problem-solving model (page 145); several copies of almanacs; a word processing-program; a database program; an already constructed database (e.g., nations of the world) using data from an almanac.

Advance Preparation

1. Introduce participants to the mechanics of database construction using a general database program. Have students construct a small database to practice the mechanics of field creation, data entry and editing, and searching and sorting.

2. Prepare in advance a small database using almanac information (e.g., nations of the world) for demonstration purposes.

3. Read both above-mentioned articles and the chapter.

Procedure

Session One   Have participants list factors that tend to result in successful database construction and classroom use, according to the articles and the database section of the chapter. Those factors will be used to evaluate the database materials developed in this activity.

Brainstorm about the range of easily accessible sources for database data, and list these on the board. As an example, use an almanac to point out the kind of data available about nations of the world. Using a computer hooked to a large monitor or an LCD projection pad, show participants your database that was built using almanac data. Have participants identify modifications you made in the data or fields (if any) in the process of transferring the almanac data to the computer database. Explain the reasons for these modifications.

Demonstrate how the database can be used to reveal patterns and relationships (e.g., what do nations with low GNPs have in common?).

Apply the list of traits of effective databases drawn from the readings to evaluate the database you demonstrated. For example, what changes/additions to this small demonstration database would be needed for successful classroom use? What question sequence, handouts, guidesheets, and the like would provide the kind of structure recommended for successful database use in social studies?

Assignment
Participants are asked to locate one or more sources of social studies data that they will use to construct a database for classroom use. Bring those sources to the next session, along with several higher-level questions that could be answered by rearranging the data from these sources.

Session Two
In this session participants will identify the specific fields for their databases, construct the files, and enter data from the source(s) they have brought to the session. You may wish to place limits on the amount they should enter initially, in order to move on to later tasks in this activity. Work with participants to refine their databases to ensure that the data can be easily manipulated to answer one or two of the proposed higher-level questions.

Session Three
Participants complete their databases. Using a word processor, participants should draft a handout that provides instructions and/or a sequence of questions that would guide students' data manipulation in pursuit of answers to the higher-level questions for which the database was designed. Print out one copy.

Session Four
Participants should load and open the database file they created and place a copy of the instructions next to the computer. All participants then move to another computer and begin working with someone else's database activity. As they do so, they should write suggestions and additional ideas on the instruction sheet. After a sufficient time has been spent working with the databases, participants should return to their original computer and study the comments of their colleagues. Debrief the activity by having participants report and discuss these comments as the basis for a broader discussion of the challenge of devising high-quality database activities.

━ Activity 3—Tropical Rain Forests ━━━━━━

Objectives

Participants will be able to:

1. Construct a spreadsheet using information from a text.

2. Manipulate spreadsheet data to answer given questions.

3. Understand the usefulness of spreadsheets in making predictions and constructing projections.

Rationale

Understanding social issues demands a higher level of mathematical and scientific knowledge. This activity will provide experience in using a spreadsheet as a tool for understanding one such issue.

Materials Needed

A spreadsheet program.

Advance Preparation

Read the chapter, especially the section titled "From Trends to Projections." Discuss the rationale for and range of technology tools that support "social mathematics." Provide participants with software to construct a spreadsheet.

Procedure

After reading the tropical rain forest information in the text on page 148, have participants identify the calculations that will be necessary in order to answer the questions posed. Participants should now construct a spreadsheet that extends over as many years as necessary and uses the basic numerical values provided; participants will then devise appropriate formulas. When the spreadsheets are finished, solicit answers to the questions and check their accuracy by comparison to the spreadsheets of others.

Explore what other questions might be answered using the basic tropical rain forest spreadsheet. What refinements could be made to the spreadsheet so that additional projections can be displayed with minimum effort? What limits do you see in using spreadsheets for modeling processes like rain forest depletion? For what other kinds of phenomena would spreadsheet-based projections be useful? Where would you look for the underlying numerical values used in such spreadsheets?

▬ Activity 4—Word-Processing Template —Critical Reasoning ▬

Objectives

Participants will be able to:

1. Use a word-processing template as the basis for a critical-reasoning writing task.

2. Critique a critical-reasoning writing sample using a word processor.

3. Propose additional templates for various writing tasks in social studies.

4. Assess the utility of word-processing templates for writing in social studies.

Rationale

To develop higher-order thinking skills in social studies, students need what researchers refer to as metacognitive guides. Word-processing templates can help provide such guidance by alerting writers to essential elements of reasoning needed to carry out high-level cognitive tasks.

Materials Needed

The chapter section "Word Processing in Social Studies," especially the "Dialectical Reasoning Template"; a word-processing program; a template created in a word-processing program; a sample essay (see handout).

Advance Preparation

Review the readings and analyze the sample essay (handout) in terms of the criteria contained in the word-processing template.

Procedure

After analyzing the sample essay, participants should draft (on paper) additional questions that could serve as a basis for a critical-reasoning writing task. With the critical reasoning template loaded into the word processor, participants should enter one of these questions at the top of the document. Participants shift computer stations and compose an electronic essay that is consistent with the template's guidelines.

When finished with the writing task, participants return to their original computer station, read the essay, and apply the template criteria for each of the four paragraphs. With the Caps Lock button active, they can enter suggestions and questions for the authors.

Participants shift for a final time, returning to the computer where they composed their essay. This time, they revise their essays based on the questions and suggestions they find. The capitalized text can be deleted (as well as the four template guides, if they wish) before printing out a final copy of the essay.

Debrief the activity by having participants report on the usefulness of the template as a guide for their writing and the utility of inserting editorial comments and revising at the computer. Participants can propose additional templates they might construct to guide student writing in social studies.

Handout—Critical-Reasoning Sample Essay

The following is one high school student's response to the following question: "Should publishers of schoolbooks use language that includes both sexes, like person and people, and avoid words like man or men when appropriate?" The essay is presented in four paragraphs, according to instructions, and was judged to have correctly followed the instructions in most respects.

1. In this age and time, women have come to the conclusion that they should have more rights, and be as equal to men as possible. In most schoolbooks today, terms such as man or men have put the ERA on the bandwagon for more neutral terms such as person or people. They feel that this is promoting a "better" sex among males, them being the "dominant" species. They feel everyone should be equal and treated as such in our schoolbooks to promote equality among the sexes.

2. Publishers of schoolbooks should avoid using words such as people and person, and continue using words such as man or men. I feel that both sexes are equal but with different characteristics, and should be treated as such. Also, if the words people and person were used, there would be confusion as to who the person was. Did a person (male or female) make the first American flag? No! Betsy Ross, a woman did. Was our first President of the United States a person? No! He was George Washington. I also can't understand what the big gripe is that the ERA has. I mean, the Statue of Liberty is a woman, and that is the first thing immigrants see when they enter this country. Ships are christened as shes. So what do they have to complain about?

   Also, to change all the books would be expensive, and education already is having financial problems. If someone is supposedly a leader of tomorrow, then they will not be swayed by the use of the male gender in schoolbooks. They would (or should) know the issues and be able to form a logical opinion for or against this idea.

3. Being a female, I can also see the other side of this controversial subject. Women have gotten very touchy and sensitive about their rights, and feel that they are still being discriminated against. So, in hopes of making the "young people" believe that women are equal to men in every way, they want to have neutral terms such as person and people substituted for man and men. And in this way they could secure that discrimination against women in all forms would cease. Look at the comparable worth issue. Women are still being paid lower wages doing the same job a man does, and he gets paid more. Is this fair? So seeing that we are the leaders of tomorrow, we should be taught equality now, in a feminist's view.

4. Although there are many strong arguments for the use of people and person in schoolbooks, I still believe that the use of man and men should be used in books. Women are being treated pretty fair these days, compared to days past, and I don't think that the Women's Libbers have anything to complain about. Also, the high cost factor of changing these books would be financially detrimental in trying to save education. It is better to have more and better trained teachers who can help us see both sides of issues without books rather than have poorly trained, small groups of teachers with books that promote neutrality and bland equality.

(from Parker et al., 1989, Appendix D, 31–32)

Using Computer Databases in Student Problem Solving

A Study of Eight Social Studies Teachers' Classrooms

Lee H. Ehman, Allen D. Glenn,
Vivian Johnson, and Charles S. White

During the last decade, many educators have encouraged the use of computer databases in social studies classrooms, because such tools are thought to facilitate higher-level thinking goals (Budin, Kendall, and Lengel 1986; Collins 1988; Ehman and Glenn 1987; Hodges 1985; and Hunter 1983, 1988). The results from a recent survey by Sheingold and Hadley (1990) indicate that social studies teachers are indeed beginning to incorporate databases into their instructional plans. In fact, 52 percent of the social studies teachers in the survey indicated that they were using computer databases with their students.

Abstract

This article describes a study in which the authors combined information from case studies of eight social studies teachers and their students to describe how teachers used computer databases to aid student problem solving, what students learned from the experience, and what enabled and inhibited effective use. Findings emphasized the importance of time constraints and pressure, prior student knowledge, use of cooperative student groups, and the use of structure by the teacher during the problem-solving process. Students also exhibited a greater confidence in using data during problem solving.

While it is encouraging to discover more and more teachers using sophisticated computer courseware in their classrooms, we are still not sure how teachers are using the databases and what the outcomes are from such use. The research reported here addresses three descriptive questions related to classroom use: a. How do teachers use computer databases in teaching problem solving? b. What do students learn during this kind of activity? and c. What are the enablers and inhibitors of successful database use during the teaching of problem solving?

To explore these questions, we decided to utilize a series of case studies in which the teachers would be free to implement a general problem-solving model.[1] Supported by a grant from the Minnesota Educational Computing Corporation, the studies took place during the spring of 1990 in eight different classrooms located in four different states: Indiana, Minnesota, Virginia, and Washington. Utilizing a common research design, teachers and their students were observed during at least 10 different class sessions; teachers and selected students were interviewed; and written teaching plans, class materials, and student projects were reviewed. By observing these actions and analyzing these materials, we sought to create an authentic picture of what happens in the classrooms of experienced computer-using social studies teachers, and describe the issues, problems, and opportunities encountered while using computer databases as part of a problem-solving instructional unit.

Previous Studies of Database Use in Social Studies

Few relevant studies on the use of databases in social studies have been reported in the literature. Those that have been documented fall into two broad categories—surveys of database use in social studies classrooms and field studies. Summaries are presented below.

Extent of Use

There appears to be a small but growing use of databases by social studies teachers and students. Hunter (1988) reported an increasing number of databases available for use in schools. Sheingold and Hadley (1990) found that social studies teachers represented the largest percentage of all subject matter teachers who reported using databases. Northrup and Rooze (1990) also found a small but significant number of social studies teachers using databases. This increased use by social studies teachers reflects the growing use of technology during the last decade. Earlier studies (Becker 1986; Martinez and Mead 1988; Ross 1988; White 1988) revealed minimal use of computers and limited student knowledge. However, while the percentage of social studies teachers using computer databases remains small, it appears that during the last six years an increasing number of experienced computer users are beginning to use databases as part of their instructional units.

Field Studies Using Databases

Field studies that exist on this subject represent a wide spectrum. Some focused on cognitive outcomes, affective outcomes or teaching and learning process factors.

---

1. The case study was an appropriate research tool, because we were investigating a phenomenon within its real-life context, because the boundaries between the phenomenon and context were not clearly evident, and because multiple sources of evidence were being used (Yin 1989).

Of these, some are impressionistic (descriptive reports of classroom use), while others are scientific studies. Summaries of the major studies are reported in Appendix A.

Cognitive Outcomes

Six major field studies reported cognitive outcomes. White (1986, 1987), Elder (1988), Rawitsch (1987, 1988), Cornelius (1986), and Underwood (1985) compared classes of students using computer databases with those working on the same data without computers. None of the studies revealed differences in achievement of factual information. White and Underwood found differences in information skills that favored computer databases, but White's findings were not replicated by Elder. Rawitsch found a difference in the number of problems solved that favored computer classes, but he also found that more time for problem solving was required by these students.

Five impressionistic studies reported interesting claims about cognitive outcomes. According to these studies, students can: 1. learn to use databases quickly (Elder 1988); 2. visualize complex historical relationships, develop critical awareness of current events, and integrate information from various library sources (Rothman 1982); 3. learn facts as well as concepts and show a deeper understanding of the concepts (Traberman 1983–84); and 4. develop an awareness of the personal reality of history (Mendrinos and Morrison 1986; Morrison and Walters 1986a, 1986b).

Affective Outcomes

Only two field studies reported results from using scientific measures of student attitude outcomes. Cornelius (1986) and Rawitsch (1987, 1988) found more positive attitudes toward the use of computer databases in problem solving among students in computer-using classes. Cornelius, however, found a difference in only one of two affective comparisons.

Impressionistic claims are made in four reports. Rothman (1982) suggested that general student motivation and involvement were increased even in heterogeneously grouped classes. Lower ability level students were also stimulated by being able to manipulate the computer and by the visual aspects of the work. Classroom discussions were also stimulated. Mendrinos and Morrison (1986) observed that student learning appeared to be more fun, interesting, challenging, and involving with the use of computer databases. Traberman (1983, 1984) found similar findings in the classrooms she observed.

Teaching and Learning Process Factors

What are the factors that influence the teaching and learning process? Few studies speak directly to this question. Rawitsch (1987, 1988) found that students with a more structured work style were more efficient in utilizing a database than those with unstructured styles. Impressionistic studies, however, reported a variety of classroom process factors relevant to the current study. Rothman (1982) and Johnson, Johnson, and Stanne (1985) all reported the positive effects of cooperative group work while using computers. Group work enhanced factual recall, application of factual knowledge, and problem-solving skills. The structure of the software program may also impact teaching and learning. Some packages may be difficult to integrate into the curriculum (Hawkins and Sheingold 1986), and others may require considerable training and practice in direct and indirect teaching methods if they are to be used successfully (Elder 1988).

Summary of the Claims

Although the research is limited and the conclusions tentative, it is possible to highlight several points related to the studies reported here. Using the three essential questions of the study as a framework, we can suggest the following conclusions:

1. *How do teachers use computer databases in teaching problem solving?* Teachers appear to use databases to develop higher-order thinking or problem-solving skills in their students. No study found a relationship between databases and lower-level knowledge acquisition or recall.

2. *What do students learn during this kind of activity?* There is some evidence that there is a positive impact on higher-order thinking skills when databases are used as part of the instructional unit. Students like to use computers to manipulate information, and student attitudes toward computer-assisted problem solving become more positive.

3. *What are the enablers and inhibitors of successful database use during teaching and problem-solving activities?* The most obvious conclusion is that cooperative student groups of two to four are effective in organizing instruction for computer use.

The Present Study

Description of Teachers, Students, and Schools

The key characteristics of the schools, teachers, and students are summarized in Table 1. It is important, however, to note some of the common features among the eight classrooms as well as the differences.

Common Characteristics

All the teachers in the study were relatively experienced computer users and all but the fifth-grade teacher in Washington had a computer and printer in their classrooms. The students were also generally experienced in the use of computers and had previous experience in the social studies classroom. Each school had a computer laboratory. These features are noteworthy because they address some of the frequently cited reasons for the lack of computer use in classrooms: lack of teacher computer literacy, access to computers, insufficient number of computers, and student computer literacy (Cuban 1986).

In addition, all teachers, with the support of their administrator, were willing to have the researchers in their classrooms; to be interviewed prior to and at the end of the units; and to take part in periodic post-lesson debriefings after classroom observations (such debriefings did not occur after every lesson). Except for the Washington teachers, all of the others had been involved in a pilot study the previous fall. Each teacher was willing to construct and teach a "problem-solving" unit of 10 or more days, using the computer and a computer database, and all units were taught during the second half of the second semester of the school year. Each used small groups of students in noncompetitive, problem-solving teams rather than individual or whole class instruction. They also agreed to have the student teams produce an oral report for the whole class, and most required a written product as well.

Table 1
Characteristics of the Eight Teachers' Classrooms

	IN #1	IN #2	MN #1 (5 classes)	MN #2 (4 classes)
Gender	Male	Male	Male	Male
Years experience	6	7	25	19
Experience with computer databases	High	Low	High	Low
School size/type	Small rural	Small rural	Large suburban	Large suburban
Grade level	12	10/11	9	12
Subject	Economics	U.S. history	American civics	Social studies problems
Student ability level	Average	Above average	Average	High
Student n	24	16	29–34	31–33
Unit topic	Classifying developed/ developing nations	Census and local social history	Foreign/domestic social/economic problems	Problems of/ solutions to MN economic problems
Unit length in days	14	11	11	19
Database used	MECC world communities	Researcher-created AW local census	Researcher-created AW world data	Researcher-created AW MN data
Computers/ printers	20 Apple IIe 10 printers	15 Apple IIe 6 printers	24 Apple IIe 6 printers	14 Apple IIe 7 printers
Student group size	2	2–3	2–3	2–4

Differences among Teachers, Students, and Schools

There were, however, many important differences among the eight teachers and their classrooms. Years of teaching experience varied widely, and their experiences with computer databases ranged from very little to extensive. The most fundamental difference among the eight teachers was their interpretation of "problem" and "problem solving," and how they incorporated these concepts into the units they planned and taught. For instance, Minnesota teacher #2 focused on contemporary social problems, while Indiana teacher #2 used a variation of the hypothetical-

	VA #1	VA #2	WA #1 (2 classes)	WA #2 (2 classes)
Table 1 (continued) Characteristics of the Eight Teachers' Classrooms				
Gender	Female	Female	Male	Male
Years experience	14	14	10+	10+
Experience with computer databases	Moderate	Low	High	High
School size/type	Medium suburban	Medium suburban	Large suburban	Large suburban
Grade level	12	9/10	5	6
Subject	U.S. government	World history	Social studies	Social studies
Student ability level	Below average	Below average/ average	Average	Above average
Student $\underline{n}$	17/21	16/25	28	30
Unit topic	Legislative executive branches over time	Current world problems	Fifty states	Geography of U.S. and Europe
Unit length in days	10	10	10	2 units spanned 45 days
Database used	Newsworks American government	Newsworks world community	MECC USA GeoGraph	MECC USA and World GeoGraph
Computers/ printers	9 Apple IIe 2 printers	9 Apple IIe 2 printers	15 Apple IIe 15 printers	12 Apple IIe 4 printers
Student group size	3	3	2–3	4

deductive method to examine economic and social historical trends over the past 40 years. Still other teacher "problems" were descriptive: collecting and displaying geographic information about the western United States for Washington teacher #1, and defining empirically the categories of developed, less-developed, and under-developed countries for Indiana teacher #1 (see Appendix B for a description of individual units). This broad array of meanings of "problem" and "problem solving" does not fit neatly into a scholarly conception of those ideas. Nevertheless, they were valid for the teachers because they used them in planning and teaching their units.

There was also a notable difference in the manner in which problems were selected by the students. Three teachers, Indiana teacher #1, Virginia teacher #2, and Minnesota teacher #1, were entirely closed. They chose the problem to be examined and students followed specific directions. At the other extreme were Indiana teacher #2 and Minnesota teacher #2, who encouraged students to address any problem they chose to define within the scope of the database used. These differences in student choice undoubtedly affected the instructional process.

Another difference among the sites was that students varied by grade and ability level. There were large and small rural and suburban schools, but none was urban. Two classes in Washington were elementary school classes while the others were at the secondary level. Class size ranged from 15 to 34, and courses taught spanned nearly all social studies subjects as did the unit topics.

Methods Used in the Case Studies

The research plan and methods for collecting the data were developed by the research team with a goal of providing a common framework for each of the eight sites in the four different states. However, depending upon local circumstances, which ranged from constraints imposed by human-subjects committees to teacher preferences, distance from the school, and the researcher's available time and assistance, variations in methodology occurred. Table 2 details some key features of the methods used.

In all cases, teachers were introduced to a problem-solving strategy, given assistance in developing a set of instructional materials to follow the model, and, if needed, given appropriate software. Researchers observed classroom activities and wrote field notes corresponding to their observations. Interviews were conducted with each teacher prior to and at the end of the units. Post-lesson debriefings also took place on numerous occasions.

Different methods were used to obtain information from students and student teams. Questionnaires to tap student perceptions about the units were used in the Washington sites, while those used in Minnesota aimed at prior student computer experience. No student questionnaires were used in Indiana or Virginia. Post-unit student interviews were conducted in the Minnesota sites with some teams while in Indiana the teachers debriefed their classes as whole groups for perceptions about the units, using questions devised by the researcher. No end-of-unit interviews or debriefings with students were conducted in Virginia or Washington. Videotaped student activities were used in Minnesota and Virginia.

The Problem-solving Model Provided to Teachers

Teachers were instructed to use a specific problem-solving model that had been adapted by the researchers. The model included these parts:

Part I: Introduction

A. Teacher introduces the unit and its objectives.

B. Teacher introduces (as much as needed) the concept of databases.

C. Teacher introduces (as much as needed) the operation of the database tool to be used.

Part II: Problem Identification

D. Students practice with the database tool.

E. Teacher introduces the problem area.

F. Students scan the database to get a feel for the problem.

G. Students focus or define the specific problem they will work on.

H. Students formulate a question or hypothesis about the problem's solution.

Part III: Problem Solution

I. Students determine what information they need in order to solve the problem.

J. Students use the database to find the information.

K. Students organize and manipulate the data as they work on their solutions.

L. Students test their information against their question or hypothesis and draw a tentative conclusion.

M. Students test their conclusion against another situation and integrate their information in drawing a confident conclusion.

Part IV: Reporting

N. Students report on the results of their problem solving; teacher evaluates the reports on the following criteria: a. clarity of problem description; b. workability of hypothesis or question; c. quality of data used—relevance, sufficiency, fairness of use, and quality of organization and display; and d. reasonableness of the conclusion.

O. Teacher leads a debriefing of the activity.

The teachers implemented the model in different ways. Differences included the meaning they placed on problems and the degree of choice permitted students in picking a problem to study. Teachers emphasized some parts more than others. We cannot claim, therefore, that each teacher put the model into practice in the same way, as would be the assumption in a field experiment where the fidelity and consistency of the treatment variable would be of the utmost importance. We made the conscious decision to let the implementation of the model vary from teacher to teacher, depending upon how the teachers themselves chose to interpret and use it in their classrooms. The variations across cases are, perhaps, the most important features of the study.

Table 2
Key Features of the Methods Used

	IN #1	IN #2	MN #1	MN #2
Dates of case study	3/22–4/20	4/11–4/23	4/16–4/27	4/26–5/24
Student interview/ debriefing (post-unit)	Whole class	Whole class	Interview of 6 teams	Interview of 2 teams
Student quest	None	None	Pre-unit	Mid-unit
Videotaping	None	None	Small-group activity	Whole-class activity
Extent of researcher unit preparation	None	Moderate	None	None
Teacher training by researchers	None	1 hour	None	2 hours
Same teachers as in fall pilot study?	Yes	Yes	Yes	Yes
	IN #1	IN #2	MN #1	MN #2
Dates of case study	4/21–6/5	4/21–6/14	3/12–3/23	3/5–4/14
Student interview/ debriefing (post-unit)	None	None	None	None
Student quest	None	None	Post-unit	Post-unit
Videotaping	Oral reports	Oral reports	None	None
Extent of researcher unit preparation	Minimum	Minimum	None	None
Teacher training by researchers	12 hours	12 hours	1 hour	1 hour
Same teachers as in fall pilot study?	Yes	Yes	No	No

Overlay Factors

Three themes run through our case studies, and transcend many of the different categories of the problem-solving model. We viewed them as "overlay factors," impinging on the whole process. These are small group work, prior student knowledge, and time pressure.

Small Group Work

Teachers and students endorsed working in cooperative, noncompetitive groups as a positive feature of the problem-solving units. Students helped one another with computers, vocabulary, and other tasks. They collaborated on generating possible problems, hypotheses, strategies for testing ideas, and developing reports. Groups generally stayed on task in both their computer work and during other unit activities.

Of course, not all groups worked smoothly. A few students complained that some group members were taking "free rides" on the work of others. Absence by some students also caused hardships on group goal attainment. Occasionally one student would monopolize the computer or intimidate others in the group.

Prior Student Knowledge

Early in the units it became clear that many students lacked sufficient knowledge about the subjects they were investigating. This lack of knowledge hindered student success at problem solving and achieving unit objectives. For example, student lack of knowledge about geography in one of the Washington classrooms meant that the teacher needed to spend additional time teaching basic geographic knowledge and students had to refer to additional materials for background knowledge as they explored the database. Such problems existed to some extent in all eight classrooms.

Time Constraints

Current classroom structures and curriculum design imposed significant time constraints on teachers and students. All felt pressure to finish the activity in an allotted time and to move on to the next one. Using computers exacerbated these problems. To do a good job, extra preparation, instruction, and practice with such mechanics as database commands were necessary. "We need more time," was a common complaint from students and teachers. Students needed more time to collect data, test hypotheses, and write reports. Teachers never appeared to have sufficient time to debrief classroom activities. Problem solving with computer databases tended to increase the amount of time needed for effective instruction and therefore pushed against other curriculum demands.

Although there were constant time pressures, we also observed time wasted by both students and teachers. For example, teachers sometimes backtracked unnecessarily because of ineffective planning, organization, or instruction. Inexperience and discomfort with using technology and a problem-solving model were significant factors. Typical classroom maintenance activities such as taking students to the computer lab or library, getting groups started on computer database tasks, and handling individual group questions also contributed to the loss of time. In some cases, students were sometimes off task for extended periods of time, and sometimes teachers knowingly permitted such behaviors to continue.

Classroom Applications of the Problem-solving Model

Each teacher followed a general problem-solving strategy. The overlay factors described above and other intervening variables shaped the outcomes of each unit. Given a general strategy, how did teachers choose to utilize the model? To explore the answers to this question, the problem-solving strategy was divided into four general areas: introductory activities, problem identification, problem solution, and reporting (see above for a summary of the problem-solving strategy).

Introductory Activities

The essentials of the introductory sequence were an introduction of the unit and its objectives, databases, operating databases, and student practice with the database. It is not surprising that each teacher chose quite different sequences, implemented them in a unique way, and emphasized different elements. Four chose to begin with the overview of units, assignment expectations, and, in two cases, the problem-solving model. The other four launched directly into the concept of databases and how to operate them. All introductory activities were concluded between one to four days.

Another common element among all the teachers was that they did not have the students practice database operations sufficiently before throwing them into the work on problem and hypothesis development or data exploration. Only one teacher, Virginia teacher #2, had carefully laid-out plans for introducing databases, and consistently checked practice exercises. Others assumed too much about student database understanding and skills. As a result, field notes repeatedly

commented on specific database problems encountered by students. Reasons for this lack of attention to sufficient practice for students may only be speculated. Time constraints obviously pushed teachers to cut short introductory activities and to move directly into major instructional activities. The lack of database knowledge and skills by the individual teacher also contributed. For example, two teachers depended heavily upon the researchers for support in using the databases, and one asked the researcher to introduce the topic to the class.

The consequences of this inadequate introduction were evident in the way students acquired information about the meaning of database categories. Most tried to rely on simple database labels rather than consult definitions of the categories in print materials accompanying the databases. This often resulted in almost comical misunderstandings of concepts like "arable land" or "gross domestic product." The result was misleading use, or complete misuse, of data. The teaching of category meanings, and insistence by the teacher that students use care in applying the categories, is an important part of database use in the classroom. Lack of attention to this issue is an inhibitor of successful problem solving.

Problem Identification

After introducing the unit and databases, and providing appropriate practice experiences, teachers were to introduce the problem, allow students to scan the database, define a specific problem and formulate some questions or hypotheses about how to solve the problem. Effective instruction put students on the right track toward systematically exploring a significant problem. Poorly structured instruction led to confusion.

Unfortunately, most teachers did not provide clear structure and expectations for students. As a result, some students were confused and overwhelmed at times, or they were unsure of what variables in their database might be related to the problem area they chose. Few teachers actually used example data to generate problems, questions, and hypotheses as a model process for what they expected of students.

In classrooms where a teacher provided a clear example to follow while exploring a problem, students were able to develop a number of problems on which to work. Effective teachers also monitored student progress, checked student work, and had students redo their work.

It is clear that teachers cannot afford to gravitate toward the mechanics of the database without first attending to the preconditions for assisting the students in problem identification. Effective teachers press students to spend sufficient time and thought on identifying and clarifying their questions and hypotheses. Monitoring, checking, and revising are essential elements during these early stages of problem identification and database exploration.

Problem Solution

After identifying the problem, students were asked to engage in a number of instructional activities geared to have them work back and forth between the database and their questions, manipulating, adding to, and eliminating data, and modifying questions. Students engaged in a number of activities requiring that they work together in small groups, use the computer database system, and complete a series of instructional activities. During this phase, human and mechani-

cal factors interacted and affected the learning outcomes. Field notes from this phase of the problem-solving process reflect the rough and tumble, nonlinear nature of the problem-solving process. The notes also provide insights into the enablers and facilitators of the problem-solving process.

Students exhibited little systematic analysis and planning behavior. Instead, they tended to "jump in" and "wade around" in the database, search through various categories to see what seemed to fit. Those students who had a clearer mental process model and an understanding of the database categories were more successful in arriving at a solution to the problem. An example from the field notes illustrates these points:

> [One] successful group spent a lot of time reading the category definitions and looking at individual years with all variables. Then they searched for patterns by "ZOOM"ing from a single year's record to multiple variable screens for successive years. They were satisfied with this strategy and made a lot of progress.

Even with a strategy students encountered difficulty with information overload. Some teachers adapted instruction to respond to this problem. In Washington, the fifth- and sixth-grade students were overwhelmed by the sheer magnitude of the data in the MECC *GeoGraph* database. As a result, the teacher reduced the number of unit objectives and provided worksheets to guide student explorations of the problem. In Indiana teacher #2's class, the teacher continued to insist that students make judgments about what data were most relevant and throw out that which was marginal or irrelevant in order to focus student attention.

While both teachers attempted to structure student problem solving, there was not much overt evidence in the classroom observations or in student debriefings that students used deliberate strategies to determine information sufficiently, even though they seemed to understand that it was important. For example, most of Indiana teacher #2's students responded during unit debriefing that they used their hypothesis as the primary criterion to determine if they had used enough information. Students in Minnesota #2's classes mentioned group discussion, following teacher directions, and trial and error as their means for judging sufficiency.

In other classes, students complained that the databases did not contain enough information to fully address their problems. They had to search out other sources of information, typically the library. Although students did not like seeking out additional information, it was a significant indicator that they were sensitive to the information-sufficiency issue, and that they were not blindly following a recipe in their work. Students wanting more information and needing to use multiple sources were positive evidence of higher-order thinking processes.

Which source of information did students prefer? Most tended to like the computer database because "all of the information is in one place"—it is convenient, easy to access, and data can be printed rather than written by hand. Students also recognized that both computer databases and reference books were equally good and should be used to complement each other. Some indicated that to depend on only one would be misleading.

Students learned to use the databases, but went through cycles of forgetting and relearning many of the commands. This was most often a problem when insufficient instruction and practice were provided before engaging in heavy computer use. Software programs that were less dependent on complex commands facilitated student use. For example, Washington elementary students learned the commands for *World* and *USA GeoGraph* quickly and did not interfere with the inquiry process. *AppleWorks*, on the other hand, with its more complex commands focused the user's attention on the database itself, and students needed to refresh their memories of the commands in order to access the database.

Nonmechanical and mechanical problems impacted the learning process. Screen limitations of the Apple IIe and software limitations permitted students to examine only a few categories of data and required students to engage in a number of cumbersome tasks in order to compare data. Other practical difficulties were brought about by time limitations. The *GeoGraph* programs took considerable time to boot-up on the Apple IIGS, and print time of the output was considerable. Mechanical problems were most often experienced with printers. They jammed, became unplugged, and caused bottlenecks when shared between computers. In only one case did an insufficient number of computers cause problems; in one classroom there were not enough diskettes.

Reporting

After identifying a problem and exploring alternatives, students were asked to report on their findings and debrief the problem-solving process. The most common report form was the oral report. The reports varied widely in format and quality. Some students used a computer word-processing program and a graphics package to complete their reports.

Feedback from teachers focused more on the content of the reports than on the problem-solving process. In fact, no evidence indicated that teachers systematically used the problem-solving criteria to give feedback to the students. Some teachers were convinced the reports demonstrated that students had used a problem-solving approach and were able to organize and synthesize information in addressing these problems. Others were distressed at what they saw as superficial and unconnected use of information just to follow an assignment.

It is clear that the reports provide a means for organizing the required thinking. The "publication" and presentation of inquiry results were important parts of problem solving and involved fruitful student-student and student-teacher interaction. In addition, teacher-led debriefings were useful; however, they appeared to be anticlimactic and it was clear that neither the teachers nor the students were seriously interested in the end-of-unit activity.

General Observations about the Problem-solving Process

Teachers made a number of general comments about the problem-solving process. They agreed that it is a difficult activity to orchestrate, but students appeared to understand the process and be able to synthesize and apply information to the problems they chose. The fifth- and sixth-grade teachers in Washington considered the process to be unfamiliar to their students; however, the researchers observed that these students were able to develop grounded, descriptive generalizations about the states and countries.

Students reported feeling more confident in their use of data and more intelligent about and critical of statistics. They generally enjoyed using the computer to access a lot of information quickly and easily. Some were positive about the break from routine class work; they had more freedom to choose problems and ask questions in which they were interested, and to work at their own pace.

Researchers repeatedly observed in the field notes and in post-observation discussions that lack of structure and organization by teachers was a major problem. Teachers who were most successful acted as "metacognitive guides." They provided students with a clear road map of the unit at the beginning, and then gave continual reinforcement and guidance to show individuals, groups, and their whole classes where they had been, where they were at the time, and where they were going. Providing clear road maps meant teachers had to be quick thinkers, especially when students were working in groups, because teachers had to assess group learning needs and provide assistance in enabling the group to move forward with the learning task. When such assistance was lacking, the quality of student work suffered and students became impatient and discouraged.

An effective guidance strategy used by some of the teachers was a regular, short debriefing in the whole class setting. The debriefing focused on specific phases of the groups' progress, and examples of ways to carry out various steps in the process. These mini debriefings gave the teacher an opportunity to reinforce and clarify expectations for the students. Based on our observations, we believe the use of regular debriefings to be far more important than unit-ending debriefings which we found not to be useful.

Conclusions and Implications for Successful Practice

Five general overarching themes emerge from these eight case studies. They are time, student knowledge, cooperative groups, structuring, and databases. Each is summarized below.

Time

Time constraints and pressures affected teachers and students alike. Teachers had to determine how much time would be devoted to the problem-solving unit and how the unit was to be integrated into the social studies curriculum. If integration was high, time pressure seemed less of a problem. When integration was low, the inclination was to hurry on to the next task. Throughout, teachers and students were confronted with other issues related to time. Precious time was lost as students moved from the classroom to the computer laboratory, loaded courseware into the computer, and puzzled over instructions or the recall of commands to operate the database. Teachers were constantly aware of the limitations of time. Secondary students had only a fixed amount of time in the social studies classroom and elementary students had to move on to another component of the curriculum. As noted earlier, students often said, "We need more time."

Based on our observations, we suggest a number of ways that teachers and students can make better use of time.

First, there are simple things like having students go directly to the computer laboratory or library rather than first coming to the assigned classroom. More specifically, more instruction can take place in the regular classroom where students are not distracted by the technology. Introductions, specific student assignments, and the answering of general questions can all occur in the regular classroom prior to computer activities. Also, clearer introductions to the components of the problem-solving model and computer use need to occur. Those teachers who provided clear introductions with opportunities for questions and feedback saved instructional time in the long run. Students need to observe the teacher practicing the problem-solving process. These issues are related to the next important theme.

Structuring

Based on our observations we conclude that structure is an essential element in problem solving. By "structure," we mean a combination of several interlocking components: unit introduction; incorporation of clear expectations with a sequence of activities; development and modeling by the teacher and practice by the students of key problem-solving elements; and provision for regular checking of student progress in accomplishing the milestone tasks of problem solving. Why is structure so important?

It may appear contradictory to emphasize structure so much when discussing problem solving in social studies. Some might argue that because true student problem solving must be open-ended and fluid in nature, teacher-imposed structure would inhibit positive outcomes. Our observations led us to disagree. We found that because of the nature of problem solving, structure provided by the teacher adds a needed source of support for students. Structure reduces some of the uncertainty for students about what to do. It can also help students develop the skills needed to solve problems. Keeping track of the overall picture of problem solving, especially when it involved computer databases, is often difficult. Clear structure assists students to find that picture and keep it in focus.

It should be noted that this teacher-organized structure need not be a heavy-handed approach, but one that assists students in focusing on key elements of the problem-solving process or in redefining the task at hand. Effective teachers in this study were able to assess student learning needs during group tasks and provide appropriate responses, and they had planned instructional activities to insure that students were on the right track and had an understanding of the problem-solving process. Examples of such activities follow.

Introductions, as we have previously noted, are the key point where the teacher familiarizes students with the big picture of the unit. The most successful teachers drew their students into the problem area without undue emphasis on the computer. The emphasis was on the problem, not on the lure of using the computer. These teachers also set forth clear expectations for student work and outcomes, including intermediate milestones in the process. Effective teachers used simple examples of problems and worked on these problems to reinforce the broad goals of the instructional unit.

Teachers also reinforced structure through the use of regular checking of individual student work at key points, as well as in whole-class debriefings of particular phases of the process. One of the teachers pointed out the wisdom of having a five-minute period each day in which the teacher leads the class to sum up where they have been, what they accomplished on a given day, and where they are going. This kind of regular debriefing was far more important for unit success than were the unit-end debriefings. Associated with the practice of regular debriefings is asking students for written products of their interim work, checking these products, and giving clear feedback and suggestions to students. The students who received this help were much more successful than those who did not.

One final component of structure is the importance of public sharing by students of the results of their problem solving and a discussion of these findings. Each group of students shared their findings with the other class members. In some cases, this sharing was quite extensive. In others, it was more informal. The public sharing, however, emphasizes one key value of inquiry—its public nature, the idea that results should be scrutinized by others.

These are all examples of what we mean by teacher "structuring." Using examples, modeling steps and processes, providing for student practice, debriefing student learning, and sharing outcomes are all essential elements of effective instructional structuring. The importance of such activities in helping students keep the big picture in focus cannot be overemphasized.

Student Knowledge

In all the classes, the lack of prior student knowledge played an important role in determining the success of instructional activities. This lack of knowledge affected the problem-solving process and student ability to use the computer database effectively. For example, student knowledge of meanings of database categories is essential if students are to use information from the databases in problem solving. Or, if students lack content knowledge about the general problem area, it seriously impedes their identification of the problem for study. Teachers who have students swim in a lake of data in the pitch dark can do little for their thinking skills. Lack of student knowledge must be anticipated by the teacher.

Small Cooperative Groups

All the classrooms involved in the study did not have enough computers to allow students to work alone on a particular problem. Consequently, small groups were the most effective instruction strategy utilized by all the teachers. Students cooperate within and across groups, teach each other, and learn important skills. Observation field notes document how students help each other with computer problems, challenge one another to think, clarify instructional tasks, and develop accurate generalizations. With interesting problems and guidance by the teacher, students make steady progress toward a solution to the problem.

Computer Databases

Two conclusions with clear implications for practice concern computer databases. First, databases with complex access instructions limit student learning. For example, the version of *AppleWorks* used

in the study required that students learn a number of keystrokes and commands to access the data. Recalling such information often slowed student activities. More graphic-oriented programs such as MECC's *World GeoGraph* allow easier access. Teachers should carefully review the database to determine how much time and practice will be needed to access the information contained in the database.

Second, even teachers with considerable computer experience cannot be expected to do the planning, design, research, data entry, and detailed checking necessary to produce usable databases in their classrooms. In this study, both commercially-developed and teacher-developed databases were used. Experience and observation suggest that well-developed commercial products will, in most cases, be much more dependable and useful problem-solving tools. More and more of these types of databases are becoming available for social studies classrooms.

Implications for Research

There is a host of possible projects that might be suggested based on this study, both qualitative and quantitative. But we are pessimistic about the worth of conducting extensive inquiry based on the typical computer "environment" now encountered in social studies classrooms. For example, the use of *AppleWorks* on Apple IIe computers tends to make the computer user the servant of the database, rather than the other way around. The teacher is equally subservient to the computer/software system, because of its limitations in numbers of variables, cases, and retrievable/display functions.

There is a glimmer of change on the horizon, however. Graphically-oriented databases like MECC's *USA* and *World GeoGraph*, running on Apple IIGS or the Macintosh, free the student and teacher from some of the limitations. Courseware that employs graphics such as maps, charts, and graphs, and permits printing them along with the raw data, can be powerful learning tools. Databases that provide more visual cues to the user and allow for multiple representations of data may provide more fertile ground for productive research.

Research employing hypermedia-based databases, for example, could yield important insights about the dynamics of problem solving with history and the social sciences. For example, hypermedia products such as National Geographic's *GTV* and Optical Data's *ABC News Interactive* series will become more common in social studies classrooms. Future research efforts may be wasted if they are based on ineffective data manipulation tools that are relics of an earlier time and that should be retired from service.

Research Topics

Drawing upon our classroom studies, a number of research topics emerge for further exploration. They are posed as questions:

1. What visual components of a database tool help the user to manipulate data efficiently and effectively? What visual metaphors make data manipulation easier and more intuitive?

2. Is student manipulation of data within the database an important part of information skill outcomes?

3. What are the differences in problem-solving outcomes between computer and non-computer databases?

4. What are the implications for problem-solving skill development of hypertext/hypermedia databases that allow unrestricted data links?

5. What are the implications for social studies teacher training? For example, what type of preservice education is needed to enable teachers to effectively integrate technology into problem-solving units?

6. What are ecological problems of modern database/computer environments? For example, can problem-solving units using computers be taught effectively in a classroom with just a few computers, rather than depending on the now-common centralized computer laboratories?

7. How much extra time, effort, and funds are required to gain how much extra benefit in terms of student learning or in terms of teacher time?

Appendix A

Summary of Research Studies Reviewed

Characteristics of the Field Experiences Reviewed			
	Cornelius (1986)	Elder (1988)	Rawitsch (1987–88)
Grade level	12	9	8
Student ability level	College prep	Low and average	NA
Total student n	36	214	339
Small groups	No	Yes	NA
Subject	World cultures	Geography	NA
Unit topic	26th amendment (18-year-old vote)	World geography	World nations
Database used	Text about legal cases	Researcher-made	Researcher-made
Treatment length in days	2	15	8
Nature of treatment groups	1. Linear research 2. Keyword search 3. No computer	1. Computer in room 2. 15 computers in lab 3. No computer	1. Computer 2. No computer
Random assignment	Yes	No	NA
Outcome measure reliability	Achievement test: 47 Aptitude test: 91	Inf proc scale: 57 Geography test: 62	1. Problem solving: NA 2. Time taken: NA 3. Efficiency: NA
Outcome measure effect size	Achievement test: +.61 Aptitude test: +1.08	Inf proc scale: +.10 Geography test: NA	1. Problem solving: +.35 2. Time taken: -.33 3. Efficiency: -.03
Significant differences	Achievement test: No Aptitude test: Yes, linear search best	Inf proc scale: No Geography test: No	1. Problem solving: Yes 2. Time taken: Yes 3. Efficiency: No

Characteristics of the Field Experiences Reviewed (continued)			
	Rawitsch et al. (1988)	Underwood (1985)	White (1986–87)
Grade level	7	NA	7–12
Student ability level	NA	NA	NA
Total student n	158	NA	315
Small groups	NA	NA	Yes
Subject	U.S. history	NA	Varied
Unit topic	1. Westward expansion 2. Civil War	NA	U.S. history U.S. government
Database used	1. Oregon Trail 2. Researcher-made CW	Factfile; seek	Scholastic PFS U.S. history/government
Treatment length in days	1. Computer simulation: 3 2. Computer database: 6	15	10
Nature of treatment groups	1. Computer simulation 2. Computer database	1. Computer 2. No computer	1. Computer 2. No computer
Random assignment	Yes	NA	Yes
Outcome measure reliability	1. Proper reasoning: NA 2. Deductive reasoning: NA	1. Classification: NA 2. Facts: NA	1. PS: .66 IPS=information process scale
Outcome measure effect size	1. Proper reasoning: NA 2. Deductive reasoning: NA	1. Classification: NA 2. Facts: NA	1. PS: +.27
Significant differences	1. Proper reasoning: No 2. Deductive reasoning: No	1. Classification: Yes 2. Facts: Yes	1. PS: Yes

Characteristics of the Impressionistic Field Studies Reviewed					
	Ennals (1985)	Hawkins & Sheingold (1986)	Mendrinos & Morrison (1986)	Rothman (1982)	Traberman (1983–84)
Grade level	Secondary British	6	6–8	11–12	10 12
Student ability level	NA	NA	NA	NA	NA
Total students	NA	1 class	NA	NA	NA
Small groups	NA	NA	Yes	NA	Yes
Subject	Local studies	NA	NA	NA	Global studies
Unit topic	Village history	NA	Irish immigrant	Revolutions	Third World geography/ economic concepts
Database used	Researcher-made on village	Used for recording information	Irish immigrant	Researcher-made; graphic output	Researcher-made in APL
Treatment length in days	NA	40	NA	NA	NA

Appendix B

Descriptions of the Individual Classroom Units

Indiana #1

The problem to be solved, chosen and presented by the teacher, was, "How do we know what country is developed and which ones are less developed?" Students used database and library reference materials to retrieve and organize data into tables, so that criteria for classifying the countries could be applied and refined.

Indiana #2

The teacher integrated information about the U.S. Census with a researcher-provided county and state database extracted from Census Bureau books from 1949 through 1985. Students developed problems and then specific hypotheses from working with the 30 database categories—social and economic variables recorded over a 40-year period.

Minnesota #1

Students used information from researcher-created databases to solve one of the following foreign or domestic policy problems that was assigned to them: a. How does a nation's wealth and population affect the living conditions of its citizens? b. What factors, other than who gets involved in politics, determine a nation's political climate? c. What are some of the effects of the continued growth of our country's population? d. How healthy is the country's economy? e. What are some of the factors that give rise to crimes? and f. What problems can result from the poverty in our country?

Minnesota #2

Students identified and proposed a solution to a problem relating to Minnesota's economic future, and then were assigned a "political perspective" by the teacher. Students also had access to print materials and conducted telephone interviews with local experts. Three times they presented drafts of written proposals to a commission of students representing each team, which critiqued the proposals. The best proposals, as determined by a student commission, were presented orally to a bipartisan commission of Minnesota state legislators in the state capitol.

Virginia #1

Students explored the interrelationship of executive and legislative branches of the U.S. government, as evidenced by study of 19th and 20th century national election data. Groups of students hypothesized about elections and electoral politics over time, and then applied data in testing the hypotheses. Oral reports were made by each of the student groups.

Virginia #2

Students applied information and ideas from their previous study of the French Revolution to current problem areas of the world. They used the database in extracting economic, social, and political data that suggested in which countries revolution might occur in the future. Student groups played the role of a citizen of the country they had chosen, in a brief simulated radio or television spot.

Washington #1

Students found and integrated information from the computer database and other print materials. They used word-processing and *Print Shop* programs on the computer to produce their written reports.

Washington #2

Sixth-grade students studied the geography of the western U.S. and the economy of Europe, by using databases plus print and nonprint sources. They focused on similarities and differences between states in the U.S. and countries in Europe. Students had the problem of describing the economy of a "perfect" country and justifying these scenarios.

References

Becker, H. J. *Instructional Use of School Computers: Reports from the 1985 National Survey*, Issues 1–3. Baltimore: Johns Hopkins University, 1986.

Budin, H. R., D. Kendall, and J. Lengel. *Using Computers in the Social Studies*. New York: Teachers College Press, 1986.

Collins, B. *Computers, Curriculum, and Whole-class Instruction: Issues and Ideas.* Belmont, CA: Wadsworth Publishing Co., 1988.

Cornelius, C. S. "A Comparison of Computer-based Database Instruction and Retrieval Strategies with Traditional Instruction." Ph.D. diss., Pennsylvania State University, 1986. Abstract in *Dissertation Abstracts International* 47: 68A.

Cuban, L. *Teachers and Machines: The Classroom Use of Technology since 1920.* New York: Teachers College Press, 1986.

Ehman, L. H., and A. D. Glenn. *Computer-based Education in the Social Studies.* Bloomington, IN: Clearinghouse for Social Studies/Social Science Education, 1987. ERIC, ED 284825.

Elder, C. L. "Development of a Social Studies Database with Accompanying Curriculum Materials to Enhance Information-processing Skills and Geographic Knowledge." Ph.D. diss., George Mason University, 1988.

Ennals, R. "Micro-PROLOG and Classroom Historical Research." In *Teachers, Computers, and the Classroom,* edited by I. Reid and I. Rushton, 130–37. Manchester, Great Britain: Manchester University Press, 1985.

Hawkins, J., and K. Sheingold. "The Beginning of a Story: Computers and the Organization of Learning in Classrooms." In *National Society for the Study of Education Yearbook,* No. 85, Part I, 40–58. Chicago: University of Chicago Press, 1986.

Hodges, J. O. "Using Database Management to Achieve Social Studies Objectives." *Virginia Resolves* 27 (1985): 6–14.

Hunter, B. "Powerful Tools for Your Social Studies Classroom." *Classroom Computer Learning* 4 (1983): 50–57.

Hunter, B. "Research and Evaluation Trends in the Uses of Computer-based Tools for Learning and Teaching." In *Proceedings of the National Education Computer Conference,* 82–94. Dallas: 1988.

Johnson, R. T., D. W. Johnson, and M. B. Stanne. "Effects of Cooperative and Individualistic Goal Structures on Computer-assisted Instruction." *Journal of Educational Psychology* 77 (1985): 668–77.

Marchionini, G. "Hypermedia and Learning: Freedom and Chaos." *Educational Technology* 28, no. 11 (1988): 8–12.

Martinez, M. E., and N. A. Mead. *Computer Competence: The First National Assessment.* Princeton, NJ: Educational Testing Service, 1988.

Mendrinos, R. B., and D. M. Morrison. "The Irish Immigrant: How the Program Works." *Classroom Computer Learning* 7 (1986): 42.

Morrison, D. M., and J. Walters. "IMMIGRANT: A Social Studies Simulation for *AppleWorks.*" In *Computers in the Classroom: Experiences Teaching with Flexible Tools,* edited by C. Thompson and L. Vaughn, 70-76. Chelmsford, MA: Northeast Regional Exchange. ERIC, ED 768013.

Noblit, G., and R. Hare. *Meta-ethnography: Synthesizing Qualitative Studies,* Qualitative Research Methods Series No. 11. Newbury Park, CA: Sage Publications, 1988.

Northrup, T., and G. E. Rooze. "Are Social Studies Teachers Using Computers: A National Study." *Social Education* 54 (1990): 212–14.

Rawitsch, D. "The Computerized Database: Not a Simple Solution." *The Computing Teacher* 15 (1987): 34–37.

Rawitsch, D. "The Effect of Computer Use and Student Workstyle on Database Analysis Activities in the Social Studies." Ph.D. diss., University of Minnesota, 1988. Abstract in *Dissertation Abstracts International* 49: 423A.

Rawitsch, D., W. M. Bart, and J. F. Earle. "Using Computer Database Programs to Facilitate Higher-order Thinking Skills." In *Research Bulletin No. 1.,* 7–9. University of Minnesota: Center for the Study of Educational Technology, Educational Computing Consortium, 1988.

Ross, E. W. "Survey of Microcomputer Use in Secondary Social Studies Classrooms." Paper presented at the meeting of the National Council for the Social Studies, Orlando, FL, 1988.

Rothman, M. "Using the Microcomputer to Study the Anatomy of Revolution." *The Computing Teacher* 10 (1982): 16–20.

Sheingold, K., and M. Hadley. *Accomplished Teachers: Integrating Computers into Classroom Practice*. New York: Bank Street College of Education, Center for Technology in Education, 1990.

Sheingold, K., J. H. Kane, and M. E. Entreweit. "Microcomputer Use in Schools: Developing a Research Agenda." *Harvard Educational Review* 53 (1983): 412–32.

Traberman, T. "Using Interactive Computer Techniques to Develop Global Understanding." *The Computing Teacher* 11 (1983): 43–50.

Traberman, T. "Using Microcomputers to Teach Global Studies." *Social Education* 48 (1984): 130–37.

Underwood, J. D. M. "Cognitive Demand and CAL." In *Teachers, Computers, and the Classroom*, edited by I. Reid and J. Rushton, 25–57. Manchester, Great Britain: Manchester University Press, 1985.

White, C. S. "Developing Information-processing Skills through Structured Activities with a Computerized File-management Program." *Journal of Educational Computing Research* 3 (1987): 355–75.

White, C. S. "The Impact of Structured Activities with a Computer-based File-management Program on Selected Information-processing Skills." Ph.D. diss., Indiana University, 1986. Abstract in *Dissertation Abstracts International* 47: 513A.

White, C. S. "Media and Technology Use in the Social Studies: A Status Report." Paper presented at the meeting of the National Council for the Social Studies, Orlando, FL, 1988.

Yin, R. K. *Case Study Research: Design and Methods*, Applied Social Research Methodological Series, vol. 5. Newbury Park, CA: Sage Publications, 1989.

*L*ee H. Ehman is Professor of Curriculum and Instruction at Indiana University, Bloomington, IN 47405.

*A*llen D. Glenn is Dean and Professor in the College of Education, University of Washington, Seattle, WA 98195.

*V*ivian Johnson is an Educational Consultant in Minneapolis, MN 55112.

*C*harles S. White is a Professor in the Department of Elementary Social Studies Education, Boston University, Boston, MA 02215.

A World Geography Database Project

Meeting Thinking Skills Head-on

Carlyn L. Elder and
Charles S. White

Numerous authors over the past few years have advanced lofty claims about the ability of databases to improve students' thinking skills, particularly those skills relating to the processing of information necessary for successful problem solving. These include the ability 1. to organize data in such a way that it make sense to them and is easy to use; 2. to glean from a large volume of information that which is relevant to a given problem; and 3. to determine whether or not they have sufficient data to solve the problem, and, if not, where they might obtain them (White 1987). As educational computing has matured as a field, so have the claims about the effects of databases. We have come to understand that databases don't teach skills, but we still believe that they can help kids learn these skills if *used effectively by teachers.*

Led by this belief, we developed a database experience in world geography for middle school and high school students (Elder 1988). We are all becoming aware of the alarming national deficiencies in geography knowledge, and in this project we hoped to help students to learn and skillfully use world geography information. At the outset of the project, however, we were met with two basic questions. What does "effective use" of databases mean? Does effective use really "produce" positive changes in students' information processing skills? We looked to see what guidance we could find from the research literature.

From *The Computing Teacher* 17, no. 3 (November 1989): 29–32. Reprinted with permission from the International Society for Technology in Education. All rights reserved.

Databases and Thinking Skills: The Research

Our exploration of existing research did not take long. While much has been written about effective use of databases, very little research has been done to see if recommended techniques really work in developing information processing skills. This was confirmed recently by the Office of Technology Assessment's (OTA) study of technology in American education. OTA noted that "while there are numerous anecdotal reports enthusiastically describing [database] use in classrooms across the country, there is very little research documenting the effects of such tools in learning" (U.S. Congress/OTA 1988, 58).

After excluding anecdotal reports and studies focusing on attitudes rather than skills, we found studies that demonstrated positive gains in students' data classification skills, question-asking skills, and the information processing skills involved in assessing relevance, sufficiency, and data organization efficiency (Ennals 1985; Underwood 1985; White 1987).

What we discovered from the existing research provided two main guidelines for database development. First, information processing skills must be taught within the database lessons, through a combination of direct and indirect instruction. Exposure to and use of a database are not enough in themselves to produce gains in skills development. Second, students have to be alerted to when specific skills should come into play as they solve problems. Learning when to use particular skills is part of improving students' metacognitive capabilities.

Figure 1.   World Geography Units

Unit 1: Population
Unit 2: Agriculture and Climate
Unit 3: Agriculture and Change
Unit 4: Work Force
Unit 5: Trade
Unit 6: Trade and Industrialization
Unit 7: Culture
Unit 8: Government
Unit 9: Comparing Governments
Unit 10: Adding Data

The next step in the project was to apply these two key ideas in developing the world geography database materials.

World Geography Database Project

The development process was divided into three phases: building the database, developing the instructional materials, and testing the resulting curriculum package in classrooms. To make the package most useful and effective, the data represented significant information as judged by geography experts and the lesson materials incorporated as much as possible the two research-based principles discussed above.

The Database

To provide sufficient breadth and depth of data to allow students to work with real-world problems, the database included 51 fields on 80 representative countries of the world. The database fields were correlated with standard world geography texts used at the middle and high school levels. This was to ensure that the data could be easily processed by students and were relevant to current world geography curriculum objectives.

Sample Unit

World Geography Database Project

Unit Seven: Culture

In the 1500s, the Portuguese began inching down the coast of Africa in what became the beginning of an explosive age of exploration and discovery, financed by the new nation-states as they vied with each other for colonies around the world. Following the Portuguese, the Spanish and Dutch, French and English sailed their ships into uncharted waters and claimed new lands in the name of their kings.

As these colonizers came in contact with new peoples, they taught them their language first, and then attempted to convert them to their religion and their customs. Some were very successful in spreading their culture, especially those who established settlements in the new lands rather than just trading posts.

Before we check the database to see just how successful these European nations were, let's include in our search a phenomenon that grew out of the area that is today Saudi Arabia. In the middle of the seventh century A.D., Muhammadan invaders burst from their Arabian desert, conquering diverse lands and peoples from India in the East to Spain in the West. How great was the impact of the Arabs, French, Spanish and English when they came in contact with different cultures?

Form into four groups, one for each of the languages. Do the exercises and share what you've learned with the rest of the class. To answer the last questions, you may need a world history book or some reference books from the library.

[Only the instructions and worksheets for the French group are included here.]

Data on population, physical geography, the economy and government of each country (see Appendix) were stored on disk for manipulation by *Filing Assistant*, a file-management program for IBM and IBM-compatible computers.

Instructional Materials

The development of 10 units followed a unit plan consistent with a world geography curriculum and with the goal of enhancing information processing skills (see Figure 1). In each unit, the teacher introduces the subject of the unit, eliciting what students already know about it, defining terms and asking students to give examples to ascertain if they understand the basic concepts they would be working with in the unit.

Students begin with one of several initiating activities: brainstorming about what they expected to find in the database, using the dictionary to define terms used in the unit, or using the database to gather data on which to base an hypothesis.

In this and subsequent activities, the teacher acts as a facilitator rather than a dispenser of information. Throughout the lessons, students are alerted to and guided in the use of information processing skills. Unit Seven (see sidebar) illustrates how this was implemented in the materials.

In Unit Seven, students are faced with problems generated by conflicting cultures. They must determine to what extent a conquering nation inflicts its culture on the people it conquers and how enduring the cultural infusion is. To work through the unit, students are divided into four groups, and each group is asked to gather data on one of

---

Worksheet

Group 1: French

Start the program, type 4, ENTER. Tab down on the first screen to % LANGUAGES and type FRENCH.., then press F10. Be sure to type the word FRENCH with two periods after it, rather than two periods before and after, because we want only those countries where French is the primary language spoken. Refer to your worksheet to answer the following questions:

1. When your first country comes up on the screen, copy down on your worksheet the name of the country, the first religion listed next to % RELIGIONS, and the first ethnic group listed next to % ETHNIC GROUPS. After you have done that, press F10 for your next country, and continue through the database until you have found all the countries where French is the primary language. Press ESC. Leave the computer to answer your other questions.

2. What do you think was the religion of France during the colonial period? What were the primary religions listed for these countries?

3. Two of these countries were not former French colonies. Can you guess which ones and whose colonies they were? (Hint: What other European country has a large French-speaking population?)

4. How many different ethnic groups did you find in these former colonies? Can you think of several reasons why this would be so?

The Whole Class

Each group is to share its answers with the other groups and answer all questions on the whole class worksheet, so make sure your group has all the answers! Discuss to what extent each conquering people—the French, Arabs, Spanish, and English—spread their culture. Refer to the worksheet for the following task:

On your worksheet, rank the four countries, with "1" being the country that enculturated (caused to adapt to one's culture) the people of the conquered countries to the greatest extent.

---

four culture groups—French, Arabic, Spanish, or English. Students in each group use the database to locate those countries where French (Group 1), for example, is spoken today as the primary language. Explicit/direct instruction is provided for the retrieval and organizing tasks required for the problem. In this case, they are explicitly instructed to organize the data by writing down the name of the country, the major reli-

gion and largest ethnic group. They then examine the data to determine if the data are sufficient for answering the questions and solving the problems.

After this explicit phase, the initial questions in the unit are designed to confront students with a lack of sufficient data for answering some questions, and additional sources will have to be sought. Students in Group 1 (France), for example, have insufficient data to deter-

Worksheet

Group 1: French

1. Countries where French is the primary language:

   Country   Religion   Ethnic group
   _____
   _____
   _____
   _____

2. The religion of France during the colonial period was:
   _____

   Primary religion listed for these former colonies:
   _____

3. Two colonies that were *not* former French colonies were
   _____ and _____ , which were both col-
   onies of the European country of _____.

4. Number of ethnic groups: _____. In your opinion, why
   are there so many?
   _____

The Whole Class

Conquering countries ranked according to which had the greatest cultural
influence on the people conquered ("1" had the greatest influence).

   1. _____
   2. _____
   3. _____
   4. _____

mine the mother country (Belgium) of the two French-speaking countries that were not colonies of France. They also have insufficient data to identify the religion of France when it was building its colonial empire. To redress this lack of data, students have to determine what data would be relevant to solving the problem and where they might be able to find the needed information.

Indirect instruction is further exemplified in the last lesson in the unit, where the class meets as a group for the final analysis of the data to determine which culture group had the most enduring impact on the people conquered. In this phase, students must discover commonalities and differences among the groups of data, analyze relationships, and pose hypotheses (Hunter 1985). Students are not told what the generalization is that they should discover from their data, and they may arrive at different generalizations. Class discussion, during which students defend their generalizations and listen to those of other students, answers some questions and generates additional ones. In sum, in Unit Seven, retrieval and organization of data were accomplished by direct instruction while sufficiency and relevancy were taught by indirect means. In other units, the mode of instruction (direct versus indirect) is reversed.

Classroom Use

The real test of these materials came when used in the classrooms. For this project, six teachers spanning grades six through nine agreed to try out the 10 units for two weeks. In all, 376 students were involved in the fieldtesting. The teachers received training in the use of the computer and the file management program, and received guidance in managing their classrooms with computer resources ranging from one to 15 computers per class. Materials were also pro vided to acclimate students to *Filing Assistant* use and to facilitate classroom logistics.

Teachers liked using the materials because the content of the units fit into their existing curriculum. They also felt that their teaching gained a new dimension by having students use computers and analyze raw data built around major geographic concepts. Teachers' reactions to computer use were positive, but those with only one computer per classroom felt a bit cramped in terms of providing enough quality time for students to use the database. Four computers at a time in the classroom seemed

to represent a threshold of comfort for participating teachers.

Students also responded favorably to the materials. Teachers reported that "computers really seemed to captivate" the students. Responses to a student critique form revealed that most students found locating data relatively easy. While the student sample contained both experienced and inexperienced computer users, the overwhelming majority of students reported that the role of "keyboarder" was equitably shared within student groups.

Conclusion

Beyond general reactions, classroom use of the World Geography Project materials uncovered two important points relevant to teaching thinking skills. First, participating teachers seemed to display increasing awareness of the need to explicitly address information skills that are essential prerequisites for effective problem solving. At the same time, using databases as part of an inquiry approach breaks with traditional classroom practice, and teachers need time to adjust and become comfortable in this very new environment.

Second, it was clear that much work remains to be done to upgrade student information processing skills. These skills do not develop automatically. In lessons where they were not given explicit instructions on what data to retrieve, many students frequently could not determine how they should proceed, largely because they failed to recognize what data might be relevant. This type of problem suggests that students do not have enough opportunities to engage in this kind of intellectual task and require more explicit instruction in fundamental information skills. Overdependence on textbooks will perpetuate the problem. Textbooks often present a problem and its solution in the same paragraph so that students are not given the opportunity to study the data and attempt to solve the problem themselves. Lessons built around a database, with activities structured to teach and to call up information skills, afford students this opportunity. ❖

Appendix

Fields in the World Geography Database Project

Population Fields

Country
Capital
Population (millions)
Birth rate per thousands
Death rate per thousands
Percent annual national increase
Doubling time (yrs)
Population in yr 2000 (mil)
Infant mortality per 1000
Percent population under age 15
Percent population over age 64
Life expectancy—all
Life expectancy—males
Life expectancy—females
Pop. growth 1950–85 (mil)
Pop. growth 1985–2020 (mil)
Percent school attendance
Yrs compulsory education
Percent literacy—all
Percent literacy—male
Percent literacy—female
Percent ethnic groups
Percent religions
Percent languages

Physical Geography Fields

Area (sq. kilometers)
Comparable size to U.S.
Percent urban population
Percent cultivated land
Density per sq. km.
Physical features
Climate
Population centers
Agricultural products
Percent GNP in agriculture

Economic/Government Fields

Type of government
Independence (year)
Budget ($ billions)
Percent budget in defense
GNP ($ billions)
Per capita ($ billions)
Work force (millions)
    Percent agricultural
    Percent industry/commerce
    Percent services
    Percent government
    Percent other
Industry types
    Percent GNP
Exports ($ billions)
Imports ($ billions)
Trading partners

References

Elder, C. L. "Development of a Social Studies Database with Accompanying Curriculum Materials to Enhance Information-processing Skills and Geography Knowledge." Ph.D. diss., George Mason University, 1988.

Ennals, L. " Micro-PROLOG and Classroom Historical Research." In *Teachers, Computers, and the Classroom,* edited by I. Reid and J. Rushton, 130–37. Manchester, Great Britain: Manchester University Press, 1985.

Hunter, B. "Problem Solving with Databases." *The Computing Teacher* 12, no. 8 (1985): 20–27.

Underwood, J. D. M. "Cognitive Demand and CAL." In *Teachers, Computers, and the Classroom,* edited by I. Reid and J. Rushton, 25–57. Manchester, Great Britain: Manchester University Press, 1985.

U.S. Congress, Office of Technology Assessment. *Power On! New Tools for Teaching and Learning.* OTA–SET–379. Washington, DC: U.S. Government Printing Office, September 1988.

White, C. S. "Developing Information-processing Skills through Structured Activities with a Computerized File-management Program." *Journal of Educational Computing Research* 3, no. 1 (1987): 355–75.

*D*r. Carlyn L. Elder, Social Studies Department Chair, Falls Church High School, Falls Church, VA.

*D*r. Charles S. White, Department of Elementary Social Studies Education, Boston University, Boston, MA.
    The materials described in this article can be ordered by contacting Dr. Carlyn Elder, 3911 Mill Creek Dr., Annandale, VA 22003.

Social Studies, Spreadsheets, and the Quality of Life

Larry Hannah

Social studies educators have begun exploring the potential of databases for teaching and learning social studies concepts. The spreadsheet is also a promising tool, though many social studies teachers may associate it with math and overlook its potential. This "Quality of Life" spreadsheet activity was designed to introduce discussion on the subjective nature of statistics. I developed it for my computer applications class of 24 junior high school students participating in a 1985 summer session program for gifted students at California State University, Sacramento. Prior to the activity, students worked with *AppleWorks* using both database management and word processing, and learned how to enter values, labels and formulas into spreadsheets.

"On the Move" (see worksheet 1) started students thinking about the livability of some quite different cities. Each student read the list and ranked the cities, one through 12. Their votes were then tallied using a spreadsheet (see figure 1). To weight the votes, each first place vote was multiplied by one, second place by two, third place by three, etc. "The best place to live" was the city with the lowest point total. This activity grabbed students' attention and demonstrated how weighting is used in statistics and how they can apply a spreadsheet in a practical situation where they have a personal interest.

When all the votes were tallied, Honolulu emerged as "the best place to live," followed by Miami and San Diego. Students voted Pittsburgh, Atlanta and Buffalo as least desirable. After the weighted spreadsheet was introduced and reviewed, students discussed the

From *The Computing Teacher* 13, no. 4 (December/January 1985–86): 13–17. Reprinted with permission from the International Society for Technology in Education. All rights reserved.

factors that led them to give particular cities high or low ratings.

The students next were introduced to the inspiration for this activity, Rand McNally's *Places Rated Almanac: Your Guide to Finding the Best Places to Live in America*. In the Rand McNally ranking of 329 metropolitan areas in the United States, the students' favorites didn't do quite as well. Honolulu was 61st rather than first, Miami was 52nd, and San Diego was the 28th ranked metropolitan area nationally. How did the students' least favorites do? Last place Buffalo was ranked 13th nationally, far better than even San Diego. Eleventh ranked Atlanta was also 11th in Rand McNally, but 11th of 329, not of 12. Pittsburgh, a city whose best rating by any student was fourth in the nation (mostly because of its football team), was rated by Rand McNally as the best place to live in America.

The discrepancies sparked a lively discussion and, much to my relief, inquiries as to how Rand McNally reached its conclusions. I gave each student a packet to read that included: 1. an excerpt from the Rand McNally study discussing its criteria and the tradition of rating places (see "Rating Places: An American Tradition"); 2. an article from the *Sacramento Bee* describing a study by a State University of New York geography professor which knocked Sacramento from 113th to 207th place; 3. two articles by a local newspaper columnist discussing errors he had found in the *Places Rated Almanac*; and 4. a 1975 *Time* magazine article showing Sacramento as rated 2nd in the nation (of 65 cities, with Pittsburgh rated 49th). Chauvinistic though they were, the articles did

Rating Places: An American Tradition

Passing judgment on different locales isn't just a current pastime; Americans have been at it for quite a while. To entice seventeenth-century colonists to pick Maryland over Virginia, promoters assembled figures showing heavier turkeys, more plentiful deer, and fewer deaths from foul summer diseases and Indian massacres, all yours if you settled in the northern reaches of Chesapeake Bay. In the nineteenth century, many northern observers connected the South's slave holding and rebellious ways with the region's broilingly hot climate and an overabundance of lunatics, drunkards and wastrels per capita.

In our own century, the process of comparing places has borrowed a great deal from statistical methods. One of America's educational pioneers, E. L. Thorndike, in the late 1930s devised a "goodness index" drawn from 39 indicators for measuring a city's day-to-day living. Since then, others have jumped into the rating game. In 1983, Prof. Murray Strauss, a sociologist at the University of New Hampshire, selected factors such as divorce, mortgage foreclosures, high school dropouts, personal bankruptcies, abortions and new welfare cases to determine the most "stressful" states. Nevada and Alaska were numbers one and two on the stress list. And the most laid-back state, according to the indicators? Nebraska.

Each of the 329 metro areas is rated (by *Places Rated Almanac*) by criteria that most people thinking of moving would deem important.

❖ *Climate* is rated on mildness; that is, how close temperatures remain to 65 degrees Fahrenheit throughout the year.

Housing is compared in terms of dollar costs. We look at prices for single homes, plus the taxes and utilities a would-be homeowner can expect to pay. We also note the supply of apartments, mobile homes and condominiums, as well as rental costs.

Health care is evaluated on the basis of the supply of general health care facilities and special options available.

Crime is measured by the annual number of violent and property crimes per 100,000 population.

Transportation measures both assets and performance, including local commuting time, public transit, and the supply of intercity travel options by way of air, rail and interstate highway.

Education ratings are based on each metro area's elementary and secondary school systems as well as options in higher education.

Arts compares cultural assets, among them museums, libraries, opera companies and symphony orchestras.

Recreation also rates assets, from good restaurants to public golf courses, zoos, professional sports teams, inland lakes and national parks acreage.

Economics looks at local living costs, household income, tax bites and the metro area's recent track record for job and income growth.

You may not agree with our rating system. If you like, you can devise your own method using the vast array of data presented. You may rule out metro areas with more than one million people. As long as summers aren't hot, you may not care a

$\Rightarrow$

spur the students' interest in the topic and a lively discussion ensued.

The students returned to spreadsheets to practice ranking and rating cities. I gave them a page from the *1985 World Almanac and Book of Facts* titled "Quality of Life in U.S. Metropolitan Areas: A Comparative Table," giving economic and climatic data (e.g., income, jobless rate, mean number of clear and cloudy days). We discussed how different assumptions, biases and value judgments led to differences between Rand McNally's and their own ratings of the 12 cities in "On the Move." These differences influence both the selection and weighting of data. I showed them how rankings can be skewed by giving enough weight to any one factor. Buffalo, for example, would come out first if we gave enough weight to average August temperature and decided cooler temperatures are better than warmer ones. In order to practice, groups of four students created their own spreadsheets to rate the cities after deciding which factors to include and with what criteria to weight the rankings. Their spreadsheets were shared and discussed.

Then the competition began.

"The Competition" (see worksheet 2) is based on events that took place in 1984 when several U.S. cities actively sought to "sell themselves" to the backers of a $150 million electronics research and development center seeking a home. That contest was ultimately won by Austin, Texas. Each team of students in our competition began by drawing from a hat the name of the city the team would represent. The cities were all closely grouped in *Places Rated Almanac,* with Sacramento added for local interest and to give them a basis for relating to the data with which they would be working. Teams were given the following tasks and rules.

Tasks

1. Devise a spreadsheet that will demonstrate that your city is the #1 place to locate the research center.

2. Prepare an argument, based on your spreadsheet, that identifies your city as #1 and includes rationale for including the data categories you selected.

3. Make an oral presentation of your team's findings.

Rules

1. All data included in your spreadsheet must be available for all the cities, including Sacramento.

2. Your data may be from any source, but must be valid.

3. You will need to document sources and provide them if challenged.

The *Sacramento Bee*, the local publisher of the *World Almanac*, has donated a class set of the *Almanac*. It includes information on such diverse areas as geography, climate and sports teams. The teams were encouraged to find other sources to augment the *Almanac*, remembering that the choice of data and use of weighting would have to be defended in their oral presentations.

After the teams prepared their spreadsheets, each group made an oral presentation. Four of the six teams prepared good spreadsheets.

hoot for relative humidity, wind speed and rainfall. You may have little interest in wildlife refuges or ocean shorelines but place a premium on good public schools. For you, a medium-sized metro area with good public transit and a record of job expansion may be more desirable than one with an abundant supply of performing arts and professional sports attractions.

Excerpts from: Richard Boyer and David Savageau, "Rating Places, An American Tradition," in Places Rated Almanac, Chicago: © 1985 Rand McNally.

One team devised a fine spreadsheet, but rated their own city fourth. (They got the "Truth in Advertising" award.) The sixth team managed to type anecdotal information into the spreadsheet. Interesting, but not a winning presentation. Primarily due to time constraints, none of the teams were able to include weighting in their spreadsheets after all.

Figure 3 illustrates how weighting and different value assumptions can completely change conclusions. The Philadelphia spreadsheet in Figure 2 has been modified to reflect assumptions that "small is better" in terms of population and a low crime rate is of utmost importance. In light of these assumptions, those two factors have been given three times the weighting of others.

As is the case with most pilot projects, there are a few things I will change the next time I teach this unit. First, I'll ensure adequate time to weight the data. Next, I'll try to incorporate a unit on statistics. Finally, I'll have students do a written presentation on their city, including use of the Clipboard function of *AppleWorks* to move data from the spreadsheet onto the word processor.

Figure 1.   Cities Ranked by Students in On the Move———————

	1*	2*	3*	4*	5*	6*	7*	8*	9*	10*	11*	12*	Points	Rank
Honolulu	11	10	12	8									41	1
Miami	5	20	12	8	5								50	2
San Diego	3	8	21	12	10	6		16					76	3
Washington, D.C.			3	8	35	36	7	16	18	10			133	4
Denver	1	4	3	16	10		27	8	27	20	22	12	150	5
Chicago	1	2	3	8	10	18		8	36	30	44		160	6
Houston			9	12	10	6	7	8		70	11	36	169	7
St. Louis					24	28	56	18	40	11			177	8
Portland	1			4	5	18	21	8	45	20	33	24	179	9
Pittsburgh			12	20	6	14	18	27		33	60		180	10
Atlanta					5	12	42	16			55	60	190	11
Buffalo						6	14	32	27	30	33	72	214	12

* Weighted by multiplying the number of votes times the rank.

Figure 2.   Students' Spreadsheets for Dallas/Fort Worth———————
and Philadelphia

Dallas/Fort Worth															
City	Unemploy	Rank	Popu-lation	Rank	Pro % Income	Rank	Per cap Income	Rank	Pop Density	Rank	Air-port	Rank	TV/Radio	Rank	Winner by Rank
Dallas	5.1	1	904078	2	3.6	1	13846	3	2715	1	2	1	63	1	10
San Jose	7.4	3	629442	3	3.6	1	14998	1	3984	4	0	3	19	6	21
Denver	5.3	2	492365	5	3.2	3	13964	2	4435	5	1	2	42	4	23
Atlanta	7.6	4	425022	6	3.4	2	11590	6	3244	3	1	2	49	3	26
Philadelphia	7.9	5	1688210	1	1.9	5	11946	5	12413	7	1	2	59	2	27
Seattle	9.8	6	493846	4	3	4	13293	4	5879	6	1	2	49	3	29
Sacramento	11.3	7	275741	7	3.2	3	11176	7	2872	2	0	3	29	5	34

Philadelphia															
Metro Area	# Of Sport Teams	Rank	Major Museum	Rank	City Park	Rank	Crime Rates	Rank	Major Zoos	Rank	Population	Rank	Hospital	Rank	Total Rank Score
Philadelphia	4	1	4	1	219	2	3785	2	2	1	1,688,210	1	124	1	9
Dallas	3	2	2	2	256	1	9821	7	2	1	904,078	2	42	3	18
Seattle	3	2	1	3	178	4	4986	3	1	2	493,846	4	27	5	23
Atlanta	3	2	1	3	164	6	7896	6	1	2	425,022	6	59	5	27
San Jose	0	7	1	3	200	3	5298	4	1	2	629,442	3	5	7	29
Denver	2	5	2	2	155	7	5362	5	1	2	492,365	5	34	4	30
Sacramento	1	6	1	3	168	5	2979	1	1	2	275,741	7	14	6	30

Figure 3.   Philadelphia Spreadsheet Modified by the Author——

Metro Area	# Of Sport Team	Rank	Major Mu- seum	Rank	City Park	Rank	Crime Rates	Rank	Rank *3	Major Zoos	Rank	Popu- lation	Rank	Rank *3	Hos- pital	Rank	Total Rank Score
Sacramento	1	6	1	3	168	5	2979	1	3	1	2	275,741	1	3	14	6	28
Philadelphia	4	1	4	1	219	2	3785	2	6	2	1	1,688,210	7	21	124	1	33
Seattle	3	2	1	3	178	4	4986	3	9	1	2	493,846	4	12	27	5	37
Atlanta	3	2	1	3	164	6	7896	6	18	1	2	425,022	2	6	59	2	39
Denver	2	5	2	2	155	7	5362	5	15	1	2	492,365	3	9	34	4	44
Dallas	3	2	2	2	256	1	9821	7	21	2	1	904,078	6	18	42	3	48
San Jose	0	7	1	3	200	3	5298	4	12	1	2	629,442	5	15	5	7	49

"Quality of Life" was a key element of a project designed to show use of the microcomputer as a tool in learning social studies concepts and skills. Both the spreadsheet and database management can be integrated into social studies instruction; "Quality of Life" illustrates just one such application.   ❖

References

1985 World Almanac and Book of Facts. New York: Newspaper Enterprise Association, 1985, 113.

Boyer, Richard, and David Savageau. *Places Rated Almanac: Your Guide to Finding the Best Places to Live in America.* Chicago: Rand McNally and Company, 1985.

Worksheet 1

On the Move

Changes require that your family move from northern California. There are 12 cities where your parent(s) have been offered employment that is inviting. As part of the family, you have been asked to rank the following cities in terms of their desirability. Rank each of these cities in order of your preference.

(1—highest; 12—lowest)

Rank	City
____	Atlanta, GA
____	Buffalo, NY
____	Chicago, IL
____	Denver, CO
____	Honolulu, HI
____	Houston, TX
____	Miami, FL
____	Pittsburgh, PA
____	Portland, OR
____	St. Louis, MO
____	San Diego, CA
____	Washington, DC

Worksheet 2

The Competition

Six cities are in competition as the site for the world's newest and largest computer research facility. Winning the competition literally will mean billions of dollars in economic growth over the next 20 years for the city selected.

As members of the Chamber of Commerce Industry Recruitment Team for your city, your task is to prove statistically that your city is the best of the six. You can use any data that is accurate and available for all six cities.

The best argument will win the competition!

Finalists

Atlanta
Dallas-Fort Worth
Denver
Philadelphia
San Jose
Seattle

L arry Hannah
P. O. Box 119
Shingle Springs, CA 95682

Do Women Live Longer Than Men?

Investigating Graveyard Data with Computers

James R. M. Paul
and Colette Kaiser

U sing computers for integrating data can play a major part in facilitating the kinds of educational change that constructivists are calling for because it can empower teachers and students by providing them with the information-handling skills required by the Information Age. The Graveyard Research Project, run by the Education Department at Rhodes University, SouthAfrica, provides teachers and senior primary students at schools in Grahamstown with the opportunity to use computers as research tools. The student groups visit regional graveyards, where they capture headstone data. Students enter this data into an electronic database provided by the university. They investigate the data using the database's various query tools. They also work with electronic spreadsheets to tabulate and graph their results, thus developing new insights from original historical data. The exercise has three main objectives:

1. To provide students with an opportunity to study history in a new way, emphasizing active learning.

2. To provide students with an opportunity to use computer database and spreadsheet software as investigative tools.

3. To develop an electronic database of graveyard information from graveyards in the Albany area of the Eastern Province, South Africa.

From *Learning and Leading with Technology* 23, no. 8 (May 1996): 13–15. Reprinted with permission from the International Society for Technology in Education. All rights reserved.

Figure 1.   Data Collection Worksheet

Location:				
Surname	First Names	DOD (dd/mm/yyyy)	Age	Comments and Other Details

Project Background

The project has involved a wide cross section of learners, but this article describes the research findings and the project as it relates to 66 standard five (12-year-old) students from Victoria Primary. These students conducted research on three local graveyards. The students focused on the Albany area, which was settled by several thousand British immigrants in an immigration scheme funded by the British government in 1820. Local inhabitants are proud of their settler roots, and many are able to trace their lineage back to these early times.

Data Collection

Students worked in pairs and collected information from specific rows of graves so that the data could be collected systematically. A data collection sheet listing specific categories of data was used (see Figure 1). This part of the project was relatively straightforward but did require the students to use their mathematical skills to check ages at death or to calculate the age when this information did not exist at the gravesite.

Data Input

After students collected the data, they were divided into three groups. Each group spent three 2-hour sessions using the computers at the university's education department. The first session involved entering the data into the database, which had already been set up to mirror the data sheet. This activity involved a simple transfer of the data into the relevant data fields. The students had recently started computer literacy lessons at their school and had a fair degree of keyboarding knowledge. Although this part of the project did not require higher order thinking skills, it was valuable because it strengthened the students' basic computer skills. Those students who had regular access to computers at home were able to complete this task with very little difficulty. For those who did not have home computers, the exercise provided opportunities for hands-on keyboarding experience and offered a sufficient number of repetitious exercises to build up their confidence.

Data Query

We asked the students to consider the type of data they had captured and to suggest what kinds of useful information they thought the data might provide. We demonstrated the basic keystrokes for ordering and selecting data and encouraged the students to scroll through the data in order to get an overall feel for it. The data were sorted alphabetically by surname to identify the families that were represented. Attempts were made to draw up family trees from the data, but the students found that the information required to do this was too scanty. We asked the students to suggest other ways of looking at the data and encouraged them to form hypotheses and then test them.

Some common hypotheses the students formulated included the following: women live longer than men, people live longer in the 20th century than in the 19th century, and most people today die in their 70s. Students sorted the data by date of death and by age at death in order to make a physical count of occurrences within specific age or year categories. They then created tables and graphs representing their findings. The software's Select feature was then used to look at the data in more detail. Data on the 19th century was selected and analyzed and then compared to similar data from the 20th century. The same process was used for data related to the age of death for men and women, and to those records showing the age at death to be less than 10.

The information was manually entered into tables (see Figures 2 and 3) for analysis and then graphed. Students worked in pairs or small groups to generate their own pie, bar, and line graphs. Categorizing and graphing the data made the information much easier to understand. Victoria Primary uses an integrated curriculum approach, and the exercise reinforced the connectedness of school subjects, particularly the ways in which history and mathematics are linked.

After the pupils had drawn their graphs, they compared and discussed their findings in a larger group. The variety of graphs the students drew indicated that the data was a valuable information source that could be examined, compared, and interpreted in many ways. It also became clear that some of the data was difficult to compare because sample sizes were very different. This led to discussion about ways to compare information fairly and the need to convert raw data to percentages. For example, it was particularly interesting to look at the difference between the number of deaths of individuals under the age of 10. While there were 22 deaths in this category during the 19th century and 35 during the 20th century, the corresponding percentages were 25.6 percent and 2.8 percent. Graphing raw data in this instance did little to bring out the real meaning of the data. Students came to understand this issue, re-examined the data, and formulated new questions.

The issue of childhood death resulted in one student suggesting that the high mortality rates in the 19th century were the direct result of poor medical knowledge at that time. This provided an ideal opportunity for a discussion that raised other issues leading in many directions—modes of transport, road conditions, and communications in general. The most valuable lesson here was that while the data could be used to support or refute the students' hypotheses, it should be carefully collected and organized, examined in the light of other factors (which may or may not be obvious), and critically examined.

Figure 2.   Age-group and Male/Female Data Worksheet———————

Age group	0-9	10-19	20-29	30-39	40-49	50-59	60-69	70-79	80-89	90-99	100-	total
no												
%												

Age group	0-9	10-19	20-29	30-39	40-49	50-59	60-69	70-79	80-89	90-99	100-	total
men												
women												
% men												
% women												

Figure 3.   19th Century Versus 20th Century Data Worksheet——

Age group	0-9	10-19	20-29	30-39	40-49	50-59	60-69	70-79	80-89	90-99	100-	total
19th C												
20th C												
% 19th												
% 20th												

The Value of the Project

Several valuable results came out of having students carrying out this project. These included the following:

1. Students cooperated with each other and used an organized approach to collect the graveyard data.

2. The students' computer literacy skills and keyboarding knowledge increased.

3. The graphing activities resulted in some lively discussion of the students' findings. They compared their findings and tried to determine the reasons for the differences.

4. The students worked with primary evidence and drew their own conclusions from the questions they formulated.

5. Primary-level students do not get many chances to work with statistical data and find it difficult to formulate questions based on it. The nature of the data, especially the fact that the students themselves had collected it, made it easier for them to pose questions that could be investigated and make hypotheses that could be confirmed or rejected.

6. Interpreting the data required students to use higher order thinking that linked statistics and history.

7. Mathematics is often taught as a subject isolated from other disciplines. At a school where the cross-curricular approach has been used for a number of years, this study initiated new links for the students between mathematics, history, and computer studies.

8. The project resulted in a thirst for further reading and research, particularly in cases where individual graves provided points of interest. For example, a poem and a bird bath on the grave of a young nature conservation officer, the names of various battles in which soldiers had lost their lives, and references to a local train disaster in which many people had been killed aroused much student interest and areas of focus for further reading.

9. Research at the primary school level usually involves regurgitating facts from reference books or electronic encyclopedias. This project actively involved the students and provided them with a chance to work like real historians, collecting and interpreting their own primary data.

The overall outcome of the project reinforced the idea that students can use their skills to work collaboratively, collect and analyze data, answer their own questions, and take responsibility for their own learning. The graveyard research project was an ideal way to encourage students along these lines, and it empowered them to use computers in a hands-on, relevant, research-oriented way. ❖

*J*ames R. M. Paul
Department of Education
Rhodes University
Grahamstown 6140
Republic of South Africa
Paul@croc.ru.ac.za

*C*olette Kaiser
Victoria Primary School
Grahamstown, 6140
Republic of South Africa
Colette@vp.ru.ac.za

R for Social Studies

Ron Wheeler

When Oxford awarded Mark Twain an honorary doctor of literature degree, he said he didn't deserve it since he had never doctored any literature. Unlike Mark Twain's literature, the field of education could use some doctors, and no part of it needs more attention than social studies.

Back in the 1960s and early 1970s—during the "Golden Age" of curriculum revitalization—the "new" social studies, as it was called by enthusiasts, advocated the development of students' thinking skills. A number of data-based, inquiry-oriented social studies projects were launched with a clearly defined goal in mind: they would teach students how to use data to build and test social concepts. In this way, social studies would help students deal with the knowledge explosion and rapid change caused by the emerging super-industrial world. Yet despite the support of many influential social scientists and educators, the new social studies was stopped dead in its tracks, primarily because no one seemed to know how to measure its effectiveness in the classroom. The field slipped quietly into a coma.

A quarter of a century later, there has never been a greater need for children to be able to process facts, tackle tough questions, and find real answers to real problems. As a society, we need energetic, goal-directed, intellectually rigorous social studies more than ever. The substance of the long-awaited social studies revival still eludes us, however, and time is not on our side.

Cynically, some might ask: if we have been able to live with unsound social studies for all of these years, why change now? To answer that question, let's look briefly at conditions then and now.

Then

To develop critical thinking skills in social studies, students needed quick access to data, yet few people back then knew what data were. What social scientists called "data" was called "information" or just "stuff" by ordinary people. And just where was this stuff, excuse me, these data, anyway? They definitely were not available through personal computers, which had not yet been invented. For the most part, they were ensconced in distant libraries, archives and research centers, or encoded on keypunch cards that only giant mainframe computers could process. The school's library, of course, was just down the hall, but for a lot of teachers, getting students there often to do sustained research was about as easy as going to Mars.

In short, the new social studies required fast access to data, but no delivery system was then in place to bring them into the classroom.

Now

We have the right tools to make students'—and teachers'—data gathering job far easier. Technology has played a decisive role. Since the initial acceptance of computers by the schools in the 1980s, "student access to personal computers has improved dramatically" (Hayes and Bybee 1995, 48). The ratio of students to computers has dropped from 125 to 1 in the 1983–84 school year to 12 to 1 in 1994–95. If this trend continues, a national student-to-computer ratio of 1:1 will be a reality early in the twenty-first century.

With a modem and electronic mail software, data can flow into the classroom at the speed of light from literally anywhere on earth. User-friendly and data-rich school-based interactive software programs are also at more and more

students' fingertips. Even if many of the parents are not data literate, their children are, or soon will be. Databases are becoming as familiar and useful to them as phone numbers and telephone books are to us.

Then

The new social studies also required access to multiple data sources. Over-reliance on a single authority or content source—either the teacher or the textbook, or both—inhibits critical thinking. Different forms of data are also important because of developmental concerns; young learners need concrete/experiential data to develop concepts. Yet back then, data sources were very limited. In 1970, textbooks had an almost monopolistic grip on the social studies curriculum. Even experienced teachers were reluctant to stray too far from them, and with good reason. The alternatives were worse, or at least untested. The most frequently used new technology in the schools was the photocopier, which was beginning to replace ditto and mimeograph machines. In-school use of television was not widespread, and commercial and public television's educational function was unclear. Too often, the school's supply of instructional materials consisted of little more than a few out-of-date maps, filmstrips and films.

The new social studies projects' materials were likewise suspect: were they just another pedagogical example of "old wine in new bottles"? Why buy these pricey projects if inside their "data boxes" was just more of the same old stuff (i.e., books, maps, photographs, records, cassettes, filmstrips, films), with only the addition of a few artifact replicas, such as an Asanti stool or ancient Greek pot, to provide the "hands-on" touch.

Now

Gone are the days of frantically scrounging for data. Everywhere we look—TV, Internet, CD-ROMs, film—data options are expanding. Thanks to computers, thousands of primary sources (charts, photographs, audio clips of speeches and music, video clips of historic film footage, literature, essays, advertisements, political cartoons, constitutions, legislation, inaugurals, Supreme Court decisions, treaties, debates, party platforms, census figures, letters, etc.) are easily accessible. Not only can students read Rev. Martin Luther King, Jr.'s "I Have a Dream" speech, they can hear and see him give it.

National polls tell us that, compared to younger Americans, older Americans are less knowledgeable of and comfortable with computers and electronic devices. But even teachers whose education did not include the new technology are teaching themselves to use it. When one considers the instructional benefits, their willingness to learn makes sense. In our growing numbers of electronic classrooms, a social studies teacher can schedule live interactive television and telephone conversations from distant sites, including Antarctica, or set up a World Wide Web page in the school so essays and research by students can be critiqued through e-mail by other students, as well as by top scholars, around the country and world. Teachers can also use interactive computer programs, like *MayaQuest* and the "trail" software simulations (*African Trail, Oregon Trail II, Yukon Trail, Amazon Trail*), to put students in the "field," where they must use data within a decision-making context. Other software resources available to teachers, like *Student Writing Center, Digital Chisel*, and *Filemaker Pro*, let students use data to create multimedia reports and presentations.

Educators today know they are making curriculum for young people who get much of their information from television and film. Indeed, film has been called "the most emotionally accessible of art forms" (Wuntch 1996, D1). Because of these insights, more and more social studies teachers are using videos that depict history, fictional renditions of historical accounts, and contemporary societal issues. But instead of accepting everything they watch as truth, students are challenged to contrast the visual media's messages and other data sources to judge their factual accuracy. By no means passé, textbooks are still an important part of the current scene. But now they are truly becoming one of many data sources, rather than the only one.

Then

We made questioners out of students, but we really didn't show them how to be inquirers. Without fast access to multiple data sources to stimulate and sustain deep thinking, rigorous inquiry in social studies is problematic. Thus, when an occasional social studies inquiry lesson was attempted by well-intentioned teachers, the results were sometimes less than what was hoped for. Instead of involved and interested, students were often off task and bored. The reasons: inquiry learning is a complex skill that takes time and patience to master; inquiry cannot be truly understood and mastered unless it is practiced within a meaningful context; and an overemphasis on inadequate or insufficient data can trivialize inquiry and result in students missing the point of the whole exercise, which is to help them see the "big picture."

Now

To paraphrase *Pogo*, "We have met the future, and it is then." Educators who are old enough to remember when the new social studies was in vogue know firsthand of its limitations. Perhaps the rhetorical excesses of those years have made all of us more skeptical about suggestions of impending change.[1] Nevertheless, the new social studies' basic goals and methodology may be just what the doctor ordered for what's ailing social studies—and society—today. Twenty-five years ago, society and the schools rejected the new social studies, which then seemed impractical and irrelevant. Today, computers, rather than duplicators, are the most influential technology in the schools. A society that is now flooded with information from many far-flung and diverse sources desperately needs clear-thinking citizens who can detect faulty data and use solid evidence to make wise decisions.

The essential assumptions about both data and society upon which the new social studies was based now accurately describe our reality. After all of these years, a meaningful context for rigorous social studies inquiry has finally arrived. No doubt, the opportunities are out there waiting, but whether they are seized or not depends on us—and on our beliefs about why and how social studies should be taught.

Conclusion

While Mark Twain may not have fancied himself a doctor, he was unquestionably a master of the art of literature. But Twain, who achieved tremendous critical ac-

claim and popular success during his lifetime, became increasingly despondent about the lack of control individuals in society seemed to have over their destiny. Like the industrial machines of Twain's time, the electronic tools of the "Information Age" can be used to enlighten people or confuse them, to expand freedom or tighten bureaucratic control, to bring the world closer together or drive it farther apart.

Today, evidence of the negative effects of massive technological change is everywhere. It is manifest in the behavior of the nostalgic and intimidated technophobes, who refuse to adapt, and who hate computers. (Of course, since they are headed for extinction, they are of no concern to us.) Much more troubling, especially for educators, are the rapidly growing numbers of aimless, point-and-click cyberkids, who treat computers like toys and use them only for their own amusement. Yet most of us remain optimistic, mainly because we believe that social studies can summon the energy and passion to play a major role in influencing the future.   ❖

References

Hayes, Jeanne, and Dennis L. Bybee. "Defining the Greatest Need for Educational Technology." *Learning and Leading with Technology* 23, no. 2 (1995): 48–50.

Wuntch, Philip. "After a Century of Cinema, Films Have Lost Passion." *Hampton (Virginia) Daily Press*, 6 January 1996, D1–D2.

1. For a strong dose of healthy skepticism, see the insightful article by James P. Shaver, "James Michener and the Historical Future of Social Studies," *Social Education* 59, no. 7 (November/December 1995): 446–50.

R on Wheeler is Associate Professor of Education at the College of William and Mary, Williamsburg, VA.

Optical Technologies and Hypermedia

Optical Technologies

- Basics of the Technology
- Videodiscs
- Digital Video
- CD-ROM

Optical Technologies in Social Studies Classrooms

- Presentations
- Developing Multimedia Lessons
- Research

Hypertext/Hypermedia

- Essentials of Hypertext
- Hypertext, Hypermedia, *HyperCard*

Issues

- Information Access/Information Use
- Thinking Skills Support
- "It's All in There" Myth
- Each Medium Used Well
- Lost in Hyperspace
- Not for Everyone

chapter 5

Optical Technologies and Hypermedia

Over the last several years, the range and power of information technologies has expanded dramatically. In this chapter, we examine in some detail optical technology, hypertext, and the marriage of the two—interactive multimedia. Each provides powerful tools for accessing and delivering information spanning diverse media. In concert, these technologies underlie a set of new "cognitive enhancers" that may significantly alter the manner in which teachers teach and students learn.

■ Optical Technologies

Perhaps our first acquaintance with optical technology was the compact disc, or CD, that brought noise-free music into our living rooms. These 12-centimeter (4.72-inch) shiny silver disks, introduced in the 1980s, have rapidly advanced in the consumer market. Both CDs and their larger siblings, videodiscs, hold information that is read by a light beam generated by a low-intensity laser—thus, their designation as "optical" technologies. How does that work?

■ The Basics of the Technology

Standard computer storage media like hard disks and floppies store information magnetically; variations in magnetism along each disk track are interpreted as strings of 0s and 1s. The traditional audio cassette tape is also a magnetic medium. Optical media store information in the form of pits and lands burned into tracks on the reflective surface of a disc. When the narrow, concentrated light beam from the laser strikes the surface of the optical disc, the reflected light varies in intensity, depending on whether all the light was reflected back by a flat land or was partially dispersed by the contours of a pit. These variations in the intensity of the reflected light are interpreted by the optical disc player as changes in audio and video signals (videodiscs) or as 0s and 1s (CDs).

Optical discs enjoy a number of advantages over magnetic media. One advantage is the amount of information that can be stored. Floppy disks contain about 100 readable tracks of information per inch; optical discs pack 16,000 tracks per inch. One CD-ROM disc (used for general-purpose data storage) can hold the equivalent of 1500 floppies. A second advantage is durability. With magnetic media, dust and fingerprints can find their way onto the surface of disks where data are stored, making some disk sectors unreadable. With optical discs, the recorded information on the reflective material is covered by a layer of clear plastic that the laser beam easily passes through. Neither fingers nor dust reach the tracks directly, so the data are less susceptible to degradation. In the past, a disadvantage of optical media was the inpossibilty for users to record information onto the discs as they do with floppy disks and video and audiotapes. But this has changed.[1] Let's take a look at the range of optical technology applications available.

▬ CD-ROMs

At the beginning of this chapter, we mentioned audio compact discs. By the early 1980s, Sony and Philips introduced CDs that stored audio in digital form and could reproduce up to 74 minutes of music.[2] Beyond the noise-free quality of the musical reproduction, users could randomly access particular "cuts" on the CD almost instantly, a feature shared by other computer media such as floppy disks.

From CDs to CD-ROMs

As a random-access medium for general-purpose storage, a CD-ROM (read-only memory) disc can store 550 megabytes (MB) of data, or about 250,000 pages of text. CD producers quickly recognized the potential power of a medium that could store that much information and could be searched so flexibly because of its random-access capability. In 1985, the first CD-ROM product of interest to the general public was released: *Grolier's Electronic Encyclopedia*. Using a computer and the software supplied with the disc, users could search the complete 21-volume encyclopedia (text-only) by entering keywords or phrases. The desired information would be found almost instantly as the computer directed the CD-ROM player to the appropriate point on the disc.

---

1. WORM (write-once-read-many) discs allow users to alter the information-recording surface of the disc one time (by burning holes in it, for example). Once recorded, the information cannot be changed, although new information can be recorded on unused areas of the disc until the full capacity of the disc is reached. Other technologies that allow for fully erasable optical discs have slowly made their way from the laboratory to the marketplace, including rewritable magneto-optical (MO) drives that can store up to 122 MB on special removable 3½-inch MO discs.

2. Attaining the goal of 74 minutes allowed Beethoven's *Ninth Symphony* to be played without changing discs.

A CD-ROM lends itself to storing reference material because of its large capacity and because the contents cannot be altered after the disc leaves the factory. Since *Grolier's Electronic Encyclopedia*, numerous reference products have appeared; some go beyond text storage to include graphics, still images, and sound.

CD-ROMs for Social Studies

Two kinds of CD-ROM products can support social studies instructional goals: general reference works and more specialized reference collections relevant to social studies topics. Specific products are identified elsewhere in this book. What is extraordinary is the proliferation of CD-ROM producers and distributors. For people interested in high-quality full-motion video on a disc, the videodisc currently is the medium of choice. We'll discuss that next.

Videodiscs

In the late 1960s, videotape machines were not judged to be commercially viable for the consumer market, given their size and expense. A number of companies pursued the idea of delivering high-quality, full-motion video to the home on a flat disc. In 1980, Philips and MCA announced a laser-based, read-only videodisc player, the result of a six-year joint effort. RCA followed the next year with a nonlaser, stylus-based format. Unfortunately for these companies and their Japanese competitor Matsushita, the anticipated home market failed to materialize. By the late 1970s, several Japanese companies had introduced small, affordable videocassette players that allowed consumers not only to view but to record movies. In the early 1980s, sales of consumer videodisc players were suspended. We can credit the explosive success of the personal computer later in that decade for the videodisc's resurrection, but that will be addressed later. The percentage of United States schools with videodisc players increased from 8 percent in 1991–92 to 35 percent just four years later (1995–96), according to Quality Education Data, Inc.

Similarities and Differences between Videodiscs and CD-ROMs

Videodiscs share their basic technology with compact discs—pits and lands read with a laser beam. Both are, for the most part, read-only media (you cannot record video onto a videodisc). The similarities end there. Videodiscs are larger—about 12 inches in diameter. They are an analog medium, rather than digital—that is, the variations in the pits and lands correspond directly to variations in the video (and audio) signal. As the name suggests, of course, videodiscs can store full-motion video (with two audio channels along each track). How much video can be stored on each disc depends on whether it is a CLV- or CAV-format disc.

CLV/CAV and Why It Matters

The information stored on a videodisc is arranged in areas called "sectors" along each track, beginning at the center of the disc and moving outward. On one kind of disc, the sectors are all the same length, so tracks on the outer rim of the disc hold more sectors than those toward the center. To be sure that each of these sectors travels under the laser beam at the same speed, the videodisc player has to speed up to read sectors toward the outer rim, maintaining constant linear velocity (CLV). Other kinds of discs store an equal number of sectors per track. To do that, of course, the sectors toward the outer rim are stretched out in comparison to those toward the inner hub. In this case, the player doesn't have to change speed when traversing the tracks and can maintain a constant angular velocity (CAV).

This variation in the length of sectors makes a difference in a videodisc's capabilities. Since sectors on CLV discs don't have to be stretched longer as they approach the rim, more sectors can be stored on the disc, and thus more video; CLV discs can store about an hour of full-motion video per side. This doesn't matter much if you intend to use the videodisc only as you would a videotape—to run video from start to finish. Unfortunately, the varying number of sectors per track makes locating the beginning and end of individual video frames more difficult—a capability required for special effects like freeze-frame, slow motion, and fast search. For CAV discs, one frame of video corresponds directly to one revolution of the disc, making random frame access and special effects possible. The cost of ever-lengthening sectors, however, is a loss of half the disc's storage capacity. Thus, CAV discs are limited to 30 minutes of full-motion video per side. That cost is worth it, since CAV discs allow the kind of flexible random access to images and video segments necessary for hypermedia applications, which we'll examine later.

Comparison to Earlier Video Technologies

What do videodiscs offer that other visual technologies do not? Beyond durability and long-term image clarity, videodiscs can offer almost instant access to individual images and to video segments—no rewinding and fast-forwarding the tape to locate the video segment of interest; no clicking through slides or spinning the tray to find the slide you want to show. CAV videodiscs can store the equivalent of 54,000 still images on each side of the disc.[3] Imagine dealing with that many slides in trays!

Controlling a videodisc and its player is not unlike controlling a videocassette and its VCR—you use a remote control device. On CAV discs, images are stored as frames, which in turn are organized into chapters. Using your remote control, you can search for a single image (push "frame," type in the frame number, and push "search") or a video clip (push "frame" or "chapter," type the starting frame/chapter number, push "search" and then "play"). To show the next image or video clip, enter the frame or chapter information and the player leaps to the desired spot on the disc. To automate the control process further, videodisc producers are providing bar codes to access images. Similar to UPC codes read at grocery store check-out counters, the alternating thick and thin lines of bar codes contain the frame information, search, and play commands you would ordinarily punch in using your remote control keypad. Instead, you use a hand-held bar code reader (about the size of an Exacto knife) to sweep a light beam across the bar code, aim the reader at the videodisc player's remote control sensor, and push the "send" button to transmit the commands to the player.

3. Don't look for slide collections that large in your videodisc catalogs in the near future. Educational videodiscs typically contain combinations of full-motion video, photographic slides (stills), and graphic images (charts and graphs). Products that provide only still images may store only 1000 to 3000 slides, leaving large areas of the videodisc unused.

Controlling a videodisc with a remote control device (keypad or bar code reader) is an example of Level I videodisc use. No other piece of hardware is required beyond the videodisc player and the video monitor. Level II videodiscs combine video images and computer software to run in self-contained systems, such as touch-screen information booths or kiosks, and are rarely seen in education. When a computer is added, with software controlling the videodisc instead of a remote control device, this is called a Level III use of the videodisc. Level III videodiscs, which are generally CAV discs that permit individual frame access, are central to hypermedia or interactive multimedia applications, which we will discuss later.

Types of Information Available on Videodiscs Relevant to Social Studies

The school market for videodiscs was barely off the ground when Optical Data Corporation launched its *ABC News Interactive* series in 1989 with *The '88 Vote*. Since then, there has been a proliferation of products targeted for social studies education, as reflected in the products described in Chapter 2.

▬ Digital Video ▬▬▬▬▬▬▬▬▬▬▬▬▬▬▬▬▬▬▬▬

The videodisc is an analog medium, whereas the CD-ROM is digital—an incompatibility of formats that stands in the way of some exciting possibilities. Because they hold information in digital form, CDs can store images and text, which can be manipulated using a computer, as well as computer programs. Wouldn't it be nice if we could digitize motion video so we could put it on a CD integrated with text, graphics, still images, and audio? Digitizing would allow us to send video through computer networks to remote sites, just like we can do now with other digital information. The big problem: full-motion video in digital form takes up a lot of storage space—about half a minute of video would fill up a CD (Salpeter 1992). So, lots of folks have been working on schemes to compress video—to get rid of redundant information in a standard video signal. The result has been the development of several formats for storing motion video in digital form on a CD-ROM disc.

CD-I, CDTV, and DVD

Three digital video formats were developed in recent years for the home market. Compact Disc-Interactive (CD-I) and Commodore Dynamic Total Vision (CDTV) products looked a lot like audio CD players. Neither presumed the use of a personal computer, just a connection to a television and a simple input device like a joystick. Video for both formats ran at about 10 frames per second, which is only one-third the rate of true full-motion video. That made for choppy video reproduction, but it represented a significant step forward. Commodore Business Machines linked CDTV closely to its Amiga computer, the company's multimedia computer marketed to schools.[4]

Digital Video Disc (DVD) is the most recent entrant into the digital video market. Introduced in 1997 as the product of a collaboration among several Japanese companies, DVD boasts picture quality that exceeds current television broadcast capabilities.

4. The CDTV format has been abandoned, however, and both Commodore and its Amiga technology were sold to a German company in 1995.

Developers found a way to squeeze seven times as many pits on a DVD disc as on current CDs while maintaining the same dimensions. Some DVDs have two layers of pits, allowing manufacturers to store up to four movies on a single disc. Interactive multimedia programs on DVD-ROMs, a successor format, will have up to 25 times the storage capacity of standard CD-ROMs.

QuickTime, PhotoMotion, and AVI

By 1992, both the Macintosh and MS-DOS computer environments enjoyed digital video capability without the expense of additional hardware. QuickTime for the Macintosh introduced a new file format, the "movie" format. This format accommodates digitized video that can be created, edited, and integrated into applications by developers and end users. This fairly inexpensive system has its drawbacks, though. QuickTime movies can play in a window that occupies only about one-sixteenth of the computer screen and can run no faster than CD-I and CDTV applications—about 10–15 frames per second. IBM's PhotoMotion and Microsoft's AVI products run at about the same speed. Also software-based, PhotoMotion is limited to 10 frames per second, but a powerful computer allows a full quarter of the computer screen to be used as the video display window. AVI matches QuickTime in display size, but it runs faster than its competitors (15 frames per second). Ongoing development will improve QuickTime's speed, even within larger windows.

DVI and MPEG

To achieve full-screen, full-motion video (at 30 frames per second) a more expensive approach, requiring additional special-purpose hardware, is necessary. Digital Video-Interactive (DVI), a compression technology developed by Intel, has been the basis for the Eye-Q board for the Macintosh and the ActionMedia II board for IBM-compatible computers. Both products create compressed digitized video files that are less than one-hundredth the size of uncompressed video files. Efforts by the Moving Picture Expert Group (MPEG) promise to achieve the same high-quality video in digitized form, without special DVI hardware.

Digital Video for Social Studies

Commercial products using digitized video appeared as recently as 1991, so the breadth and depth of applications are currently narrow but growing. Numerous reference materials have been upgraded across the range of formats to include digitized video. New titles are also gradually appearing.

Videodiscs and CD-ROMs in Social Studies

For social studies teachers and students, optical technology carries both current benefits and future potential. We want students to find and use a wide range of information as they study social studies topics and issues. With print-based reference material, students pay a high price in the effort to search for relevant information. The current searching capabilities of CD-ROMs reduce the search time by providing a more flexible tool in a single package (rather than the multivolume package of other reference materials). That kind of flexibility extends to videodiscs as well.

The potential of videodiscs and CD-ROMs (and their offspring) for social studies teaching and learning hinges on two elements: what collections of information will become available and in what forms the information will be stored (the range of media). Student use of primary source materials has long been a priority in social studies education, but the effort to collect such materials in a form that is useful for students has been a perennial challenge. Imagine the range of primary historical documents that could be placed at a student's fingertips on a single CD-ROM disc and that could be searched so quickly! What primary documents would you archive for teaching U.S. history or government, or world history (no more than 250,000 pages)? And what kind of information beyond text would you want available on disc? CD-ROM products today are outpacing traditional reference texts in the kinds of material one can retrieve, including sound and pictures (up to 2000 pictures per disc).

What CD-ROMs can do for textual information, videodiscs can do for visual information. We noted above that 54,000 slides could be stored on each slide of a CAV videodisc. These might include not only still photographs, but also graphs, charts, diagrams, and maps that can be accessed and displayed on your video monitor. Videodiscs can also store audio and full-motion video, providing a highly manipulatable visual database to support instruction. Digital video is forging a marriage of CD-ROM and videodisc capabilities, combining the best of both worlds.

Optical disc resources can place an enormous archive of primary source and support materials, textual and visual, in the hands of social studies teachers and students. Wading through such material requires some thoughtfulness and skill. Fortunately, new computer-based software tools are available to help us navigate within large and complex collections of information.

■ Hypertext/Hypermedia ━━━━━━━━━━━━━━━━━━━━━━━

Imagine that you are about halfway through reading an 850-page book on the Civil War. The author is leading you through events of the war in the eastern theater of operations. At one point, you read a general's name that is only somewhat familiar to you—someone briefly discussed 150 pages ago in the western theater of the war. To better understand this person's role, you hold your place with one finger and take a couple of minutes to look back. Sometimes just flipping through the pages gets you there, but not this time. You decide to use the book's index, where several page numbers appear for the general. The first one doesn't help enough, but the second location has what you need—a page or so that helps clarify why this general's role in the western war effort had an impact on the east. Your memory refreshed, you return to the place at which you paused (assuming your finger didn't slip).

In this common practice, the reader has interrupted a linear presentation of text to pursue a line of inquiry in a non-linear fashion, skipping around in the text using two information tools—the book's index and his or her own memory. This is just one small subset of what Ted Nelson had in mind when he coined the term "hypertext," based on an idea advanced first in 1945 by Vannevar Bush, President Franklin Roosevelt's science advisor during World War II. To get a better understanding of hypertext, let's put our Civil War opus in a computer so that it can be read at a monitor. When you reach the point in your reading where the general is mentioned, you see that his name is in boldface. In fact, the names of all the people, events, places, concepts, principles, and documents are highlighted. You use a mouse to point to the general's name and click the mouse. A new screen appears with information about the general as well as a menu of other information you can retrieve in similar fashion. When you've located the information you need, you move the pointer to a return arrow and you are instantly transported back to your starting point.

Let's take this a step further. Consider that the Civil War (and history in general) is a collection of themes, events, people, ideas, and the like that are all related in a web of interconnections. Our author has strung these pieces of information together into threads—paths through this web—and is trying to present these threads in a way that reflects the overall knowledge of the war she has woven for herself over the years. Rather than being tied solely to the author's knowledge structure, imagine a Civil War information database that consisted of this web of interconnected information and a tool for you to piece together your own threads and to weave your own knowledge about the war. Such a tool allows you to view a visual representation of the information web and to traverse it at will, or to follow the paths of the expert (the author) if you wish. This is the essence of hypertext.

A Hypermap of Fundamental Values in Civics

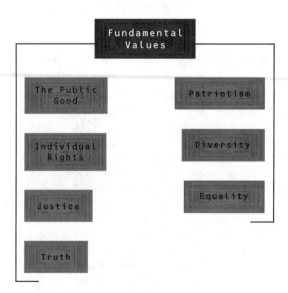

Essential Features of Hypertext

Underlying the concept of hypertext are two powerful ideas: that structures of knowledge can be made more understandable if they can be represented visually, and that the ability to navigate external knowledge structures can help learners construct and elaborate their own internal knowledge structures.

Visualization

Hypertext tools can display a diagram of the concepts, people, documents, and other elements of a knowledge structure and how they are interconnected, as illustrated by the hypermaps presented in in the preceding and following figures.[5] In the first figure, seven concepts are linked to the larger idea of "Fundamental Values," part of the larger knowledge structure of civics. A click on one example of these—"The Public Good"—transports the user along the web to a deeper level of detail or complexity (see the following figure). While exploring the information, the user is continually exposed to the connections among ideas through a visual metaphor.

Hypermaps and other visual representations can help students understand the structure of disciplines in a way that linear presentations cannot. Conceptual structures are also readily portrayed. Using Gardner's notion of multiple intelligences (1985), learners can draw on both their linguistic and spatial intelligences within hypertext environments as they grapple with complex content.

Connections to the Learner's Knowledge Structure

Knowledge represented as connections or relationships among concepts is based on the principles of schema theory derived from current cognitive psychology. Like the hypermaps described above, learners possess their own internal maps, or semantic networks—schema and the connections among them. Learning is reorganizing the structure of this network, refining relationships among concepts, and adding new concepts to the existing network. Proponents of hypertext environments suggest that, since it resembles semantic memory, hypertext material can help learners refine and expand their internal cognitive structure. This notion derives from constructivist cognitive theory, which posits that learners are actively involved in constructing personal knowledge, rather than simply ingesting the knowledge of an information giver (Bednar, Cunningham, Duffy, and Perry 1992).

---

5. Organization of these hypermaps is based on the Center for Civic Education and the Council for the Advancement of Citizenship's *CIVITAS: A Framework for Civic Education*. Bulletin No. 86. Washington, DC: National Council for the Social Studies, 1991.

A Hypermap of One Fundamental Value: The Public Good

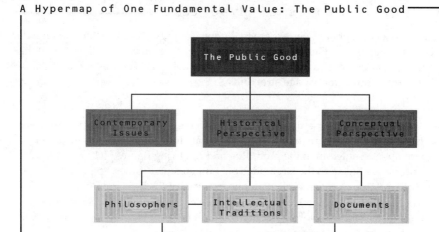

From Hypertext to Hypermedia to HyperCard

So far we've been focusing on text-based material and imagining how one might travel around interconnected textual material. Let's return to the example of the Civil War text via computer and your search for that general. When you clicked on the highlighted name of the general, suppose you got more than just text. Suppose a graphic timeline appeared on the computer screen that showed your current location in the history of the war in the eastern theater, with a parallel line for what was happening in the west. Suppose also that a Mathew Brady photograph of the general appeared on a video monitor, retrieved automatically from a videodisc. Or even better, how about a brief full-motion video excerpt about the general from a television documentary.

All of this moves us beyond hypertext to hypermedia—the ability to traverse a web of information in diverse forms: textual, graphical, audio, and video. Hypermedia, mentioned briefly at the conclusion of Chapter 4, is best thought of as an environment within which we can draw upon information stored on videodiscs and CD-ROMs and take advantage of digitized video in whatever format emerges. But the environment must be created by a tool, and efforts to develop simple, inexpensive hypermedia software for personal computers led to *HyperCard* for the Macintosh in 1987, and a variety of MS-DOS-based products, such as *LinkWay* for the IBM (released in February 1989). The following table lists a variety of hypermedia software tools.

One metaphor that can be applied to hypermedia software is that of index cards organized into stacks. Information from a particular card in one stack can be linked to other information on any other card in any other stack. A button on the first card might display information needed to go to the desired destination card, or a button might contain commands to retrieve images from a videodisc or audio from a CD attached to the computer. So, in your computer text of the Civil War, an invisible button on top of the general's boldfaced name brings up a graphic timeline on your computer screen (a card from the "timeline" stack). At the same time, it sends a command to the videodisc player to display frame number 45,392 on the video monitor—the Brady photograph (assuming you had a videodisc that contained such information).

Sample of Hypermedia Tool Producers[6]

Product	Producer	Computer Required
Digital Chisel	Pierian Spring Software 5200 SW Macadam, Ste. 570 Portland, OR 97201 503-222-2044	Macintosh, System 7.X, 68040-based color Macintosh, 4 MB RAM
GUIDE HyperText Authoring System	Information Access 15821 NE Eighth St., Ste. 200 Bellevue, WA 98008-3905 425-201-1915, fax 425-201-1922	IBM and compatibles
HyperCard	Apple Computer, Inc. One Infinite Loop Cupertino, CA 95014 800-282-2732 (U.S.), 800-637-0029 (Can.)	Macintosh
HyperStudio	Roger Wagner Publishing, Inc. 1050 Pioneer Way, Ste. P El Cajon, CA 92020 800-497-3778 619-442-0522 (tech support)	Macintosh PC (Windows)
LinkWay, LinkWay Live! (supports IBM's DVI system)	IBM Corporation P.O. Box 16848 Atlanta, GA 30321-6848 800-426-2255	IBM and compatibles
MediaLink (freeware)	University of South Carolina (see http://web.csd.sc.edu/medialink) Contact: Dr. Oakman, 803-777-2401	Macintosh, System 7.X, 68040-based color Macintosh, 4 MB RAM (Windows beta version available)
ToolBook	Asymetrix Corporation 110 110th Ave. NE, Ste. 700 Bellevue, WA 98004 206-462-0501	IBM and compatibles and Windows
Tutor-Tech Hypermeida Toolkit	Techware Corporation P.O. Box 151085 Altamonte Springs, FL32715-1085 888-832-4927, 407-695-9000	Apple IIe, IIc, IIc+, IIGS

6. For a more complete list of hypertext/hypermedia tools, including high-end products, see *T.H.E. Journal* 18, no. 1 (August 1990).

Many current videodisc products are used in hypermedia applications. They are marketed to be used at both Level I (no computer) and Level III (computer-driven), so they are packaged with the necessary computer software. Hypermedia use of videodiscs are, by definition, Level III applications, marrying the videodisc and the hypermedia software (*HyperCard*, *LinkWay*, or some other similar tool).

A Screen from ABC News Interactive's In the Holy Land ————————

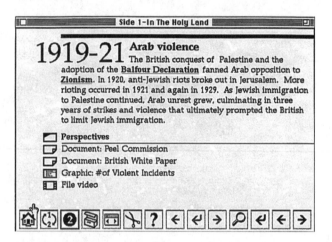

The *ABC News Interactive* series marketed by Optical Data Corporation is a good example of current, commercially available hypermedia material for social studies. The above illustration displays a computer screen created with *HyperCard* software used in conjunction with a videodisc for *In the Holy Land*. Let's look at what you can access from this screen. You see a picture (icon) of film, meaning that a full-motion video excerpt is available for viewing. The document icon will access text, perhaps primary source material, which you can choose to print out by clicking on a printer icon. Buttons are also available to let you search events by name or date, and boldfaced text indicates a link to related information on another card. The control bar along the bottom provides you with several tools, including a documentary maker for composing your own presentations.

■ Using Optical Technology and Hypermedia in the Social Studies Classroom

In the hands of creative teachers and energized students, optical technology alone, or contained within hypermedia environments, can be used in virtually unlimited ways. Most uses break down into two areas: research and presentations.

■ Research

Not surprisingly, CD-ROMs and videodiscs are likely to reside in a school's media center. CDs and videodiscs are reference material in a small package. When assigning research or writing projects, teachers can encourage students to investigate a wide range of appropriate information sources in traditional text form and in electronic form. Level III videodisc stations can be established in the media center as well, with videodisc players, video monitors, and computers—allowing teachers and students to conduct research in a hypermedia environment. Depending on the product, retrieved information can be printed out or saved in a computer file. Teachers, too, can find CD-ROM products of great value, providing access to the entire text of historic documents, for example, as well as a wealth of detailed data on topics ranging from countries of the world to Desert Storm.

Presentations

If the library is the only place where hypermedia research stations are set up, each station should be on a mobile cart for transfer to the classroom from time to time. Teachers and students will want to make class presentations, and they should be encouraged to do so.

Presentations by the Teacher

A videodisc player, large monitor, and videodisc of choice can make for effective whole-group instruction. Be sure the videodisc player is placed high enough so you can use a remote control device as you move around the classroom. This level of use feels like instruction with a slide projector or a VCR, but you may now be using a bar code reader to flash frame numbers to a videodisc player, alternating between still images and full-motion video instantly.

Using a hypermedia workstation in the classroom adds another dimension of information, providing both high-quality images from a videodisc and text/graphics from a computer. For whole-group hypermedia instruction, another piece of equipment is highly desirable—an LCD projection pad. Computer screens are notoriously small and ill-equipped for large groups to view. Connected to the video output port of your computer, an LCD pad sits on top of a regular overhead projector, and it displays an image of the computer screen—similar to a dynamic overhead transparency.[7]

There are difficulties in using hypermedia for whole-group instruction, however. Depending on the LCD pad, you may have to lower the lights a bit (or shut off one bank of lights) to improve the readability of the display. If you are operating a mouse, you are more tied to one place in the classroom. Some teachers address the latter problem by enlisting a student to operate the mouse, or by using a remote mouse (another kind of remote control device, but this time for the computer).

7. Many hypermedia applications for schools are two-display products; that is, the computer output is seen on one display (computer monitor or LCD pad), and the output from the videodisc appears on another display (a video monitor). Some products, however, display both the computer output *and* video on the computer screen using a video overlay card inside the computer.

Developing Multimedia Lessons

How are multimedia presentations planned? At the simplest level, as you develop your lesson plan, you write down the frame numbers of stills or video you want to use at certain points in the presentation. Or you note what bar codes you'll use. As you teach, you'll be walking around with either a remote control keypad or the videodisc's Teacher's Guide with the bar codes and the bar code reader.[8] Many products have sample lesson plans already prepared.

Developing hypermedia-based lessons can be almost as simple. Numerous commercial products include presentation- or documentary-making tools that automate the selection and organization of visual materials. Together with the text of your lesson plan (or text you want displayed to your students), these multimedia presentations can be stored on the computer's hard disk and retrieved at class time.

For the adventurous who crave maximum flexibility and creativity, there are the hypermedia development tools like *HyperCard, HyperStudio, LinkWay,* and others. Build your own stacks. Compose cards with your own text. Create buttons to call up videodisc images or CD music. Use a scanner to digitize your own photographs and display them on the computer. Use your VCR to capture video segments and digitize them with QuickTime, PhotoMotion, or some other video digitizer. Add music or speech to your presentation using an audio digitizer.

Share this adventure with your students. According to Eliot Soloway, we should "let students use [multimedia] to generate a sense of ownership, self-expression, participation, and communication" (Bruder 1991, 23). Thinking about how to construct a multimedia presentation encourages students to deeply consider how elements of information are interconnected—to construct their own knowledge of the content. This brings us back to the underlying power of hypertext/hypermedia.

Issues

Achieving the benefits ascribed to optical technology and hypermedia environments depends on skillful and thoughtful use of these tools. A number of issues should be considered before, during, and after using optical technology.

Information Access Versus Information Use

CD-ROMs and videodiscs allow students to access a tremendous volume of information. Much attention has been paid to technologies that allow students to access distant databases—to search through thousands of documents and retrieve data from huge archives. But what does the student do with this information? As Naisbitt (1982) put it, we are "drowning in information but starved for knowledge." Students need to develop information-handling and problem-solving skills to construct knowledge from information. (See the discussion of databases in Chapter 4.)

---

8. Inexpensive software is available for you to generate your own bar codes so you don't have to lug around the Teacher's Guide and you won't be limited to the bar codes provided by the producer.

Look for Thinking Skills Support in Evaluating Commercial Products

This is a corollary of the prior point. Many commercial producers of CD-ROMs, video-discs, and hypermedia products are caught up in the "information access" mindset. Few have achieved what Nelson envisioned as the power of hypertext, and few producers have created products that address the cognitive supports students need to make meaning of hypermedia information. What they leave out, you'll need to supply.

Look for Products That Use the Various Media Well

Film and video are at their best when they tell a story and evoke emotion. Text is good at conveying information. Each medium should be used for what it does best. Thirty-second video clips are not powerful uses of video. Good hypermedia products avoid creating what some have referred to as "desktop MTV."

The "It's All in There" Problem

It seems that when you integrate a large body of information with a computer, students believe that everything they need to look for about a topic "is all in there." Novice problem solvers frequently make the mistake of ending their inquiries when they find the first relevant piece of information or the first plausible answer. This is especially true when the computer is used as a tool; after all, this is a computer! It ought to have everything I need. Students sometimes need to be reminded to employ other, more traditional, information technologies—such as print.

Teachers who review commercial hypermedia products discover the fallacy of "it's all in there." Many products suffer from the swiss cheese effect—a delectable resource, but with lots of holes in it. Those you'll have to fill yourself.

Getting Lost in Hyperspace

We've talked about using hypertext/hypermedia to navigate large and complex collections of information. Navigators sometimes get lost, and this can happen to students (and teachers) who use hypermedia. A good hypermedia product provides a compass of some kind—a "you are here" map, for example—that is always on the screen or a mouse click away. From wherever you are in the product, you should be able to return to your starting point quickly. Good navigation aids are essential to efficient and effective use of hypermedia products.

Hypermedia Is Not for Everyone

Gathering information by traveling along webs of interconnected textual and visual information is different from traditional, book-based data retrieval. It takes some getting used to. For some students, visual cues such as hypermaps, arrows, and icons are meaningless, even distracting. While hypermedia maximizes individual choice in exploring information, the visual nature of the environment itself may not be universally beneficial.

Summary

The raw material for social studies—our primary source material—is multimedia. What we know of ourselves, our history, our cultural and political values, is stored not only in the Declaration of Independence and the Federalist Papers, but also in the reassuring radio fireside chats of Franklin Delano Roosevelt and the stirring oratories of Martin Luther King, Jr. It appears on the ceiling of the Sistine Chapel, in Mathew Brady's photographs, and in pictures of Auschwitz. And it appears on the nightly news. Optical technology may help us make better use of this broad range of material in the teaching of social studies.

Dede (1987) referred to hypermedia as a "cognition enhancer," which he defined as a tool that forges a partnership between the cognitive strengths of a person and an information technology. The tools to harness the multimedia resources of optical technology extend beyond just streamlining visual presentations. The complex and interwoven threads of history and geography and the array of interrelated abstract concepts in the other social sciences have presented perennial challenges to social studies teachers and students. How can we make sense of the complexity? How can we see the connections and relationships? The ability to construct visual representations of the complicated knowledge structures within the social studies makes hypermedia-as-cognition-enhancer an appealing notion.

References

Articles/Chapters

Bruder, Isabelle. "What's New in Multimedia." *Electronic Learning* 12, no. 1 (1992): 16.

Bednar, Anne K., Donald Cunningham, Thomas M. Duffy, and J. David Perry. "Theory into Practice: How Do We Link?" In *Constructivism and the Technology of Instruction: A Conversation*, edited by Thomas M. Duffy and David H. Jonassen, 17–34. Hillside, NJ: Lawrence Erlbaum Associates, 1992.

Duffy, T. M., and David H. Jonassen. "Constructivism: New Implications for Instructional Technology?" *Educational Technology* 31, no. 5 (1991): 7–12.

Greenfield, Elizabeth. "Authoring Systems Focus on New Structure and Users." *T.H.E. Journal* 18, no. 1 (1990): 7, 10ff.

Horney, Mark. "Reviews: A Hypertext Bookshelf." *HyperNEXUS: Journal of Hypermedia and Multimedia Studies* 3, no. 1 (1992): 14–17.

Mageau, Therese. "Software's New Frontier: Laserdisc Technology." *Electronic Learning* 9, no. 6 (1990): 22–28.

Swan, Karen. "History, Hypermedia, and Criss-crossed Conceptual Landscapes." *Journal of Educational Multimedia and Hypermedia* 3, no. 2 (1994): 120–39.

Walkenbach, John. "Personal Rewritable Optical Drives: A World of Unlimited Storage." *PC World* 10, no. 9 (1992): 136–40ff.

Books

Gardner, Howard. *Frames of Mind: The Theory of Multiple Intelligences.* New York: Basic Books, 1985.

Memory and Storage. Understanding Computers Series. Alexandria, VA: Time-Life Books, 1987.

Naisbitt, John. *Megatrends.* New York: William Morrow, 1982.

Other Resources

Apple Computer, Inc. and the National Council for the Social Studies. *Making Connections: Social Studies through Technology.* 1992. Nine-minute videotape about using interactive multimedia in the social studies classroom. Order from Apple Computer, Inc., telephone 800–825–2145.

Emerging Technology Consultants, Inc. *The Videodisc Compendium for Education and Training.* Order from P.O. Box 120444, St. Paul, MN 55112, telephone 612–639–3973.

International Society for Technology in Education (ISTE): Hypermedia/Multimedia Special Interest Group and *HyperNEXUS: Journal of Hypermedia and Multimedia Studies.*

Ztek Company. Annual catalog of videodiscs and CD-ROMs. Order from P.O. Box 1055, Louisville, KY 40201–1055, telephone 800–247–1603, 502–584–8505.

Discussion Questions

1. How does the optical disc compare to magnetic storage media? What are the advantages and disadvantages of each?

2. How is hypertext different from traditional text? What does hypertext allow readers to do that book-based text does not?

3. How is information access different from information use? What do students need to develop, in light of this difference?

4. In what ways is hypermedia an example of what Dede called a "cognition enhancer"?

Additional Readings and Questions

Adams, R. C. "Cool Moves: Teaching Geography and History with *HyperCard.*" *The Computing Teacher* 22, no. 7 (April 1995): 31–33.

1. According to Adams, what capabilities did the electronic material (in this case, a *HyperCard* stack) provide that traditional instructional materials could not?

2. In what ways does the Cool Moves *HyperCard* stack capitalize on the power of visualization?

3. What information, beyond that described in the article, would you want students to have in order to enrich their knowledge of the topic?

Ayersman, David J. "Reviewing the Research on Hypermedia-based Learning." *Journal of Research on Computing in Education* 28, no. 4 (summer 1996): 500–525.

1. How does the author characterize the bulk of writing to date about hypermedia-based learning?

2. Based on current research, what conclusions can be drawn about the effects of hypermedia-based learning? In what areas? For what student populations?

3. Based on current research, what claimed benefits of hypermedia-based learning have yet to be demonstrated convincingly?

Brown, Adrian. "History, Digital Imaging, and Desktop Video." *Learning and Leading with Technology* 22, no. 8 (May 1995): 19–21.

1. What benefits did the author claim for the multimedia approach taken in the desktop video-making project? After reading this chapter and its associated readings, how plausible do you think these claims are?

2. How would you weigh the costs and benefits of engaging students in the project described in this reading?

McMahon, Teresa A., Alison A. Carr, and Barry J. Fishman. "Hypermedia and Constructivism: Three Approaches to Enhanced Learning." *HyperNEXUS: Journal of Hypermedia and Multimedia Studies* 3, no. 2 (winter 1993): 5–10.

1. What is the constructivist cognitive theory (or constructivism), and how does it relate to hypertext/hypermedia?

2. Pick one of the three prototypes in the article and describe what constructivist ideas were incorporated into its design.

3. What design characteristics of the hypermedia prototypes described in the article are evident in other social studies-related hypermedia/multimedia products you have seen or used?

Patton, Susannah. *"Choosing Success*—From Idea to CD-ROM." *Electronic Learning* 15, no. 4 (January/February 1996): 26–28.

1. What conflicting views were held by the filmmakers, multimedia designers, and educators who were part of the product's development team? What issues do these conflicting views raise with respect to the evaluation of multimedia intended for social studies classrooms?

2. What advantages did the developers see in the "MTV approach to life skills" described in the article? Did they recognize any potential disadvantages that they would need to remedy? Do you see any?

Scheidler, Kay. "Students Cross Discipline Boundaries with Hypermedia." *The Computing Teacher* 20, no. 5 (February 1993): 16–20.

1. What conditions helped make this project a success, according to the author? Would these conditions be difficult to replicate in other schools?

2. In what ways did this project encourage less gifted students to succeed? How much of this success was based on the technology used, and how much was based on other, nontechnology aspects of the project?

3. What other cross-disciplinary projects can you envision for hypermedia development?

Activities

1. Select a topic or concept that is taught in social studies and make a list of several related subtopics or subconcepts. Depict the interrelationships among these ideas in a hypermap. The first two figures in this chapter are examples of hypermaps.

2. Using a videodisc related to a social studies topic, make a class presentation or deliver a lesson that requires you to show visual material from the videodisc. Use a remote control device (Level I) or a computer (Level III) to control access to the videodisc.

3. Apply the problem-solving process presented in Chapter 4 (databases) to a lesson plan that integrates videodisc or CD-ROM material.

Cool Moves

Teaching Geography and History with HyperCard

Richard C. Adams

D id you ever have the feeling that *everybody* knows how to do something but you? Are you the sort of person who reads *The Computing Teacher*, and therefore everyone at your school expects you to be the expert? And you're certain they're overestimating how much you *really* know?

Like many of you, I feel like a fraud. Here I am, the computer coordinator for a small, rural school district, and until a short time ago I had never made a *HyperCard* stack on a Macintosh.

I could plead that economic factors caused my ignorance; budget reductions for the last five years had made it so that our high school didn't actually *have* any Macintosh computers except for the old Mac 512K machine on the secretary's desk. But the truth is, even after I got my hands on a Mac Classic, I didn't use the *HyperCard* program that came with it. I could see no reason to.

Then came an announcement of a grant program for science teachers who wanted to study the relationship between the sciences and the humanities. I had a geography/history project in mind that would be ideal for the grant program. I was awarded one of the grants, so now I had a reason to learn about *HyperCard*.

An Approach to History

As a science teacher at a small (400-student) high school, I'm not forced to teach the same thing twice each day— every period is different. Thus, while I teach first- and second-year chemistry, physics, and computer science, I also teach photography and a Talented and

From *The Computing Teacher* 22, no. 7 (April 1995): 31–33. Reprinted with permission from the International Society for Technology in Education. All rights reserved.

Figure 1.   HyperCard Buttons Let Students
            Retrieve Information on Various Groups

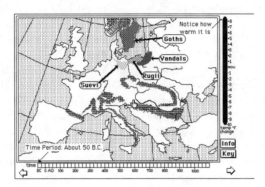

Gifted class that includes history, literature, philosophy, Latin, German, Italian, … and geography.

In my role as both a science and history teacher, I can't see history merely as a collection of events brought about by purely human motivations. In my courses, I have always taught the idea that technology, geography, and climate have had major influences on human history. Some scholars would have us believe that people really aren't affected by those things; they believe that human thoughts and desires alone determine people's actions.

As someone who has studied physical things and can appreciate temperature and geographic differences, I'm sure that one of the major factors in the development of democracy in Greece was the fact that Greek mountains kept people close enough together that everyone could know everybody else. I think the reason Egyptians had such a stable culture with friendly gods was because the Nile didn't flood without warning. I also feel that the barbarians who invaded the Roman Empire did not do so simply out of greed for all those Roman goodies, such as hot baths, gold trinkets, and honeyed sparrow brains in wine sauce ala Nero.

The trouble was that I had difficulty organizing and presenting weather and geography information in a historical framework that would hold the interest of a class of fidgeting 10th graders. That's when I realized that *HyperCard* would allow me to teach something better than I could with a bunch of handwaving and wonderful lectures.

Animation will grab kids' attention. Movement of any kind fascinates this generation of "vidiots." But I wanted to convey some real information along with the moving pictures. *HyperCard* allowed me to show the movement of barbarian tribes wreaking havoc around the Roman Empire, show temperature changes that were occurring, and allow students to get more information about the tribes by pressing *HyperCard* buttons at any time. Figure 1 shows an example of a *HyperCard* card from my lesson.

Building the Project

I spent a summer researching this project thanks to a National Science Foundation Sci-Mat Fellowship administered by the Council for Basic Education. The fellowship, funded by the DeWitt Wallace/

Reader's Digest Fund and the William H. Donner Foundation, allowed me to get a suitable Macintosh computer and to have time to really dig into the libraries and current research on this subject.

The earth seems to have two cold cycles—one occurring about every 80 years and another occurring about every 180 years. When these two cold cycles match up, it gets very, very cold. My first task was to analyze periods of extreme cold that were well documented. I chose the early 1600s, when the Thames River froze over so regularly that Queen Elizabeth strolled *on* the river during her daily walks. Using this period as a base, I used the *WordPerfect Works* spreadsheet to calculate backward in 20-year increments, and used somewhat arbitrary temperature values of plus 10 degrees to minus 10 degrees. I then used *WordPerfect Works* to make a graph that showed temperature patterns. My graph showed that it should have been very cold in about the year A.D. 100 and really warm around A.D. 900 and 50 B.C.

I continued my cold-weather/warm-weather research using historical accounts. The Romans evidently had warmer weather than we do now. During the "Little Optimum" years around A.D. 900, Europe had a climate estimated to be 10 degrees Fahrenheit warmer than it is today. Predictions that global warming will raise the temperature by one degree within the next century look less threatening when we consider how warm it used to be.

The historical records seem to correspond to what glacier records showed. But what was happening in the lives of people during these times? Around A.D. 100, the Goths left Sweden, where glacier records show it had been getting colder. During the warm years around 50 B.C., the population probably increased

as the growing season got longer and longer. The Goths landed in the area now called Poland and displaced the people called the Sueves and the Vandals. But it still got colder and the Goths went farther south—all the way to the Black Sea. They were doing fine there until the Huns, moving out of the Steppes that had dried out with the decrease in moisture always associated with colder weather, started crowding them. The Goths split into two groups: the Ostrogoths in the east and the Visigoths in the west.

With the *HyperCard*'s animation capabilities, successive versions of European maps can be produced in which students can see groups of people moving around like amoebas and bumping into each other. After everybody had settled down from the cold-weather moves and rearranged themselves, the Polish Vandals were in North Africa, the Swedish Visigoths had set up kingdoms in Spain, the Swedish Ostrogoths were taking it easy in the south of France, the Middle German Lombards had control of Italy, the German Burgundians had moved near Switzerland, the German Franks had taken over France, and the Huns and Magyars had combined to form the Hungarians. A number of the groups had sacked Rome and shaken up institutions in general, destroying the Western Roman Empire. Figures 2a, 2b, and 2c show a typical sequence of *HyperCard* cards charting the movements of some of these groups.

The warming that occurred between A.D. 800 and A.D. 1000 resulted in increasing populations in Scandinavia, but customs of primogeniture gave land only to the eldest son, no matter how large the family. Thus, it was the younger sons who went "a-viking" and settled in England, Scotland, Ireland, northern France, Iceland, and Greenland. (Greenland re-

Figure 2a.   Map for A.D. 140

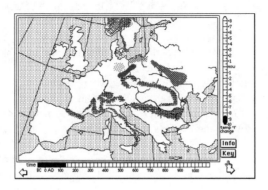

Figure 2b.   Map for A.D. 375

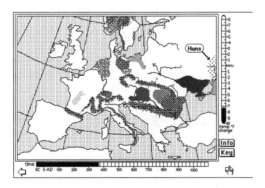

Figure 2c.   Map for A.D. 420

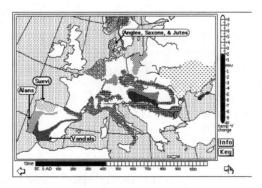

ally *was* greener at this time.) Swedish Vikings had moved south again, about where the Goths crossed over, where their

oarsmen ("Rus") gave their name to the area then called Rusland, now called Russia. These Vikings ended up being

Varangian guards for the city of Constantinople and the Byzantine Empire. As the weather started cooling again, the Norsemen Normans invaded England and southern Italy, and the Crusaders found the warm Holy Land attractive. When it got really cold in the 1400s, 1500s, and 1600s, Europeans found that establishing colonies in warmer lands around the globe made very good sense.

Using HyperCard as a Teaching Tool

My *HyperCard* stack "Cool Moves, or Even Barbarians Know When to Come Out of the Cold" allows students to see an animated map showing more movement than I ever could achieve waving my hands in front of a map taped to a blackboard. Tribes are identified and their names are made into "hot spots" so that students can get further information about the character, lifestyle, and history of any particular group (see Figure 1). Clicking on the Info button provides an explanation of what was happening during that time with the weather and other groups. A moving time-bar and thermometer give constant correlations with time and temperature.

The stack can be used as a lecture display tool or in a computer lab where students can explore and draw their own conclusions. It can also be given to individual students who are researching barbarians, weather patterns, or geography.

One of the main lessons I learned in creating this stack was that it isn't very difficult to make a useful teaching tool with *HyperCard*. I had programmed in BASIC long ago, and programming in *HyperCard* turned out to be much easier than I expected. To make the arrow button that allows the user to go to the next card, you simply choose a new button from a menu and type a script that says "Go next." To make the name of a tribe into an "active" spot, you write a script that says "Go card [name of tribe]," i.e., "Vandals." (It did help to have a friend show me how to do just a few cards—manuals can be valuable but intimidating.) I discovered that I had been avoiding the use of a valuable teaching tool just because I was unfamiliar with it.

Yes, it took some time to create this tool, but I learned a great deal about teaching this subject, discovered new relationships between temperatures and the migration of people, and can now educate students about this fascinating time period in a much more detailed and interesting way than if I had never made a *HyperCard* stack about it.

Teaching is something I do because it's fun. The fact that the school district pays me a salary allows me to have fun and eat too. Teaching tools like *HyperCard* allow me to get better at what I do, keep my interest alive, and keep me as fresh as the new faces I see each year in my classroom.   ❖

*T*o receive an electronic copy of this stack and the author's research paper on the project, send a blank, Macintosh-formatted 1.4 MB disk, a self-addressed disk mailer, and sufficient return postage to Richard C. Adams, Pleasant Hill High School, 36386 Highway 58, Pleasant Hill, OR 97455.

Reviewing the Research on Hyper-based Media

David J. Ayersman

Computers have only been seriously impacting education for 10–15 years; hypermedia is one of the more recent forms of computer-based learning tools to develop. Functional hypermedia systems have only been in existence since the late 1980s, and many consider the development of *HyperCard* in 1987 to be an important milestone in this development (Burton, Moore, and Holmes 1995). Synthesizing the research from such a brief period of time might seem an easy task with an expectation that very little would need to be summarized. In one regard, this assumption is valid. There is clearly not

Abstract
This article synthesizes the research on hypermedia-based instruction while providing a meaningful framework for categorizing the research to date. Two very general groupings that are used posit hypermedia as a tool that learners consume information from and as a tool that learners use to produce and structure information. Research relating to individual differences, attitudinal measures, systems analysis, and performance is examined. Concomitant changes in pedagogy are also addressed. (Keywords: computer-assisted instruction, hypermedia, literature review.)

enough research on hypermedia-based learning to merit a meta-analysis. An attempt at conducting a meta-analysis would result in too little of the research being considered because of the diversity of formats and designs that have been utilized to examine this area of computer-based education. The nature of

From the *Journal of Research on Computing in Education* 28, no. 4 (summer 1996): 500–525.
Reprinted with permission from the International Society for Technology in Education.
All rights reserved.

hypermedia has led to combinations of qualitative and quantitative methodologies and to a majority of the research originating from action-research, classroom-based samples that many would argue do not constitute generalizable data because of the small sample sizes and uncontrolled extraneous variables. On the other hand, few would disagree that hypermedia is effective for teaching and learning. Providing a research-based foundation to what many appear to already know is the purpose of this article.

Hypermedia-based Learning

The history of hypermedia has been well documented and definitions of hypermedia abound (Burton, Moore, and Holmes 1995; Maddux 1994; Myers and Burton 1994). Recent developments in computer-mediated communications have taken hypermedia and provided it with a limitless source of media-based information through networks. In many ways, this has heightened the attention and the impact of hypermedia on learning. What was too costly or prohibitive just a few years ago as memory-hungry applications or as blank slates of authoring applications is now a gateway to the Internet. Hypermedia has come to include remote databases and online resources accessible by way of the World Wide Web and other networks using Web browsers. In numerous ways, a shift has occurred so that the balance of power is more equal between the reader and the author. Although the author has control of the actual content of a program or document, the reader can control the sequence and presentation of the information so that it suits his or her needs. But what does the literature say about hypermedia?

Although much has been written about hypermedia-based learning, very little of the writing has been research based. Much of the available literature on hypermedia consists of predictive views of hypermedia's potential, descriptive essays explaining various hypermedia systems, and narrative tomes opining reasons why hypermedia is an effective tool for teaching and learning. The majority of this literature is generally more promotional than investigative. "The research evidence on enhancing learning with multimedia is understandably sparse" (Toomey and Ketterer 1995, 474). Admittedly, hypermedia is a relatively new technological learning tool and it takes time to provide a research base. Making efficient use of time can accelerate the development of this research base and can be accomplished by understanding where the research has been, what has been proven, what remains to be proven, and how hypermedia has been applied to learning. This study will begin to provide this record of the hypermedia research.

Using Hypermedia

Hypermedia can be used in the classroom in several ways. Perhaps the approach used least often, but thought of most frequently, is hypermedia as a stand-alone commercially available software program. An increasing number of commercial software programs are being developed, and they are targeting many content areas. Unfortunately, many of these programs are recognizably ill equipped for the needs of the classroom because of poor design (Stanton and Baber 1994). Arguably, commercial hypermedia software is improving, but other uses of hypermedia might be more appropriate for many educational purposes. Open software designs allow the purchaser to construct the content using hypermedia-based tools and formats. Many educators are adopting hypermedia as a construction tool for collaboratively creating their own software suited to their particular disciplinary needs. Hypermedia software created in this fashion can generally take two forms. Educators can combine efforts with instructional designers, computer programmers, other specialists, and other educators to create software suited to their particular disciplinary needs and individual instructional approaches. A second, and more common, approach to noncommercial hypermedia software development is for students to work collaboratively to develop their own software projects that focus on specific disciplinary topics. Research shows that taking this social constructivist approach offers many benefits.

There are many diverse areas in which hypermedia is effective for providing information to learners. Hypermedia has been successfully used to teach about sexually transmitted diseases on college campuses (McKillip and Baldwin 1990) and for promoting problem-solving skills and understanding social behavior (Holland, Holyoak, Nisbett, and Thagard 1986; Stevens 1989, as cited in Kozma 1991). Multimedia case studies have been developed for exploring moral dilemmas (Covey 1990, as cited in Kozma), enhancing classroom management skills (Overbaugh 1994, 1995), and teaching engineering design processes (Hsi and Agogino 1994). Many libraries, museums, and information kiosks utilize hypermedia search engines for quick and easy access to information. The use of hypermedia for instruction is not limited to learning semantic and cognitive information; it also expands to address learning procedural information as well. Learning complex procedural knowledge is enhanced by practice and the use of rule statements presented through hypermedia instruction (Kim and Young 1991). For example, Waddick (1994) effectively taught chemistry students to operate a spectrophotometer using *HyperCard*.

Researching Hypermedia

Throughout the literature, the use of hypermedia as an instructional resource has often been compared to alternative instructional strategies where more traditional methods (lectures) have been used. A typical comparison is for students to be assigned to one of two groups where one group receives hypermedia-enhanced instruction while the control group receives traditional lecture instruction. This comparison invites some skepticism for several reasons. First, the instructional strategies differ so greatly that the hypermedia-enhanced instruction often utilizes vastly different approaches to teaching and learning. This comparison then becomes one of instructional strategies and philosophical differences in teaching and learning rather than a clear focus on hypermedia as a tool for learning. Some clarity is needed between the method and the medium being used and compared by such studies. A broader interpretation of research on hypermedia-based learning is the clear result. In this broad interpretation, the focus is not just on the equipment or tools being used in the classroom, but also on the instructional strategies that seem to go hand-in-hand with them.

Concomitant with the growth of hypermedia systems in education is the resurgence of learning theories focusing on subjectivist principles—interactivity, social and cultural processes, critical thinking, peer collaboration, and learning by doing. The importance of social interactions as a process whereby learning occurs through constructing and reconstructing one's own interpretation of the environment is often credited to Vygotsky (1962, 1978). An integration of the medium (hypermedia) and the method (cognitive learning theory) has occurred, and this is evident in how the tools are being applied and in the outcomes from such applications.

Generally speaking, the results from these comparative studies range from no significant differences for the two groups of students' performance levels to differences significantly favoring the use of hypermedia-enhanced instruction. While comparative studies involving hypermedia continue, they also are present within each of the trends that the research has experienced to date. One interpretation of these trends is that hypermedia was initially explored using affective measures. What do teachers think of hypermedia? What are students' attitudes toward it? Answering these questions created a wave of attitudinal and perceptual research attempting to convey the reaction to hypermedia on the part of learners and teachers. The wave did not achieve tidal proportions though because of the high number of non-research-based writings that intermingled with it. As the research continues, however, it does so with an increasing complexity that is evident in multiple independent variables and questions that cut across the strands spoken of in this review. This research is the foundation for one (Attitudinal/Perceptual) of four such strands.

A second strand of research (Individual differences) has been an exploration of individual differences and hypermedia. Although the research is somewhat scarce, it is a widely held belief that the multimodal attributes and the high level of learner control inherent in hypermedia may accommodate various learning style differences. Research is beginning to surface that proves this notion of satisfying the diverse needs of students with a singularly robust hypermedia environment.

A third strand of the hypermedia research (Systems analyses) has analyzed hypermedia and its components while also looking toward patterns of user actions. By looking at how various hypermedia attributes relate to students' learning, we gain invaluable insight into how hypermedia systems ought to be designed as well as how the learner engages in the learning process. In most cases, this area of the research also examines students' metacognitive decisions as they experience hypermedia-based learning.

A fourth strand of research (Performance), based on hypermedia's effects on skill level and performance, has been conducted in a variety of content areas and for different age-level groupings. This body of research begins to answer questions pertaining to cognitive and procedural development. While many await the solid research base to emerge in the area of performance, the research has already shifted slightly toward more sophisticated examinations—intricately detailed studies that often use creative, multiple-level analyses to investigate the process of learning with hypermedia.

Figure 1. Categories of Research on Hypermedia-based Learning

Category	Explanation
Perceptual/Attitudinal	Examinations of learners' opinions and feelings (affective) toward hypermedia
Individual differences	Learning style and cognitive style comparisons within hypermedia environments
Systems analyses	Examinations of pathways, navigational preferences, and node and link structures, information/knowledge systems
Performance	Investigations of skill-level from consuming premade hypermedia software (cognitive/procedural) Pre-collegiate Collegiate Investigations of skill-level from producing one's own hypermedia software (cognitive/procedural) Pre-collegiate Collegiate

Research on Hypermedia-based Learning

There are many possibilities for grouping research on hypermedia-based learning. Often, hypermedia is categorized as having three potential applications: a. knowledge/information presentation, b. knowledge/information representation, and c. knowledge/information construction (Ayersman and Reed 1995; Nelson 1994; Nelson and Palumbo 1992; Palumbo and Bermudez 1994). Although this grouping is comprehensive, it is perhaps a bit too broad for the purposes of understanding research on age-level and content-area-specific applications of hypermedia. Examining each content area and the hypermedia research in that area might be difficult to summarize because of the large number of categories derived from the dozens of content areas utilizing hypermedia. For these reasons, I have chosen to group the research on hypermedia-based learning into four broad categories:

◈ Perceptual/Attitudinal

◈ Individual differences

◈ Systems analyses

◈ Performance

The central focus of this review is to examine the literature that explores performance of both cognitive and procedural skills and hypermedia. The Performance literature has been subdivided into uses of hypermedia as a tool for construction of knowledge and as a tool for presenting knowledge. Furthermore, the Performance literature has been grouped with age-level subheadings. These subheadings are used only for the research exploring performance and hypermedia; they include pre-collegiate and collegiate learners. Because much of the literature on hypermedia focuses on something other than performance,

I have also included the three previously mentioned broad categories of a. Attitudes/Perceptions, b. Individual differences, and c. Systems analyses (see Figure 1). Non research-based literature has largely been excluded from these analyses. An important outcome of using these categories is that age-level groups that have been underemphasized in the research are easily identifiable.

It must be recognized that the research is not as clearly delineated as this division suggests. A clear trend developing very recently has been toward more complex research designs. Researchers are beginning to progress toward examinations of multiple independent variables within single studies. As a result, the Perceptual/Attitudinal research begins to merge with the Individual differences research. As performance is increasingly included, the divisions begin to become indistinct. For now, these four categories create a meaningful way of examining the research on hypermedia-based learning.

Perceptions and Attitudes

Generally speaking, positive attitudes are reported following hypermedia-based learning situations. Perceptions and attitudes toward hypermedia are fundamentally important because they often accompany effective learning. That is, as experience with hypermedia is acquired and as learning occurs, perceptions and attitudes toward hypermedia change, often becoming more positive. Instruction using hypermedia to teach about the use of hypermedia systems in education significantly affects the attitudes toward hypermedia of preservice and inservice teachers (Reed, Ayersman, and Liu 1995a, 1995b). These attitudinal changes consist of increases

in other-based concerns and decreases in self-based concerns; it is desirable to progress from self-based concerns to other-based ones. Greater degrees of experience with authoring languages and hypermedia influences the reduction of self-based concerns while increasing other-based concerns.

Undergraduate students with differing backgrounds in hypermedia and with varying attitudes toward hypermedia tend to view the features of hypermedia differently (Liu, Ayersman, and Reed 1995). Based on an examination of novice students' descriptive statements of a hypermedia program, nine domains emerged. For the group as a whole, nearly two-thirds of the features cited referred to some form of learner control. When examining the applications of these domains in relationship to attitudinal changes toward hypermedia, the researchers found that larger changes in self-based concerns coincided with an emphasis on learner control citations (95 percent) while smaller changes in self-based concerns coincided with more variety and less reliance on learner control citations (40 percent). The high-change learner was inexperienced with computers, and the low-change learner was more experienced with hypermedia and computers. As a result, the more experienced learner was able to identify a greater variety of hypermedia features rather than focusing on only a few general features, like the less experienced learner did. One conclusion of this study is that, as hypermedia experience is gained, the features of hypermedia that are identified by learners tend to be more detailed and specific while encompassing a greater variety of descriptive features.

Students using hypertext as a tool for learning have experienced an increased sense of control and increased levels of intrinsic motivation (Becker and Dwyer 1994). Undergraduate students in a computer architecture course identified the computer simulations as being helpful in understanding concepts and making learning more concrete (DeNardo and Pyzdrowski 1992). Teacher trainers have been found to have more positive attitudes toward interactive multimedia than either computer-assisted instruction or video (Kizzier, Ford, and Pollard 1994). When used in conjunction with collaborative learning, sixth-grade language arts students completing a two-week unit where they used an authoring tool to create multimedia materials reported that the freedom to design their own presentations and the use of multiple media forms were two of the most satisfying aspects to the experience (Finkelman and McMunn 1995). Undergraduates using hypermedia-based simulations to learn classroom management skills unanimously enjoyed using the programs because of their realism. Many also described the programs as self-explanatory and easy to use (Overbaugh 1994). Students working in collaborative groups have reported significantly more favorable attitudes toward both math and computer math lessons than students working individually with the same software and information (Brush 1996).

That students enjoy using hypermedia systems is no great surprise. That teachers are gaining more positive attitudes toward hypermedia suggests a realization of its potential for learning. It has been shown that experience with hypermedia results in improved attitudes and perceptions toward its use. Collaborative learning seems particularly suited to working in hypermedia environments, and the research suggests that attitudes are more favorable as a result.

Individual Differences

Some findings about the learning style advantages of hypermedia environments have been tempered with qualifications about programs that are inadequately robust. That is, the programs did not truly allow for nonlinear linkages among concepts that learners might prefer. When comparing a hypermedia treatment that incorporated a robust presentation of material in multiple contexts emphasizing multiple facets of the information to a less robust program, Jacobson and Spiro (1993) found that the control group led to higher performances on measures of memory while the hypertext treatment led to superior knowledge transfer and higher order cognitive activity. Some have included random links among information as nonlinear (Lin and Davidson 1994), when, in fact, nonlinear links are anything but random. Confusing linearity/nonlinearity with the degree of structure within a hypermedia program has taken the hypermedia research off course.

There are benefits to both linear and nonlinear organizations of information. Linear sequences are thought to be most beneficial for conveying details and cause-and-effect relationships. Nonlinear structures allow a broader context and additional information that augments global learning (Gordon and Lewis 1992). Students with different learning styles and differing degrees of computing experience have been shown to differentially prefer linear and nonlinear pathways through a hypermedia program (Reed, Ervin, and Oughton 1996). While students may choose to engage in the learning process differently, research using robust hypermedia programs has shown that students can ultimately achieve comparable levels of performance. To develop hypermedia programs with various features suited to multiple learning styles requires that the software designer view the content material from multiple perspectives. Having preservice teachers engage in such processes is thought to develop an understanding of multiple organizations of information that might enhance the ability to instruct individuals who perceive information differently.

Combining text with animation and hypertext captions results in greater recall, inference, and comprehension (Large, Beheshti, Breuleux, and Renaud 1995). The dual-coding theory introduced by Paivio (1979, 1986) provides a partial explanation of why many think that hypermedia-enhanced instruction will be so effective for learning. If each person is capable of processing information through both verbal and imaginal systems, then providing information that has contextual meaning to both of those systems would seem to augment one's ability to store and retrieve that information. The information would then have two memory codes rather than one, and, if they are contextually related, one may help to trigger the other. These multimodal approaches to education are thought to be particularly effective for accommodating students with diverse styles and preferences for learning. For those students who rely predominantly on one of the two systems, having it available would certainly be beneficial. In a study comparing the use of animation with two types of explanations, students were found to generate more creative solutions for solving problems when explanations accompanied the animation than when they followed the animation (Mayer and Sims 1994).

A growing body of research is showing that students may choose to take dif-ferent paths and use different media, tools, and learning aids while ultimately acquiring information that allows them to perform at comparable levels (Hsu, Frederick, and Chung 1994; Liu and Reed 1994; Toro 1995). For example, females have been shown to review videodisc segments more frequently and spend more time on task than males in an interactive video learning environment (Braswell and Brown 1992). An exploration of students' choice of media from within a hypermedia program for fashion merchandising students indicated that 56 percent of the students chose visual, 30 percent chose text, and 14 percent chose auditory media (Frey and Simonson 1993). Providing students with navigational options and greater levels of learner control can allow them to learn using their preferred approaches. While empowering the learner in a hypermedia environment can be beneficial for addressing individual differences, it can also be detrimental to those students lacking effective metacognitive learning strategies and the capability to take advantage of the options available to them.

When discussing the use of hypermedia as a learning and teaching tool, the importance of one's instructional approach cannot be overstated. Providing metacognitive cues to students that allow them to pause for reflection can be especially beneficial for performance on far-transfer tasks (Lin, Newby, and Foster 1994). This approach encourages students to better understand the process of problem solving rather than simply deriving the right answer.

Metacognitive decisions for how to go about learning are closely related to individual differences. Realizing that learners may choose to go about the process of learning differently, one could infer that the ability to learn is not diminished if the environment includes the options and information preferred by each learner. Within a hypermedia environment, learning is then enhanced for all learning style groups if the software is robust enough to offer the preferential forms of information for each learner. Unfortunately, many programs that are available are not robust and offer few media choices and limited user options. Examinations of learner differences within a hypermedia environment can be the foundation for creating these more robust programs. Deliberate attempts to target the metacognitive abilities of students might enhance their ability to learn in this type of environment as well.

One prediction—primacy of print theory—has been that information will be recalled better when presented in print than in another media form (Thompson 1994). Recent findings do not support this theory, however. A survey of undergraduate journalism students and university library employees revealed no significant effects for text as a function of modality (Thompson 1994, 1995). McCorduck (1992) aptly stated that the equivalence between mastery of text and mastery of knowledge is one of the unacknowledged assumptions of education for the past few centuries. She also described exceptions to this assumption that involve other forms of representing knowledge, including visual images and non-text-based media. Hypermedia environments are ideal examples for countering primacy-of-print philosophies. Because hypermedia incorporates multiple forms of information, it is especially suited to conveying knowledge that is not easily conveyed solely through print or verbal explanations. It is not difficult to imagine a physics student having difficulty with a particular

concept. Using video to slow down a physical process to the point where the learner can identify the steps leading to a particular result could certainly be seen as beneficial. Incorporating contextual links that allow the student to expand on the process that was learned can then allow the learner to transfer that understanding to other situations and environments.

A review of research (Daiute and Morse 1994) shows that the inclusion of images and sounds can improve comprehension and production of text while more fully bringing culture into the classroom. Students are better able to recall information when multiple modes of information are combined. When talking head video is combined with voice and text, students are better able to recall information than when using primarily audio (Ottaviani and Black 1994). College students studying French comprehend authentic linguistic input better and produce more comprehensible communicative output as a result of including subtitles (Borras and Lafayette 1994). The basis for incorporating multiple media formats into the learning environment is evident.

Marrison and Frick (1994) examined learning style and attitudes toward instruction of undergraduate economics students using hypermedia instruction, hypermedia instruction with lecture, and lecture only. While students had similarly positive perceptions toward the hypermedia instruction, field independent students found the hypermedia instruction easier to use and more exciting than field dependent students. In other studies, field independent students have been found to achieve significantly more than field dependent students when using particular search tools available within the hypermedia program (Leader and Klein 1994). It is not surprising that people vary in their approaches to processing and organizing information. Individual preferences are especially obvious when students construct hypermedia environments and choose to create links. Although not as unique as a signature, each student tends to develop links that seldom match those of other students (Ayersman 1994; Ellis, Furner-Hines, and Willett 1994). For students consuming previously designed hypermedia environments, the patterns for preferred methods of navigation have also been found to differ (Horney and Anderson-Inman 1994).

Eighth-grade field independent students have been shown to learn computer ethics more effectively than their field dependent peers regardless of whether advance organizers or structural organizers were present (Weller, Repman, and Rooze 1994, 1995). Scores for the field dependent students were highest when the structural organizers were absent. Examinations of the pathways taken by the two learning style groups showed that the learners chose different methods for seeking information and the data suggest that field dependent students may be more affected by the presence or absence of advance organizers and structural organizers.

Much of the sparse hypermedia and learning style research has shown no significant differences in performance for learning style groups examined (Ayersman 1994; Liu and Reed 1994; Overbaugh 1995). When significant differences have been found, there have typically been qualifications. In one study, significant differences were found using a text-only form of the treatment (Wey and Waugh 1993). In some studies the treatment has been very brief (Weller,

Repman, and Lan 1993) or the sample size has been insufficiently small (Wang and Jonassen 1993).

As the many various individual differences come into consideration, the development of a hypermedia instructional program that addresses them all begins to border on intelligent tutoring systems and artificial intelligence. Research has shown that active-learning and passive-learning students differentially interact with hypermedia software and that active learners are more apt to spend more time on task, more frequently view video and other information sources, and, as a result, tend to achieve more than passive learners within such an environment (Yung-Bin 1992). To overcome this, one could foresee more active prompts and cues on the part of the software program as it attempts to elicit more active participation on the part of the learner. The interface for hypermedia systems will change in this direction.

Analysis of Systems

In 1991, Kozma stated that there was little research on hypertext to date and that, of the studies that had been done, the focus was more on rudimentary functions of hypertext and relatively simple tasks rather than on learning or problem solving. It is now five years later, and a focus on investigating the distinct attributes of hypermedia still exists. This is not necessarily a negative observation. While there are numerous studies that have explored features and attributes of hypermedia systems without factoring in learning or performance, other studies have begun to link these analytic investigations with performance. Important insight is derived from both areas of the literature in regard to optimal design structures of hypermedia systems. Greater understanding of hypermedia systems and of human learning systems has resulted. For the most part, this category of research on hypermedia-based learning (Systems analyses) is devoted to examinations of pathways, navigational preferences, and node and link structures.

Harmon and Dinsmore (1994) evaluated how graduate students chose to link nodes of information within a hypermedia system using subject matter pertaining to the Holy Lands in the Middle East. They found that students identified eight types of links. Insight gained from such studies is particularly helpful for authors of hypermedia software in that it reveals probable mechanisms and options that learners might most likely use. An interesting outcome from the Harmon and Dinsmore study was that subjects tended to describe the video nodes as detrimental to their purposeful thinking. To explain this disruption to the subjects' thought processes, the authors suggested that the video clips may have been too lengthy; they lasted from 45 seconds to 120 seconds in duration. Perhaps the main point, however, is that individuals chose various linking mechanisms and that not all individuals processed and categorized the information uniformly.

Students differentially structure the knowledge that they gain through learning with and about hypermedia systems (Ayersman 1995). Moreover, the type of hypermedia software influences how students apply theoretical models to specific features of the software (Ayersman and Reed 1995). When examining the pathways chosen by undergraduate students using a hypermedia program based upon their background experiences with computers, Reed and Giessler (1995) found that some types

of experiences are better predictors of nonlinear pathways while others are better predictors of linear ones. One might then conclude that having both options available could conceivably accommodate a greater diversity of learner preferences.

Regardless of the type of node and link organization used for information within a hypermedia program, context should be the deciding factor for links among nodes of information. Often, this creates the need for multiple paths to a single node and the allowance of nonlinear organizations of information. Consensus has not yet been reached as to the number and type of possible structures within a hypermedia environment. There is growing support for a four-quadrant matrix of possible information structures (Ayersman 1994; Ayersman and Reed 1995; Reed, Ayersman, and Liu, in press), but research exists that has utilized other formats. The development of common fundamental structures might be beneficial to both software developers and learners. The benefit will be that a common understanding of options will then be available to both users and developers of hypermedia.

Performance

The advent of hypermedia requires reconfiguring students for the nonlinear possibilities it offers (Landow 1992). Because of this, achieving positive gains in student performance from implementations of hypermedia treatments is not necessarily an immediate result. The fundamental difference between structuring information in linear and nonlinear organizations can require adaptation on the part of the learner. Traditional organizations of information (linear) have persisted for quite some time and to expect students to quickly adapt to nonlinear organizations might be unrealistic. Studies comparing the two structures of information in a computer environment have generally found that nonlinear structures can result in initially lower levels of achievement for some students until they become comfortable and proficient with hypertext formats (Schroeder 1994). For example, Ayersman (1995) found that students completing a 15-week course in hypermedia did not necessarily progress toward choosing nonlinear formats for representing their knowledge structures even though clear gains in hypermedia knowledge were evident.

Consumers of Hypermedia

When hypermedia software is commercially developed or made by the teacher, the role of the student is typically to interact with the program in a somewhat limited fashion. Although many options may be available to the user of the program, the information portrayed by the program is already organized and selectively limited by the creator of the software. In many ways this can be a tremendous benefit to the student who requires structure imposed on the information to be studied. Knowing when to impose structure and when to allow learner control makes the development of hypermedia software sufficiently difficult. Applying such programs to various age levels of learning can not just enhance the process of learning, but it can also lead to the development of more effective hypermedia software as we quickly realize what works and what does not.

Pre-collegiate Consumers

There is not a great deal of research for applications of hypermedia with children in kindergarten through grade 12. This may be partially because teachers of these grade-levels are seldom engaged in publishing the results of the action-research that they engage in daily. Based on the available research, K–12 students seem to benefit from using hypermedia in a variety of ways.

Deep comprehension is promoted by the use of Multimedia Environments that Organize and Support Text (MOST) for at-risk kindergarten children (Mayfield-Stewart et al. 1994). Listening comprehension, story production, and decoding skills are enhanced as well. Hypermedia programs are effective at teaching third-graders effective study skills and strategies (Temme 1991). Using 80 fourth-grade students and two forms of a hypertext social studies program, Mack (1995) found no significant effects for performance or attitudes between the two treatments, indicating that both groups increased similarly.

Low-ability students have traditionally been one group of students that finds computer-assisted instruction beneficial. A three-year longitudinal study using hypermedia software to provide reading lessons for 300 K–3 students found that low-ability subjects realized significantly higher levels of achievement than did control students (Boone and Higgens 1993).

As previously discussed, the technological transformation that brings us hypermedia is operating hand-in-hand with a pedagogical transformation that more often targets innovative approaches for instruction. Addressing both of these areas, fifth graders who worked collaboratively using Jostens mathematics software performed significantly higher on a posttest achievement measure than peer students working individually (Brush 1996).

Moore-Hart (1995) examined the effects of a hypermedia program (*Multicultural Links*) on fourth- and fifth-grade students vocabulary development; reading and writing performance; and attitudes toward writing, culture, and computers. She used comparison groups to examine whether students using *Multicultural Links* and the *Multicultural Literacy Program* would increase their reading comprehension, vocabulary, and attitudes more than groups of students using either the *Multicultural Literacy Program* or traditional reading programs. Descriptively examining the mean scores and gain scores of the three groups revealed that the students using the *Multicultural Literacy Program* with computers outperformed the other two groups in reading performance and vocabulary development.

Hypermedia applications are effective for increasing seventh- and eighth-grade students' abilities to discover links among people, places, events, and issues within historical contexts while developing clearer and more empathic understanding (Swan 1994). Kinzer, Hasselbring, Schmidt, and Meltzer (1990) found that video-based anchors are effective for learning disabled language arts students to acquire writing and comprehension skills.

Collegiate Consumers

In a self-report study using 168 undergraduate students, two-thirds of the students reported that they learned more when multimedia presentation materials were used as compared to traditional lecture materials (Pearson, Folske, Paulsen, and Burggraf 1994). The remaining one-third of the students were neutral, and there was no apparent relationship to the students' styles of learning and their preferences for multimedia presentations over lecture. Students representing all learning style types were present in both the two-thirds who favored multimedia and the one-third who remained neutral.

Educational Psychology students receiving instruction augmented by a hypermedia-based program created by the instructor used more research and theory to support their analyses, and they integrated their presentations of observation and theory better than those students in the traditional course (Delclos and Hartman 1993). Engaging students in a multimedia program employing concept maps and hypertext to teach *Hamlet* resulted in higher performance levels for the experimental group than for the control group (Barnes 1994). Hypermedia software has been shown effective for undergraduate remedial math students' success solving math word problems (Henry 1995).

Overbaugh (1995) examined the efficacy of interactive video for teaching classroom management skills to preservice teachers. Participants used an interactive video computer-based simulation program that combined a commercial videodisc that had been repurposed to correspond to a *HyperCard* program developed by the author. He found that students significantly had improved achievement scores following the three-hour treatment.

Fitzgerald (1995) examined the effects of an interactive video program on classroom observation skills. She had students use the program in one of two ways: either as a teaching tool or as a learning tool. She found that the interactive video program was more effective in developing classroom observation skills for special education graduate students when used within independent, learner-controlled conditions.

Chen (1993) developed two interactive multimedia systems to teach preservice educators basic classroom teaching skills and classroom management. Students were found to improve their knowledge, understanding, and confidence for both areas while boosting their sense of preparedness to enter the teaching profession.

Undergraduate students have been shown to significantly increase their Spanish proficiency by using hypermedia-based learning materials within a 16-week course (Toro 1995). When these students' gains in proficiency were examined based on learning style, using the Group Embedded Figures Test, the two groups of students were found to learn differentially. That is, field independent students tended to prefer different learning strategies and methods of accessing and organizing the same information used by the field dependent students. Field independent students scored significantly higher than the field dependent students (Toro).

A hypermedia-based learning tool used for teaching inferential statistics was compared to graduate students using non-computer-based learning tools for performance scores and time needed to complete the exercise (McCoy 1994). She found no significant differences for the two groups on performance score or for time needed to complete the exercise. There were also no significant differences in participants' perception of helpfulness of the materials used, aid in improving understanding of statistics, or improvement in confidence in either immediate or future decisions. There was a significant difference in participants' perception of ease of use of the materials; however,

the *HyperCard* group reported their materials as easier to use than those who used traditional paper (McCoy).

A study using three computer simulations, involving interactive text and graphics with nonlinear navigational possibilities, to teach computer science students computer architecture examined student achievement and differences among ability groups (DeNardo and Pyzdrowski 1992). Using quality point averages within computer science to distinguish low-, medium-, and high-ability groups, the study found that the simulators were beneficial to all three groups for increasing performance levels, but that it was particularly beneficial for those in the low- and medium-ability groups.

Combining the two categories of Analysis of systems and Performance, Lidwell, Palumbo, and Troutman (1994) examined types of interfaces for hypermedia systems and the effect on students' performance on a measure of their knowledge of Doppler Effect. Thirty-six college students were randomly assigned to either the global interface group or the local interface group. The global interface design consisted of a two-dimensional map displaying links and their respective semantic relationships with nodes providing additional hypermedia sequences of information. The local interface design represented only two nodes from the network at a time. The general difference in the two interface designs was that global interface users were able to view the entire map and all of its correctly identified links and nodes while the local interface design required the users to select the correct relationship to identify it as correct; their view was limited to partial aspects of the overall map. The global interface group experienced a significant decrease in performance, while the local interface group significantly increased their performance scores on the Doppler Effect measure. The authors interpreted this outcome as an indication that depth of knowledge (local interface design) was more helpful on the performance measure than breadth of knowledge (global interface design).

Not all of the research has shown results favorable to the use of hypermedia with college-age students. Using a sample of 212 undergraduate special education students, comparisons have been made between groups receiving class lecture alone and those receiving class lecture in combination with either hypertext-based instructional programs or linear drill-and-practice programs (Rojewski, Gilbert, and Hoy 1994). That no significant differences were found for academic achievement or problem-solving ability indicates that hypermedia treatments are no less effective than nonhypermedia treatments. Supporting the notion that a lifetime of linear-style learning experiences is difficult to overcome, students in this study preferred the linear-style program to the hypertext approach.

Azevedo, Shaw, and Bret (1995) utilized hypermedia tutorials for radiology education over an eight-month period for a group of 12 students while a second group of 12 students received lectures on the same subject material. Posttest comparisons indicated no significant differences in the two instructional conditions.

When adults use hypertext with the goal of answering specific questions, different hypertext reading strategies are developed by successful and unsuccessful users. Successful readers more often choose only the most important nodes to read and then spend more time read-

ing them, a depth-first approach, while less successful adults traverse more nodes and spend less time on each, a breadth-first approach (Gillingham 1993). These strategies are similar to those evidenced by Bazerman (1985) using physicists and simple printed text. The participants read parts of the text, skimmed, jumped, reread, and generally traversed the material in nonlinear ways while selectively attending to relevant sections. A combination of prior experience and domain knowledge causes each learner's preferences to be somewhat different as he or she consumes hypermedia-based information. Having a variety of options available for the learner can be even more beneficial for some than others.

Gretes and Green (1994) compared the use of a multimedia adult literacy instructional program to traditional classroom instruction by replacing conventional learning tools with multimedia materials. For low-literacy adults, the multimedia software group surpassed those who had used nonmultimedia materials. In numerous studies, there is evidence that low-ability students and certain learning style groups perform better when their preferences are accommodated. Providing semantic descriptors for the links used within a hypermedia-based learning system can significantly improve adult learners' performance scores while also resulting in more positive attitudes toward the system used (Zhao, O'Shea, and Fung 1994).

In summary, using hypermedia in a manner that places the student in the role of consumer has shown significantly positive effects on performance. This is true for both age-level groupings. Apparently, even when results do not significantly favor hypermedia formats, they tend to show no significant differences. Overall, this can be interpreted as meaning that hypermedia treatments are no less effective than other methods of instruction. In a majority of cases, however, hypermedia has been shown to result in significantly higher levels of performance in a variety of content areas for college-age students.

Producers of Hypermedia

Producing robust hypermedia programs requires skills in many areas. The creator(s) of the software must have knowledge of learning theory, instructional design, and the software/hardware being used. Few educators possess all of the requisite skills for producing commercial-quality hypermedia programs. Fortunately, this does not pose the problem that one might initially expect. The fact that individuals rarely possess the sum of these requisite skills provides a fundamental opportunity for collaborative endeavors that often leads to cross-disciplinary projects. One teacher's curricular materials rarely match the needs of another teacher. The particular needs of these instructors qualify them for developing hypermedia-based learning materials that incorporate their preexisting materials while supplementing them with additional information based on various media forms that may have been previously inaccessible. An increasing number of instructors are converting course materials to digital formats that are suited to hypermedia-based environments and are then consolidating and possibly distributing these materials on CD-ROM. However, the time, energy, and planning involved in this approach generally provides a disincentive to most educators, who might prefer to spend their time addressing only the most immediate concerns of their profession. Using commercial or teacher-made hypermedia software focuses on only one attribute of hypermedia—its merit as a tutor for students. Computer-based instruction is generally recognized as offering three functional roles to educators. Computers and, thus, hypermedia can serve as a tool, a tutor, and as a tutee. It is the role of tutee that these former approaches overlook. Active learning theory, constructivism, constructionism, and many other theories of learning that have at their core the axiom that learning is doing are particularly suited to using hypermedia in the role of tutee.

Pre-collegiate Producers

Introducing students to hypermedia educational technologies is not just highly successful for supporting learning, but it also promotes small-group interactions and allows for the development of original projects reflective of the groups' collaboration (Wilson and Tally 1991). A descriptive qualitative study examining fourth-grade students' methods of expression using both hypermedia and using paper and pencil indicated that a single media format (paper and pencil) limits students' ability to convey insight and individuality (Riddle 1995). The same students were found to develop new ideas and more actively engage in peer collaboration when using hypermedia software. The students showed greater descriptive detail, unique perspectives, and more diversity among backgrounds, interest, and skills when using the hypermedia software to create and add graphics, animation, and sound to their textual communications.

Toomey and Ketterer (1995) conducted a case study in which they observed three elementary teachers using hypermedia as a tool for students to construct knowledge. Their observations indicated that the introduction of hypermedia into the classroom as a tool for students to use in their learning created a classroom context in which the instructors' roles were somewhat changed. Teachers adopted constructivist learning approaches and became "influential mediators and facilitators by working collaboratively with the other mediators in the room, namely other children and technology" (Toomey and Ketterer, 480).

McLellan (1992) explored how fifth graders adapted to the nonlinear structures of information presented by way of *HyperCard*. The students interacted with previously developed software and then began to develop their own stories utilizing *HyperCard* and working in two-person teams. Her results show that children can quickly adapt to the nonlinear structures offered by *HyperCard*. Admittedly, this does not occur without practice at designing stories for a hypertext medium and training in the features of story structure. Gaining insight into the analysis of stories at the level of detail present through hypertext productions maximizes the nonlinear features of hypermedia.

A descriptive study of ninth-grade American History students who worked collaboratively on hypermedia software projects revealed dramatic decreases in off-task behaviors when introduced to constructivist learning with hypermedia (Lehrer, Erickson, and Connell 1994). Based on measurements of these students' self-reports of their perceptions of the design process, they also emphasized higher level skills while identifying positive aspects of the design process including: a. mental effort and involvement, b. interest, c. planning, d. collaboration,

and e. individualization. The skills gained by these students went beyond content-area knowledge and abilities with the hypermedia authoring software to include abilities of finding and interpreting information, articulating and communicating knowledge, and using computers as cognitive tools. The students progressed to the creation of complex hypermedia documents of history while engaging in deeper explorations of the content and substantive conversations with peers. As a result of the experience, students began to see themselves as authors of knowledge as they completed the hypermedia projects.

Reed and Rosenbluth (1995) used hypermedia with high school seniors to teach humanities, science, and technology subjects. The students experienced significant increases in number of values, number of social reforms, and number of events relating to the humanities (Reed and Rosenbluth). The students also showed significantly more detailed concept maps as a result of the treatment.

The benefits of using hypermedia as a knowledge construction tool are numerous and go well beyond gaining content area expertise. Students work cooperatively and without teacher supervision to search out and remember science materials during multimedia-based instruction (Beichner 1994). Using hypermedia to construct individual and small group projects, K–12 students admit not only to learning the content of science and mathematics, but also to gaining technological expertise (Volker 1992). In this project, teachers' roles became that of providing resources and clarifying questions of content. Again, we find that concurrent changes in the means and in the method coincide most effectively.

Collegiate Producers

Surprisingly, the amount of research that examines college-age students using hypermedia as a knowledge construction tool is minimal in comparison to the much larger group of research using this age-level group as consumers of hypermedia. While some treatments have involved opportunities for students to act initially as a consumer of hypermedia and later as a producer of hypermedia, more treatments have not.

It is generally accepted that programming languages can be effective for increasing problem-solving skills. With the advent of hypermedia and authoring languages, Reed and Liu (1994) investigated the comparative effects of programming versus authoring language instruction on problem-solving skills, computer anxiety, and performance. While problem-solving skills significantly increased for the group learning BASIC programming, the *HyperCard* group did not show a significant increase. Computer anxiety significantly decreased for both groups, and the *HyperCard* group outperformed the BASIC group on both of the performance measures, but the authors suggested that the ease of use for *HyperCard* might simplify programming/authoring so much that critical thinking processes required for problem-solving skills did not occur. It is important to note that this ease of use enabled the *HyperCard* group to achieve higher levels of performance than the BASIC group (Reed and Liu).

Although the research is limited, having students construct hypermedia software has benefits beyond increases in performance or attitude. Students begin to learn both content area information and social skills as they cooperate in teams to collaboratively develop hyper-media software. Finding that construction of hypermedia is easier for students than programming languages provides encouragement for using hypermedia as a knowledge construction tool. There is an obvious need for a greater research emphasis in this area.

Summary

Despite the fact that hypermedia is relatively new as an educational tool, the research results to date appear very promising. As the interface becomes more user friendly and as progressive technological changes occur, it can be expected that hypermedia will gain ground as a commonly used tool in classrooms. The merger between hypermedia and computer-mediated communications seems imminent and in many cases has already begun. As this change continues, the balance of power between user and developer can be expected to more closely resemble equality.

Negroponte (1995) explained that the multimodal nature of an effective computer interface would have many different and concurrent channels of communication, "through which the user could express and cull meaning from a number of different sensory devices (the user's and the machine's). Or, equally important, one channel of communication might provide the information missing in the other" (98). Largely, the hypermedia research results are consistent with Paivio's dual-coding theory (Mayer and Anderson 1992) in that this deliberate multimodal redundancy is proving effective for accommodating various learners' needs in a hypermedia environment.

Hypermedia is at least as effective as lecture, and this is especially so for remedial and learning disability students

(Higgins and Boone 1992). Comparisons of hypermedia treatments to lecture no longer seem to warrant a research focus. Investigations of specific types of hypermedia treatments and various individual differences still offer many questions to be answered as the most effective structures of information within a hypermedia system are not yet conclusively known.

Although teachers are more frequently engaging students in exercises and projects that involve creating hypermedia software reflecting the content areas, clearly the majority of research centering on performance has originated from teachers using hypermedia as a tool for information/knowledge presentation and representation rather than construction. Although the quality of commercial hypermedia software can be expected to improve, there are added benefits to using hypermedia as a knowledge construction tool that certainly warrant a more solid basis in the research.

An often overlooked benefit of teachers using hypermedia in their teaching is that frequently action research has resulted. Authentic classroom-based research that educators find most directly applicable to their profession is being conducted with hypermedia treatments; because of this, the findings are that much more meaningful to them. If hypermedia is promoting this type of research activity, it is a tremendous bonus when coupled with the promotion of more positive attitudes and perceptions, the accommodation of individual differences, the development of more clarity of the learning process, and increases in performance. Combine the many positive outcomes evident in this review, and there are numerous advantages and benefits to incorporating hypermedia as a tool for teaching and learning.

Future Research

In spite of the promising findings evident in this review, there are many areas in need of additional research. Some age-level groups used in this study have had very little research focus. If we were to examine individual content areas, there would certainly be many more gaps in the research. Having seen where the research has taken us, we can now more ably direct its future. With so many areas to examine and so many wonderful developments occurring so frequently, the research on hypermedia-based learning promises to be a very interesting place to invest one's research interest and energy.   ❖

References

Ayersman, D. J. "Cognitive Psychology and Hypermedia: Merging the Disciplines." Ph.D. diss., West Virginia University, 1994.

Ayersman, D. J. "Effects of Knowledge Representation Format and Hypermedia Instruction on Metacognitive Accuracy." *Computers in Human Behavior* 11, no. 3/4 (1995): 533–55.

Ayersman, D. J., and W. M. Reed. "The Impact of Instructional Design and Hypermedia Software Type on Graduate Students' Use of Theoretical Models." *Computers in Human Behavior* 11, no. 3/4 (1995): 557–80.

Azevedo, R., S. G. Shaw, and P. M. Bret. "The Effectiveness of Computer-based Hypermedia Teaching Modules for Radiology Students." Paper presented at the annual meeting of the American Educational Research Association, San Francisco, CA, April 1995. ERIC, ED 385187.

Barnes, W. G. "Constructing Knowledge from an Ill-structured Domain: Testing a Multimedia *Hamlet*." Paper presented at the annual meeting of the American Educational Research Association, New Orleans, LA, April 1994. ERIC, ED 372743.

Bazerman, C. "Physicists Reading Physics." *Written Communication* 2, no. 1 (1985): 3–23.

Becker, D. A., and M. M. Dwyer. "Using Hypermedia to Provide Learner Control." *Journal of Educational Multimedia and Hypermedia* 3, no. 2 (1994): 155–72.

Beichner, R. J. "Multimedia Editing to Promote Science Learning." *Journal of Computers in Mathematics and Science Teaching* 13, no. 2 (1994): 147–62.

Boone, R., and K. Higgens. "Hypermedia Basal Readers: Three Years of School-based Research." *Journal of Special Education Technology* 12, no. 28 (1993): 86–106.

Borras, I., and R. C. Lafayette. "Effects of Multimedia Courseware Subtitling on the Speaking Performance of College Students of French." *Modern Language Journal* 78, no. 1 (1994): 61–75.

Braswell, R., and J. Brown. "Use of Interactive Videodisc Technology in a Physical Education Methods Class." Paper presented at the annual meeting of the American Educational Research Association, San Francisco, CA, April 1992. ERIC, ED 348936.

Brush, T. A. "The Effects on Student Achievement and Attitudes When Utilizing Cooperative Learning with ILS-delivered Instruction." Paper presented at the annual meeting of the Eastern Educational Research Association, Cambridge, MA, February 1996.

Burton, J. K., M. Moore, and G. A. Holmes. "Hypermedia Concepts and Research: An Overview." *Computers in Human Behavior* 11, no. 3/4 (1995): 345–69.

Chen, A. Y. "The Use of Interactive Multimedia Systems to Improve the Learning of Classroom Practices." *Education Research and Perspectives* 20, no. 2 (1993): 24–32.

Covey, P. "A Right to Die?: The Case of Dax Cowart." Paper presented at the annual meeting of the American Educational Research Association, Boston, MA, April 1990.

Daiute, C., and F. Morse. "Access to Knowledge and Expression: Multimedia Writing Tools for Students with Diverse Needs and Strengths." *Journal of Special Education Technology* 12, no. 3 (1994): 221–56.

Delclos, V. R., and A. Hartman. "The Impact of an Interactive Multimedia System on the Quality of Learning in Educational Psychology: An Exploratory Study." *Journal of Research on Computing in Education* 26, no. 1 (1993): 83–93.

DeNardo, A. M., and A. S. Pyzdrowski. "The Effects of Teaching a Hypothetical Computer Architecture with Computer Simulators." Paper presented at the annual meeting of the Eastern Educational Research Association, Hilton Head, SC, March 1992. ERIC, ED 351000.

Ellis, D., J. Furner-Hines, and P. Willett. "The Creation of Hypertext Links in Full-text Documents." *Journal of Documentation* 50, no. 2 (1994): 67–98.

Finkelman, K., and C. McMunn. *MicroWorlds as a Publishing Tool for Cooperative Groups: An Affective Study* Report No. 143. Charlottesville, VA: Curry School of Education, University of Virginia, 1995. ERIC, ED 384344.

Fitzgerald, G. E. "The Effects of an Interactive Videodisc Training Program in Classroom Observation Skills Used as a Teaching Tool and as a Learning Tool." *Computers in Human Behavior* 11, no. 3/4 (1995): 467–79.

Frey, D., and M. Simonson. "Assessment of Cognitive Style to Examine Students' Use of Hypermedia within Historic Costume." *Home Economics Research Journal* 21, no. 4 (1993): 403–21.

Gillingham, M. G. "Effects of Question Complexity and Reader Strategies on Adults' Hypertext Comprehension." *Journal of Research on Computing in Education* 26, no. 1 (1993): 1–15.

Gordon, S., and V. Lewis. "Enhancing Hypertext Documents to Support Learning from Text." *Technical Communication* 39, no. 2 (1992): 305–8.

Gretes, J. A., and M. Green. "The Effect of Interactive CD-ROM/Digitized Audio Courseware on Reading among Low-literate Adults." *Computers in the Schools* 11, no. 2 (1994): 27–42.

Harmon, S. W., and S. H. Dinsmore. "Novice Linking in Hypermedia-based Instructional Systems." *Computers in the Schools* 10, no. 1/2 (1994): 155–70.

Henry, M. J. "Remedial Math Students' Navigation Patterns through Hypermedia Software." *Computers in Human Behavior* 11, no. 3/4 (1995): 481–93.

Higgins, K., and R. Boone. "Hypermedia Computer Study Guides for Social Studies: Adapting a Canadian History Text." *Social Education* 56, no. 3 (1992): 154–59.

Holland, J., K. Holyoak, R. Nisbett, and P. Thagard. *Induction: Processes of Inference, Learning, and Discovery*. Cambridge, MA: MIT Press, 1986.

Horney, M. A., and L. Anderson-Inman. "The Electrotext Project: Hypertext Reading Patterns of Middle School Students." *Journal of Educational Multimedia and Hypermedia* 3, no. 1 (1994): 71–91.

Hsi, S., and A. M. Agogino. "The Impact and Instructional Benefit of Using Multimedia Case Studies to Teach Engineering Design." *Journal of Educational Multimedia and Hypermedia* 3, no. 3/4 (1994): 351–76.

Hsu, T. E., F. J. Frederick, and M. L. Chung. "Effects of Learner Cognitive Styles and Metacognitive Tools on Information Acquisition Paths and Learning in Hyperspace Environments." Paper presented at the national convention of the Association for Educational Communications and Technology, Nashville, TN, February 1994. ERIC, ED 373721.

Jacobson, M. J., and R. J. Spiro. *Hypertext Learning Environments, Cognitive Flexibility, and the Transfer of Complex Knowledge: An Empirical Investigation* Report No. 573. Urbana, IL: Center for the Study of Learning, 1993. ERIC, ED 355508.

Kim, E., and M. F. Young. "Multimedia Football Viewing: Embedded Rules, Practice, and Video Context in IVD Procedural Learning." Paper presented at the annual meeting of the Northeast Educational Research Association, Ellenville, NY, October 1991. ERIC, ED 345705.

Kinzer, C. K., T. S. Hasselbring, C. A. Schmidt, and L. Meltzer. "Effects of Multimedia to Enhance Writing Ability." Paper presented at the annual meeting of the American Educational Research Association, Boston, MA, April 1990. ERIC, ED 318030.

Kizzier, D., J. Ford, and C. Pollard. "Perceived Appropriateness of Technologically Mediated Systems in Educational and Business Learning Environments." *Delta Pi Epsilon Journal* 36, no. 1 (1994): 32–48.

Kozma, R. B. "Learning with Media." *Review of Educational Research* 61, no. 2 (1991): 179–211.

Landow, G. P. "Hypertext, Metatext, and the Electronic Canon." In *Literacy Online: The Promise (and Peril) of Reading and Writing with Computers,* edited by M. C. Tuman, 67–94. Pittsburgh: University of Pittsburgh Press, 1992.

Large, A., J. Beheshti, A. Breuleux, and A. Renaud. "Multimedia and Comprehension: The Relationship among Text, Animation, and Captions." *Journal of the American Society for Information Science* 46, no. 5 (1995): 340–47.

Leader, L. F., and J. D. Klein. "The Effects of Search Tool and Cognitive Style on Performance in Hypermedia Database Searches." Paper presented at the national convention of the Association for Educational Communications and Technology, Nashville, TN, February 1994. ERIC, ED 373729.

Lehrer, R., J. Erickson, and T. Connell. "Learning by Designing Hypermedia Documents." *Computers in the Schools* 10, no. 1/2 (1994): 227–54.

Lidwell, W. M., D. B. Palumbo, and T. Troutman. "Promoting Learning through Hypermedia: Local Versus Global Interfaces." *Computers in the Schools* 10, no. 1/2 (1994): 189–98.

Lin, C. H., and G. Davidson. "Effects of Linking Structure and Cognitive Style on Students' Performance and Attitude in a Computer-based Hypertext Environment." Paper presented at the national convention of the Association for Educational Communications and Technology, Nashville, TN, February 1994. ERIC, ED 373734.

Lin, X., T. J. Newby, and W. T. Foster. "Embedding Metacognitive Cues into Hypermedia Systems to Promote Far Transfer Problem Solving." Paper presented at the national convention of the Association for Educational Communications and Technology, Nashville, TN, February 1994. ERIC, ED 373735.

Liu, M., D. J. Ayersman, and W. M. Reed. "Perceptions of a Hypermedia Environment." *Computers in Human Behavior* 11, no. 3/4 (1995): 411–28.

Liu, M., and W. M. Reed. "The Relationship between the Learning Strategies and Learning Styles in a Hypermedia Environment." *Computers in Human Behavior* 10, no. 4 (1994): 419–34.

Mack, M. "Linear and Nonlinear Hypertext in Elementary School Classroom Instruction." Paper presented at the national convention of the Association for Educational Communications and Technology, Anaheim, CA, February 1995. ERIC, ED 383324.

Maddux, C. D. "Multimedia, Hypermedia, and the Culture of Schooling." *Computers in the Schools* 10, no. 1/2 (1994): 21–26.

Marrison, D. L., and M. J. Frick. "The Effect of Agricultural Students' Learning Styles on Academic Achievement and Their Perceptions of Two Methods of Instruction." *Journal of Agricultural Education* 35, no. 1 (1994): 26–30.

Mayer, R. E., and R. B. Anderson. "The Instructive Animation: Helping Students Build Connections between Words and Pictures in Multimedia Learning." *Journal of Educational Psychology* 84, no. 4 (1992): 444–52.

Mayer, R. E., and V. K. Sims. "For Whom Is a Picture Worth a Thousand Words? Extensions of a Dual-coding Theory of Multimedia Learning." *Journal of Educational Psychology* 86, no. 3 (1994): 389–401.

Mayfield-Stewart, C., P. Moore, D. Sharp, F. Brophy, T. Hasselbring, S. R. Goldman, and J. Bransford. "Evaluation of Multimedia Instruction on Learning and Transfer." Paper presented at the annual meeting of the American Educational Research Association, New Orleans, LA, April 1994. ERIC, ED 375166.

McCorduck, P. "How We Knew, How We Know, How We Will Know." In *Literacy Online: The Promise (and Peril) of Reading and Writing with Computers*, edited by M. C. Tuman, 245–59. Pittsburgh: University of Pittsburgh Press, 1992.

McCoy, L. P. "Decisions in Inferential Statistics with *HyperCard*: Design and Field Test." *Computers in the Schools* 10, no. 1/2 (1994): 69–77.

McKillip, J., and K. Baldwin. "Evaluation of an STD Education Media Campaign: A Control Construct Design." *Evaluation Review* 14, no. 4 (1990): 331–46.

McLellan, H. "Narrative and Episodic Story Structure in Interactive Stories." Paper presented at the annual meeting of the Association for Educational Communications and Technology, Washington, DC, February 1992. ERIC, ED 348012.

Moore-Hart, M. A. "The Effects of Multicultural Links on Reading and Writing Performance and Cultural Awareness of Fourth and Fifth Graders." *Computers in Human Behavior* 11, no. 3/4 (1995): 391–410.

Myers, R. J., and J. K. Burton. "The Foundations of Hypermedia: Concepts and History." *Computers in the Schools* 10, no. 1/2 (1994): 9–20.

Negroponte, N. *Being Digital.* New York: Vintage, 1995.

Nelson, W. A. "Efforts to Improve Computer-based Instruction: The Role of Knowledge Representation and Knowledge Construction in Hypermedia Systems." *Computers in the Schools* 10, no. 3/4 (1994): 371–401.

Nelson, W. A., and D. B. Palumbo. "Learning, Instruction, and Hypermedia." *Journal of Educational Multimedia and Hypermedia* 1, no. 3 (1992): 287–99.

Ottaviani, B. F., and J. B. Black. "The Effects of Multimedia Presentation Formats on the Spatial Recall of a Narrative." Paper presented at the national convention of the Association for Educational Communications and Technology, Nashville, TN, February 1994. ERIC, ED 373772.

Overbaugh, R. C. "An Example of Software Development and Authoring with *HyperCard*: Creating an Interactive Video Simulation for Teaching Basic Principles of Classroom Management." *Computers in the Schools* 10, no. 3/4 (1994): 313–38.

Overbaugh, R. C. "The Efficacy of Interactive Video for Teaching Basic Classroom Management Skills to Preservice Teachers." *Computers in Human Behavior* 11 no. 3/4 (1995): 511–27.

Paivio, A. *Imagery and Verbal Processes.* Hillsdale, NJ: Lawrence Erlbaum, 1979.

Paivio, A. *Mental Representations: A Dual-coding Approach.* New York: Oxford University Press, 1986.

Palumbo, D. B., and A. B. Bermudez. "Using Hypermedia to Assist Language Minority Learners in Achieving Academic Success." *Computers in the Schools* 10, no. 1/2 (1994): 171–88.

Pearson, M., J. Folske, D. Paulsen, and C. Burggraf. "The Relationship between Student Perceptions of the Multimedia Classroom and Student Learning Styles." Paper presented at the annual meeting of the Eastern Communication Association, Washington, DC, April 1994. ERIC, ED 374482.

Reed, W. M., D. J. Ayersman, and M. Liu. "The Effect of Hypermedia Instruction on Stages of Concern of Students with Varying Authoring Language and Prior Hypermedia Experience." *Journal of Research on Computing in Education* 27, no. 3 (1995a): 297–317.

Reed, W. M., D. J. Ayersman, and M. Liu. "The Effects of Students' Computer-based Prior Experiences and Instructional Exposures on the Application of Hypermedia-related Mental Models." *Journal of Educational Computing Research* (1996).

Reed, W. M., D. J. Ayersman, and M. Liu. "The Effects of Three Different Hypermedia Courses on Students' Attitudes." *Computers in Human Behavior* 11, no. 3/4 (1995b): 495–509.

Reed, W. M., J. R. Ervin, and J. M. Oughton. "Prior Computer Experience, Learning Style, and Linear Versus Nonlinear Navigation in a Hypermedia Environment: Comparison of Low- and High-experience Users." Paper presented at the annual meeting of the Eastern Educational Research Association, Cambridge, MA, February 1996.

Reed, W. M., and S. F. Giessler. "Prior Computer-related Experiences and Hypermedia Metacognition." *Computers in Human Behavior* 11, no. 3/4 (1995): 581–600.

Reed, W. M., and M. Liu. "The Comparative Effects of BASIC Programming Versus *HyperCard* Programming on Problem Solving, Computer Anxiety, and Performance." *Computers in the Schools* 10, no. 1/2 (1994): 27–46.

Reed, W. M., and G. S. Rosenbluth. "The Effects of *HyperCard* Authoring on Knowledge Acquisition and Assimilation." *Computers in Human Behavior* 11, no. 3/4 (1995): 605–18.

Riddle, E. M. *Communication through Multimedia in an Elementary Classroom* Report No. 143. Charlottesville, VA: Curry School of Education, University of Virginia, 1995. ERIC, ED 384346.

Rojewski, J. W., J. P. Gilbert, and C. A. Hoy. "Effects of a Hypertext Computer Program on Academic Performance in a Special Education Course for Nonmajors." *Teacher Education and Special Education* 17, no. 4 (1994): 249–59.

Schroeder, E. E. "Navigating through Hypertext: Navigational Technique, Individual Differences, and Learning." Paper presented at the national convention of the Association for Educational Communications and Technology, Nashville, TN, February 1994. ERIC, ED 373760.

Stanton, N. A., and C. Baber. "The Myth of Navigating in Hypertext: How a 'Bandwagon' Has Lost Its Course." *Journal of Educational Multimedia and Hypermedia* 3, no. 3/4 (1994): 235–49.

Stevens, S. "Intelligent Interactive Video Simulation of a Code Inspection." *Communications of the ACM* 32, no. 7 (1989): 832–43.

Swan, K. "History, Hypermedia, and Criss-crossed Conceptual Landscapes." *Journal of Educational Multimedia and Hypermedia* 3, no. 2 (1994): 120–39.

Temme, D. L. *A Computer Approach to Teach Study Skills to Third Grade Students and Parents* Report No. 143. Fort Lauderdale, FL: Nova University, 1991. ERIC, ED 343600.

Thompson, D. R. "The Digital Daily: How Will Readers React?" Paper presented at the national meeting of the Association for Education in Journalism and Mass Communication, Gainesville, FL, March 1995. ERIC, ED 380840.

Thompson, D. R. "New Technology and the Newspaper of the Future: Some Effects of Modality, Story Type, and Search Experience on Information Location." Paper presented at the annual meeting of the International Communication Association, Sydney, New South Wales, July 1994. ERIC, ED 374407.

Toomey, R., and K. Ketterer. "Using Multimedia As a Cognitive Tool." *Journal of Research on Computing in Education* 27, no. 4, (1995): 472–82.

Toro, M. A. "The Effects of *HyperCard* Authoring on Computer-related Attitudes and Spanish Language Acquisition." *Computers in Human Behavior* 11, no. 3/4 (1995): 633–47.

Volker, R. "Application of Constructivist Theory to the Use of Hypermedia." Paper presented at the convention of the Association for Educational Communications and Technology, Washington, DC, February 1992. ERIC, ED 348037.

Vygotsky, L. S. *Mind in Society*. Cambridge, MA: Harvard University Press, 1978.

Vygotsky, L. S. *Thought and Language*. Cambridge, MA: MIT Press, 1962.

Waddick, J. "Case Study: The Use of a *HyperCard* Simulation to Aid in the Teaching of Laboratory Apparatus Operation." *Educational and Training Technology International* 31, no. 4 (1994): 295–301.

Wang, S. R., and D. H. Jonassen. "Investigating the Effects of Individual Differences on Performance in Cognitive Flexibility Hypertexts." Paper presented at the annual meeting of the American Educational Research Association, Atlanta, GA, April 1993.

Weller, H. G., J. Repman, and W. Lan. "Do Individual Differences Matter? Learner Characteristics and Achievement in Hypermedia-based Instruction." Poster presented at the annual meeting of the American Educational Research Association, Atlanta, GA, April 1993.

Weller, H. G., J. Repman, W. Lan, and G. E. Rooze. "Improving the Effectiveness of Learning through Hypermedia-based Instruction: The Importance of Learner Characteristics." *Computers in Human Behavior* 11, no. 3/4 (1995): 451–65.

Weller, H. G., J. Repman, and G. E. Rooze. "The Relationship of Learning, Behavior, and Cognitive Style in Hypermedia-based Instruction: Implications for Design of HBI." *Computers in the Schools* 10, no. 3/4 (1994): 401–20.

Wey, P., and M. L. Waugh. "The Effects of Different Interface Presentation Modes and Users' Individual Differences on Users' Hypertext Information Access Performance." Paper presented at the annual meeting of the American Educational Research Association, Atlanta, GA, April 1993.

Wilson, K., and W. Tally. *Designing for Discovery: Interactive Multimedia Learning Environments at Bank Street College* Report No. 15. New York: Bank Street College for Technology in Education, 1991. ERIC, ED 337147.

Yung-Bin, B. L. "Effects of Learning Style in a Hypermedia Instructional System." Paper presented at the convention of the Association for Educational Communications and Technology, Washington, DC, February 1992. ERIC, ED 348008.

Zhao, Z., T. O'Shea, and P. Fung. "The Effects of Visible Link-types on Learning in the Hypertext Environment: An Empirical Study." *Computers in the Schools* 10, no. 3/4 (1994): 353–70.

*D*avid Ayersman, EdD, is the director of instructional technology at Mary Washington College, where he also serves as a senior lecturer in teacher education. His research interests include hypermedia and computer-mediated communications. (Address: Dr. David Ayersman, Instructional Technology, Trinkle Hall B-8, Mary Washington College, Fredericksburg, VA 22401; e-mail: ayersman@mwc.edu.)*

History, Digital Imaging, and Desktop Video

Adrian Brown

K en Burn's series on the American Civil War has been the inspiration for experimenting with presentations using desktop video in history classes at De La Salle Senior College, Cronulla, in New South Wales, Australia. Using Amiga computers and the school video camera, students have recorded on the computer screen the results of their investigations of the experiences of the young Australian soldiers who went off to war in 1914. Through this process, they are able to make a permanent document for public presentation of their historical inquiries while creating resources their peers can use. As a result, they have come to value history and the inquiry process.

D esktop videomaking brings the power of professional videomaking to classroom desktops without the need for powerful editing suites, complicated splicing routines, and special processing units.

Today, most people's knowledge of the past comes from film and television, but the medium of communication for most professional historians is the written word. If history is to maintain its appeal in schools and at the same time keep in contact with the findings and methods of historians, then it is our duty as history teachers to train our students to retell the stories of the past in the medium of the future.

History is an inquiry-based discipline, and through presentations students are able to communicate the results

From *Learning and Leading with Technology* 22, no. 8 (May 1995): 19–21. Reprinted with permission from the International Society for Technology in Education. All rights reserved.

of their inquiries. Over the years, I have witnessed many good presentations drawing on much original and interesting primary source material. But after the presentations were given, they were gone, lingering only in memory. Using computers to digitize primary source material students gather, shaping the resultant files with paint programs, utilizing presentation software to link the material, and transferring the results to video offers a way of making student presentations permanent and public.

This is desktop videomaking. It brings the power of professional videomaking to classroom desktops without the need for powerful editing suites, complicated splicing routines, and special processing units.

Desktop video provides students with new opportunities for developing other valued historical skills, such as empathy, i.e., getting in touch with how people in the past experienced the events they went through. In the process of scrutinizing the photos, documents, and other memorabilia, students gain new perceptions about and feelings for the people who underwent the terrible experiences the students describe.

Furthermore, by using computers to generate videos, students learn to master significant aspects of modern media. They learn how to tell stories through images, balance words and pictures, and use technology to extend our repertoire of oral and written communication.

The process of putting together a program requires the pooling of a significant range of skills. Therefore, desktop video is very well suited to the development of cooperative learning strategies. Because the resources students create can be interactive, students' learning opportunities are extended. Desktop videomaking can help create a strong motivational environment for learning because students create resources that their peers can use to further their learning.

Planning and Creating the Videos

The students involved in the evolution of this program were year 11 students (ages 15–16) taking a New South Wales Modern History course. Many of them had used computers, but mainly for word processing or games. However, all students adapted easily to the desktop video processes used in the program.

Working in groups, students were charged with the task of investigating the effect of World War I on the lives of young Australians, both on the frontline and at home in Australia. (These individuals were often the students' grandparents.) Using photographs, documents, various memorabilia, interviews, letters, and diaries, the students reconstructed the impact the war had on the lives of individuals and thus gained a broader understanding of the context in which the war was fought.

The inquiry also focused on discovering how the war affected the lives of young people who between 1914 and 1918 were almost at the same age as the students themselves. Although there was rich source material already available in the school resource center, community libraries, and various war museums, the young researchers found their most interesting source material in the memories of relatives and friends, interviews with members of the local league of returned soldiers, and conversations with the residents of a nearby home for elderly people. The stories these people told and the objects and photos they shared provided the basis for the students' weaving of their own narratives.

Preparation for presentation began with storyboarding and scripting. Storyboarding required the students to translate the narratives they created into a series of quickly sketched images that encapsulated the key elements and the progression in the stories being retold. Each image was roughly drawn on a separate page, with a panel allocated to include the spoken words that would accompany the images when they appeared on screen. Previous experience had taught us that careful planning of storyboards and constant rewriting of scripts ensured a much better final product.

During storyboarding and scripting, students selected the appropriate visual source material from the photographs, postcards, line drawings, and various memorabilia they had gathered from their families and friends. An interesting by-product of this process was that the visual evidence often caused the students to refocus their investigations in ways that the exploration of written evidence did not. For example, they often became aware of the importance of significant detail—a look, the crumpled state of clothing, the choreography of groups.

All the visual documentation was digitized and saved to disk using the school video camera connected to an Amiga 2000 through an analog-to-digital converter. The images were then edited using *Dpaint* (Electronic Arts). Where necessary, *Dpaint* was also used to supplement the digitized images with drawings, maps, and diagrams. The image files were then linked using *Scala* (Scala Software), which was also used to create titles, credits, and "wipes" between the images.

Some students quickly learned to use the animation capacity of *Dpaint*.

Using this feature, they were able to include animations of soldiers coming up to the trenches and crossing no-man's-land. By stamping each of the frames taken from a movie about "going over the top" in the Battle of the Somme, they were also able to create a film-like presentation of the worst moment of trench warfare. Adding music drawn from the time also enhanced the impact of the presentations.

Completed scripts were recorded on a multitrack tape recorder, allowing students to integrate sound effects and music with the narrative. A tape recorder was then connected through an audio jack to a VCR, and the computer program was fed through a genlock onto the VCR so that the final presentations could be made on the classroom video monitor. The *Scala* software proved especially useful at this stage because transitions between shots could be controlled by a mouse.

Dumping to video had the added advantage of providing students with a product they could give to their family members and community members who helped them gather the original research material.

Discussion

The multimedia approach taken in this project was designed to make students active creators of their own interpretations of historical events instead of being sifters of the interpretations of others. One of the drawbacks of much of the software used in the social sciences is that even when it includes a multitude of interesting material and approaches, it often casts students in the role of receivers rather than givers. Instead, multimedia in education should liberate students' talents.

Although the concept of creating resources that other students can use validates students' work, it is in the process of creating those resources that student learning really occurs. The awareness that their investigations would receive public display in video gave additional impetus to the students' initial research. As a consequence, they scrutinized the visual evidence more thoroughly as they selected material for inclusion. For example, a postcard of King George inspecting the trenches, which in other circumstances may have been taken at face value, was discovered to represent a very sanitized view of trench warfare.

The storyboarding and scripting processes helped to refine the concepts the students were attempting to express. Recasting their stories in visual form assisted in the mastery of detail that otherwise may not have occurred. Because images cannot be held for long on the screen, the dialogue had to be kept as taut as possible, forcing students to separate the important detail from the unimportant, the relevant from the irrelevant.

As part of their research brief, students were encouraged to include as much primary source material as possible. Many students were able to garner all sorts of memorabilia from older relatives and friends. Digital imaging led them to value this material, both for the connection it enabled them to make between life on the Western front and their own lives, as well as for its value in conveying something of the texture of the war. Editing the images led to further inspection, awareness of significant detail (for example, the whiteness of the uniforms in what was reputedly a field hospital), and a reexamination of the links between images.

In addition to developing their historical skills, students were training themselves in visual literacy. They were learning to speak a language that combines images, words, and music. They were creating their own maps from the maze of visual images with which they were constantly bombarded. In evaluating their work, the students themselves noted that they had learned to use many of the techniques they had previously seen in film clips and video. For example, they discovered the morphing capacity of *Dpaint*, a feature they had seen used for sophisticated results in film and television. One group decided to achieve greater identification between narrator and audience by using morphing to turn themselves into the soldiers and nurses whose stories they were telling. At the end of the program, they disengaged by turning back into themselves. Others were able to use 3-D rendering to portray the dimensions and look of the trenches.

In all these tasks, the students proved ready learners and competent users—learning best from one another. We kept the equipment and software as simple as possible. Although there was a significant use of technology, its use was never allowed to interfere with the basic processes of discovery, analysis, and judgement. Perhaps the best testimony to the success of this program was the glow of delight on the faces of the program participants as their presentations appeared on the classroom monitor.   ❖

*A*drian Brown
De La Salle Senior College
Cronulla, NSW
Australia 2230

Hypermedia and Constructivism

Three Approaches to Enhanced Learning

Teresa A. McMahon, Alison A. Carr, and Barry J. Fishman

A significant dialogue about constructivism was begun at the 1991 AECT convention in Orlando. As a society of educational professionals, we talked about what constructivism was and what it was not; we struggled with the underlying belief system that constructivism embraces; and we tried to integrate these beliefs into our existing structure of theories about how human learning occurs. At the 1992 AECT convention, Indiana University continued the discussion by demonstrating three prototype hypermedia systems designed to play an integral role in constructivist learning environments: *Perspectives '48*, *Lockermedia*, and *TruMedia*.

Each of these systems was developed by one of three groups from the Instructional Systems Technology program working in association with the Indiana University Multimedia Instructional Design Lab. The groups were challenged to design a 10th grade U.S. History course that instantiated constructivist learning theory. Although this paper will attempt to briefly describe the major elements of each group's curriculum design, the major focus will be on the three hypermedia systems at the center of each.

General Tenets of Constructivist Theory

There has been so much controversy surrounding constructivism in the instructional design field that we feel it is important to review the basic tenets of the theory. The most basic tenet of

From *HyperNEXUS: Journal of Hypermedia and Multimedia Studies* 3, no. 2 (winter 1993): 5–10. Reprinted with permission from the International Society for Technology in Education. All rights reserved.

267

constructivist epistemology is that learning is indexed by experience (Bednar et al. 1991). Learners *construct* personal meanings based on their life experiences, both in and out of school. The context in which learners construct understandings is also important. Learning should take place in an environment consistent with what students will face outside of school. Authentic experiences (apprenticeships, on-the-job experience, etc.) are therefore the most powerful. An extended discussion of the theoretical underpinnings of constructivism can be found in two recent issues of *Educational Technology* (see particularly Duffy and Jonassen 1991; Cunningham 1991; Molenda 1991).

What does constructivism mean in practice? Cunningham, Duffy, and Knuth (1993) identify seven pedagogical goals for constructivist learning environments:

1. Provide learners with experience in the knowledge construction process.

2. Provide learners with experience in and appreciation for multiple perspectives.

3. Embed learning in realistic and relevant contexts.

4. Encourage ownership and voice in the learning process.

5. Embed learning in social experience.

6. Encourage the use of multiple modes of representation.

7. Encourage self-awareness of the knowledge construction process.

These goals suggest three major principles for designing instruction. First, it is imperative that learners be placed in authentic learning environments. This means providing opportunities for learners to have real uses for information and make decisions in a complex learning environment. Second, research

on cognitive apprenticeship (e.g., Collins, Brown, and Newman 1988) stresses the importance of modeling, coaching and scaffolding as instructional strategies. Third, collaboration and multiple perspectives are central to constructivism.

Several design implications became apparent to each group as they progressed through the task of designing constructivist learning environments. Primarily, it was found that traditional models of instructional design (e.g., Dick and Carey 1990) no longer provided a useful orientation. One group, for example, began with a traditional outcomes-oriented task analysis. As they attempted to determine learning objectives for U.S. History they realized that traditional task analyses seemed contradictory to a constructivist pedagogy. Pre-determined objectives are simply not consistent with an environment that "encourages ownership and voice in the learning process" (Cunningham et al. 1993).

Once it became apparent that traditional ID tools were no longer adequate, the teams sought a new angle on the design process. The solution that each eventually found was to begin the course design by determining the context for the authentic activity. In a hypermedia system, that context is represented most logically in a central metaphor. Once a metaphor was selected, interface design began. The development of student tasks then naturally followed from the construction of each interface.

Another common design decision was to provide depth in place of breadth. We perceived the hypermedia systems as opportunities to really "dig in" to the content and actively engage learners in the pursuit of their own knowledge. The teams all met with several subject matter experts (SMEs), including a high school history teacher and two experts on history education from Indiana University.

Although each of the hypermedia systems designed was different than the other two, they all shared some common features. First, they are all contextually rich, and use authentic materials whenever possible. Second, the systems situate learners in real world tasks. Third, they each embody the principles of constructivism outlined above to varying degrees. Fourth, the role of the teacher is dramatically altered from current conceptions. In all three designs the teachers' role shifts from information-giver to guide and facilitator.

Even with these commonalities, the differences in the three prototypes are striking. Each system emphasizes one or another of the constructivist principles. Portions of each principle are in all designs, but some designs instantiate certain principles more effectively than others.

The Prototypes

The specific content domain for each hypermedia prototype was limited to the Truman Doctrine. This was intended both to make the vast domain of U.S. History more manageable and to provide a basis for comparing the three projects. Interestingly, none of the prototypes present the Truman Doctrine explicitly. Instead, they explore the issues and events surrounding its creation. Each team created a contextually rich environment in which learners could construct their own understanding of the Truman Doctrine and the culture of American society at that time in history.

Our SMEs informed us that students often complain that history is boring and irrelevant to their lives. In our prototypes, we explored two methods for making history more relevant. First, our SMEs encouraged us to make history *personal* for our students. Second, our learning theory drove us to create authentic tasks in which students must filter, synthesize, and analyze historical information for real uses.

Perspectives '48

Perspectives '48[1] (see Figures 1 through 3) is based on events of the 1948 presidential election campaign. It is a simulation, and students are assigned roles as candidates and constituents. In these roles they research and debate important issues of 1948. To learn about and support their positions students investigate the hypermedia system. The interface is designed around the homes of five demographically different American families. Each household represents a different socioeconomic, geographic, and ideological point of view (see Figure 1). This provides multiple perspectives on events of the time, emphasizing history as an interpretive activity and down-playing the role of "objective" fact memorizing. Information is obtained through the metaphor of each family's living room, providing a familiar and realistic interface instead of imposing libraries of information (see Figure 2). This illustrates the notion that history is an everyday occurrence witnessed in everyday objects.

Perspectives '48 uses primary source materials including: speeches, photographs, movie newsreels, personal accounts, magazine articles and

1. *Perspectives '48* was designed by Buck F. Brown, Wook Choi, Lon Goldstein, and Teresa A. McMahon.

Figure 1. Perspectives '48 Household Demographics
Are Revealed by Clicking on Family Names;
Living Rooms by Clicking on Household Sketches

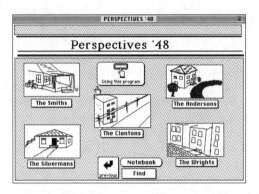

Figure 2. Items in Living Rooms Represent
a Range of Information Sources

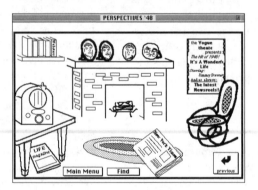

Figure 3. An Example of One Medium in
Perspectives '48: A Newspaper Clipping

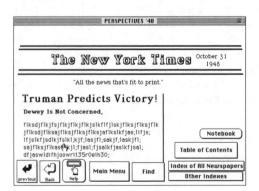

newspaper editorials (see Figure 3). Students are encouraged to share, debate, and challenge the validity and usefulness of all information sources. The students' roles (as candidates and voters) force them to confront multiple perspectives and to use critical thinking skills. The teacher's role is critical. The teacher takes on the role of expert voter and expert historian, modeling various techniques for evaluating, synthesizing and supporting arguments.

Evaluation of the activity is based on a reflection paper that the students prepare at the end of the week's activities. This paper examines the student's own perspective on how to become an informed voter. Also, as the teacher moves from group to group offering guidance, she or he can observe each student's involvement and understanding. Evaluation is not based on student success in the election nor on their ability to choose the winning candidate. Success in *Perspectives '48* is based upon how well students are able to explain and defend the choices they make.

Lockermedia

The central metaphor of *Lockermedia*[2] (see Figures 4 through 6) is the student locker. The locker was chosen because it represents a personal space for students. In this way, *Lockermedia* stresses that history is personal, a point emphasized by our SMEs. What could be more personal to a high school student than their locker?

There are a number of tools within the *Lockermedia* locker. These include an electronic mail system for teacher/student communication (the reminder clipboard); a navigational tool for retracing one's steps (the tape recorder); and a timeline for accessing various points in history (the yo-yo) (see Figure 4).

There are many activities that are available to *Lockermedia* users; we will focus on two. The Class Pennant stresses inquiry skills necessary for authentic history making. Throughout the year the teacher poses questions that require students to interview family and community members. The data they collect are entered into the *Lockermedia* database and become the basis for class discussions. Through this activity they become real historians and experience how traditional history is formed from the accumulated experiences of individuals like themselves. A timeline (see Figure 5) is constructed from the collected data of individual class members and from textbook sources. All the data are joined in this timeline, so that the labor unrest in Chile is juxtaposed with Sarah's dad graduating from high school. This helps students to situate their own experiences in the larger historical context while seeing that history can be viewed as a succession of personal events.

The entire *Lockermedia* database is organized around people, particularly lesser known historical figures. In the second activity we will look at the murder of George Polk, a CBS news correspondent during the late 1940s. One way students enter this *Lockermedia* activity is by clicking on the people poster (see Figure 4). A list of historical personalities appears and George Polk is selected (see Figure 6). Polk was found murdered in Greece during the Civil War of 1948,

---

2. *Lockermedia* was designed by William Brescia, Alison A. Carr, Pai-Lin Chen, and Robert Garfinkle.

Figure 4. Lockermedia Uses the Metaphor of a School Locker

Figure 5. The Timeline Juxtaposes Public and Private History

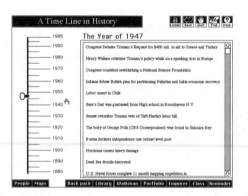

Figure 6. A Variety of Authentic Sources Are Used to Solve Polk's Murder

Figure 7.   TruMedia Puts Students in the Role
            of an Advisor to President Truman

Figure 8.   There Are Many Resources Available
            for Research by Presidential Advisors

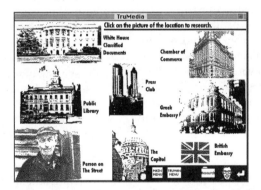

Figure 9.   Electronic Mentoring Provides Online Modeling
            for Students; Teachers and Peers Are Other
            Sources for Modeling in the TruMedia System

and his story grounds the students in the culture that prevailed during the time which led to the creation of the Truman Doctrine. In this activity, *Lockermedia* provides a number of authentic resources (digitized audio, video and print materials) for students to investigate in trying to gain an understanding of American History during the late 1940s. This activity again emphasizes the complexity of real world problems. The students are given information which they must sort, synthesize, and evaluate in order to build their case and identify Polk's murderer.

TruMedia

TruMedia[3] (see Figures 7 through 9) offers a unique perspective on the curriculum development of history courses. *TruMedia* departs from traditional chronological approaches to history and works in a backwards fashion. Current events are the first topic covered in the course, and each new topic is discussed both in terms of its own times and in terms of its implications for present day events.

TruMedia asks students to explore the Truman Doctrine through two activities. In the first, the students are asked to take on the role of an advisor to President Truman on the situation brewing in Greece and Turkey in 1948. The student task is to prepare an opinion brief for President Truman. Students begin the activity by visiting the Oval Office to receive instructions from President Truman (see Figure 7). After choosing an area to investigate, students are able to

investigate a number of data sources that would have been available to real presidential advisors at that time. They are offered such options as the Turkish Embassy, the British Consulate, and the White House Classified Document Library (see Figure 8). Students are cautioned about the danger of trusting documents just because they are in the database. An important lesson of all three hypermedia systems is that "historical" or "factual" documents must be considered on their own merits and weighed against other evidence.

There are three levels of mentoring in *TruMedia*. Using the computer's audio and animation capability, actual advisors to President Truman (see Figure 9) demonstrate their problem-solving processes to students. Second, students are expected to act as peer advisors to each other. Students work in groups to create the synergy of multiple perspectives on issues. Third, and most importantly, the teacher is expected to be an expert both in the content of history and the problem-solving processes that students use in *TruMedia*.

A second activity of the *TruMedia* system is a letter writing campaign to political officials on a topic of current U.S. or local policy which interests them. This activity is based upon the first activity, but this time their task is that of an active participant in our community and country. The letter writing task helps students integrate their knowledge of history with the needs of the present.

---

3. *TruMedia* was designed by Siat-Moy Chong, Barry J. Fishman, Peter C. Honebein, and Younghwan Kim.

Summary and Conclusions

It is our belief that hypermedia is an ideal tool for working in constructivist learning environments. Accordingly, we have explored a wide variety of issues associated with hypermedia, constructivism and the learning of history. We have presented three hypermedia prototypes and associated activities. We believe that the prototypes offered here are good examples of learning environments in which learners' *own* constructions of history are encouraged. The richness and flexibility of these hypermedia systems allows learners to explore multiple paths to multiple solutions.

There is much work yet to be done. We need to explore the implications of constructivist theories for the underlying goals and structure of U.S. education. We need to develop a set of guiding principles for the design of constructivist learning environments. The results of our work highlight the ability of hypermedia and constructivism to transform history from a simplistic linear cause and effect study to a relevant and authentic engagement with our past.   ❖

References

Bednar, A. K., D. Cunningham, T. M. Duffy, and J. D. Perry. "Theory into Practice: How Do We Link?" In *Instructional Technology: Past, Present and Future*, edited by G. Anglin. Denver, CO: Libraries Unlimited, 1991.

Collins, A., J. S. Brown, and S. E. Newman. "Cognitive Apprenticeship: Teaching the Craft of Reading, Writing, and Mathematics." In *Cognition and Instruction: Issues and Agendas*, edited by L. B. Resnick. Hillsdale, NJ: Erlbaum, 1988.

Cunningham, D. J. "Assessing Constructions and Constructing Assessments: A Dialog." *Educational Technology* 31, no. 5 (1991): 13–17.

Cunningham, D. J., T. M. Duffy, and R. A. Knuth. "The Textbook of the Future." In *Hypertext: A Psychological Perspective*, edited by C. McKnight. London: Ellis Horwood, 1993.

Dick, W., and L. Carey. *The Systematic Design of Instruction*. 3d ed. Glenview, IL: Scott, Foresman and Company, 1990.

Duffy, T. M., and D. H. Jonassen. "Constructivism: New Implications for Instructional Technology?" *Educational Technology* 31, no. 5 (1991): 7–12.

Molenda, M. "A Philosophical Critique of the Claims of 'Constructivism.'" *Educational Technology* 31, no. 9 (1991): 44–48.

*T*eresa A. McMahon,

*A*lison A. Carr, and

*B*arry J. Fishman are graduate students in the Instructional Systems Technology program at Indiana University. They can be reached at Wright Education Building, Indiana University, Bloomington, IN 47405–1006.

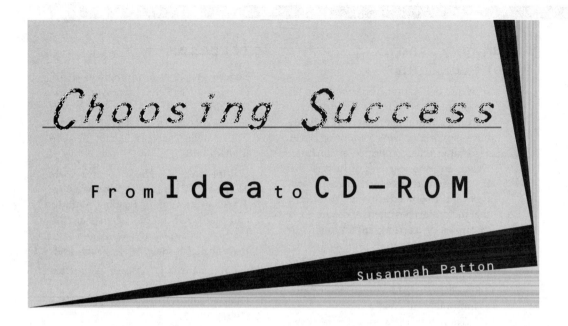

Choosing Success

From Idea to CD-ROM

Susannah Patton

When Computer Curriculum Corporation (CCC) first gave teenagers a look at its new multimedia curriculum in 1992, the audience was less than impressed. The interactive program, designed to help teens face issues ranging from low self-esteem to drugs and violence, left high schoolers in Dade County, Fla., rolling their eyes.

"We were showing them Dick and Jane on video," says Michael Chertok, a senior curriculum developer at CCC and a multimedia producer for the project. "They wanted something more like MTV. They told us, 'If this isn't real, we'll tune out.'"

For Chertok and the other members of the development team, it was back to the drawing board.

Students, educators, filmmakers, and designers hash over presentation of at-risk-teen issues.

Three years later, a team of 65 multimedia specialists and a cast and crew of 150 completed *Choosing Success*, a year-long multimedia course for at-risk teens. The production brought together software developers, filmmakers, and educators, who sometimes clashed over how realistic to make the project. In the end, a documentary filmmaker directed real kids, not actors, in dramas that closely mirror their own experiences in inner-city neighborhoods. And the team of multimedia specialists gave the program the slick, hard-edged look of a news report on MTV.

The $8 million curriculum was paid for by a partnership between CCC and the state of Florida. Royalties from sales outside of Florida will go to the state's department of education. Florida set aside $1 million for the project, its most extensive involvement with an outside software company.

An MTV Approach to Life Skills

The eight-unit program draws students in with hip graphics and an upfront approach, but the content tries to make young people think hard about characters' problems and discover logical solutions. Students assume the role of investigative reporters, gathering information from a "virtual city" and by "telephoning" people who discuss how the characters should handle challenges from drug addiction to getting a job. Students then use the material to put together their own multimedia presentation. A mystery—the death of Janina, one of the character's friends—threads the units together, but is never solved.

"It's kind of like the O. J. [Simpson] trial in that way," says Denise Daniels, a creative director for *Choosing Success*. "There's a soap opera element with scenarios left hanging. The story motivates the kids to go on."

Eight Characters, Five Themes

But the similarities to the Simpson trial or *Beverly Hills, 90210* shouldn't overshadow the course's educational backbone, the developers say. Throughout the stories of eight main characters, five major themes are underscored: building literacy, self-esteem, multicultural awareness, computer literacy, and media awareness.

Students are asked to evaluate the characters' predicaments and figure out solutions. They are also expected to answer a series of questions at the end similar to those in a traditional life-skills curriculum.

Teachers and students who have tried *Choosing Success* say the realistic scenarios set it apart from other courses aimed at kids at risk of dropping out or who face life-threatening problems. In a culture dominated by slick media messages, the best way to help young people, they say, is to speak to them in their own language.

"Our competition is no longer a textbook," says Mike Eason, chief of educational technology for the Florida Department of Education. "We needed to find another way to reach the kids."

Teachers and Students Have Their Say

The production team for the CD-ROMs relied in part on Florida teachers and students to find the best way to meet young people's needs. Bernard Broussard, a teacher at Corporate Academy, a Miami public high school, worked with 15 Florida colleagues to advise them. He and the other teachers told the producers that they needed to bring greater diversity to the cast to be more realistic.

"We felt strongly that *Choosing Success* needed to reflect the needs of all students," Broussard says, noting that in the early scripts, the cast lacked racial and economic diversity. "Our kids were the best judges," Broussard says. "If they don't relate to the characters, it can't work."

When Broussard's students saw the final product, they approved. "Most of the kids said it reflected their experience and environment," he says.

Crossing the Line?

The realism, which includes scenes of marijuana smoking, some street slang, and violence, crossed the line for some educators involved in the project. It veered off the traditional, safer path of much educational software, leaving some unsure whether schools would use it.

In the end, the team decided not to soften the stories and to present real scenarios with subtlety. "Some of us felt strongly that we couldn't patronize the kids," says Rob Nilsson, an award-winning documentary filmmaker who directed the dramatic footage in *Choosing Success*. "We had a lot of emotional debates, but we eventually won the argument."

Florida education officials reviewed each unit, raising some objections but finally agreeing with the production team. "There was some profanity and some subjects we didn't like," says Chris Master, executive director of instructional technology and media support services for the Dade County public schools. "But we felt it all worked."

The first unit tells the story of Ruth, a teen struggling with a drug problem and trying to cope with her best friend's suicide. With an unresponsive father and a mother who is addicted to pills and alcohol, Ruth's self-esteem is at low ebb. The unit asks students to find out more about Ruth's life in order to find solutions.

By clicking around a map of Ruth's community, students can hear from her friends, peek into her diary, and consult experts. Piecing together the information, students are encouraged to come to the conclusion that talking to her friend Marcus and getting involved with activities will help Ruth build her sense of herself. While the main body of the story is freewheeling multimedia, after students put the video together, they have to go through a series of multiple-choice questions to demonstrate what they have learned.

A Long Time Coming

The Florida legislature came up with the idea for the multimedia curriculum in 1989, as an attempt to stem an escalating high school dropout rate. The state put out a 90-page request for a proposal for the project and asked its largest school district, Dade County, to evaluate the three plans received. Florida had previously produced two social studies videodiscs with ABC Interactive and others with National Geographic. But none compared with *Choosing Success* in cost or scope.

After the state chose CCC, known for its integrated learning systems, it set up a state committee and a national advisory panel to write an outline. The panel of education professors, teachers, and administrators from urban school districts across the country worked with CCC to come up with 24 topics ranging from dating pressures to handling family conflicts. The company put together an initial prototype and set off to schools in Dade County and the San Francisco Bay Area to gauge reaction.

When teachers and students called it "silly," the team members knew it was time to change direction. Students said they had come closer with a second prototype that introduced the concept of the user being a cub reporter assigned to writing and creating a video of the events. They hired Rob Nilsson, brought in as a screenplay writer, and got ready to inject a higher dose of reality into the project.

Going to the Source

Nilsson, along with Irena Yershov, the executive producer, insisted that the filmed portions include real drama, not "drama that tries to prove a point," says Nilsson.

"The film was supposed to be about kids at risk, so we needed kids at risk, not the drama class," he says. "We had kids come in with guns and others with a look in their eyes like their senses had been dulled." Nilsson and writer Don Bajema went first to a community center in the low-income neighborhood of North Richmond, in the San Francisco Bay Area. There they found kids and adults interested in working and learning about filmmaking. They spent time in the area to gain trust and acceptance; they also recruited cast members and hired technicians and assistants for the project.

The film crew chose a diverse group of cast members from area high schools. The film's cast and crew at this point joined with a team of multimedia specialists to start production. Meeting at alternating homes around the Bay Area, the creative team brainstormed how to fit the stories together.

From Debates to Beta Test

The meetings, stretching out over hours and meals, often included heavy debates. "The biggest struggle was multimedia versus film," Daniels says. While filmmakers were thinking about how to best

tell the story, the multimedia people were picturing teenagers at a computer, where short video segments were more likely to keep their attention. Education and entertainment also clashed, with filmmakers and educators scrambling to resolve the desire for reality versus the limits of the classroom.

Hours of film and audio and hundreds of still photos and graphics were eventually edited into the CD-ROM. After all the material was digitized, the technical director brought it into the shell of the interactive design. The technical team and producers then spent several months going through the program, checking for glitches and cleaning up stray details.

After months of intense work, the first two units were ready to go. One, "Employability," tells the story of Jimmy, a sophomore who loves art, but needs to make money to help support his family. The story leads the student through Jimmy's life, in which his mother moves out and leaves him with an alcoholic father. The student who played Jimmy was actually dealing with some similar conflicts, Daniels says.

By the fall of 1994, with two units completed, *Choosing Success* was ready to face a real test: kids. The creators brought the curriculum to high schools in California and a correctional facility in nearby San Mateo. "We brought two computers to the recreation center at the correctional facility and held our breath," Daniels says. "Kids sat down and said, 'Yeah, it's cool.'"

Into the Classroom

A Palo Alto, Calif., middle school teacher used parts of the curriculum last spring with several students, and noticed the program encouraged the kids to talk to people about their problems. "It's the first program of its kind I've seen," says Mary Sause, a counselor at Palo Alto's Jordan Middle School. "The situations are believable and kept students' attention."

Sause did note, however, that *Choosing Success* lacks flexibility in the question-and-answer sections. Students are asked to respond to the stories much as they would in a traditional workbook or an integrated learning system. "Kids who are 14 are more willing to take their word for it," Sause says. "But older students may be impatient with some of the answers."

Sequels to *Choosing Success* aren't out of the question, say the producers. The curriculum could be extended with another eight modules; a Web site, a TV series, or even a feature film could also be germinated. "There's a lot more material," says Nilsson. "You haven't seen the last of these kids."   ❖

S usannah Patton is a freelance writer based in New York City.

Students Cross Discipline Boundaries with Hypermedia

Kay Scheidler

The world of buttons, links, text fields, digitized sounds, and graphics provided by hypermedia allows us to create new worlds for our students. Such class environments can stimulate even the normally tuned-out student to research and develop a personalized electronic presentation, and can spur the more motivated student to delve into broad, skillful research and to forge original connections.

Our cross-discipline project with hypermedia has encouraged students to use higher level thinking skills that bridge conventional course subjects.

Hypermedia Encourages Creativity

Our interdisciplinary hypermedia project began three years ago when I started to create *HyperCard* stacks in American studies with three other teachers working with the ACCESS Project—American Culture in Context: Enrichment for Secondary Schools—headed by Professor Kathryn Spoehr of the Cognitive and Linguistic Sciences Department at Brown University. For two years, we four teachers created stacks for students to use in our courses. Then the focus of the project became student-developed stacks. Last semester, each student in two of my heterogeneously grouped English classes in a city high school created stacks. My students disregarded conventional sub-

From *The Computing Teacher* 20, no. 5 (February 1993): 16–20. Reprinted with permission from the International Society for Technology in Education. All rights reserved.

ject-area boundaries to research an area of their own interest and design a stack representing their learning. Creating stacks encouraged students to be creative with the types of information used because the links are nonlinear. Student-designed buttons allow and even encourage a student to incorporate another type of information into the stack.

As the emerging stacks drove them to new research, the students used a widening range of resource material to create their stacks—physics readings, poetry, history, music, rap, graphics, mythology, student surveys, laserdisc segments, sports magazines, anthologies, comics, literary criticism, biography, and oral history. The students broke through the barriers of separate disciplines to represent their subjects as fully as their research allowed them. Their stacks crossed conventional course subjects to make connections with their focus that emphasized the stack theme rather than the discipline, allowing them to demonstrate relationships across the disciplines. Their stacks are now available for other students to use.

Hypermedia allows us to create a presentation of our ideas, our research, and our creativity. It stimulates us to do our best because it's so easy to modify or redesign, and as the final stack takes shape, we want it to be one of our best efforts because others, not just one teacher, will be able to see this creation of ours.

Stimulated by access to his or her own powerful, networked Macintosh computer, though constantly comparing notes with fellow students, each student in my project was able to research and shape a stack that in the end he or she was proud of: "I worked hard on this," several said in final interviews. "I put a great deal of time into it." "I feel good. I

like it!" "I love me!" said Karama, delighted with a breakthrough connection. "Can I have a printout of this to show my mother?" said another eleventh grader. "Maybe then she won't always think I'm stupid."

Fitting the Pieces Together

The cross-disciplinary nature of almost all the students' stacks allowed them to see the value of the different perspectives offered by what we think of as separate disciplines. In a stack on "Dance," for example, Adrienne chose to use a section on "History of Ballet," in addition to "Ballet Today," "Choreography," and "Emotional Aspects." Tracee used poetry and correspondence, original documents, in her stack on black Civil War soldiers. As Derek researched his stack on "Immortality" and learned more about biological studies of prolonging life, he asked if he could change his research question from, "How can we achieve immortality?" to "How do we think we can achieve immortality?" His exploration of his subject led him to the poems of Emily Dickinson on death, and to readings on death in classical mythology. He conducted a student opinion survey on immortality to add a math component and a chart. As with many others, Derek's self-direction constantly propelled him to new areas of study.

Debbie and Brian worked together, using a historical perspective on a literary subject. Having read *Native Son* and *Black Boy*, they wanted to learn more about the author, Richard Wright. One researched biographical information, while the other compared literary criticism of the 1940s, when his work was published, with current criticism of his work. These students found numerous pictures of this little-photographed writer to incorporate into their two linked stacks, and they collaborated on the scanning and placement of the pictures. Brian, a less academically oriented student, was able to use his computer understanding to assist the scholarly Debbie, helping her to overcome her computer phobia. Debbie's responsible work habits helped stimulate Brian to hold up his end of the work. Two others collaborated on a stack on Malcolm X where one selected the information, the other typed it in, the first then proofed the work. While a less complex stack, their level of dedication to their project and pride in the finished work was among the highest.

In creating stacks, students gained new insights into organization and rationale, while creating new designs of knowledge for others. "I see history is a collection of pieces of a puzzle," said one student, "and I want to create my own piece of the puzzle." "A balanced tree structure is the best way to present information," said Xiao Hai. "This is why I organized my information on my buttons on my main overview card this way."

Teachers Have Trouble Crossing Disciplines

These students' openness to research in other disciplines was in contrast to the work of their teachers when we were given the same opportunity for a couple years. Professor Spoehr initiated the ACCESS project in 1988, to study the effects of using computers on student learning and on schools, with support from the James S. McDonnell Foundation, with computers from Apple Computer, Inc. She and two teachers from Lincoln School in Providence began by first deciding on the modification of

HyperCard that would be most useful for creating American Studies stacks in English and history. Programmers adapted *HyperCard* to a basic format including some predefined buttons that also make creation of cards, buttons, fields, and links easier. The next year, a history teacher and I in our large urban high school joined the project. These two English-history teams in two different schools were supported for two more years to create stacks for use in our courses.

Even though each of us had studied and/or taught both English and history, our primary training inhibited our movement into new territory. We were restrained by our years of teaching the separate disciplines and by our courses for which we were creating these materials. When I was given the opportunity to create stacks in hypermedia for my English classes, working with the history teacher, we had many stimulating discussions over the two years on how we would develop our stacks in order to foster the merging of understanding across the disciplines for our shared students. Our project started with our combining English and history in one stack during the pre-colonial period. Our early stacks each had one overview card, with buttons leading to separate sections, but more and more we each created the stacks for our separate disciplines rather than developing them together. The merging of stack development across the disciplines required more time and effort than we had bargained for. Creating the stacks was demanding enough, we found.

So when our stack development had reached the end of the first quarter of the twentieth century I had retreated to my safe discipline harbor, talking with the English teacher at the other school about which famous American authors

Figure 1.   Discipline Specific Stacks Convey the Structure of the Field to Students

A Hierarchically Organized Stack (e. e. cummings)

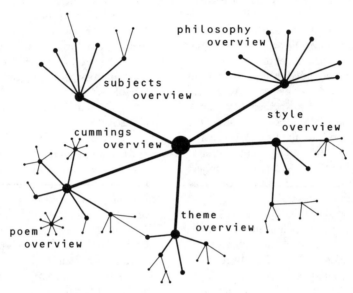

needed to be "done." I ransacked university libraries and created stacks with current criticism on conventional and emerging literary "greats," Ernest Hemingway, e. e. cummings, Robert Frost, Emily Dickinson, Zora Neale Hurston, and Alice Walker. Of the 52 stacks the four of us have created, the great majority are subject-matter specific, directly related to our own disciplines. We didn't even bother linking to the stacks of the other disciplines very much, other than throwing in World War I and II buttons on the cummings and Hemingway stacks.

Teacher-created Stacks Help Students

This separate discipline focus hasn't been harmful to the students. Maps of the organization of my stacks drawn by Professor Spoehr illustrate that the stacks convey to students the structure of the discipline. I had created the stacks from my own expertise of over twenty years of studying and teaching English. The stack structure reflects this subject-matter expertise. The five suboverview cards of the cummings stack, for example, present information on the poet's philosophy, themes, subjects, writing style, and various textual analyses of specific poems. Teachers know what they want students to understand, and this can be usefully demonstrated through a teacher-created stack, through "showing" rather than "telling." By exploring such a stack, students get a fuller sense of the discipline and of the ways to look at a literary text (Figure 1). As such, our stacks provide contexts for our students to understand the disciplines of English and of history.

Still, students use our stacks to take small ventures across the disciplines. Although each subject teacher has created separate stacks on his or her own discipline, the stacks are available for students to use in any course. Stacks on authors incorporate biographical information that relates to the history of the period, as in Emily Dickinson's poems during the Civil War and the effect of the wars on e. e. cummings and Ernest Hemingway's work. With the various stacks, students are aided in seeing how a writer is in part the product of the period in which he or she lived and how a piece of literature stands alone in addition to being a product of a period in history. As the stacks create contexts for understanding, the students who use them are able to bring an understanding of history to their learning about the writing of a period, an understanding of literary analysis to readings of a period.

Our corpus of teacher-created stacks in English, history, and art allows students to browse through stacks that represent the structure of the discipline through individual writers, themes, and readings. The student-created stacks allowed students to use similar skills of collaborative and independent research, organization of materials, and design of stacks and cards, but moving across the disciplines.

Students Forge New Links

We were fortunate to have double-period classes which met on alternate days for students to use the computers over the 10-week period of the project. Still, since creation of a stack is limited by access time to the computer, students were constantly making choices about what material to include. The final stacks are skeletal representations of the students' varied perspectives on the subject. As Dion said in explaining her pop-up button that gave her bibliographic information on her source, "This section is just short. If you want to read more information you can look in this book."

The stacks were both a product of research and an impetus to research. As stacks began to grow and take shape, students realized the need to find more material, to turn to other sources. Paulo didn't get started really researching his stack until he saw the accomplishments of his peers taking shape. Then, as others were finishing up, he took off, madly researching and creating his own project. "I want to finish this, because other students will be using it," he said.

The graphic nature of the stacks was also an impetus to the development. As pictures began to enhance the text, more and more pictures appeared, and, to my surprise, were researched and used most responsibly. When I was creating stacks, I could only find one poor picture of the author Richard Wright to use. Debbie and Brian improved immensely on this, with pictures of Wright and his family at nearly every stage of his life. Through such photos they brought the writer to life for us.

The one area most researched was black history and literature. Sixty-five percent of the students who created stacks were black. Many had a strong interest in capturing their cultural heritage in the stacks. For the weaker students in particular, this search for information on black history and literature became a driving force in their research, helping them to hone the skills of research, selection of material, and organization through the motivation of cultural pride. All of the link buttons created to connect to other stacks were with the black history stacks, with students often linking to stacks from other classes, usually of students whom they didn't know. They were seeking to reinforce and connect their work with the work of other students. And the strongest work was done on a black writer, Alice Walker. "I read seven books by and about her for this stack," Charity reported. An optical character recognition scanner was used to scan the entire text of Walker's first published short story into the stack, which Charity chose to place in a scrolling text field.

In a neat division of disciplines that still allowed a strong cross-discipline connection, Karama created a stack on the Reconstruction Period during her work in her history class, then chose to research the literature of the period in her English class work. To her surprise, the anthology she selected had only work by white writers. We located a black literature anthology to research black writers of the period. Both were combined, along with the history, under a single overview card on the Reconstruction Period. In Karama's presentation of her stack at the end of the project she exuded a new self-confidence.

Sandra, of limited English proficiency, agreed to do a stack on her native Portugal, though at first she was reluctant. Her father wrote out some information on the farming industry for her, in Portuguese, and with some help she translated this and incorporated it into her stack. We got photographs from travel agents. Her motivation to enlarge her stack increased when she was the first to incorporate music. Sandra brought in a tape of Portuguese music to place in her stack. In fact, after Sandra initiated the use of sound in the stacks, other tapes soon appeared and sound was brought into buttons on stacks. In her normal classroom work, Sandra's head would often fall quietly to her desk in withdrawal. Creating the stack meant she had to constantly interact with others and with her material. This helped to improve her English language ability.

Because the stacks were public displays of their learning, students chose areas that they wanted others to learn about. Xiao Hai said about his stack on China, "Students here know very little about Eastern history. There are 5,000 years of Chinese history. You can learn something from it. I hold the responsibility to inform people."

Assessing the Stacks

At the end of the 10-week period, each student presented his or her stack to the class, using a computer screen projection. Each described why he or she chose the subject, and demonstrated how the stack was organized. Besides being a valuable experience for the presenter, the other students said they learned from these presentations. I would use such presentations mid-way through the work another time, so that students can focus on their progress and direction earlier and compare notes, and so we can catch problems earlier.

Our project team is also working on a more reliable means of assessing the stacks. While teams of English and history teachers at three schools had students creating stacks, we each used our own grading criteria, and we want to refine our criteria. We found at a later summer meeting that the two of us from my city school, the two private school teachers, and a team of teachers from

Sheldon High School in Eugene, Oregon, rated student stacks from all of our three schools similarly on a 10-point, 10-question scale. There was little variability among the ratings of the teachers in two subjects, from three very different schools. But we're still developing a mutually agreeable assessment tool that can be given to students at the start of such a project to provide them with better direction. A written mid-point project assessment using this form would also provide quantitative and qualitative evaluation that would be useful to direct revisions.

We had an ideal work situation. We had the time, curricular freedom, hardware and even support staff needed for such an extended creative project. Two programmers from the research project were available to assist the students on technical matters on a regular basis over the project period, and to troubleshoot the inevitable hardware and software problems. The students relied heavily on the programmer assistance at first, but soon some students began assisting others. Students had little difficulty using the version of *HyperCard* modified by the ACCESS Project programmers. A couple of students quickly mastered the graph-ics scanner, and assisted others with scanning and placing pictures in their stacks. Students brought in audiotapes of selected sound, usually music, and a digitizer allowed the sound to be incorporated into the stacks.

A formal written survey of the two classes and my one other larger class of the same grade and similar composition which did not do hypermedia projects, verified significant positive findings. The students who created stacks reported that they felt they had learned more, enjoyed the work more, and felt others were more engaged than the students who did traditional English class work. The students who created stacks did harder work but enjoyed it more and felt they had learned more.

This project suggests that with the right support all students can perform at higher levels, applying learning across disciplines to create "personalized" demonstrations of learning. The valuable tool of hypermedia provides students with a way to think about a subject that is important to them, and to present it to others in a way that demonstrates their own learning at a level beyond the constraints of separate disciplines. ❖

*K*ay Scheidler
Hope High School
Providence, RI 02906

Building Community in the Computer Age

Four Traditions of Teaching Values

- Values Analysis and Problem-based Learning
- Moral Dilemma Discussion
- Values Clarification
- Values Inculcation

Computers as Threats to Democratic Principles

- Computers and Censorship and Free Speech
- Computers and Rights to Privacy
- Equity of Access Issue

chapter 6

Building Community in the Computer Age

At the turn of the century a technology burst onto the American scene that had a profound effect on society and traditional values—the automobile. The mobility provided by this invention inalterably affected American culture, from the way business was done to moral conduct. Prior to the automobile, trucks that haul products across highways and back-seat sex were not concepts people had considered. The computer has the same potential to alter our ways of interacting commercially, politically, and interpersonally. Let us look at three examples:

1. During the Tiananmen Square democracy movement of May 1989, it was widely reported that the Chinese students used computer-based technology, such as fax machines and electronic mail, to transmit ideas, seek support, and provide information to sympathetic student groups both within the country and abroad. More recently, various groups involved in the conflicts throughout the eastern European region of the Balkans have used the World Wide Web to communicate their plight or position in struggles to resist ethnic cleansing or repressive regimes.

2. The electronic bulletin board service, Prodigy, was in the national news when its management reacted to the use of the service to transmit anti-Semitic points of view espoused by neo-Nazis. The competing issues ranged from the principle of freedom of speech to the potential violation of human rights.

3. A computer was used by two American scholars to create a complete, but bootlegged, edition of the Dead Sea Scrolls. Access to complete editions of the original Scrolls—the oldest known copies of the Old Testament and other religious or legal writings dating back to 50 A.D.—has been monopolized by a tightly knit group of scholars. Computer-based technology has intruded on what they consider sacred ground.

The above examples illustrate two dimensions of civic-moral education in relation to the advent of microcomputers in our world: teaching about civic and moral issues with technology, and the moral and ethical use of computer-based technology in a democratic society. The purpose of this chapter is to consider how social studies teachers can address these two dimensions of civic-moral education in their teaching.

The first dimension is concerned with helping teachers use computers in social studies education to more effectively teach about civic-moral issues. The computer will be considered as a tool for changing and clarifying values about real-life issues. Four specific strategies and appropriate software will be described and critiqued in relation to civic-moral education.

The second dimension is concerned with the ways computers will change our concept of ethics and values in the Information Age. This dimension considers issues of access based on gender and class, such as the issue faced by the Prodigy service, and freedom of speech and copyright as a personal property right, as in the scholarly squabble over the computer-generated, unauthorized version of the Dead Sea Scrolls. In the broadest sense, this dimension is concerned with what it means to be human and interact with others via computer-based technology.

This chapter begins with a consideration of the first dimension. It looks at how social studies software and the Internet reflect the four traditional approaches to civic-moral education: values analysis, cognitive moral development, values clarification, and values inculcation. We will then consider the second dimension, which is concerned with how computer-based technology effects a society committed to democratic principles. Could this technology be a threat to what we, as a society, espouse in documents such as the Declaration of Independence and the Constitution regarding our inalienable human rights and form of self-government?

Computers and Four Traditions of Civic-Moral Education

Before beginning a description of the relationship between various approaches to civic-moral education and computers, a point of clarification is in order. As established in Chapter 1, the responsibility of social studies teachers to promote the thoughtful acquisition of civic and moral values is primary because of the nature and definition of social studies. There is considerable social and educational debate, however, about the field of civic-moral education as it is played out in classrooms. Theorists and practitioners cannot agree on the best approach to help students acquire values and arrive at moral decisions. This disagreement is evidenced by the fact that different scholars call the field by different names, including values, moral, affective, civic, or most currently, character education (Ryan and McLean 1987; Benninga 1991; Beane 1990; Massey 1993; Kohn 1996). Without resolving the arguments about the best label, or what is the best pedagogical approach, the term civic-moral education will be used. Regardless of what it is called, the intent of the social studies curriculum in this dimension is concerned with cultivating a sense of community in the classroom (Noddings 1984). The goal is to promote the cultivation of civic-moral values and provide guides to action that uphold the principles of our democratic beliefs. This involves using technology to study history and geography in regards to decisions people have made (or are facing), and studying ourselves in regards to how technology is used—in the classroom, the school, society in general. Questions about who has access to technology and how it is controlled are important issues for students to discuss.

One reason the argument about the best approach to civic-moral education cannot be put to rest is that there appears to be no one way to teach civic-moral values, even when using a computer. As Ryan (1991, 9) points out,

> Different people learn to be moral in different ways. The approach of one theorist or practitioner may be wonderfully effective with one group of students and have no impact on the next. Operationally this means that teachers should know several ways to teach values and moral heritage.

Keeping in mind that these approaches are best used in some combination to have the maximum impact on students' learning, the following are four different theoretical orientations to civic-moral education and computer-based applications. The selected strategies illustrate the various tools that are available to social studies teachers for teaching civic-moral values. All have a place in a social studies program that integrates computer-based technology as part of the curriculum.

Tradition 1—Values Analysis and Problem-based Learning

Engaging students in a systematic inquiry of a problem or question was originally presented as values analysis by Fraenkel (1976). This method is particularly well suited to helping students deal with current events and public policy issues (Kuse 1991). Essentially, the process asked students to think of value-laden issues, such as reducing federal funding for the arts and humanities or eliminating private ownership of handguns. Students then research the issue to develop data from which they project consequences regarding how different decisions would affect various parties both in the short and long term.

More recently, a refinement of this approach is being labeled problem-based learning (PBL). In addition to a technology emphasis (much of the information and communication is WWW-based), there are three other characteristics that distinguish PBL from values analysis: 1. the instructional model is more elaborate; 2. there is more cross-curricular emphasis; and 3. the assessment of learning is tied to a student production portraying their understanding of the problem (as well as their proposed solutions). In outlining the PBL process, some examples of projects and their relationship to computer-based technology will be described.

The instructional model for PBL is recursive, i.e. the various stages of the model spiral and are repeated as you move through them. It begins with sufficient discussion about concepts such as community or technology to lead to the identification of specific problems such as these:

◈ How can we improve the image of our community?

◈ How will the economic and ecological problems facing our community be impacted by increased recreational use of waterways?

◈ How is technology changing and improving our lives?

A broad topic can be broken down into subtopics that groups pursue as lines of inquiry. Taking the last question on the previous page as an example, different subtopics could be: How can we impact the educational process so that technology is used for students who are incapacitated through illness? How can accuracy claims of advertisers be assessed? What are the technology needs of the community and how can we meet them? Although student discussion is conducted throughout a PBL project, the goal at this stage is student involvement and ownership of the problem.

The second stage is developing a plan of inquiry. Here teachers help students think through the collection and analysis of the various types of data that they might examine. At this stage teachers should seek correlation to other areas of the curriculum, such as mathematics to calculate averages or language arts to write and design questionnaires.

As students conduct inquiry and analyze data in the third stage, computer-based technology comes into play in a number of ways. Word processors and page layout software are used to construct questionnaires and surveys. QuickTime movies and digital cameras record visual data (this is particularly useful in promoting geographic learning and understanding). Internet interviews and other data collection is accomplished via *CUSeeMe* and e-mail technologies, including chat rooms and listservs. Databases and spreadsheets (see Chapter 4) are created to store and analyze data.

The fourth stage of PBL centers on preparing and presenting findings. Students employ multimedia applications such as those described in Chapter 5 (*HyperStudio* or *LinkWay*). Graphic applications (software with drawing and paint tools) can be used to create presentations of the data and possible solutions. The cost of producing CDs is dropping dramatically and CDs could now be considered an affordable format for storing student presentations. Of course, as explained in Chapter 7, developing a WWW homepage about a project is becoming easy enough for an elementary class to plan and produce.

Finally, debriefing and consolidation is conducted. Here students are led to examine the overall process and the results. Suggestions for future inquiry are solicited and results reported to the school and community as appropriate. Needless to say, overall this is a very open-ended curriculum process—one that is negotiated with students. Therefore, teachers must be able to deal with the ambiguities inherent in this inquiry approach.

Cultural Debates, a program on CD-ROM from Tom Snyder Productions, exemplifies the values analysis tradition. The software provides a context in which students take positions on an issue facing a rain forest community. Students use *Cultural Debates* in the process of examining the similarities and differences between the rain forest culture and their own. This CD-ROM is used to help students gather data in preparation for a debate on one of six possible topics: cultural values, modern medicine, education, land management, technology, and ecotourism. As with the other Tom Snyder products described in this text, this software is used to help students develop their thinking about the issue using a problem-solving and cooperative-learning format.

Tradition 2—Cognitive Moral Development—The Moral Dilemma

Other software by Tom Snyder Productions uses a moral dilemma to help young children consider possible courses of action.

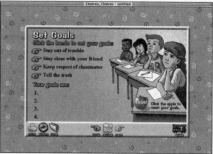

These screen shots of *Taking Responsibility* (from the *Choices, Choices* series) sets the stage for a dilemma about a trick gone astray and the choice between affiliation (keeping friends) versus telling the truth to the teacher.

The *Choices, Choices* series has several different dilemmas. In the program *Taking Responsibility*, a student and a friend are playing a joke and accidentally knock over the teacher's favorite pot while the teacher is out of the room. The dilemma is whether you would tell the truth and reveal your friend's identity or keep silent about the culprit. A second dilemma from the *Choices, Choices* series, *On the Playground,* involves a new kid at school who is a little "different," and the choice must be made between playing with your old friends or playing with the new kid, which will affect your relationship with your classmates. Both of these programs provide ample opportunities for teachers to use the type of Socratic dialogue that Kohlberg and his colleagues indicated as imperative to promoting cognitive moral development with students.

The *Decisions, Decisions* series by Tom Snyder Productions, which is described in the Chapter 2, also provides opportunities for students to stretch their cognitive moral reasoning as they examine emerging dilemmas and consider courses of action based on the goals they establish as they begin the program. In addition to the historically oriented programs reviewed in Chapter 2, other programs that deal with current civic-moral issues in our culture are available and worthwhile in helping students explore the various values and moral issues presented. The titles of these programs describe the nature of the civic-moral dilemma that students must make decisions about: *Lying, Cheating, and Stealing; The Environment; A.I.D.S.; Violence in the Media; Substance Abuse; Drinking and Driving*; and *Prejudice*. It should be noted that these programs all relate closely to the thematic strands presented in the NCSS standards. Specifically, the first six programs are tied to the theme of science, technology, and society, while the seventh program addresses the multicultural theme. So how do programs like *Decisions, Decisions* promote cognitive moral development?

Student growth in cognitive civic-moral reasoning results from exposure to more sophisticated discussion about courses of action that involve higher stages of moral reasoning. Through the discussion process, students assimilate a more encompassing cognitive structure for solving a moral problem, i.e., a cognitive structure that considers the perspectives of all the people who might be involved in the dilemma. Just as Piaget suggested stages of growth to understand how the child's mind unfolds,

Kohlberg identified three levels of moral reasoning: preconventional, conventional, and post-conventional. At the preconventional level, students are able to consider the perspective of only one party, most likely themselves. At the conventional level, students are able to see the perspective of a number of groups simultaneously. At the post-conventional level, students are able to consider the perspective of a multiplicity of groups while also taking into account basic human rights (Kohlberg 1987; Power 1989).

Kohlberg's theory and research, as well as classroom activities, center on the belief that moral thought and discourse is grounded in law and justice. An important debate about Kohlberg's theory and research emerged when researchers began to look at cognitive-moral development from other dimensions besides an orientation to law and justice. As measured by Kohlberg's research, higher stages of development around a law and justice orientation were observed in males more frequently than females. Different orientations seem to suit women better, a fact that supports Kohlberg's findings in his work with law and justice. Gilligan (1962) and Noddings (1984) advocate the theory that men and women may develop differently because of differences in upbringing based on gender: women's upbringing leads to an orientation toward moral decisions based on considerations of *care and nurture*; men's moral decision making is based on considering what is *lawful and just*. Thus, men and women can both make moral decision using the highest stages of thought, but different orientations are used in the thinking process.

Parker, in attempting to reconcile the work of Gilligan and Noddings with the theories of Kolberg, avers both orientations should be taught. "One cannot mount a comprehensible argument *for* caring *instead of* justice or the reverse. Clearly, the two dimensions are equally critical, like the two wings of a bird, and are needed for and from both males and females" (1997, 228). *Decisions, Decisions* and *Choices, Choices* reflect these two wings: *Decisions, Decisions* is grounded in a law and justice orientation and *Choices, Choices* is grounded in caring.

Parker's bird analogy is also applicable to thinking about computers and teaching civic-moral values: we use computers as an instructional tool (what we teach with—the left wing) and we can use computers as a source for curriculum (what we teach about—the right wing). Having described some software that showed us the instructional wing, let us look at the curriculum wing.

The role of the computer in our society becomes a great source for teacher-created moral dilemmas. Access to pornographic material through the Internet and potential conflict with first amendment rights comprise a dichotomy with which our culture must come to grips. Another dilemma lies in what, if any, limits should be placed on governmental agencies that potentially have the ability to monitor the nature of information citizens access through the Internet and with what frequency. Kohlberg maintained that the life of any individual school, i.e. the interactions among its constituents, is an ideal source for dilemmas regarding civic-moral values (Kohlberg 1987).

The unauthorized transcription of the Dead Sea Scrolls described at the beginning of this chapter places moral claims of property in conflict with liberty. Do the scholars' rights to keep the historical data to themselves outweigh the public's right to have access to antiquated documents? Kohlberg suggested eight other moral issues around which dilemmas could be posed: authority, affiliation, conscience, contract, law, life, punishment, and truth. To be a dilemma there must be two or more competing moral claims that make choosing a course of action difficult. The key is enabling students to explain their reasons for whatever choice is made. This is always the focus of dilemma discussions—*why* do students believe a particular course of action should be taken. As discussed above, it also is key that students look at a dilemma from both a Kohlbergian justice orientation and the Gilligan and Nodding orientation of caring.

To promote thoughtful discussion about a moral dilemma Kohlberg identified the following typology of questions for a teacher to use to promote discussions. The italicized text represents the direction a question would take based on the "Quest for the Wizard" dilemma found on page 323 of Reading 3.

1. Universal consequences: "What if everyone *illegally copied software*?"

2. Switching roles: "How would you feel if you were *the author of the software and you needed the income to support your family*?"

3. Issue-related: "Is it ever all right to *violate copyright laws*?"

4. Seeking reasoning: "Why do you say *violating copyright* is wrong?"

5. Definitional: "What does the concept of *copyright* mean to you?"

6. Checking perception: "Can you tell us what the two competing claims are in this dilemma?"

7. Student-to-student interaction: "Jonathan, can you tell us in your own words what you think Allison meant by that statement?"

A good discussion about moral issues should include as many question as are appropriate from the above list. Obviously, the last two questions can be used during any teaching situation. For the previous five, a teacher need only switch the content that is italicized to fit the facts of the dilemma being discussed.

In an exciting project currently underway at Carnegie Mellon University, videodiscs are being developed that present students with moral dilemmas. The project is called Theoria (pronounced Tay-o-ree-a), a name derived from the Greek word for theater. The project director explains that the discs represent a sort of ethical theory. A dilemma is presented, and emotional contexts for the situation make the game come alive. For example, one videodisc contains the dilemma of Mr. Cowart, who in 1973 received severe burns on 65 percent of his body and requested doctors to end his suffering and let him die. Mr. Cowart is a practicing attorney, but he is disabled. He has been able to resume a "normal" life (he married after the accident), but he still maintains he should have been allowed to die. Students debate the right to die as they watch scenes of the crash, the victim's physical and psychological therapy, and interviews with various people involved.

More projects like this one will produce a wealth of source material for moral dilemmas. The *ABC News Interactive* series *In the Holy Land* and *Martin Luther King* offer ample opportunities for teachers to introduce a dilemma and hold a discussion about it. The above questions are a vehicle for promoting the kind of discourse that leads to cognitive moral growth. Many resources are available to teachers for learning more about leading dilemma discussions. (See Reading 5 in this chapter for more information on this topic.)

Tradition 3—Values Clarification

Using values clarification as a means for teaching children to understand civic-moral values and analyze reasons for choosing certain courses of action is considered the most problematic approach for several reasons (Stewart 1976; Lockwood 1978). First, it originally espoused a philosophy of ethical relativism, i.e., teachers should be neutral about student values. The important thing was that students be taught to cherish and act on their own values (Metzger 1986). Those who originally espoused the values clarification approach have revised their theory and acknowledge that in some matters, such as stealing, a teacher must provide explicit moral guidance to help students live an ethical life and adopt societal values (Harmin 1988). A second criticism has not been addressed by those advocating the values clarification approach to civic-moral education: there is little distinction between real values, such as those identified by Kohlberg, and matters of public policy, such as whether smoking should be allowed in public.

The values clarification approach draws from a wide range of strategies that are used to help students traverse the seven steps of fully integrating a value into their way of life. These steps are opening one's mind, anticipating consequences, sensing one's inner guidance, choosing, acting, persisting, and speaking up. The absence of any recommended sequence of activities, however, is the third criticism of the values clarification approach.

Despite these criticisms, the technique has merit and includes the most widely used strategies for helping students come to grips with civic-moral values. A computer can be adopted to many of these strategies. In fact, computer use for collecting student responses would overcome a fourth criticism: when these strategies are used in class discussions, students' rights to privacy can be violated when they are forced to take positions on value-laden issues as a result of peer pressure. Using database or word-processing programs, teachers can create files where students anonymously record their responses to moral dilemmas. One of the articles that follows this chapter (see "Computers, Kids, and Values" by Stephen J. Taffee) includes seven value-laden issues to which students respond based on values they hold about the uses of computer technology. Similarly, the Tom Snyder Productions program *TimeLiner* could be used by students to develop a more effective time management plan for their daily activities. This is only one values clarification strategy from a seminal book that contains over 80 different strategies. (Simon, Howe, and Kirschenbaum 1972).

Tradition 4—Values Inculcation

Values inculcation is the most common and longest standing approach to teaching values. This approach instills certain beliefs and attitudes in students by exhorting them and modeling the kind of values adults wish young people to adopt. Your parents have been inculcating values all your life, such as "say please and thank you" or "be respectful to elders." Similarly, your teachers have probably urged you to do things, such as bring your materials to class and don't be late. Values inculcation was originally attacked as futile when new approaches, theory, and research about values education gained ascendancy during the 1970s. The original opponents of values inculcation are rethinking their views, however, as schools again turn their attention to promoting values and ethics in society's future adults. There is now a growing recognition that values inculcation is not inherently futile. Furthermore, it is a reasonable approach that should be used with values clarification, values analysis, and moral discussion so that civic-moral education is undertaken from a variety of perspectives (Harmin 1988; Kirschenbaum 1992).

An example of a computer-based simulation that could be a vehicle for inculcating values is a decade-old project supported by the University of Michigan. The Interactive Communications and Simulations (ICS) program is a set of telecommunications exercises for elementary, secondary, and middle school students. (A more detailed explanation of how computers are used in telecommunications can be found in Chapter 7.) *Arab-Israeli Conflict* is the best known of these telecommunications exercises. The purpose of the exercise is to immerse participants in the complex dynamics of multifaceted international political reality. Sixty roles are represented in the current version, and these roles are organized into 12 teams representing various countries—seven are directly involved in the conflict, and the rest are representative parts of political entities that are also involved. All of the roles are high-level governmental or political figures. Participants engage in three basic activities (or levels of communication) through the computer: messages, press releases, and action forms. Correspondence is sent from one school to another via a modem, and the activity is mediated by a "mentor" group at the University of Michigan. This particular exercise is a powerful tool for social studies teachers in secondary schools, but it is time intensive once a school becomes involved. As with most telecommunications linkages among schools, the value of this program is the interaction that is generated with students from different geographic areas.

A second exercise from ICS that is appropriate for students as young as fifth grade is *Earth Odysseys*, an interdisciplinary e-mail program that has two principal intents: to provide an engaging form of vicarious travel and to simultaneously provide curricula activities in the areas of environmental sciences and social studies. The following are examples of topics addressed: societal diversity, political boundaries, clothing and mores, European expansion, material culture, transportation, and recycling. During the course of an odyssey, each traveler/correspondent sends an e-mail report of the broad array of phenomenon that can be encountered when one travels. These reports are made available to student participants on a daily basis.

An example of an *Odyssey* experience that inculcates values is an exercise that centers on a varied group of people from Canada, the United States, and Germany who undertook a three-month trip through 12 countries of central, southern, and eastern Europe. In one of the reports a student describes the practice of "black riding," which means using public transportation without paying—an easy enough thing to do, but a practice in which most people don't engage. Twenty responses to this report were received. The one from mentor Mike at the ICS center urged participants to compare the moral judgment of those who do not black ride with the moral judgment of those who do in regards to people who commit similar low-level illegal activities, such as speeding on the highway when the police are not around. Another report, and a great number of responses, dealt with the moral issues of the Holocaust.

A classroom teacher can use exercises like those offered by the ICS to make students consider certain basic values such as the dignity of human life or the value of honesty. The minimal expense and modest time commitment associated with participating are greatly offset by the opportunities students have to engage in dialog with participants from around the United States and the world. The ICS exercises allow students to use the telecommunications capabilities of the computer as they consider value-related issues under a teacher's and the ICS staff's tutelage.

To date there lacks compelling evidence that any one approach to values education is clearly superior to another or that combining theoretical approaches hinders student growth. Each approach has a different theoretical basis and focus for learning, but these do not necessarily work against one another. The case can be made for just the opposite—each of these various approaches can play a legitimate role in the development of students' values. Recalling Parker's "wings of a bird" analogy for reconciling different orientations to civic-moral development, let us extend the analogy and consider that in addition to a set of wings, a bird has two feet; it uses all of these limbs in conjunction to travel from place to place (Parker 1997). Thus, all four of these traditions can and should be used.

When using social studies software, an effective teacher will see opportunities to consider underlying civic-moral and value-laden issues and will take the time to discuss them with students. It must be noted, however, that discussion should take place before, during, and after the use of *any* software. It would be professionally irresponsible to have a student interact with a computer without drawing out what they learned and felt during the experience. The next section considers the second dimension of the relationship between civic-moral education and computers: the civic-moral issues associated with the use of computer-based technology in a democratic society.

Computers as Threats to Democratic Principles

Social studies is the part of the curriculum that is most concerned with preparing students to become responsible citizens. The preceding section described four approaches for preparing students to become conscientious citizens. Another aspect of values education is helping students understand the issue of technology as an intrusion into the democratic way of life (Rossi 1996). Computer-based technology infringes on principles that we consider central to our society. This section identifies three democratic principles and the issues they face in regards to computers. Social studies teachers should be aware of these so they can better help their students prepare for citizenship in a democracy.

One basic principle of our democracy is that all people are created equal. This raises the issue of equity of access to the vast amounts of information available through computer-based technology. This equity issue potentially affects students in a number of diverse groups such as the economically disadvantaged, females, and the physically challenged. Equal opportunity for all students to learn how to comprehend, generate, and communicate information through computer-based technology is imperative to ensure all citizens are responsible members of our society.

A secret ballot is part of the essence of our electoral process. Over the course of our nation's development, citizens' rights to privacy as a fundamental democratic principle have been maintained by our legal system. Computer-based technology and the flow of information made possible by computers raise the issue of how much information should be available to the government and other groups. Too much information about our private lives in the hands of totalitarian forces could be used to undermine our democratic way of life. As Halal points out, our democratic way of life could also be threatened by forces who wish to use computer-based technology to wreak havoc with the large information systems that run the military, airports, financial markets, and other functions of our society (1992). Coates reports that in a survey conducted in businesses that use electronic mail and other computer-based telecommunications, over 60 percent of the respondents think it's OK for management to surreptitiously access and read an employee's files (1993).

A third democratic principle comes into play regarding computer-based technology—freedom of speech. Should limits be placed on what people can communicate via electronic mail and bulletin boards on the Internet? Who should be responsible for monitoring telecommunications processes to prevent the Internet from being used as a medium for denying civil rights to ethnic or religious groups?

The issue of labeling computer simulations has recently surfaced. Just as movies are rated for parental discretion based on violence and other themes unsuitable for young children, should Nintendo and other computer-based action games be rated and labeled? The recording industry vigorously opposed the labeling of its products a few years ago. Will there be a different outcome when it comes to violence or sexual fantasy in computer games? World Wide Web links make it simple to access sexually explicit information and photographs. (See Chapter 7 for a description of the World Wide Web and how to access the vast amount of information available. Addresses for sexually explicit sites are not provided, however.) It doesn't seem possible to prevent students who know how to navigate the Internet from viewing pornographic material. What should schools do about this issue?

Equal opportunity, right to privacy, and freedom of speech are certainly not new issues in our evolving practice of democracy. The power of computer technology, however, puts them in a very different light. The instant access to a vast audience, the data storage potential of computers, and the alluring visual power of computer-based technology are of great benefit, but they also pose certain questions our culture must consider: How can all citizens best benefit from computer technology? What can be done to prevent this technology from being used to spy on citizens? What limits should be placed on the information and communications available through the Internet?

◼ Summary ━━━━━━━━━━━━━━━━━━━━━━━━━━━━━

A primary goal of school in general, and social studies in particular, is to help young people think about civic-moral issues and develop the kinds of values and that will allow them to participate in a democratic community. Two dimensions of civic-moral education in relation to technology were considered: the use of the computer as a tool to promote civic-moral development, and civic-moral issues raised by computer use in regards to basic democratic beliefs about freedoms and rights. In either case, a social studies teacher's role is to promote thoughtful discussion of the issues and serve as a "moral compass" for students. Computers serve as a tool or springboard for such discussions.

This chapter identified four different approaches to civic-moral education and outlined what each has to offer in the way of unique software and applications. A tension exists, however, in regards to civic-moral education: social studies teachers have a responsibility to inculcate certain basic human values in students, but they also have a responsibility to help students find their own answers to civic-moral dilemmas when there is no clear-cut answer. The four approaches to values education present different means for addressing the tension of teaching students values while letting them make their own decisions. The issue of which approach to use (and when) is best decided by individual teachers. The goals and the learning situation will dictate which approach to employ. Social studies teachers need to seize opportunities for promoting civic-moral growth as they occur, particularly within the context of the life of the school itself (Kohlberg 1987).

This chapter also considered the role of technology in a democratic society. Three democratic principles and the issues they face in regards to computers were also explored.

Building community is richly illustrated in the next chapter, which deals exclusively with the Internet. The illustration focuses on an online conferencing system from San Francisco called the WELL that was founded by a group of "old hippies." The evolution of the WELL parallels the evolution of the Internet in that they both started out with a well-defined purpose that changed and broadened into something quite different from what its originators ever imagined.

■ References

■ Articles

Coates, J. "Computer Privacy? It's Not a Given." *Chicago Tribune* (23 May 1993): sec. 7, pp. 1, 6.

Halal, William E. "The Information Technology Revolution." *The Futurist* (July/August 1992): 10–15.

Harmin, Merril. "Values Clarity, High Morality: Let's Go for Both." *Educational Leadership* (May 1988): 24–30.

Kohn, Alfie. *Phi Delta Kappan* 78, no. 6 (1996): 429–39.

Kuse, Loretta, and Hildegard Kuse. "Values Analysis in the News." *Social Education* 55, no. 5 (1991): 331.

Lockwood, Alan L. "The Effects of Values Clarification and Moral Development Curricula on School-age Subjects: A Critical Review of Recent Research." *Review of Educational Research* 48, no. 3 (summer 1978): 325–64.

Massey, Mary. "Interest in Character Education Seen Growing." *Update* (May 1993): 1,4.

Metzger, D. J. "Viewing Values Education from Two Perspectives." *The Social Studies* (October 1986): 80–82.

Parker, Walter C. "Democracy and Difference." *Theory and Research in Social Education* 25, no. 2 (1997): 220–34.

Rossi, John A. "Creating Strategies and Conditions for Civil Discourse about Controversial Issues." *Social Education* 60, no. 1 (1996): 15–21.

Watkins, Beverly T. "Videodiscs Bring Dimension of Emotion to Ethics Education." *Chronicle of Higher Education* (March 4, 1992): A22–24.

Books

Fraenkel, J. R. "Teaching about Values." In *Values of the American Heritage: Challenges, Case Studies, and Teaching Strategies*, edited by Carl Ubbleohde and Jack Fraenkel. Washington, DC: National Council for the Social Studies, 1976.

Gilligan, C. *In a Different Voice: Psychological Theory and Women's Development*. Cambridge, MA: Harvard University Press, 1982.

Kohlberg, Lawrence. *Essays on Moral Development*. Vol. 3 of *Education and Moral Development*. New York: Harper and Row, 1987.

Little, T., and W. B. Goldsmith, Jr. *Policymaker: A Decision-making Model for Selecting Policy Options to Resolve Social Issues*. New York: Newsweek, 1990.

Noddings, Nel. *Caring*. Berkeley: University of California Press, 1984.

Power, F. C., A. Higgins, and L. Kohlberg. *Lawrence Kohlberg's Approach to Moral Education*. New York: Columbia University Press, 1989.

Simon, Sidney B., Leland W. Howe, and Howard Kirschenbaum. *Values Clarification: A Handbook of Practical Strategies for Teachers and Students*. New York: Hart Publishing Company, 1972.

Stewart, John S. "Problems and Contradictions of Values Clarification." In *Moral Education: It Comes with the Territory*, edited by D. Purple and K. Ryan. Berkeley: McCutchan, 1976.

Discussion Questions

1. What are the two dimensions to the issue of teaching values to students in relation to the increasing use of technology?

2. What is values analysis? Describe a social issue that might be appropriate for students to discuss in class. Identify possible solutions and their consequences.

3. How does a dilemma discussion promote cognitive moral growth according to Kohlberg? What are the benefits of using multimedia technology in projects such as Theoria to promote cognitive moral growth?

4. What are the criticisms associated with values clarification as an approach to teaching values? How can the computer help overcome the criticism regarding invasion of privacy?

5. What are the democratic principles threatened by the use of computer-based technology in our society? As a social studies teacher, what can you do about this?

Additional Readings and Questions

Glenn, Allen. "Democracy and Technology." *The Social Studies* (September/October 1990): 215–17.

1. What are some of the characteristics of a democratic nation? What impact is technology having on information?

2. Identify three areas of knowledge/skills that citizens must have in light of technology.

Taffee, Stephen J. "Computers, Kids, and Values." *The Computing Teacher* 12, no.1 (August/September 1984): 15–18.

Hannah, Larry S., and Charles B. Matus. "A Question of Ethics." *The Computing Teacher* 12, no.1 (August/September 1984): 11–14.

1. What two basic points about the structure and use of dilemmas are illustrated with the "What's the Harm" dilemma?

2. How can a teacher determine when a dilemma discussion such as the one prompted by "Right or Wrong" is degenerating into a problem-solving exercise?

3. When would it be appropriate for a teacher to use a dilemma for the purpose of a problem-solving exercise?

Carpenter, Cal. "Online Ethics: What's a Teacher to Do?" *Learning and Leading with Technology* 23, no. 6 (March 1996): 40–41, 60.

1. What are some of the ways that hackers inflict damage, and what are some of the tools they use?

2. What four things can teachers do to promote proper attitudes about online activities?

3. What are copyright laws designed to do? What is the constitutional basis for such laws in this country, and how is the interpretation of copyright laws in other countries becoming a problem in relation to the Internet?

Milone, Michael N., Jr., and Judy Salpeter. "Technology and Equity Issues." *Technology and Learning* 16, no. 4 (January 1996): 38–42.

1. Compare the different levels of computer access (at home and at school) for children from low-income families and children of high-income families.

2. In addition to socioeconomic differences, are there also gender differences in access to and uses of technology?

▬ Activities ▬▬▬▬▬▬▬▬▬▬▬▬▬▬▬▬▬▬▬▬▬▬▬

1. Construct and administer a 15-item survey that would help students in your class get to know each other better. Questions should emphasize value-laden issues ("Are professional sports overemphasized in our culture?" or "What is the biggest problem facing public education today?") over matters of personal taste ("What is your favorite pizza topping?" or "Who is your favorite male singer?"). Enter the data from the survey into a database and analyze the results for trends or anomalies by applying different relational strategies available with the database.

2. Obtain a copy of one of the programs from the *Choices, Choices* or *Decisions, Decisions* series by Tom Snyder Productions. Preview it, critique it, and write a rationale for its use in your curriculum. Decide whether you would use the program at the beginning, middle, or end of a unit and support your decision. Also, describe what other instructional activities (computer activities and exercises away from the computer) you would develop to complement the learning experience.

Democracy
and
Technology

Allen D. Glenn

I am no longer a provider and controller of information. I must teach these students the skills they need to use information. I have to rethink how and what I teach." These words belong to Jack Webber, a sixth-grade teacher at Samantha Smith Elementary School in Redmond, Washington.[1] He was talking about his teaching experiences during a social studies unit in which students had used two computer databases, one on the fifty U.S. states and another on the countries in the world community. His students' class activities of the last several weeks confirmed in Mr. Webber's

mind what he had thought all along—new technologies are changing teaching and learning. What had happened in Mr. Webber's class?

The class was studying a typical social studies unit, the United States and Europe. A basic understanding of America served as the foundation for the study of a country in Europe and then of the continent. In fact, all the sixth grades were studying the same unit. In Mr. Webber's class, however, students used new, powerful computer databases. Working in cooperative groups, students first developed basic computer

---

1. Mr. Webber is part of a study on the use of computer databases and problem solving in social studies. The study, taking place in Virginia, Indiana, Minnesota, and Washington, is sponsored by the MECC/University of Minnesota Research for the Study of Educational Technology.

The Social Studies (September/October 1990): 215–17. Reprinted with permission of the Helen Dwight Reid Educational Foundation. Published by Heldref Publications, 1319 Eighteenth Street, NW, Washington, DC 20036–1802. Copyright © 1990.

database skills and knowledge about the fifty states. Next each group selected a European country for in-depth study. Each group had access to print materials, video materials, and a computer database. Through a series of learning activities developed by Mr. Webber, students in each cooperative group acquired new technology skills and knowledge about the United States, Europe, and the world. For the first time in their learning, students had ready access to a large database of information, were taught skills needed to access the information, and were led through a series of exercises designed to help them develop generalizations. The information and the ability to access the databases influenced their decision making, the way they cooperated with each other and the teacher, and their knowledge of the subject. It also changed the way Mr. Webber thought about his teaching and the skills he needs to develop in his students.

In classrooms across the globe, microcomputers, computer networks, laserdiscs, CD-ROMs, videotape, television, and satellite communication are changing the nature of the classroom, student learning, and the information available to students. The National Foundation for the Improvement of Education, for example, speculates that tomorrow's social studies experience may be somewhat like this:

> Diana's Social Sciences class is studying about past civilizations and cultures. Diana's class is using telecommunications to search databases on topics and artifacts they have discovered. She has just sent a message through her laptop computer at her student workstation to a

student in the foreign language class to help translate a script found scrawled on one of the objects. She then calls up the interactive videodisc surrogate field trip of Cancun. She travels through the ruins, choosing many different paths. She selects in-depth information on digging techniques (Bruder 1990, 29).

The social studies classroom of tomorrow will be one rich with information that will be easily accessed, manipulated, and analyzed. Walt Tremer (Bruder 1990), teacher at Southern Lehigh high school in Center Valley, Pennsylvania, sees tomorrow's classroom as one in which students can "sit in their classroom and ... [can] interact 'face-to-face' with kids all over the world." Access to information will be "a window on the world to my students."

But what do these new technologies have to do with democracy? The answer is "a lot." The articles in this issue of *The Social Studies* suggest that a democratic nation is founded upon a common set of values, citizens with a knowledge base, individuals who can make decisions, people who believe in the rights of others, and men and women who are able to act on their beliefs. At the center of these characteristics is information. Information is power, and technology is dramatically changing the information available to citizens and governments, altering how it may be used in a political system, creating moral issues, and demanding that citizens develop new skills to use information in the decision-making process. In a democratic society where all citizens have the right to participate equally in the political process, technological skills and the ability to use information may lead to a power gap between those who know how to use technology and those who do not. Technological advances, therefore, are changing the nature of information in society and the skills citizens need for the information age.

The Changing Nature of Information

If a political system is to meet the demands placed upon it by its citizens and by external forces, it must collect information. The process is as old as government. What has changed is the speed by which information is collected, accessed, and analyzed. Hard discs and magnetic tape have replaced the sheet of paper and the file cabinet. High-speed digital computers process information from a variety of sources, including satellites far above the earth. Databanks and simulations for system analysis based on the capabilities of the computer are used by government officials to make decisions about who gets what. For example, census databanks are used to determine the number of representatives for each state and serve as the baseline for other federal allocations to individual states. Social security databanks keep track of the tax payments of working citizens and the amounts due to qualified persons. Data are also used to develop models or simulations used in various system-analysis activities. Public policy and military decisions are often explored through system-analysis techniques. Through simulation, it is possible to test different hypotheses and explore alternatives. For example, what would be the impact on public schools if all children between the ages of three and five were to attend preschool?

Through system-analysis techniques, public officials can test various alternative strategies before proposing a particular policy. Data manipulated by supercomputers are the lifeblood of the modern political system.

Citizens in any political system must also rely on information about the political process. In authoritarian societies, political rulers control the information as an effective means of controlling the citizens. For forty-five years, citizens of eastern Europe were denied access to accurate information about the status of the political system. Through advances in technology, especially global television, the truth about political, economic, and social conditions became known. The end result was knowledge that the political system no longer met the demands of the people, and dramatic changes occurred.

Citizens throughout the world have access to more information than ever before. As the dramatic events occurred in Eastern Europe, people across the world witnessed them through live television broadcasts beamed via satellite. "Live from…" is a phrase common to broadcast news and has shaped people's views about information. More and more adults rely on television as their primary source of information. Mary Hepburn (1990) suggests that television has become the most powerful citizen educator. How this media shapes citizens' ideas of the truth has dramatic implications for a society.

Richard Remy (1980) noted in *The Handbook of Basic Citizenship Competencies* that a competent citizen must be able to acquire and process information, assess involvement, make judgments and decisions, communicate, cooperate, and promote interests because "societies without significant numbers of citizens who can, for example, acquire information, make independent judgments and communicate their opinions to public officials are less likely to be able to maintain democratic traditions and forms of governance than societies with such individuals." If new technologies are causing changes in the information available to citizens and the skills they need to understand it, democratic citizens must learn more about information and develop appropriate skills. For example, the students in Mr. Webber's class had access to more information than ever before. They did not need to rely on one textbook or on the knowledge of their teacher. Data, easily accessed on their classroom computer, were available on 177 countries in the world! And videotapes and printed materials were also available to enhance the information from the database. The knowledge learned was then presented in a special format designed by the students via a computer word-processing program. Based on their own analysis of the data, students developed descriptive and explanatory generalizations about the world community. These students experienced life in the information age and the challenges of abundant information.

A Democratic Citizen in a Technological Age

Democratic societies depend on the knowledge, skills, and attitudes of their citizens in order to maintain the stability needed to grow and prosper. In a technological age, democratic citizens also need the knowledge and skills appropriate for the time. The concepts presented throughout this issue are critical; however, they must be extended to include the following:

Citizens in a democracy must:

◆ understand the role of information in a democratic society and the issues related to the balance between the ideals of freedom and privacy and the need for information;

◆ comprehend how data are collected, stored, analyzed, and used in policymaking decisions;

◆ gain the technological skills needed to access and manipulate information on various technology systems—computers, videodiscs, networks, and CD-ROMs;

◆ be able to assess the quality of the information being presented to them, whether it be in digital or visual databases or presented visually via electronic devices;

◆ develop analytical skills needed to develop descriptive and explanatory generalizations drawing upon a varied database;

◆ explore topics related to technology to gain an understanding of how technology is affecting social, political, and economic issues;

◆ be able to work cooperatively with others in examining data, developing possible solutions, and making decisions; and

◆ believe that they have the ability to access the information they need to make decisions.

To be participants in the democratic process, tomorrow's citizens must understand the changing nature of information and develop the individual and group skills needed to use information in an effective way. Almost forty years ago, Hubert Evans and Ryland Crary (1952) wrote, "A free society is free because its citizens, past and present, have made it free; it will remain free only as long as citizens keep it free." The challenges for today's democratic citizen are to understand how technology is changing society and to develop the skills needed to use these technologies effectively. ❖

References

Bruder, I. "Education and Technology in the 1990s and Beyond: Visions of the Future." *Electronic Learning* 9, no. 4 (1990): 24–30.

Evans, H., and R. W. Crary. "The Citizen as Problem Solver." In *Education for Democratic Citizenship: Twenty-second Yearbook of the National Council for the Social Studies*, edited by R. W. Crary, 29. Washington, DC: National Council for the Social Studies, 1952.

Hepburn, M. A. "Americans Glued to the Tube: Mass Media, Information, and Social Studies." *Social Education* 54, no. 4 (1990): 233–36.

Remy, R. C. *Handbook of Basic Citizenship Competencies*. Alexandria, VA: Association for Supervision and Curriculum Development, 1980.

Computers, Kids, and Values

Stephen J. Taffee

The computer revolution has brought with it a host of related ethical and moral concerns which have been given little more than lip service by educators. These concerns include privacy issues, equality of computing opportunity, violence and stereotyping of characters in computer games and computer crime. There are reports of students becoming engrossed in computers at the expense of their relationships with others and/or their school work. Educators wanting to address these concerns find their efforts confounded by a lack of legal certainty about hardware and software copyrights and patents; the availability of sophisticated copy programs and hardware designed to reproduce even copy-protected software; software rental agencies (which allegedly contribute to illegal copying); the hero image accorded computer "hackers" (a la *War Games*) who make unauthorized entry into computer systems; and a great deal of confusion and conflict in society at large about the appropriate place for computers in our daily lives.

While answers to what is "right" or "wrong," "good" or "bad" about computers may be elusive, a means for making such judgments is not. Educators have been using values clarification for many years to help students acquire more meaningful, socially constructive guides to decision making. While this process and technique is widely known (Raths, Harmin, and Simon 1978; Simon, Howe, and Kirschenbaum 1972; Simon and Clark 1975), values clarification has seldom been applied to computer-related issues.

From *The Computing Teacher* 12, no. 1 (August/September 1984): 15–18. Reprinted with permission from the International Society for Technology in Education. All rights reserved.

Values Clarification

Values clarification is a process for helping students make better informed decisions about values and moral issues. It is neither morally absolute nor morally relativistic ("everything goes"). Instead, it requires that students reflect on available value choices, the consequences of each choice, how they act on their values and how they feel about their values. Students are encouraged to develop the interpersonal communications skills necessary to explore such issues with each other in meaningful ways. Teachers, through the use of carefully constructed values clarification exercises and class discussion, can help students wrestle with many important issues involving computers, without lecturing and nagging on the one hand, or simply avoiding the subject, hoping students will somehow work it out on their own.

Here are several values clarification strategies which focus upon values and moral issues concerning computers or which use computer terms as a means of stimulating discussion of broader issues. Remember—each strategy is meant as a stimulus for discussion and is not an end in itself. Clarification of values occurs when students have an opportunity to reflect and to share their thoughts and feelings over a period of time. Teachers must guard against their own as well as students' moralizing and try to keep the class free from pronouncements of right and wrong which can end class participation prematurely.

The new user of values clarification strategies is strongly encouraged to read one of the many introductions to the use of the technique which are available (see References). While the techniques are not difficult to use, it is important that they be used in a manner which will reduce the tendency to moralize or otherwise influence students to respond in ways which they believe would be acceptable to their teacher. Teachers are encouraged to share their own responses to any of these strategies with their students, but it is best done toward the end of class so as not to unduly influence students.

Strategies about Computers

Strategy #1: Values Continuum

One of the mainstays of values clarification, the values continuum, encourages students to see that values often are not absolute, and that there can be a wide range of opinions on a given topic.

Directions: Explain the extremes represented by each end of the continuas in Figures 1 and 2, and ask students to consider where their values fall on those continua. The strategy may be processed using any of the outlined discussion techniques.

In Figure l, "Lock-it Louise" believes that all software should be extensively copy-protected and that violators should be prosecuted to the full extent of the law. Copy programs and devices, and software rental enterprises would be outlawed. "Copy Kate," on the other hand, would do away with all copy-protection schemes, and would support legislation to allow all software to be listed and modified as the user sees fit. In the meantime, the copying of software is seen as a perfectly legitimate alternative.

Figure 1.   Software Protection Continuum

Lock-it Louise   Copy Kate

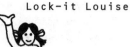

Figure 2.   Purpose of Computers Continuum

Gaming Gabe

Serious Cyril

In Figure 2, Gaming Gabe is a computer game freak who defines computers as "toys" and is only interested in using computers for fun. Serious Cyril sees computers as "tools" and takes a work-oriented approach to them. Cyril is interested in computers to the extent that they can make his life more productive and profitable.

Discussion: The continuum strategy may be processed in several ways.

1. Designate ends of the classroom as ends of the continuum and ask students to walk to the part of the room which best represents their position on the continuum. Once there, they may discuss their choices and reasoning with nearby students and adjust their position if necessary.

2. You can draw a continuum on a chalkboard or overhead transparency and ask several students to write their name on the continuum at the spot representing their position. A class discussion can follow.

3. You may keep this activity (and any of those which follow) at a more "private" level and encourage students to interact with each other in small groups or to write about their experiences in a journal.

Strategy #2: Rank Order

In this strategy, students are asked to prioritize a list of alternatives. The choices may be constructed to be mostly attractive or unattractive (thus making choosing more difficult), or neutral to encourage a range of opinion.

Directions: Explain to students that they are to rank order the following classes of programs. (Some may need to have the meaning of rank order explained to them.) Students are to place the number 1 next to the type of program most important to them, a 2 next to the next most important, and so on.

___ Arcade-type games

___ Communications utilities

___ Copy utilities

___ Educational games/drills/tutorials

___ Fantasy games

___ Graphics/drawing (including Logo)

___ Programming utilities

___ Spreadsheets

___ Word processing

Discussion: The activity may be processed by asking students to share their rank orders with the rest of the class or a small group. Students may also make private journal entries.

Rank orders may also be applied to situations involving people. For example, teachers could read the following anecdote to their class, and ask students to rank order the characters' behavior from most ethical to least ethical:

Mary recently was given a new computer system for her birthday. Prior to that, she was very interested in computers, but mostly because her friend, Brad, was president of the school's computer club. Mary would like to join the school's club, both to learn more about her computer and to be closer to Brad. However, the club has an unofficial initiation requirement that one "pirated" program be submitted to the club's software library by every new member. Brad tells Mary that if she wants to join, she needs to provide the group with a copy of *Martian Mania* (a copy-protected game that came with her new computer). Mary refuses, telling Brad that to do so would be wrong, and even if she wanted to she wouldn't know how to copy it. Another club member, Ann, tells Mary that she could borrow any one of her nibble copying programs or even use her "duplicard"—a hardware device for copying protected software. Disgusted with both Brad and Ann, Mary secretly lets the club's advisor know about the pirating and illegal software library. The advisor subsequently disciplines Brad and Ann, and erases all the club's illegal programs.

Rank the behaviors of the following persons or groups from most ethical to least ethical:

Ann

Brad

Club Advisor

Duplicard, Inc. (manufacturers of software and hardware copying devices)

Martian Mania's producers

Mary

A discussion—quite likely a lively one—can follow. Be sure to insist that students respect each other's right to an opinion and try to keep the discussion focused on what the characters did or should have done. You can also ask students to consider the ethics of the situation from a perspective other than their own, e.g., the school, the publisher of copy-protected software, the makers of copy-protection breaking devices or a judge.

Strategy #3: Either/Or

This strategy forces students to consider how they perceive the computer, often with very interesting and insightful reasoning. (See Strategy #8 for an example of either/or statements which ask students to make judgments on a more personal level.)

Directions: Ask students to respond to the following statements. Discussion may follow the techniques suggested in Strategy #2: Rank Order.

Which is a computer more like?

❖ Friend or foe?

❖ Hard or soft?

❖ Threat or savior?

❖ Male or female?

❖ Pleasure or pain?

❖ Puzzle or solution?

❖ Work or hobby?

❖ Person or machine?

❖ Fire or ice?

❖ Tool or resource?

❖ Monster or Messiah?

Strategy #4: Values Sheets

Values sheets are among the most adaptable and available of the values clarification strategies. They are reasonably easy to construct and may be processed in a variety of ways.

Directions: Provide students with a short quotation, portion of a magazine or newspaper article, a picture, cartoon or similar "stimulus." They are then to respond to a series of carefully constructed questions which you have prepared. For example, you might distribute the following, well-known quotation from Evans (1979):

> Suppose for a moment that the automobile industry had developed at the same rate as computers.... Today you would be able to buy a Rolls Royce for $2.75, it would do three million miles to the gallon, and it would deliver enough power to drive the Queen Elizabeth II. And if you were interested in miniaturization, you could place half a dozen of them on the head of a pin (76).

1. What three words best describe your reaction to this quotation?

2. What would the world be like if progress in automobiles had indeed matched that of the computer industry?

3. What progress would you like to see in computers during the next twenty years?

4. If you had been given a choice twenty years ago between being able to produce a Rolls Royce quality car for $3.00 or an advanced computer, which would you have chosen? What would have been the consequences of your choice?

5. How is your life different because of microcomputers?

The following cartoon could also be used as a discussion starter:

'I KNOW ITS GREAT FOR THEIR HAND/EYE COORDINATION... IT'S THEIR BRAIN/REALITY COORDINATION THAT CONCERNS ME...'

© 1981, The Philadelphia Inquirer/Washington Post Writers Group. Reprinted with permission.

Potential processing questions might include:

1. What do you think is meant by the term "brain/reality coordination"? What concern is the speaker revealing by this statement?

2. Which would you rather do with a computer: write a letter, solve a problem or play a game? How might you modify the quality and amount of time you spend using a computer?

3. What kind of computer game would you rather play? Pick one quality from each column:

Difficulty

___ Computer wins more than 50 percent of the time.

___ You win more than 50 percent of the time.

Outcome

___ Enemy (or you) destroyed.

___ Treasure gained (or lost).

Display

___ Lots of animation and color

___ Lots of text

Input Device

___ Joystick or paddles

___ Keyboard

4. Which would you rather do (or be able to do)?

❖ Play a computer game.

❖ Write (program) a computer game.

❖ Be a character in a computer game (like *Tron*).

❖ Watch an expert play a computer game.

Strategy #5: Inventory

Computers and technology enter our lives in hundreds of ways almost every day. Many of us use the world's largest computer network every day (the telephone system) without even thinking of it as computer-driven. Similarly, we receive mail generated by computer mailing lists and buy groceries which are classified and priced by a computer.

Directions: Students are to keep a journal of the number and type of computers and technologically-related devices (e.g., calculators) which they encounter in one week. The activity may be processed individually, in small groups or by the whole class.

Strategy #6:
Unfinished Sentences

Like the values sheet, this activity can be spontaneously constructed by a teacher, or suggestions can be elicited from the students themselves. It is an excellent warm-up activity for more in-depth activities, and can remain viable indefinitely if the sentence stems are varied and the strategy itself not overused.

Directions: Students are to complete the following sentence stems. Process the activity through techniques previously identified.

- ❖ I wish computers were more _____ and less _____ .

- ❖ Computers are _____ .

- ❖ I'd rather work with a computer than _____ , but I'd rather _____ than work with a computer.

- ❖ Copying programs _____ .

- ❖ "Hackers" _____ .

- ❖ The best thing I've ever done on a computer was _____ .

- ❖ Computers are never _____ but they're always _____ .

- ❖ Ten years from now, I hope computers _____ .

Strategies that Use Computers

As students become more computer literate, educators will be able to use computers as examples and symbols for other aspects of life. Strategies 7 and 8 make use of the computer as a means of stimulating discussion about a range of values-related issues.

Strategy #7:
Ask the Computer

Directions: Tell students that they have been given a rare opportunity to ask questions of the world's largest, fastest and smartest computer. However, they will each be allowed to ask only one question. While the computer is the world's smartest, it is limited and may not be able to answer "impossible" questions such as, "How many stars are in the universe?" Care should be taken, therefore, to construct a question which is both reasonable and personally meaningful to the student.

Students can be encouraged to work alone or in groups. If you wish, you might ask students to write an essay about their question and how it is important to them. Questions can be shared, with a class discussion held on the types of questions asked and which ones a computer could really answer.

This strategy could easily work into an extended discussion pertinent to computer literacy. You might discuss which is more important: asking good questions, providing good answers or having good information. This would provide an excellent opportunity to discuss the limitations of computers and whether "logical" answers are always "right" answers.

Strategy #8: Either/Or

Which are you more like?

- ◆ Dot-matrix printer or a letter-quality printer?
- ◆ Timex/Sinclair or a Cray supercomputer?
- ◆ Floppy disk or a hard disk?
- ◆ RAM or ROM?
- ◆ Input or output?
- ◆ Bit or a byte?
- ◆ Hardware or software?
- ◆ BASIC or assembly language?

General Comments and Conclusion

Our knowledge and skills in working with computers are progressing at breathtaking speed. If computers are to become fully integrated into our lives and our society, then concerted efforts must be made to encourage progress concerning the many value-related concerns accompanying the computer revolution. Computers are inherently apolitical, unbiased and unthinking machines, yet they may be used in ways which dehumanize and oppress people, or in ways which personalize and liberate people. Values clarification offers us a mechanism for beginning a dialogue with students about such issues. Like the computer itself, it is not a panacea, but it is an exceptional opportunity and resource. ◆

References

Evans, Christopher. *The Micro Millenium.* New York: Viking Press, 1979.

Raths, Louis, Merrill Harmin, and Sidney B. Simon. *Values and Teaching, Working with Values in the Classroom.* 2d ed. Columbus, OH: Charles E. Merrill Publishing Company, 1978.

Simon, Sidney B., and Jay Clark. *Beginning Values Clarification.* San Diego: Pennant Press, 1975.

Simon, Sidney B., Leland W. Howe, and Howard Kirschenbaum. *Values Clarification: A Handbook of Practical Strategies for Teachers and Students.* New York: Hart Publishing Company, 1972.

S *tephen J. Taffee, Associate Professor of Education, North Dakota State University, Fargo, ND 58105.*

This article will also appear in a forthcoming book, edited by the author, entitled Annual Editions: Computers in Education 84/85. *Dushkin Publishing Group, Inc.*

A Question of Ethics

Larry S. Hannah
and Charles B. Matus

Not all the computer news these days involves announcements of new technological breakthroughs, machines, or even new software. Recent headlines in the News section of *InfoWorld* point out some of the other computer-related issues facing our society.

> "Louisiana legislation would punish software pirates" (March 19, 1984, p. 16).

> "Apple wins copyright appeal: Australian court bolsters international law" (June 25, 1984, p. 12).

> "Quakers condemn violent video games" (April 2, 1984, p. 18).

> "Police raid worries sysops: bulletin board shutdown raises debate" (July 9, 1984, p. 30).

> "Video arcades meet stiff community opposition" (December 26, 1983/January 2, 1984, p. 18)

Another issue ran as its cover story, "Preschool computing: are we pushing our kids too hard?" (February 20, 1984, pp. 24–27).

Background

The strategy for cognitive development of moral and social reasoning as discussed in this article is based largely on the work of Professor Lawrence Kohlberg of Harvard University. A dilemma such as "The Final Project" depicts an issue or situation in which at least two alternative courses of action are available, neither of which clearly represents a socially determined or approved response.

From *The Computing Teacher* 12, no. 1 (August/September 1984): 11–14. Reprinted with permission from the International Society for Technology in Education. All rights reserved.

The Final Project

"Sue, you're not listening. You have to come over and help me. If I don't get the program finished before tomorrow morning, I'll get an 'F' on the programming project and may not pass the course." Tom was pleading for what he dearly hoped was the last time. If only he hadn't waited until the last night to get started. "Look, I tried everything, but somehow the darn thing just won't sort properly. I know that it's something small, but I just can't get it to work."

After listening to more reasons why Sue felt she shouldn't help him, Tom tried again. "I know that it may seem like cheating, but it's really not. It has to be some silly little error. I've done all of the important work myself. Besides, the whole idea is to learn and I'll be learning how to do it. I'm not asking you to write the whole program, just to find the bug. You're supposed to be a friend. What kind of friend are you if you won't help out when I really need it?"

Should Sue help Tom?   Yes   No

Why or why not?

Is it a friend's duty to help even if that help might be considered cheating?

Is it fair of Tom to request Sue's help on his project? Why or why not?

What would you advise Sue to do in this situation? Explain.

Each of these items is an indication that the widespread use of microcomputers has brought with it new social and moral issues, issues that must be faced by young people as well as adults. How can we as teachers work with moral and social issues such as these in our classrooms? How can we prepare our students to handle such questions? The sidebar represents a discussion that might take place in a classroom where a teacher is working with these issues.

The students' task in this discussion is *not* to reach group consensus on Sue's proper action, but rather to examine the moral and social consequences of different courses of action that Sue might take. Each student is encouraged to think about and express possible actions focusing on the reasoning behind the choices. This is the dilemma they are discussing.

As students participate in a discussion group, they have an opportunity to practice reasoning and decision-making skills. The student may examine consequences of various responses within the relative "safety" of the group. The focused discussion provides a structured opportunity to reach and test tentative conclusions as well as to be exposed to the ideas of others, an experience which enhances the development of complex reasoning skills.

Dilemmas are designed to present situations relating to course content, current social issues, or the lives of the students in which the central character has to decide between alternative possibilities for action on a moral or social issue. Discussion is to focus on what the central character(s) *should* do and *reasons* supporting that action, not on what the character would do or what the student would or would not do. Probe questions are used to elicit student responses that include both a recommended course of action and a reason for that action.

Extensive research by Dr. Kohlberg and others has demonstrated that during structured, yet open, discussions of dilemma situations, students benefit from examining their own reasoning and that of other participants. Through interaction during discussion of these dilemmas, people naturally move toward more complex, broader reasoning. While Kohlberg bases moral education on universal principles of justice, there is no preaching a set of "appropriate" virtues. The method is based on the concepts that morality develops in stages and that everyone passes through the same stages of moral development. The discussion group provides the necessary interaction to enable growth to occur.

Using Dilemmas in the Classroom

Dilemma discussions may be used at any grade level—however, one must account for varying levels of sophistication in reasoning. Vocabulary, topic selection and time allotment will vary with age and grade level. The younger the group, the more similar reasoning will be; as age advances, so do the variety and complexity of responses to dilemma situations.

The following guidelines will lead to an active, productive dilemma discussion.

◈ Establish a nonthreatening atmosphere where students feel free to express their opinions and are not intimidated when their ideas are challenged by others.

Alicia: I don't think that Sue should help Tom. After all, he did wait until the last minute to start.

George: I go along with Alicia. If Tom had started earlier, he would have been able to debug the program. And if he couldn't, then he didn't understand the algorithm and shouldn't pass anyway.

Mary: I disagree. If he turns it in and gets an "F," he won't learn how to do it—which he might if Sue reviews the program with him. It's the end of the year and he won't get to see the corrected program. I think that he probably has learned his lesson about waiting until the last minute. And anyway, that's not the main point. Don't forget that he did write most of the program.

George: He may have written most of the program, but the sorting element probably is the key routine. If he hasn't learned it or can't figure it out, that's his problem, not Sue's. It's his assignment.

Harley: To heck with the program. Either she's Tom's friend or she's not. If she's a friend, she'll help. If she isn't, she won't. It's as simple as that.

◈ Present the dilemma clearly by reading it to the class. Ask the class to verbally reconstruct the dilemma. This serves as a reinforcement and summary of the major components in the dilemma.

◈ Encourage student interaction and avoid the tendency to respond with your own opinions. Any early expression of teacher ideas can influence the reasoning of some students

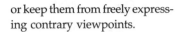
W h a t ' s   t h e   H a r m ?

"What's wrong, Sue? You look as though something is bothering you."

"Jim, do you know what Bill, Mary and the others are doing in the computer lab? They were scanning the Keymakers' Bulletin Board and found the telephone number and access code of the Security Credit Bureau. I thought it was funny when they called the credit bureau and found out that the principal was three months behind on his car payments. But then, somehow, it didn't seem right. They're checking on Mrs. Henderson, our English teacher, right now. Did you know that they can find out how much anyone owes on their credit cards, house, car, anything? ... I know that they don't plan to do anything special with the information, but it just doesn't seem right."

"Well," Jim asked, "what do you plan to do? You know that if you tell any of the teachers about it, we'll just get banned from using the lab after school. You remember that Mrs. Roberts warned us about calling that bulletin board last week. Did you try to get them to stop?"

"Yes, but they think that it's just a game. They won't quit. I really think that I should tell Mrs. Roberts, but you're right. They will start closing the lab after school and the group will blame me. I don't know what to do."

Should Sue report the group? Yes No

Why or why not?

Is it actually right or wrong for Bill, Mary and the others to be getting credit information on people using the computer access code from the Security Credit Bureau? Explain.

⇒

or keep them from freely expressing contrary viewpoints.

The discussion begins after you ask the initial probe question. Respond to a rationale-supported response by accepting it non-judgmentally. When a student gives an unsupported response, you must probe for the rationale before accepting the answer. If you do not understand a student's response, seek clarification before accepting or probing further.

Keep the discussion flowing by intervening with appropriate questions. Be careful not to dominate the discussion with too many questions, and do not allow any one student or small group to dominate.

Keep the discussion open-ended. The conversation should focus on the *reasons* used to justify recommended actions relating to the issues in the dilemma—not on the actions themselves. Focusing on the reasoning helps to emphasize the point that there are no inherent right or wrong answers. Do not attempt to force the class to reach agreement on an answer or solution to the dilemma.

A few minutes before you are scheduled to stop, or when it appears that the group has exhausted the subject, bring the discussion to a close. A non-judgmental summary of the viewpoints expressed during the discussion is very helpful and vital in leaving the group with a sense of accomplishment. It also serves to clarify the various positions expressed by students. You may wish to have them summarize points raised by others, or ask the students to continue the discussion with their parents/family after providing a copy of the dilemma and questions to take home. You also may use the discussion as a lead-in for other activities, e.g., creative writing, analysis of historically similar situations, etc.

It is important that you express your appreciation to the group for their efforts, cooperation and accomplishments.

Here are three additional dilemmas for your use, followed by a general discussion of the dilemmas which place them in a classroom context. The probe questions at the end of each dilemma are used to regenerate a discussion that has begun to stall or become one-sided. The intent is not to seek a specific response or force a position, but rather to challenge students' thinking and require them to re-examine their position(s) based upon additional data. There is no magic involved in conducting moral dilemma discussions—just follow the guidelines given, keep the discussion open and focus on reasons. Students and teachers who have been involved in discussions on dilemmas such as these have found them to be exciting, informative and productive.

Each dilemma presented addresses one or more social and moral issues. In "The Final Project" students are asked to examine the concepts of friendship, obligations, honesty and

If Sue told Mrs. Roberts about the group's activities, would it be fair for Mrs. Roberts to close the computer lab to all students after school? Why or why not?

Should Sue's decision to tell or not to tell be affected by her classmates' feelings toward her? Explain your answer.

If the majority of students agree that Sue should tell, then probe further with:

Would it change the situation if Sue knew that the students accessing the Credit Bureau would be suspended from school if their activities were discovered? Explain.

If the majority of the class agrees that Sue should not tell, then probe further with:

Would it change the situation if the students accessing the Credit Bureau records started to gossip about the information they were obtaining, and even started getting information on the parents of students in the school? Explain your answer.

If you were Sue, what would you do? Explain.

Write or Wrong

Ms. Garcia, the school principal, was preparing for a discussion on the district's interim word-processing policy with the faculty. She had been told by her supervisor to reaffirm the interim policy stating that "no major assignments are to be done with the aid of microcomputer word-processing programs." Ms. Garcia also was aware that the policy was controversial with faculty members, students and parents. Already, one student had refused to comply with the policy and had received a failing grade on a term paper written on a word processor. The student was challenging the policy and had appealed to Ms. Garcia.

Ms. Garcia knew it was her duty as principal to enforce the interim policy even though she was personally undecided about its fairness. She felt badly that a student at her school was getting an "F" based on a policy that even the school board had declared as "interim" while they studied the issue further.

Should Ms. Garcia enforce the policy? Why? Why not?

Is the policy fair to everyone? Should students who have a computer at home have an advantage over those who do not? Explain. Is the student who received an "F" right in challenging the policy? Explain.

If the majority of the class agrees that Ms. Garcia should not enforce the policy, probe further by modifying the dilemma as follows:

Would it change the situation if Ms. Garcia knew that non-enforcement of the policy would lead to a protest by several students and parents? They already had argued that allowing one student's violation of school policy to go unpunished is unfair to those who had complied and not used word processing. Explain.

fairness as they relate to the dilemma of whether or not to help a friend on a school assignment.

"What's the Harm?" illustrates a couple of basic points concerning the use and structure of dilemmas in the classroom. Real-world, topical issues can be used to stimulate interest and debate. The dilemma is based on a news story that broke on June 20, 1984. In this case, unauthorized individuals used home computers to access TRW Information Services, a credit data bank with information on over 90 million persons. The access was made using a phone number and access code listed on a computerized bulletin board. The only other information required was the name and address of the person on whom they were seeking information (*The Sacramento Bee*, June 21, 1984).

Although the dilemma focuses on a computer-based topic, students are asked to reason around age-old questions regarding friendship and responsibility to a group versus responding to an ideal. A direct focus on whether or not one should make unauthorized entrance into a data bank is too easily responded to with a "no" answer. Topics which have obvious "right" or "wrong" answers do not lead to productive debate. In the course of the debate on whether Sue should or should not report her friends, much information will be shared on information services, data banks in general, data security, modems, bulletin boards, etc. The debate on the dilemma topic can be followed by a valuable discussion of these related topics and others such as the issue of privacy.

"Quest for the Wizard" requires discussion participants to examine their beliefs in a situation which tests personal and professional ethics. Scott is caught between keeping a promise and sharing with a friend. The issue is further complicated by the potential violation of copyright laws. Scott is tempted by a devious request to violate his promise and is reminded that he has not refused programs in the past that were reproduced in violation of copyright. These are complex issues with which to wrestle, but ones that are commonly faced and responded to without a great deal of thought.

Often during the course of a dilemma discussion such as with "Write or Wrong," participants will want to "solve" the dilemma. They may respond to probe questions by requesting more details or by proposing solutions. When this happens, be aware that the discussion could easily slip into a problem-solving exercise unless you refocus the discussion on the moral issues involved. If you repeatedly find it necessary to refocus on the issues, remind the group of the distinction between solving a problem and examining the issues.

When a dilemma discussion has been exhausted and there is a desire to pursue the topic further from another approach, it is entirely appropriate to shift to problem solving. The objective then is to achieve a solution or solutions which are fair and just. If a true dilemma has been presented, problem solving may be quite difficult and no universally acceptable solution may be found. This, of course, leads to other issues such as the political process of compromise and its inherent ethical and moral implications.

Quest for the Wizard

"WOW! You got *Quest for the Wizard*! How did you ever get that? I've got to get a copy." Indeed, Scott had finally gotten a copy of the game he and everyone else wanted, but it wasn't his to keep. A friend at Software City had felt sorry for him after seeing Scott longingly try out the program for the third Saturday in a row. As a favor, he loaned Scott the store's demonstration copy to play with over the weekend.

"Jerry at the computer store let me borrow it. I had to promise him that I wouldn't make a copy for myself. Sorry, Manny, we can't do that."

"Hey, look, you're not going to hold out on me now, are you? Where do you think you got all your games? You certainly didn't buy them. Without me, you would still be sitting there writing your BASIC programs. Tell you what. You let me make a copy for myself, and then you won't be breaking your promise to Jerry. Then, a few days from now, I'll make a copy for you. Remember, you owe me a lot more than you owe Jerry."

Should Scott make the copy for Manny?   Yes No

Is it Scott's duty to keep his word to Jerry (the software salesperson) and not make himself a copy? Why?

Would it actually be wrong for Scott to let Manny make a copy for himself? Explain your answer.

Does the fact that Manny has shared many programs with Scott obligate Scott to share this program with Manny? Why or why not?

Is Manny being fair in demanding that Scott let him make a copy of *Quest for the Wizard*? Explain your answer.

If the majority of the discussion group agrees that Scott should make a copy of *Quest for the Wizard* for Manny, then probe further with:

Would it matter if Jerry found out and told Scott that he was no longer welcome in the store because he had broken his promise? Explain your answer.

If the majority of the discussion group agrees that Scott should not make a copy of *Quest for the Wizard* for Manny, then probe further with:

Would it matter if Manny told Scott that he would stop sharing his programs if Scott did not share *Quest for the Wizard* and, furthermore, he did not think he was much of a friend if he would not let him make the copy? Explain your answer.

Summary

During the course of each day, young people are faced with a number of decisions requiring social and moral reasoning. These decisions frequently are made without sufficient data, an awareness of alternatives or an understanding of the possible consequences associated with a given course of action. Through the use of dilemma discussions, students are provided the opportunity to examine their beliefs about personal morals and social ethics, and to develop an intrinsic sense of personal and social responsibility without having a set of predetermined virtues thrust upon them.

As educators, we can influence the future by providing young people the opportunity to polish their reasoning skills, to develop fairer and more just positions regarding social and moral issues. The use of the open-ended, moral dilemma discussion is a way of developing cognitive skills that are in keeping with the inherent democratic principles of fairness and justice.   ◆

Resources

For a further discussion of Lawrence Kohlberg's theory of moral reasoning and instructions on writing and using dilemmas, see Ronald E. Galbraith and Thomas M. Jones, *Moral Reasoning: A Teaching Handbook for Adapting Kohlberg to the Classroom.* Minneapolis, MN: Greenhaven Press Inc., 1976.

Dilemmas in this article may be reproduced for classroom use.

*D*r. Larry S. Hannah
School of Education
California State University
Sacramento, CA 95819

*C*harles B. Matus
Sacramento County Office of Education
9738 Lincoln Valley Dr.
Sacramento, CA 95826

On Line Ethics

What's a Teacher to Do?

Cal Carpenter

The National Information Infrastructure (NII), more commonly known as the Internet, is rapidly expanding around the globe and bringing unprecedented interpersonal opportunities to students and teachers whether they be from elementary schools or universities. As a teacher with the Lesley College Graduate School Computers in Education Program, I come into contact with K–12 educators from around the country who are eager to join the online community of the Internet.

As with any young community, however, problems with crime and antisocial behavior from those who lack moral principles are present on the Internet and must be dealt with by those who seek educational opportunities. Due to the spiraling growth of network traffic and the increase of potentially serious problems, businesses, individuals, government offices, and educational institutions have all begun to address ethical issues from their own perspectives. Legislation, codes of conduct, and moral precepts have been suggested as means of keeping the network civilized. A stable moral code for the new technology of interpersonal communications needs to be established for educators. Educators at all levels should initiate and model a standardized role of ethical behavior for all Internet users.

The State of the Net

The recent dramatic growth of the Internet is seen by some as a "feeding frenzy" and by others as a fulfillment of the prediction of technology's impact on

From *Learning and Leading with Technology* 23, no. 6 (March 1996): 40–41, 60. Reprinted with permission from the International Society for Technology in Education. All rights reserved.

society. The exponential growth of the World Wide Web (WWW) has been one of the most significant aspects of the Internet's growth. Bournellis (1995) notes that the Web was introduced in 1992 and began its rise in 1993. The maintainers of the *WebCrawler* search tool conducted a count finding that 38,796 Web servers were in use at the end of June, 1995. Graumann (1994) states that America is moving steadily toward a national communications system capable of carrying many times the volume of information flowing today.

At present, however, the same technology that has brought society so many benefits has created a new criminal element: the hacker. The crimes are varied, but the goal is always the same—the hacker abuses the available technology to gain entry into a secure computer system. Once into a system, a hacker may engage in a number of crimes, such as damaging programs, changing or erasing memory, stealing information, and transferring funds. Hanson (1991) has described some of the tools hackers use.

- Phreaking: Hackers engage in illegal activities having to do with phone lines and accounts. By accessing a company's 800 system or by transferring billing information to another account, phreakers are able to use the phone system without payment.

- Virus: The virus is a computer program containing instructions that copies itself onto, or infects, another program. When triggered, a virus may replicate itself, taking up memory.

- Logic Bomb: This type of virus may be destructive in nature, causing system failures or deleting files from memory. It may be set to trigger on a specified date or when the infected program runs a particular function.

- Worm: A worm is much like a virus in that it will infect a system or program by copying itself and then move on. Unlike a virus, a worm does not attach itself to a program; it remains independent.

- Trojan Horse: This is a program that appears to serve some useful purpose but secretly contains a destructive bit of programming code. While one is using the program, such as a popular game, the hidden Trojan horse may be erasing memory or damaging files. Unlike a virus, the Trojan horse does not replicate itself.

The criminal element in the society of cyberspace is a concern for all members of the community. As user awareness and preventive measures grow, the current problems that frequent the Internet may eventually be replaced by a new renaissance of intellectual development guiding our society into the next century.

Piracy, Privacy, and Security Issues

Most of today's industrial felons do not engage in their criminal behavior with guns or crowbars; they commit their crimes with computers, modems, and loopholes in security systems. Businesses and the appropriate authorities are working to stop the criminal hacker, but they are almost helpless against the millions of software pirates who "steal" from companies by duplicating programs and giving them away to their friends and colleagues. The Software Publishers Association (1993) in Washington, D.C., states that in 1991, the year of the most recent statistical analysis, the software industry in the United States lost an estimated $1.2 billion due to piracy. Most who pirate software, especially educators, do not consider their actions criminal. Teachers often rationalize illegal duplication as the only means to cope with underfunded and overcrowded classroom situations, or believe they are making "fair use" of a product in order to bring technology opportunities to their students.

Copyright laws are designed to protect the intellectual property rights of individuals and are based on Article I, Section 8 of the United States Constitution. These laws are becoming blurred when applied to the Internet. Sivin and Bialo (1992) state that while there is a firm sense of right and wrong when it comes to fair use of physical property, the fair use of computers and related technology often involves the idea that information is property, and we are often confused about how to regard nonprint information. To compound the problem, copyright laws vary greatly from country to country, and the global nature of the Internet allows a user to access information in many countries at one sitting.

But just because a file is available on the Internet doesn't mean that taking it is legal. Making sense of these complex issues is difficult, and trusting our intuition regarding what is ethical and legal is not always the best path to follow. Sivin and Bialo (1992) contend that it is up to educators to become informed about the relevant legal and ethical issues and provide the guidance students need throughout their education.

Privacy in the Information Age is evolving into a technological oxymoron. The gathering and sharing of personal information has become a common practice for business and government. Pillar (1993) indicates that the advent of telecommunications, the growth of centralized government, and the rise of massive credit and insurance industries that manage vast computerized databases have turned formerly modest records into an open forum of data available to nearly anyone for a price. While the United States Constitution does not specifically guarantee personal privacy, Americans have come to believe that their privacy rights extend to their personal mail. But can we expect the right to privacy to extend to our private electronic mail? This is an issue that has particular ramifications for education.

Educators must make their students aware that the security of electronic mail is particularly low. Krol (1994) explains that e-mail messages may be read intentionally, as by system operators, or by mistake, as in the case of a computer-routing error. For example, messages that were thought to be deleted may reappear years later as a result of a system backup. Since e-mail can be traced to its originating machine, proper conduct and ethical activities online must be instilled in users from the outset of telecommunication use. Freedom to use the mail resources of the global Internet must be tempered with common sense and good judgment.

Screening Electronic Sites

In speaking of electronic networks, Vice President Al Gore has said, "To accommodate all the uses for which a free and democratic society needs a national electronic network, the network must be built by the federal government and managed for the benefit of all. It is as much a right for a citizen in this country to use such a national network as to breathe the air and walk the public streets." While many Internet users agree with the democratization of the network, however, metaphorically speaking, the air and streets of America's online networks are not without their own set of problems.

In 1995, Congress passed the Communications Decency Act, which calls for government regulation of the Internet and commercial online services. Total government control of the network will have its detractors. Many believe that full implementation of such regulations constitutes censorship and conflicts with First Amendment rights.

The controversial nature of some material on the Internet often attracts the most attention from the general public. One example is *Time Magazine*'s expose of pornography in cyberspace (Elmer-Dewitt 1995) which spurred government concerns to protect innocent children from the evils of the Internet. Blamed for playing a role in everything from kidnappings to the terrorist attack in Oklahoma City, the Internet has been portrayed as a villain by those who wish to control it. However, another movement that is gaining momentum seeks not to regulate the Internet but rather find ways to develop controls that parents and teachers can use to keep children away

from adult-centered areas of the Internet. Individual computer-based programs such as *SurfWatch* and *Net Nanny* can be used to monitor the information being accessed on the Internet and block transfers from sites carrying offensive material. The list may be amended by parents or teachers. Another program, *SafeSurf* ensures child-safe Web sites by encoding "safe" homepages with an identifiable coding, which in turn are linked to other approved sites. Whatever the method, it is important for parents and teachers to establish ground rules for online use. The global capabilities of the Internet and its use by all students and teachers is a reality that educators are confronting more and more.

Ethics Education and the Internet

As the Internet expands to all aspects of community life, education remains the first line of defense against unethical attitudes that can grow into criminal behavior. Beginning in elementary schools, students and teachers should be exposed to appropriate ethical behavior for using the Internet. To promote proper attitudes about online activities teachers should:

- Establish a clear set of expected behaviors.
- Make each concept real to anchor understanding.
- Model appropriate behaviors.
- Reinforce proper behaviors and attitudes.

Generally, each host service that connects students posts a list of expected behaviors, do's and don'ts, or network etiquette, commonly called netiquette.

The list varies according to local system operators and institutional requirements; however, themes of responsibility, respect, and e-mail management tend to dominate. Some host services and institutions, such as the Cleveland Free-net and Colgate University, require network users to sign ethical compliance forms in which the users agree to uphold established values and behaviors while connected to those resources. Many other institutions—Boston University, Columbia University, James Madison University, Michigan State University, and Purdue University, to name just a few—post their ethics codes online as models for others to examine.

Ethical issues are complex. A list of rules is not adequate to help enhance a student's understanding until the concepts behind them become real. Sivin and Bialo (1992) state that schools can take action on technology ethics on two fronts: 1. setting school policy that provides a model for students to follow and 2. incorporating technology ethical issues into the curriculum. It is through the creativity and resourcefulness of the teacher that the issues may be integrated into the curriculum.

Topics to Explore

Dealing with ethical issues related to using a network is not necessarily easy. Discussions have been successful in some situations, role playing in others. Sometimes the local news or a school event offers a spark to introduce an issue. The key is to allow the student to internalize the concept by experiencing the issue in the focused light of reality. Generally there are a number of themes that can be the focal point for discussions or role playing:

❖ Theft of information: This includes intellectual property and the rights of authors to their material.

❖ Theft or destruction of property: This includes criminal hacking as well as spreading viruses and making unauthorized entry into commercial online services.

❖ Piracy: Students should be informed about issues related to making illegal copies of software.

❖ Privacy: Privacy issues involve accessing private information about people, businesses, or organizations without permission.

❖ Access to technology: This category includes issues of gender, ethnicity, and economic differences that impact access.

As technology expands through all facets of society, so too should the training that will establish a broad awareness of acceptable activity.

An Ethics Model

Educators play a central role in bringing order to the new frontier of electronic networking. As educators learn and accept new paradigms, standard codes of behavior for proper use of the Internet, and technology in general, will be developed, taught, and modeled throughout a student's education. The following 10 rules might serve as a set of guidelines and help generate a discussion of ethics in the use of the Internet and related technologies:

1. Be responsible in your use of the network.

2. Respect the rights and privacy of others.

3. Respect the property of others.

4. Respect authors' rights to their ideas.

5. Be honest and law-abiding in online activities.

6. Assume that your e-mail is public.

7. Don't use vulgar or offensive language.

8. Before downloading material to disks, check for viruses.

9. Monitor how much memory your Internet activity uses.

10. Follow the netiquette of your host computer.

Our awareness about proper Internet use is growing, but only when our actions reflect a proper ethical attitude will society be able to attain the full potential that this evolving technology offers. ✦

References

Bournellis, C. "Internet '95." *Internet World* (November 1995): 47–52.

Elmer-Dewitt, P. "On a Screen Near You: Cyberporn." *Time* 146 (July 1995): 1.

Graumann, P. J. "The Road to the Information Highway: Are We Almost There Yet?" *Technology and Learning* (March 1994): 28–34.

Hanson, G. "Computer Users Pack a Keypunch in a High-tech World of Crime." *Insight* 15 (April 1991): 8–17.

Krol, E. *The Whole Internet User's Guide and Catalog.* 2d ed. Sebastopol, CA: O'Reilly & Associates, 1994.

Pillar, C. "Privacy in Peril: How Computers Are Making Private Life a Thing of the Past." *MacWorld* (July 1993): 124–30.

Sivin, J. P., and E. R. Bialo. *Ethical Use of Information Technologies in Education: Important Issues for America's Schools.* Washington, DC: U.S. Government Printing Office, 1992. DOJ Publication no. OJP–91–C–005.

Software Publishers Association. *Education Software Management: The K–12 Guide to Legal Software Use.* Washington, DC: Software Publishers Association, 1993.

Software

Use these Web addresses to obtain more information on the following screening software.

Net Nanny

http://www.netnanny.com/netnanny/

SafeSurf

http://www.safesurf.com

SurfWatch

http://www.surfwatch.com/surfwatch/

*C*al Carpenter
38 Dunster Road
Bedford, MA 01730
CalCarpent@aol.com;
calcarp@tiac.net

Technology and Equity Issues

Michael N. Milone, Jr.
and Judy Salpeter

Are computers widening the gap between the "haves" and the "have nots" in this country? Or is technology helping to level the playing field? Some of our conclusions might surprise you.

Among the issues that face educators in the next decade, perhaps none is more important than providing all students with comparable educational opportunities, particularly with respect to technology. To understand how important schooling—and indirectly, exposure to technology—is to a student's future, one need look no further than the U.S. Department of Labor's 1992 publication, *What Work Requires of Schools: A SCANS Report for America 2000*. In the report, the authors assert that "More than half of our young people leave school without the knowledge or foundation required to find and hold a good job." The report was not addressing technology specifically, but given the rapid infiltration of technology into all careers, the infer-

ence one can draw is that today's young people are not being prepared as well as they should be to succeed in tomorrow's highly technical careers.

Inadequate access to technology not only makes it difficult for young people to find and keep a decent job, it also prevents them from participating completely in civic discourse, a problem noted by Cherry McGee Banks in the September 1993 issue of *Phi Delta Kappan*. Although McGee Banks had no way of knowing how accurate her prediction would be, the election of 1994 proved her prescient. The outcome of the election was due in great measure to the Republican party's ability to mobilize voters through technology—television, talk radio, voice mail, online services, and fax communication. Whether you agree or disagree with the outcome of the election, the fact is that those who best controlled technology came out on top. It is in the best interest of both today's young people and the nation as a whole that *all* students have an opportunity to master the elements of technology they will need to have a productive future. Further, it is also clear that technology should be one of the principal tools by which students learn to manage the ever-increasing base of knowledge they will need to achieve success. After all, today's students are tomorrow's mechanics and doctors, teachers and political leaders. Given this indisputable need, the issue then centers on access and quality: Do all students have equitable access to technology, and is the quality of their access comparable?

From Home to School

If we begin with a look at the home scene, it becomes clear that there is a serious gap between higher-income students, many of whom have access to personal computers, and children from families that lack the resources to purchase such hardware.

The Link Resources Home Media Consumer Survey found that, in 1995, almost 42 percent of households with children had a personal computer. As computer prices drop, middle-income homes are gaining greater access. For example, a new study from Dataquest indicates that 52 percent of the people planning to buy a home computer during the next year have household incomes of $40,000 or less. Nevertheless, this leaves a sizable group of children whose families still cannot afford a home computer.

How can schools deal with this inequity? As *Technology and Learning* columnist Daniel Kinnaman pointed out in his April 1994 "Leadership Role" column, some educators might be tempted to respond by forbidding students to use home computers to complete assignments. After all, he quotes one teacher as saying, "Not every student has a computer at home, so it's unfair for those that have computers to use them." Kinnaman's response: "That's not equity. That's foolishness. Not every child has two parents at home either. Should we tell those who do that they can get help from only one parent?"

Taking away access from one group is clearly not the solution. But the inequality of home access does place a greater burden on schools to provide technology resources to students (and families) with the greatest need for them. How are we doing with this difficult task?

The School Numbers

A look at the condition of education in general might lead us to worry. The funding differences between rich and poor schools are both statistically significant and educationally meaningful. The National Center for Educational Statistics' Indicator of the Month for September 1995 points out that the wealthiest districts in terms of household income have access to about 36 percent more revenue per student. Similarly, school districts with less than five percent of children living in poverty have about 27 percent more revenue than those with many children (more than 25 percent) living in poverty.

To some degree the same sort of pattern holds true for technology. In a recent conference paper entitled

"Equality and Technology," Jeanne Hayes, President of Denver-Colorado-based Quality Education Data, reported socioeconomic and ethnic differences in access to new technology. A closer look at the QED numbers, however, reveals that the inequities are smaller than one might fear. For example, schools with the lowest percentage of Title I students (10 percent or fewer) had a student-to-computer ratio of approximately 12:1, while schools with the highest number of Title I students (26 percent or more) had a ratio closer to 14:1. Analyzing by ethnicity yielded almost identical results—schools with "low multicultural" populations (more than 80 percent white) averaged 12 students per computer, while those with "high multicultural" ratings (50 percent or more nonwhite students) had a 14:1 ratio. In both cases, that's a difference of about 15 percent—significant but smaller than in other areas of education, and less than half the discrepancy found by Henry Jay Becker a decade ago. (In his 1983 report, *School Uses of Microcomputers: Reports from a National Survey*, Becker showed ratios of 155:1 for students in high socioeconomic status (SES) schools, 215:1 in low SES, predominantly minority schools—a 33 percent average difference.)

A 1992 study conducted by the Instructional Association for the Evaluation of Educational Achievement (IEA), and edited by Ron Anderson, found a disturbing 25 percent discrepancy in computer ratios when comparing low and high multicultural settings at the middle school level, but only 11 percent in elementary schools and no difference at all in high schools. Even better news is the fact that in responding to interview questions, ethnic minority students were slightly more likely than white students to report using computers at school. The authors of the report conclude, as we do, that the increased access is probably related to the success of targeted programs such as Title I (formerly Chapter I).

Our conclusions concerning computer access: We still have a long way to go, but we do seem to have made considerable progress over the past decade.

Inequitable Uses?

Perhaps an even greater concern than *access* is the question of *how* computers are being used by different students. In recent years, many writers have contended that poor, minority, and inner-city students are given fewer opportunities for higher-level applications and thus are not reaping the full benefits of technology. In many cases, this contention has been based on research conducted by Henry Jay Becker back in the 1980s.

In both the 1983 and 1985 national surveys conducted at Johns Hopkins University, Becker looked at the two most common types of computer use at the time—programming and drill and practice—and found that students in the lower SES schools were approximately three times as likely to be using drill-and-practice software as those in the higher SES schools, while students at the higher socioeconomic level were three times as likely to be learning to program the computer. As Rosemary E. Sutton summarized in "Equity and Computers in the Schools: A Decade of Research," published in the *Review of Educational Research* in 1991:

> This means that the low-SES children, who are disproportionately African-American

and Hispanic, were gaining most of their experience with a computer when it was in control, asking questions, expecting a response, and informing the student when he or she was correct. In contrast, the high-SES students, who are disproportionately White, were gaining considerable experience when they were in control, giving the computer a series of instructions, and observing the consequences of these instructions.

If such a discrepancy in types of use continues to be true, that is indeed a serious concern. One of the few recent reports that addresses the topic of how computers are used by different groups of students is the 1992 IEA study mentioned above. According to the IEA numbers, differences do persist, although they are far less dramatic than they were in the past. For example, while students from high-SES families were pretty close to the national average in time spent using computers for skill-building, they were 13 or 14 percent more likely than average to use computers for higher-order activities and 26 percent more likely to experience what the study called "diverse" use (a mix of skill-building and higher-order thinking).

Another relevant study, also from 1992, is Henry Jay Becker's paper "How Our Best Computer-using Teachers Differ from Other Teachers." He focused on "exemplary computer-using teachers" (those who, based on their responses on a questionnaire, appeared to "provide intellectually exciting educational experiences" to students rather than using the computers as "substitutes for paper-and-pencil worksheets and for 'enrichment' to reward the completion of other work"). His conclusion was that "exemplary computer-using teachers are as likely to be found in low-income districts and low socio-economic-status schools as they are in other schools."

Our own anecdotal evidence confirms the observation that—with leadership from creative computer-using teachers and school administrators—much is going *right* for at-risk students. In attending conferences, reviewing article submissions to this magazine, and judging our annual Teacher of the Year contest, we have found an overwhelming number of success stories coming from schools in low-income areas. Of our eight national Teacher of the Year winners this year, for example, four worked with at-risk students of one kind or another, including minority and rural or urban poor.

This is not to suggest that the technology education offered to poor and minority students is consistently as good as it should be. It is clear that we have a long way to go before *all* students receive a quality education on a predictable basis. Nonetheless, for once, the news on the education front appears to be better than many people believe.

Making Equity a Reality

Here are just a few examples of schools that have overcome economic obstacles to provide their students with a quality education in which technology plays an important role. These and many other success stories demonstrate that technological inequity need not be a fact of life for this generation of young people.

At the Perry Middle School in Miramar, Florida, a multicultural school that falls at the low end of family incomes in Broward County, high-risk students participate in a "school within a school," the A.C.E. Academy. School/business partnerships are key to the A.C.E. program. The students broadcast the school morning news with help from one of their business partners, Telecommunications International, and regularly visit the training and repair departments of another partner, CompUSA, to learn about technology applications in the real world. In addition to serving as cross-age and peer tutors within the school, A.C.E. students even offer introductory computer classes to new employees at partner businesses.

Judy Shasek, resource teacher at the school, tells about one student who at age 15 was still in eighth grade because he'd been at home (in one of the poorest, roughest Broward County neighborhoods) caring for his mother, who was disabled with cancer. Shasek describes how the A.C.E. program inspired him to move on to high school, participate successfully in the academic program (during the day and at night and summer school), become A.C.E. Academy's first graduate, and head for community college on a basketball scholarship. She has all sorts of helpful tips for others, but perhaps her best explanation for A.C.E.'s success is that, "Everyone else told these kids, 'You can't,' but A.C.E. said, 'You can'—and they believed it and proved us right."

Chinle Elementary School, located on the huge, rural Navajo reservation in Chinle, Arizona, is a true technology success story. Tribal leaders made a commitment to integrating technology into the curriculum and instituted a "saturation" program that equipped the

Other Equity Issues

In addressing the questions of educational fairness in this article, our focus has been on socioeconomic differences—traditionally those resulting in the most dramatic inequities. However, this is not to say that poor and minority students are the only young people who have suffered from below-average access to computers over the years. Many of the 1980 studies also pointed to inequitable access by girls and students with disabilities.

Although a more in-depth analysis will need to wait for another article, here's a quick look at the issues and resources available to help in these areas.

Girls and Technology

Female students are in a unique circumstance since they enjoy virtually equal institutional access to computers when compared with their male peers, but appear to have very different attitudes about computers. Suzanne Lavon Burgo, who completed an interpretive analysis of more than a hundred studies on gender, computers, and education as her doctoral dissertation at the University of Virginia in 1993, found that female students are less likely to be exposed to out-of-school computer activities, less likely to participate in optional computer activities in school, and less likely to major in computer science at the university level.

Despite these attitudinal differences, the female and male students had comparable performance on post-instructional measures. Burgo also found that experience with computers had a greater effect on students' attitudes than did gender differences—supporting the idea that we like what we can do well.

This finding suggests that looking for ways to encourage additional technology use by girls at crucial periods in their education can have a long-term positive impact on their attitudes.

One of the best ways to locate resources to help address issues of gender and equity is to visit the Women in Technology World Wide Web site (http://gseweb.harvard.edu/TIEWeb/STUDENTS/STUDENTGROUPS/WIT/withtml), established by the Harvard Graduate School of Education. It contains a wealth of information about various organizations' efforts to promote female students' interest and achievement in technology-related fields, including the Society of Women Engineers, the Ada Project, the International Network of Women in Technology, and Women and Computer Science.

Technology Help for Students with Special Needs

Students with disabilities are arguably the kids who can benefit most from educational technology, and yet their access has not always been what it should be. Although special education programs were some of the first to obtain technology for use with students, equipment budgets have often lagged, causing those programs to continue to function with extremely outdated equipment. Although little hard data exist to define the current status of technology access for disabled students, signs indicate that the situation is improving because of legislation, changing attitudes, and the advances that have been made in technology itself. Nevertheless, we believe we have a long way to go before all students with special needs have adequate

⇒

school with a 30-station lab and five-station mini-labs in each classroom. The 700 students in the school now have access to 200 computers, which they use for everything from mastering the basic curriculum to compiling research-based writing portfolios.

Fifth-grade teacher Camala Natay feels the writing portfolio activities have motivated her students more than any other activity and have improved their achievement significantly, as measured by scores on the Iowa Test of Basic Skills. Since the Chinle students rarely have computers at home (many of them come from traditional homes where electricity is unavailable), another important venture is the school's "lab night," during which students and their parents work together at the computer. Natay and her colleagues hope the school's technology saturation approach will help the students break the cycle of poverty, which runs about 49 percent among Native peoples in Arizona.

Clear View Elementary School, located just a few miles north of the Mexican border in Chula Vista, CA, has been featured in a number of publications (including this one) in recent years. The highly multicultural, low-income school made a serious commitment to technology and went, in just one year, from being barely computer literate to defining the term "cutting edge." Introduced to technology in kindergarten and first grade, students are experts at logging onto the Internet, creating multimedia projects, and using integrated application software by the time they reach grade six. They've also had the chance to explore the interface between computers and ham radios, edit videos, use laptop computers, and gain experience with many other aspects of technology.

Clear View's principal, Ginger Hovenic, explains, "We have an attitude here that our students can excel if given the proper motivation and opportunity. That's what our teachers do, and that's how we view technology."

The Nixon Elementary School in El Paso, TX, uses technology in concert with peer tutoring and other interventions in its Dual Language Program to teach Spanish to English-speakers and English to Spanish-speakers. A border school with high numbers of poor, non-English-speaking students, it has made headlines with its creative technology solutions, earning a Texas Successful Schools Award and recognition by *Redbook* magazine as the best school in Texas and one of the best in the nation.

At Rowland High School, situated in a low-wealth district about 25 miles east of Los Angeles, some of Hollywood's future stars are now in training. Started by *Technology & Learning*'s 1991 national Teacher of the Year, Dave Master, Rowland's filmmaking program is one of the best in the nation. Almost every piece of equipment in the school was donated, a result of successful partnerships with community, businesses, and industry groups. In the early days, Master solicited additional needed equipment by bringing student products to the community to show what they could accomplish with donated technology resources.

Students in the program, which is open to anyone in the school, have won almost a thousand awards, and typically go on to successful (and lucrative) careers in the film industry or related fields.

The C. Melvin Sharpe Health School in Washington, DC, serves mentally and physically disabled students from

access to the types of adaptive devices and other technologies that can make a major difference in their lives.

Fortunately, there are numerous organizations and clearinghouses to help educators, students, and parents looking for technology for special needs. Here are two of the best places to start:

❖ ABLEDATA (The National Database of Assistive Technology Information) offers extensive listings of commercially and noncommercially available assistive technology. You can reach ABLEDATA at 8455 Colesville Road, Suite 935, Silver Spring, MD 20910–3319; (800) 227–0216; BBS line (301) 589–3563 (you need to set your modem to 2400, 8–1–N).

❖ Alliance for Technology Access is a national network of community-based service providers with 44 resource centers across the country. To learn the location of a center near your district or to order their comprehensive 1994 book, *Computer Resources for People with Disabilities*, call (800) 455–7970; or write to Alliance for Technology Access, 2173 E. Francisco Blvd., Suite L, San Rafael, CA 94901; or send e-mail to atafta@aol.com.

throughout the city. With a limited budget but boundless enthusiasm and dedication—and some generous help from business partners AT&T and the Internal Revenue Service—the school's staff has put together one of the best adaptive technology centers in the country.

It's not unusual for Ramona Medane, the technology coordinator, and her colleagues to work well into the evening doing whatever is necessary to make technology accessible to their students. According to Medane, "Most of the technology we have here was donated or obtained through grants the teachers have written. We have a lab and computers in every classroom, all of which have been adapted to the needs of various students. We hold a computer fair at the school yearly and work with satellite schools throughout the city. I think people hear too much of the bad news about education in the cities. If anyone thinks our students are getting shortchanged, they should come and visit us."

The Keys to Success

Ask the teachers and administrators at the schools described above how their programs were made possible and you're likely to hear a multi-faceted response like this one from A.C.E. Academy's Judy Shasek: "We do everything you can imagine, including writing grants—constantly—for additional public and private support, seeking out community partners, promoting parent and community involvement, pairing up with community-based social service providers, and changing our school culture. We stiffened up our rules, upgraded our curriculum, and raised our expectations for all students. If there is something we aren't doing, we aren't aware of it. And as soon as we find out what it is, we'll try it."

Here's a closer look at some of the successful approaches used by educators we interviewed for this article.

❖ **After-hour open labs.**

It's helpful to have computers available before and after school and in the evenings, for families that don't have them at home. Chinle's Camala Natay says of her school's lab night, "It is one of the most important things we do at our school. Most of the time, the students are teaching their parents. This gives the children a chance to build their confidence and gets their parents more interested in what's going on at school."

❖ **Loaners.**

Another response to inequities in home access is to allow students to borrow computers for specified periods of time. Although the risk of equipment being lost or stolen is a real one, the schools that are involved in this type of program generally report very few problems—and a highly positive response on the part of parents and students. The Indiana Buddy System Project, a partnership among the state education department, the Indiana Corporation for Science and Technology, the Lilly Foundation, Apple, and IBM, is a great example of what can be accomplished with outside funding. This statewide effort so far has provided 2,000 students with technology in their homes. Many individual schools have initiated similar take-home programs for their own students (see "Notebooks for Learning on the Go" by David Hoffman, *Technology and Learning*, February, 1995).

❖ **Teacher training.**

In a survey recently completed by Cable in the Classroom, lack of knowledge was cited as one of the most significant barriers to widespread implementation of technology in classrooms. There is no question that an ongoing staff development program is necessary not only to maintain teachers' technology skills but also to develop awareness and ensure that poor, minority, female, and disabled students are receiving a fair deal.

❖ Seeking additional funding.

Since technology is expensive, schools that have developed successful equity programs have generally obtained additional funding from state and federal grants or private foundations. Many programs are targeted at communities with the greatest economic need. Even when equity is not a stated goal, granting organizations are likely to look favorably on a well-conceived proposal that also happens to serve a population with limited economic means.

A few good resources for learning about available grants include the following:

❖ *Aid for Education*, a semi-monthly newsletter covering education funding and news (CD Publications, 8204 Fenton Street, Silver Spring, MD 20910; (800) 666-6380).

❖ *The Annual Register of Grant Support* (Marquis Who's Who, Inc., 200 East Ohio Street, Chicago, IL 60611).

❖ *The Foundation Grants Index*, which matches grant seekers with foundations (The Foundation Center, 79 Fifth Avenue, New York, NY 10003; (800) 424-9836). Another publication from the Foundation Center is the *National Directory of Corporate Charity*.

❖ "Grants, Contests, Etc.," a monthly column appearing in this magazine.

❖ Local partnerships.

Partnerships between schools and local businesses are central to many equity success stories. Sometimes these partnerships are initiated by the company. For example, AT&T has set up Community Involvement Councils (CICs) in many cities where it has 1,000 or more employees. Each CIC oversees philanthropic efforts focused on the specific needs of that community—including its schools. In other communities, partnerships are initiated by parents or school personnel approaching businesses (in the immediate or neighboring communities) with ideas about mutually beneficial educational programs. The local Chamber of Commerce can often put you in touch with organizations that are willing to provide schools with financial assistance or volunteer hours.

❖ Using telecommunications to connect.

Giving students a chance to "chat" or exchange electronic mail with their peers and adult experts from other schools, states, or countries allows them to build a sense of community that transcends economics and other factors that sometimes separate young people within a school.

❖ Mentors and role models.

Nothing gives students a better understanding of what technology can do for them than showing them potential careers and allowing them to learn from individuals who are using computers in their daily work. Some schools set up annual career days that focus on technology-related fields and include everything from word processing in an office to programming or working as a computer chip fabrication technician.

Others recruit community members to serve as ongoing mentors to students. It's important to find role models who are both male and female and represent a broad range of ethnic groups—including those groups most common in your student population.

❖ Rethinking your expectations.

Far too often, well-meaning educators make decisions about technology use that impact negatively on the success of the lower-achieving or less-advantaged students in the school. When an innovative new program or approach—portfolio assessment, for example, or a project involving multimedia authoring—is being piloted in your school, do you find yourself automatically starting off with the "honors" students and others who have traditionally done well in school? If so, it's time to rethink your approach. All the equity success stories we know of involve a "Can do" attitude on the part of teachers and students alike.

❖ Nurturing internal leadership.

A key success factor present in virtually every successful educational technology program is an individual or small group of people who are leading the way. The notion of the "champion" and the "skunk works," a highly motivated group of people dedicated to solving a common problem, was highlighted in Thomas Peters and Robert Waterman's classic text, *In Search of Excellence*. Although the book focused on America's most successful companies, the lessons it contains are just as valuable in educa-

tion. It is essential for us to nurture and encourage those teachers and administrators who have the vision, energy, and enthusiasm to help all children reach lofty goals.

Maintaining the Momentum

Although we've seen real progress in the movement toward equitable technology access and use, the battle is far from won. If all students are to be given an opportunity to become productive adults who are both self-fulfilled and capable of contributing to the common good, then the entire school experience must be restructured to maintain equity and promote students' respect for themselves and one another.

The goal of equity is to empower all students to make the most of their lives. Unfortunately, past efforts toward this goal have often exacerbated the problems they were intended to solve. We who are involved in technology-based education have a unique opportunity to expect a great deal from students while being able to provide them with the tools they will need to meet these high expectations. Our field is still young and vibrant, and we are not saddled with the baggage of the past that has hampered others within and outside education. It is an opportunity that does not present itself often, and we should certainly do our best to take advantage of it so that all of our students can achieve the fullness of their potential. ❖

*M*ichael N. Milone, Jr., is a Contributing Editor to Technology and Learning, *and a freelance author, consultant, and software developer.*

*J*udy Salpeter is Editor in Chief of Technology and Learning.

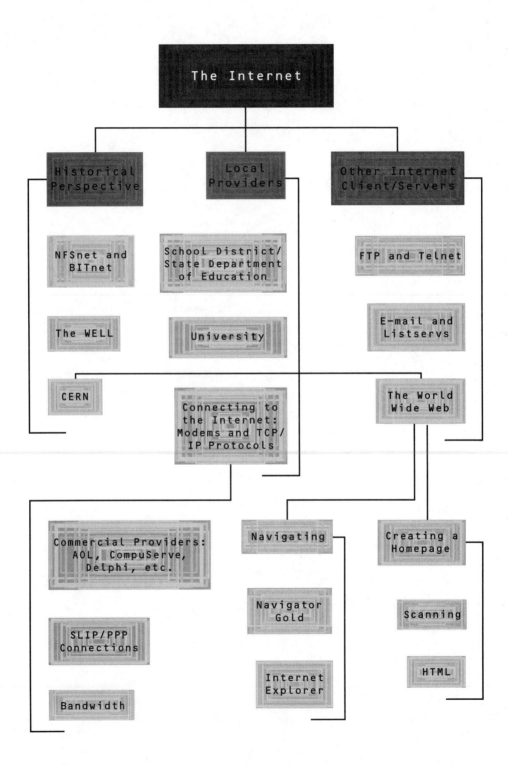

chapter 7

Technology and the Future

The Internet: A Forerunner to the Information Superhighway

Woodstock was an art and music festival held in upstate New York in 1969 that became a label for a whole generation. A counterculture commune known as the "Hog Farm" first gained notoriety at Woodstock. As recounted in a documentary film of the concert, the Hog Farm made arrangements for the security at the festival and "whipped up breakfast in bed for 400,000." What could a member from this commune and a former "Merry Prankster" (a group immortalized in Tom Wolfe's *Electric Kool-Aid Acid Test*) have in common with the Department of Defense (Wolfe 1968)? This chapter will begin by answering this question and providing an introduction to one of the more exciting applications of computers as a tool for sharing information—the Internet.

We begin with the history of the Internet, a term for a global interconnection of a variety of computer networks whose linkages permit computer-mediated communications (CMC), such as e-mail, discussion groups, and hypermedia links. A description of some of the terms (client, server, TCP/IP, World Wide Web, and Java) and tools used for navigating on the Internet (Eudora, Telnet, FTP, and Netscape) will be explained. Internet resources that social studies teachers can use with elementary and secondary school students will be highlighted. This chapter will conclude with a real-world application of the Internet's powers in telecommunications—citizens from many different countries using the Internet in international efforts to control the serious global health issue of malaria.

The Internet—A Historical Perspective

Stewart Brand and Larry Brilliant were two of the founding fathers of a computing conferencing system known as the WELL, which is an acronym for Whole Earth 'Lectronic Link (Rheingold 1993). During the 1960s, Brand was one of the Merry Pranksters, a troop of early hippies who were followers of author Ken Kesey. Brand later

343

became a faculty member of the Western Behavioral Sciences Institute (WBSI), which was experimenting with the effectiveness of computing conferencing. It was through WBSI that he became acquainted with Brilliant, who had migrated from the Hog Farm commune to medical school before becoming a leader in the World Health Organization's fight against smallpox. Both men became involved in using computers as a means to "facilitate communication among interesting people in the San Francisco Bay Area . . . and to bring e-mail to the masses" (Rheingold 1993, 42). With startup money from Brand's successful counterculture magazines *The Whole Earth Catalog* and its spinoff *The Whole Earth Software Review*, the WELL was founded as a computer conferencing system in San Francisco in 1985, and it soon after posted a site on the Internet. It became legendary as an online community where people came to know and care about each other while collaborating on common interests via the Internet.

The Internet is the largest computer network in the world, consisting of thousands of smaller regional networks that are interconnected—hence the name Internet. Each computer network linked to the Internet has its own address that allows individuals outside the network to access it. More specific information for logging onto the Internet and using some of the navigational tools, such as Netscape Navigator, will be described after a brief discussion of the Internet's origins and development.

In 1964, as the Merry Pranksters were roaming the United States in their psychedelic bus, the RAND think tank was examining top-secret thermonuclear war scenarios for the Department of Defense's Advanced Research Projects Agency (ARPA). Paul Barand was a RAND Corporation researcher who proposed that under a thermonuclear attack, decentralizing authority for maintaining national and local communication was imperative. Specifically, he proposed "that messages be broken into units of equal size and that [a computer] network route these message's units along a functioning path to their destination, where they would be reassembled into coherent wholes" (Rheingold 1993, 74). This idea was realized a few years later with the genesis of the Arpanet, which was designed for ARPA, the agency after which it was named.

At the same time as the Woodstock festival was happening in 1969, the Arpanet was the first computing conferencing system in operation. The Arpanet's original function was to allow computer data to be transferred to one of the four nodes that comprised the original links. This soon changed, however. As Rheingold points out, "a continuing theme throughout the history of CMC is the way people adapt technologies designed for one purpose to suit their own, very different communication needs" (1993, 7). Once the Arpanet existed it was easy to develop electronic mail capabilities. By the early 1970s, the United States government had imposed wage and price freeze policies to address the inflationary economic crisis at that time, and it was crucial to send information relative to enforcing these policies to geographically distant local headquarters. It was then that computer conferencing began to encompass other forms of discourse including social, commercial, and scientific.

By the mid 1970s, CMCs were appearing in corporations such as Xerox, which developed an inexpensive and flexible local area network (LAN) protocol named an Ethernet. This and other networking technologies that were being developed, such as ones developed at Digital and IBM, spawned the idea of networking these LANs so people could access them all. The Arpanet became so popular that ARPA declassified it from a research project and handed over operational control to the Defense Communications Agency. Mailing lists began to appear on the Arpanet. Among them was SF-LOVERS, a mailing list about science fiction (clearly a non work-related theme) that spread rapidly throughout business networks despite the attempts by some administrators overseeing the system to stamp it out.

The experimental Internet began in 1977 with the development of TCP/IP protocols. IP is the Internet Protocol that permits communications among different types of underlying networks, such as Ethernets and token rings. TCP is an acronym for Transmission Control Protocol, which provides for communications to end users (people or programs at the receiving end) of IP data transmissions.

More and more people, largely scientists in academic and research institutes wishing to share information, were thwarted from doing so because they had not been authorized by the Defense Department to use the Arpanet. Thus, in 1979 an imitation of the Arpanet mailing lists called Usenet was created between Duke University and the University of North Carolina, Chapel Hill. Usenet spread like a wildfire from campus to campus, and eventually around the world, with the help of sympathetic computer center managers who saw the enormous potential Usenet offered in transmitting information.

At about this time, an operating system called UNIX was becoming a standard and the UNIX-to-UNIX copy program (UUCP) was developed and distributed by AT&T. This permitted any computer using UNIX to automatically dial into any other UNIX computer and share information via a modem. By 1983 a version of UNIX was developed at the University of California, Berkeley that included the TCP/IP protocols. Computers could not only share data with each other via modem, but they also could encode and decode Internet data that traveled at much higher speeds.

On January 1, 1983, all hosts and networks connecting with the Arpanet were required to use the TCP/IP protocols, and the Arpanet was split into two networks: Milnet, which was used for operational military communications, and the Arpanet Internet, which consisted of many different networks able to communicate using one common overarching protocol—Internet Protocol (IP). Within the next year, the various federal agencies participating in and funding the Arpanet Internet dropped the acronym and the network became known as the Internet.

The federal breakup of the AT&T monopoly into regional companies in 1985 began the competition for long-distance service and created the need for these companies to start laying fiber-optic cable across continents and oceans. Thus, international links for faster data transmission came into being. Concurrently, the National Science Foundation (NSF) funded five supercomputer centers and a couple dozen regional networks, all of which were intended to interconnect with a national NFSnet. A year later, this NSFnet was implemented and became a major network on the Internet. In response to scholars from disciplines other than science who wanted access to CMC, IBM and NSF established BITnet, which spread rapidly throughout higher education institutions. By 1988 both the Internet and BITnet were about the same size in terms of the number of users: approximately half a million each worldwide.

Several factors already described converged to generate the exponential growth of the Internet. These factors included the implementation of TCP/IP in the latest versions of UNIX, the continuing spread of fiber-optic cable, and the development of the NFSnet regional centers. Funding for the Internet shifted from the government to the private sector; in the hands of the private sector, the main focus of the Internet changed from academic research to global communication.

By the beginning of this decade BITnet started to shrink and be overshadowed by the Internet. Various clients (another word for software) available for surfing the Internet were gaining popularity with the 2.8 million Internet users: Gopher and Telnet were used extensively at this point in the Internet's evolution.

In 1989 CERN, a European computer science laboratory, proposed the most dramatic development for the Internet: a graphic way of searching for information. Mosaic was a graphic browser developed at the University of Illinois in 1993, and millions of people had a "browse, search, and retrieve" tool that allowed hypermedia to be conducted on the Internet. This revolutionary interface made the technology interactive. The creators of Mosaic were soon lured to a new commercial venture called Netscape Navigator, where their ideas continued to evolve as they developed a browser that incorporated several tools for searching the Internet under one graphic interface (an interface that is easy to become comfortable with). Bill Gates and his giant Microsoft Corporation soon developed Internet Explorer, which is now locked in competition with Netscape for market dominance in WWW software browsers.

A variety of uses are now possible with the Internet: accessing distant library catalogs, visiting exhibits in art museums, reading the latest editions of popular magazines, communicating with like-minded individuals about a topic of mutual interest. The United States presidential candidates in the 1996 election used homepages on the World Wide Web to spread their platform. Citizens in former communist countries, including the former Soviet Union, Poland, and Hungary, are all connected to the Internet and are daily sending messages and reading the information shared by newsgroups. The quality and speed with which audio and video data can be transmitted is revolutionizing the communications industry (Negroponte 1995).

From a simple network of some 23 computers on the Arpanet in 1973 to a global network of networks with an estimate of 20–30 million users worldwide, the Internet has inalterably changed human communication patterns just as the printing press did several centuries ago. The difference between these two revolutionary technological developments in human communication is that where it took considerable time (as long as two centuries) for large numbers of people to learn how to read and for the true impact of the printing press to be felt, much of today's world population is prepared to consume and publish multimedia information, making the Internet's impact more readily apparent.

A dramatic and touching example of how the Internet is affecting peoples' lives was reported in a recent *Time* article describing the Internet (1994). It involved the WELL, the San Francisco-based computing conferencing system founded by Brand and Brilliant. It involved a woman who posted messages regarding her impending death due to cancer. Those who read her messages and responded were deeply touched by her musings on the meaning of life and its inescapable end for each of us. The relationships that developed between her and the many people she never met face to face are a profound testament to the connective power of the computer as a communication device and its potential to build community.

The next section will include a description of how to become more familiar with the Internet and the possible resources a social studies teacher can find. The chapter will conclude with a case study of how the Internet has the potential to promote global linkages that permit people to solve a major health problem in third-world countries. It is this potential to connect people to solve human problems that makes the Internet such an important aspect of computer technology for social studies teachers to learn about and share with students.

Connecting to the Internet

The preceding section described the origin and evolution of the vast backbone of computer networks known as the Internet. How does one get on the Internet and gain access to the vast amount of resources and communication possibilities found there? And once you get on, how do you get around and what are some of the interesting sites and resources you'll find? What follows will begin to answer these introductory questions. More in-depth information on resources available for social studies teachers is listed in Chapter 8.

The equipment required to connect to the Internet is readily available in most schools: a modem and a computer. The modem accesses telephone lines, and the data available from different sites on the Internet can be transmitted as bits (digital information coded as 0s and 1s) through the telephone line to a computer. The development of TCP/IP protocols described in the previous section made it possible for different computers to communicate effectively with one another. The level of data interpretation depends on the computer receiving information. Thus, displaying graphic or audio data, such as a picture of Martin Luther King, Jr. and a digital recording of his "I Have a Dream" speech, requires a computer with multimedia applications and adequate memory for operating the software. Modems used in conjunction with less sophisticated computing equipment still permit access to textual data and personal communications capabilities through the Internet.

The effectiveness of a modem is determined by the speed at which it can transmit encoded digital information and is measured in bits per second (bps). Currently, a good modem will operate at 36,600 bps, which is a fast transmission of data. (Actually, the amount of information transmitted is determined by dividing the bits per second by 10 because any character is made up of a combination of 10 bits or 0s and 1s.) Of course, related to the speed of the transmissions of bits is the bandwidth across which the information travels. Bandwidth has been compared to the diameter of a pipe or number of lanes on a highway. The development of fiber-optic cable (T-1 or T-3 lines) as a conduit for transmitting information gives us an almost infinite bandwidth compared to the conventional copper wire of most telephone connections (Negroponte 1995). At this point, however, the cost of dedicated data-grade phone lines, such as ISDN or T-1, is prohibitively high for most schools. One promising approach is wireless Ethernet transceivers, a reasonable investment given the bandwidth that it creates among schools connected to the Ethernet system (Van Horn 1997).

With a computer and an inexpensive modem, or with a pricier means of data transmission like fiber optics, a social studies teacher has the necessary hardware to access the Internet, but that is not all that is needed. A telecommunications link must be established, and the software tools that allow one to explore the various resources on the Internet must be available. Negroponte compares the establishment of a telecommunications link to handshaking. As with a fraternal group, there are certain nuances to shaking hands that must be observed for communication to be established properly.

There are two means by which a teacher can establish a telecommunications link for accessing the Internet. The first is to gain free access through an account with a university or for your school district to establish an account with a State Department of Education server (which is a computer dedicated as a gateway to the Internet). If no one at your school district can help you establish access, many universities are interested in working with schools to provide access to the Internet, and an inquiry to an administrator from the computer center staff at a university might help you establish Internet access. Once you establish an account you will be given a user identification, which is composed of letters from your name, and you'll have to choose a password, one which is easy for you to remember but too obtuse for anyone else to figure out.

The second way to gain access to the Internet is through a commercial online service. Currently, America Online, AT&T, Prodigy, CompuServe, and Delphi are among the nationally known Internet providers that offer a gateway to the Internet. There are also local Internet providers who charge roughly the same amount as nationally known providers for an Internet connection. The advantage of any commercial service is that the telecommunications link is easily established (the handshaking process is straightforward), but the browser software packages offered are sometimes limited compared to what Netscape Navigator offers. Netscape Navigator has become the industry standard and can be downloaded from the Internet. Microsoft includes Internet Explorer in its Windows 95 software package. Phone numbers for large online services are provided in Chapter 8. Local providers can be found through telephone directories or ads in the local paper.

Connection to the Internet through a modem comes in two forms: SLIP (Serial Line Internet Protocol) or PPP (Point to Point Protocol). Either of these protocols links your modem to the server (the host computer that serves as a gateway) and then to the Internet. Linkages such as SLIP or PPP are important to have because they allow you to use all the client software needed to get around on the Internet without having to set the modem communications parameters for every application. (Each software client has a specific application to the Internet, e.g., e-mail, reading newsgroups, or Web browsing.) Proper configuration of SLIP or PPP on your computer can require some expertise, but someone at the computer center where you are establishing the Internet connection should be able to help. Establishing the telecommunications link (figuring out the proper handshake) and finding out who might help you could be a bit tricky, but it is worth pursuing.

Once the telecommunications link is established a number of software tools (called Internet clients) can be used to find the various resources on the Internet. As mentioned above, commercial online services that are Internet providers, such as CompuServe or Prodigy, have their own unique client software that subscribers use. Because this book is written for students enrolled in a university course, the names of client software commonly found in higher-education environments will be described. These clients are usually available from the server (host computer on campus) or can be downloaded from sites on the Internet. Readers using a commercial online service as an Internet provider can find out the type of client software offered and where it will get them on the Internet by contacting the service to which they subscribe.

A final note about telecommunications and the Internet regards Internet addresses. An Internet address has two forms: an IP address and a domain name. The IP address is the numeric form, the one read by the computer. Domain names are easier for people to remember and are comprised of the following elements: **userid@machine.subdomain. organization.domain**. The IP address appears in reverse order and looks like this: 124.95.9.7. The domain name is automatically translated to the IP address by software called Name Server. This software package also permits the use of abbreviated domain name addresses that may only need the elements **userid@organization.domain**. The domain portion of the address divides Internet users into the following categories: universities (.edu), commercial enterprises (.com), nonprofit organizations (.org), government (.gov), and networking organizations (.net). International codes for domains are based on the first letters of the country involved, such as Australia (.au), Canada (.ca), or the United Kingdom (.uk). Although case is not critical, most addresses are written in lowercase letters. The use of a period (.) is critical, however, as is the elimination of spaces. Underlines and dashes may be used as well as digits 0 through 9. Precise addresses are a critical detail in sending and requesting information along the nodes of the Internet. There is no friendly postal worker who might be able to decipher a slight misaddress; a file for transmission across the Internet must be carefully addressed to be sent and received successfully.

▬ Internet Clients/Servers and the Resources They Provide ▬▬▬▬

A whole lingo has developed around the Internet, such as nethead (one who uses the Internet a great deal), surfing the net (spending time looking at different resources and repositories of information and news), flaming (sending angry messages to someone through the Internet), and information superhighway (a metaphor for the Internet). The term Internet client refers to software that is used to carry out specific applications on the Internet. Metaphorically, one could think of a client as a way to merge into a lane on the information superhighway, i.e., certain clients run in certain lanes. This metaphor breaks down, however, as clients are not necessarily "lane bound" and some clients switch lanes. Clients access servers, which are computers that store and share text, graphic, and sound files with client computers connected to the Internet. A computer that operates as a server can retrieve information and function as a gateway by which local users access the Internet. In the next section we will consider the application of different types of clients and servers: electronic mail and listservs, newsgroups, Telnet and file transfers, and databases. A separate section is devoted to the most intriguing and rapidly developing lane on the information superhighway, the World Wide Web (WWW).

E-mail and Listservs

Sending messages through the Arpanet, the Internet's precursor, was one of the original reasons people began using the Internet and why it grew popular so quickly. Sending someone electronic mail (e-mail) has become as easy as composing text with a word processor. Eudora is the name of the most popular e-mail client; commercial service providers, such as America Online, have their own name for this lane of traffic on the Internet. Recently, WWW browsers such as Netscape Navigator and Microsoft Internet Explorer have started including an e-mail feature built into the capabilities of their software.

Eudora offers users a variety of features, including an automatic signature that appears at the bottom of every message, a file system (mailboxes) for storing and classifying messages, and an address b ook for storing nicknames and addresses of people to whom e-mail is sent frequently. Eudora has a graphical user interface (GUI) that is menu driven. This means that program commands are grouped into categories (just as a menu in a restaurant categorizes various courses, such as appetizers, salads, entrees, and desserts), and the user accesses a particular category to select individual features.

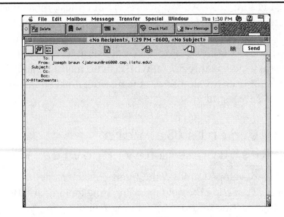

Eudora is an e-mail client that offers a variety of user-friendly features for sorting and sending electronic communications.

A listserv is a special format of e-mail where messages about a topic of common interest are sent to groups of subscribers. Subscription to a listserv is easily obtained by sending an e-mail to the person in charge of the list. There is a Web site that will conduct a search of known listservs at **http://www.liszt.com**. (See Chapter 8 for this and additional social studies resources available on the Internet.) Specific information about where and what to say in a subscription message is provided through this homepage.

Once you are a subscriber you will automatically receive any messages posted to the listserv every time you open your mail. Conversely, you can send a message to everyone on the listserv by posting a message. A listserv is a wonderful way to maintain communications with a large number of people about a subject of common interest, but if there are a large number of postings, it becomes a little like sorting out junk mail. One has to open each message to see what is said, and if one subscribes to a number of listservs, time must be taken to determine what is worth saving and what should be deposited in the trash. In the event that a subscription to a listserv is no longer wanted, a message can be sent to the person in charge, and your subscription is canceled. NCSS and many state affiliates post messages through listservs. This is an excellent source for receiving and requesting information and opinions. (See Activity 1 at the end of this chapter to enter a subscription for your e-mail account to the NCSS listserv.)

Opinions and information are also available through another e-mail feature that is more commonly associated with commercial online services—chat rooms or online discussions. On the Internet there is a chat room known as Internet Relay Chat (IRC) and one available through the Web called CUSeeMe, which allows a video display. Chat rooms function differently from e-mail in that the communication occurring is in real time (although there is some delay, participants are online as the conversation occurs). The WELL, the computerized conferencing system described at the beginning of this chapter, has a number of chat rooms available where like-minded individuals hold discussions using their computers as a substitute for being together in person to carry on a conversation. In time, chat rooms like CUSeeMe may become common ways of carrying on conversations, and the telephone may fade as an outdated communication technology just as the telegraph did a century ago.

Newsgroups

Like-minded individuals who wish to exchange information and points of view are not limited to just e-mail and listservs on the Internet. Newsgroups are another common way for people to discuss topics of interest ranging from social history to folk music lyrics. Newsgroups are accessed through client software that connects to a server. Unlike listservs, newsgroups require no subscription message; the user simply selects whatever newsgroup appears interesting and begins reading messages that have been posted about a particular topic. In this way newsgroups prevent the participant from receiving unwanted messages posted to listservs. Newsgroups can be preselected so that only stipulated ones appear and you don't have to sort through thousands of newsgroups.

Another distinguishing factor of newsgroups is the way postings are grouped into a thread of discussion within the general topic of the newsgroup. For example, within the newsgroup alt.bikeriders, a thread of discussion might develop on scenic paths in a particular region of the country or upcoming bike races. Similar to a listserv, users can easily post a response or new message that is available to everyone accessing that particular newsgroup, and that posting becomes part of the discussion thread.

Thousands of newsgroups are available through the Internet, with Usenet being the best known set of newsgroups. Although it contains over 2000 newsgroups, it is not the only collection of newsgroups available. Commercial newsgroups have also come into being. Usenet categorizes newsgroup messages according to a three-letter prefix (alt stands for alternative, k12 for education). For each category there may be anywhere from 30 to 100 newsgroups; within each newsgroup, a similar number of threads of conversations may be occurring as users post messages and responses. Client software for accessing newsgroups offers features such as checking articles already read (so you can keep track of what has been previously explored) as well as automatically posting any selected newsgroups into a personal newsgroup file. (The latest versions of Netscape Navigator and Microsoft Internet Explorer offer access to newsgroups.)

Newsgroups are a vast repository of information that may be easily accessed for retrieving other people's thoughts about a topic or adding your own.

The power of newsgroups lies in the fact that a particular problem posed by a newsgroup user may receive dozens of responses from around the world within hours. Needless to say, this is a powerful way to globally exchange information and ideas almost instantly, and this exchange of information accounts for the countless hours of netsurfing, which people describe as addictive.

─ Telnet and FTP

Suppose you want to access a card catalogue at a university or obtain information (such as your e-mail) that is stored in a computer across the country (or even on another continent). Telnet is a software client that allows you to connect to other computers on the Internet and gain access to what is stored there. It allows the user to run a program on a distant computer from his or her own computer while paying only a phone charge for the computer that serves as the Internet connection. Thus, Telnet is a client that permits interactivity between servers. It is a simple and inexpensive way to seek and explore information resources stored in distant sites. The only trick to using Telnet successfully is that you must know the address of the server you wish to access.

To transfer files from another server file transfer protocol (FTP) clients are employed. Fetch (on the Macintosh platform) and FTP (on the IBM platform) are two popular FTP clients that allow you to download the resources found at distant FTP sites to your own computer. In other words, you can obtain and download a file from a server on the other side of the world to the computer on your desk (or you can upload a file). There are many Internet sites that have publicly accessible repositories of information available, such as the Library of Congress, that can be accessed using FTP by logging in using the account name "anonymous." These sites are called anonymous FTP servers.

The data in a file that is found on a server can come in a variety of forms: graphic, audio, text, or program. The type of data that is contained in a file can be determined by the two- or three-letter abbreviation that follows a file name.

Types of Files

Text files:	.txt or .doc
Graphic files:	.pcx, .gif, .wmf, .bmp, .tiff, .jpeg, .mov, or .emp
Audio files:	.au or .wav
Program files:	.exe or .com
Compressed files:	.sea, .zip, .arc, or .sit

In the process of transferring files to or from a server, FTP client software takes care of translating the format to one that can make sense to all computers involved. FTP has two modes for transmitting files: ASCII and binary. ASCII is used to transmit text (but not word-processed documents since they contain control codes imbedded by the word-processing software). Binary is the mode used for most data files other than text. This eliminates part of what would be a major problem for Internet users—transferring files across different platforms. Thus, a Macintosh user can go to an FTP site that runs UNIX and transfer data in binary or ASCII format. Once obtained, this file can be converted so that it can be read by software designed for the Macintosh or PC.

In the following section, the WWW, perhaps the most intriguing development in the Internet, is described. What makes the WWW so interesting is that many of the distinct client functions discussed above, such as e-mail and newsgroups, are now merged in a single client. As Netscape Navigator and Microsoft Internet Explorer continue to compete for market dominance, their e-mail functions will improve. Later versions of Navigator and Internet Explorer will include an FTP function. Thus, separate e-mail programs such as Eudora (or FTP programs such as Fetch) will decline in popularity as software that can handle all Internet activity becomes more readily available. In other words, everything is becoming WWW-based, and clients such as those for specific functions will be working behind the scenes of the WWW browser you use.

■ The World Wide Web (WWW)

As you may recall from Chapter 5, hypermedia is described as an environment for learning that allows you to view a visual representation of a web of textual, graphic, and audio information and to traverse it at will. The WWW is an array of hypermedia programs from computers around the world. This section will describe how to access the WWW, how it functions, and some of the most intriguing sites for social studies teachers to visit.

What makes the WWW the fastest growing component on the Internet is its ease of use. The GUI for the WWW is easy to understand and use. The figure below shows a screen shot of Netscape Navigator, currently the most popular client software. Examples of other Web browsing software are Microsoft Internet Explorer, Mosaic, and MacWeb. The description below will focus on Netscape Navigator; the other browsers operate similarly. The differences occur in the way the information is displayed to the viewer. A homepage written in Netscape Navigator will appear differently when viewed with Mosaic as the browser; for example, pictures may appear on the right side of the screen instead of the left, or text may not wrap around images.

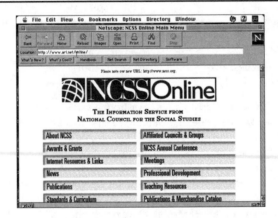

Navigating the World Wide Web with the Netscape browser is remarkably simple given all the information that it is put at one's disposal.

■ Menu Selections

The menu choices at the top of the screen provide the user with a way to access various software functions. For example, Edit allows you to cut, paste, or copy various information found when using the WWW. View allows the user to see the programming code used for creating a WWW document. The programming code is known by its acronym HTML, which stands for Hypertext Markup Language, and will be discussed in more detail later in this section. Bookmarks allow the user to categorize and keep track of various sites that have been visited. The Directory and Help menus will aid the novice in seeking information about using the client for its optimal effectiveness. The Window menu gives the user access to the e-mail and news clients of Netscape Navigator. The mail client that Netscape Navigator provides is adequate, but lacks certain features that Eudora offers, such as mailboxes and filters for processing and sorting incoming mail.

Buttons, Boxes, and Links

Below the pull-down menu choices is a row of buttons that allow access to common commands. As one explores the various links that are available at a Web site, the need to go backwards and forwards (or return to the homepage) becomes imperative. There are buttons devoted to these functions, and there is a Stop button if you decide not to establish a link. The Images button lets the user choose whether to include graphics; it takes more time to transmit graphic data, and the user might choose to forego the graphics and establish a link expeditiously. The Reload button requests Navigator to update a page after changes have been made to the source document. Finally, there is a Print button for making a hard copy of the active screen.

Below this row of square buttons is a dialog box titled "Location." In it appears the URL, which is the address of a particular server and name of the Web page on that server. URL stands for uniform resource locator, and it is a primary means of navigating around the Web; the URL for NCSS is **http://www.ari.net/online**. Underneath the Location dialog box is a row of buttons in the shape of rectangles. These buttons offer users additional features, such as a list of interesting links to visit (What's New and What's Cool), and access to search engines. A number of search engines are available through Netsearch; just click on the box with that title to access different search tools. Among the most popular are Yahoo, Alta Vista, Lycos, and WebCrawler. Buttons for Handbook and Net Directory provide additional information about using Netscape Navigator. There is also a box titled Newsgroups, but not all servers are set up for this Internet function (the same is true for the e-mail function).

There are two primary means of establishing a link to a homepage on the Web. If a particular URL for a link is known (a URL can be found through searches under Netsearch), it can be entered in the Location dialog box at the top of the screen. Other times, you may be viewing a homepage that contains underlined text that is a different color than the rest of the text. These are hot links, and by clicking the mouse when it is over one of these hot links, the Web browser searches for the server of that link. The requested page is then transmitted via modem and appears on the screen, replacing the page from which it was accessed. If the user wishes to view this previous page or others before that, the Back button will retrieve them quickly. On any given homepage there may be several hot links that will take the user to related sites and from these more hot links may be available. It is by browsing the Internet and following related links that the power of hypertext as a communication medium becomes evident. Thus, the Web is an array of homepages and links existing in hyperspace and available through the Internet.

A Homepage and Its HTML Document

A homepage is constructed using a set of codes called tags and a text-editing program designed specifically for HTML. The software programs for editing a homepage are menu-operated and the codes are inserted by the software when a particular function is selected. For example, in selecting the "establish a link" function from the editing software BBedit Lite or PageMill (on the IBM platform the analogous software is called HTM Editor Assistant or Frontpage), the tag (see below) will automatically be inserted after you provide the URL for the link. The latest version of Navigator Gold (and also the Microsoft product Frontpage) allows the user to view a word-processed file as a Web document. This program inserts all the HTML tags for the user automatically. Inserting graphics, formatting letters in bold, centering a title, creating tables, and all the other graphic elements that make homepages visually appealing are created with relative ease through this special editing software. The simplicity of creating homepages has caused their proliferation throughout the Web. While HTML appears to be a complicated coding language, its syntax is much easier than it looks. Below is a section of an HTML document for a homepage on China. Any homepage's HTML document can seen by selecting Source from the View menu in Netscape Navigator.

Creating HTML documents is rapidly becoming as simple as word processing. Programs are evolving that insert the coding (HTML tags) automatically. The <> are used to bracket codes that govern the way a Web page is displayed.

Any homepage's success is due to a number of factors. The ease in navigating around the page (also called the interface) is important. The visual appeal of the page's layout and typography, the incorporation of photographs and audio, and the quality of links to other related Web sites from around the world are other important factors that make a user want to add a site to his or her Bookmarks file for a future visit or share it with others. The secret behind a homepage's success is not so secret since the HTML document used in constructing the page can be easily accessed (select Source from the View menu). Coding tags, sources of graphics, and worthwhile URLs are readily available to anyone who wants to see them. Copyright infringement notwithstanding, many designers of Web sites have traveled in the same footsteps as those who went before and borrowed the ideas and work of other designers.

When designing a Web site in which you want to incorporate original work, such as a photograph, video footage, or audio recording, you'll find that the steps to accomplish this are not that daunting. The graphic or audio selection must be translated into digital data. An optical scanner is a computer-mediated device that allows one to take a photograph and reconstruct it as a digital image. In other words, color or black-and-white photos are converted into bits of information, which appear as pixels on the computer screen, and the converted digitized image can be saved as a computer file. Graphic conversion software can then save the computer file of a digitized image in a format that can be read by a Web browser such as Netscape Navigator.

The exact steps for digitizing an image and storing it in a format for transmission on the Internet are available with the documentation accompanying whatever scanner and graphic conversion software being used. Similarly, with appropriate application and editing software (some of which can be downloaded from the Internet), audio and video files can be saved in a digital format and transmitted across the Internet.

One of the more fascinating ways of transmitting images is made possible by the recent development of Virtual Reality Markup Language (VRML). With this software, it is possible to take a series of photographs of an image (or a place such as a room in a museum) and seamlessly weave the series of photos together. The browser uses the mouse to navigate around the image. Thus, the user can view a room as if he or she were actually there. In the case of using an image of a vase for VRML, the user can turn and manipulate the object in almost any direction with the mouse. The implications of this software for allowing access to museum resources and geographic studies is remarkable. Unfortunately, there is a downside to the wonders of using the Internet—transmitting auditory and video data.

At this point, the transmission of audio and video files is limited by the bandwidth that is available. Auditory and video files must be compressed because they are large. In the process, the speed with which the data is recorded (and played back) is not the same fidelity as the original source. Thus, video footage looks jerky (or is displayed in a small viewing area on your screen), and audio files are not as clear as they would be on a CD. This issue of auditory and video file size and quality is going to change, however. Currently, programmers are working with a programming language called Java to enable the use of audio and video files on the Internet.

What makes Java remarkable is that it will provide the user with applets (short for application software) embedded in the file. Applets will allow the user to break down auditory and video files as they are received and play them without having to wait to download the entire file from the server. When a user accesses a homepage that includes Java, the files are transmitted and displayed simultaneously without the user having to wait for the entire file to be received and then accessed with an application residing in the user's hard drive. Java will speed up the transmission of graphic and auditory files and improve the quality of the transmission.

All of the client-servers described above have been involved in a humane effort to combat a worldwide health plague. This effort represents the ways the Internet can be used to promote positive social goals on a global scale.

▪ Rotary Against Malaria—Using the Internet to Combat Deadly Disease ▬▬

Rotary International is a service club dedicated to the ideal of "service above self." It has over 1.2 million members in over 27,000 clubs located in over 150 countries. In 1978 Rotary undertook to eradicate polio by the year 2000 (for certification by 2005). Rotary Against Malaria (RAM) formed in the early 1990s to organize Rotarians to work to help control malaria. With Rotary Against Malaria, individual clubs built on the relationships formed during the PolioPlus campaign. With effective networking, the parent Rotary International may not need to adopt RAM as their next program.

In October of 1992, the World Health Organization named malaria their first priority tropical disease because it has become so widespread and dangerous. The tragedy is that malaria is preventable and treatable at low costs. The solution is primarily one of logistics. Malaria treatment and prevention involves providing mosquito netting, drugs, and education to target populations.

RAM's use of the Internet breaks new ground for Rotary International and for fighting against a widespread, deadly disease. Rotarians specifically designed the RAM homepage to provide information resources on malaria by country and to coordinate efforts by individual clubs in diverse countries that pair up to do charitable projects with the help of the Rotary International Foundation. The Internet allows Rotarians to locate projects, find donor clubs, and educate all involved. For example, projects in Tanzania targeted items for a grant, and within hours most of the necessary information for submitting a proposal was transmitted over the Internet to individuals in different parts of the world who helped prepare the grant online.

Similarly, the Internet helps Rotary International collect and send out information on malaria. Mail to developing countries is spotty at best. Considering how few people in the developed world understand the serious threat posed by malaria, a RAM volunteer developed a Web page to provide information. Other volunteers contributed to the creation of a database cataloging who, where, and what is being done in this worldwide effort to combat malaria. This helps avoid duplicate projects and allows the pooling of efforts. In addition, malaria workers can share information on drug resistance and availability and access to nets and educational materials. Once malaria workers educated the public threatened by malaria, demands mushroomed for insecticide-soaked nets.

What makes the Internet so unique in this effort is that historically, antimalarial efforts were so fragmented and uncoordinated that few systematic programs could be attempted. Help from the public sector, aided by fast, accurate communication, has renewed hope that deaths from malaria may stop. The URL for the RAM homepage is **http://www.bednet.org**.

▪ Assessment—The Missing Link ▬▬

There are a number of aspects to consider when evaluating a Web page for instructional use in social studies. The first is the topic of *theme*: how appropriate are the ideas and content for promoting significant social studies goals? Certainly the RAM page cited above is ideal in this regard. An effective Web page should show *organization*: the layout and structure of pages should be clear and easy to follow. The Web provides some unique ways of looking at how information is presented and it is important to consider how easy a page is to read and view. Are language uses and conventions, such as spelling and grammar, correct? The technical quality of a Web page is important and can be determined by examining whether external and internal links function. All of these criteria are important to consider when evaluating a Web site for use in social studies instruction.

As rich as the possibility is for promoting significant learning through the Web, there is one fundamentally disappointing aspect of most worthwhile homepages (including the RAM homepage): there is little provided to help the teacher with the crucial task of assessment. In other words, while a Web page may have a lot of information readily available, students are not usually asked to do anything with the information. Thus, the teacher must figure out how to determine what, if anything, an individual student has learned from spending time at a site.

Up to this point, most Web pages have not given teachers much direction in assessing student learning. Hopefully this will change as teachers become more savvy in using the Web as a learning resource. Developers of Web pages often provide an e-mail link for the user, but most do not ask the user to respond to the content encountered. Moreover, few Web sites engage the student in analyzing data found at one site with similar data from another site and drawing a conclusion from such an analysis. As more curriculum is specifically developed around the Internet, this assessment issue will have to be addressed. Until then, social studies teachers using the Internet for instructional purposes will be on their own when it comes to determining what students have learned from visiting a Web page and what difference that learning might make.

Summary

John Perry Barlow has been described as the "current poet-laureate to cyberspace" and was the subject of a recent full-page feature article in *The Wall Street Journal*. He is also a contributing lyricist for the Grateful Dead as well as a co-founder of the Electronic Frontier Foundation, a nonprofit organization that is devoted to protecting free expression, guarding individuals' rights to privacy, and maintaining online access to the masses with regard to the Internet (Berger 1995). As Barlow has noted, the advent of a technology is often filled with unintended consequences. (Who would have imagined the pollution and lifestyle changes brought about by the automobile?)

Future scenarios (some rather alarming) are being forecasted regarding how the Internet will affect us as a society and as members of the world community (Negroponte 1995; Rheingold 1993; Stoll, Turkle, and Talbott 1995). But the truth is no one knows for sure how factors such as copyright, democratic principles versus totalitarian infringements, human communication and social interaction, and teaching and learning will be impacted. All we can say with certainty is that we have been, and will continue to be, inalterably changed by our venture into cyberspace.

Barlow points out that our familiar realities are about to be altered, and if we don't like the confusion, we can dig a hole and hide for 20 years. Instead, he advocates a blind faith—an inclination toward optimism and belief that, like those involved in the RAM project, we will take advantage of the potential that lies at our fingertips. As social studies teachers, it is our charge to prepare students to become global citizens imbued with a spirit of democracy and able to accommodate the accelerating changes that computer technology is bringing about. Hopefully, our history will reveal to future generations that changes made by computer technology were humane and helped create a better world.

References

Articles

Berger, Bob. "The Circuit Rider." *NetGuide* 2, no. 9 (1995): 30–32.

Van Horn, Royal. "Power Tools: FTEC-97, Push/Pull, and New Tools." *Phi Delta Kappan* 9 (May 1997): 675, 731.

"WELL: Wishers on the Internet." *Time* 144, no. 10 (September 1994): 18.

Books

Negroponte, Nicholas. *Being Digital*. New York: Alfred A. Knopf, 1995.

Rheingold, Howard. *The Virtual Community: Homesteading on the Electronic Frontier*. Reading, MA: Addison-Wesley, 1993.

Stoll, Clifford. *Silicon Snake Oil: Second Thoughts on the Information Highway*. New York: Doubleday, 1995.

Talbott, Stephen L. *The Future Does Not Compute: Transcending the Machines in Our Midst*. Sebastapol, CA: O'Reilly and Associates, 1995.

Turkle, Sherry. *Life on the Screen: Identity in the Age of the Internet*. New York: Simon & Schuster, 1995.

Wolfe, Tom. *Electric Kool-Aid Acid Test*. New York: Farrar, Strauss and Giroux, 1968.

Discussion Questions

1. What are TCP/IP protocols and why were they so important to the development of the Internet?
2. What are the similarities and differences between listservs and newsgroups?
3. What are some of the factors that can make a homepage successful, and what role does HTML play in constructing a homepage?

Additional Readings and Questions

Marcus, Stephen. "Avoiding Road Kill on the Information Highway." *The Computing Teacher* 22, no. 1 (1994): 38–41.

1. Why is lurking considered acceptable Internet behavior while flaming is not?
2. In what ways can telecommunications be viewed as a "place to go" rather than as a simple application of technology or method of communication?

O'Neil, John. "Technology and Schools: A Conversation with Chris Dede." *Educational Leadership* 53, no. 2 (October 1995): 6–12.

1. What is the biggest barrier to better use of technology in schools?

2. Why is it important to strive for generative knowledge in helping students make use of the vast amount of information that technology brings into the classroom?

McCarty, Paul J. "Four Days that Changed the World (and Other Amazing Internet Stories)." *Educational Leadership* 53, no.2 (October 1995): 48–50.

1. In what ways can school districts fund access to telecommunications and the Internet?

2. As a classroom teacher, what are some management strategies you can use to provide access to a computer linked to the Internet for a large group of students?

3. How are conceptions of teaching and learning changing in relation to the amount of information available to students through the Internet?

■ Activities

1. Subscribe to the NCSS listserv. Make sure you send your subscription request to the address of the listserv owner (**listserv@bgu.edu**). Leave the subject heading blank and uncheck a signature if yours is automatically appended. In the message type only the following: **subscribe ncss-l <your name>**. Remember, don't post anything to the list that you don't want everyone to read, and use the listserv owner address (**listserv@bgu.edu**) to seek information about how the list operates.

2. Subscribe to a newsgroup and follow a thread of a discussion for a week. Post your own comments to the conversation.

3. Visit the RAM at **http://www.bednet.org** and answer the following questions:

   ❖ How many people are killed by malaria each year, and who is particularly susceptible to contracting it?

   ❖ Name three aims of RAM.

   ❖ What is the Malawai project?

   ❖ Who is the coordinator of RAM in the United States? Send him an e-mail with your comments about the project.

Avoiding
Road Kill
on the
Information
Highway

Stephen Marcus

Q: "What's the largest man-made [sic] structure in the U.S.?"

We have the responsibility to help ourselves, our colleagues, and our students acquire continuing "driver's education," to avoid the unpleasant consequences of speeding down the digital highway.

A: "The Interstate Highway System."

—Traditional bar bet

Q: "What's the largest co-authored text in the world?"

Hint: It's a trick question.

Several years ago, in a discussion of telecommunication, I noted how the unique nature of electronic conversations generated a wide range of interesting issues peculiar to the medium. These included questions regarding language, gender, ethics, and "the host in the machine." I wondered, however, if I were "looking for more complexity and nuance than the situation or the technology warrants" (Marcus 1989).

Would that were the case.

In the intervening years, there has been enormous growth in educational online services, writing-related telecommunication projects, electronic teacher networks, and, perhaps most significantly, attention at the federal level to the creation of an "information highway." These activities, both within and related to educational settings, have been preceded by and concomitant with developments that are by turns intriguing, exciting, and deeply disturbing.

There seem, in fact, to be ample reasons for applying the advice of educational philosopher Paul Nash regarding anticipating a previous crisis. That is, we would do well to understand and to prepare ourselves and our students for coping with the problems and fulfilling the promise of yet another supposed improvement in our lives wrought by technology.

It will be enough here, I hope, to introduce some of the relevant terms, practices, and notions that are evolving from a new world that is both strange and familiar.

Let's begin by exploring some history and territory.

Browsers, Hunters, and Database Fascination

In the early days, large computers (mainframes and mini-computers) were used for organizing, storing, and retrieving information—thereby putting at our disposal so-called databases. Different preferences for using these systems soon became evident. Some individuals were quite content to browse through a database, looking for anything that was interesting and following lines of inquiry that evolved from the information retrieved. Other individuals preferred a more goal-oriented approach. They came to the computer knowing what they were looking for, and they enjoyed the hunt for a specifically defined target (i.e., the information relevant to a particular question or problem).

Both browsers and hunters soon became familiar with a phenomenon that came to be called "database fascination." People would sign on to a system, start retrieving information, and "suddenly" realize that a lot of time had passed. They had succumbed to the mesmeriz-ing effect of looking into (or "through") their computer screen, entering a world that consisted entirely of information.

This was certainly something akin to the experience of those who loved going into libraries or bookstores. However, as pointed out by media critic Neil Postman, there are important consequences to changing the form of information, its quantity, speed, or direction. The eventual proliferation of microcomputers engendered a booming population of database junkies.

Flamers and Lurkers

With the growth of electronic mail systems, bulletin boards, discussions, and conferences, people had access to "databases" that consisted of more immediate and personal data, that is, the ongoing exchange of ideas, conversations, and other information, whether stored or emerging in "real-time" interactions.

In this new setting, known generally as telecommunication, two particular behavioral patterns emerged. Some individuals would join a conference or free-wheeling discussion and just "listen in" or "observe" what was going on. They contributed rarely or not at all. They were known as lurkers, although the term didn't connote any necessarily nefarious intent. Some people just didn't seem to have much to say, but they enjoyed—or at least were content with—hanging around the fringes of the activity.

Other individuals, however, became known as "flamers," characterized by extremely hostile, angry, and often personal attacks on others in the group or on the topic being discussed. Flaming continues to be a problem—for others and sometimes for the flamers themselves. In the business world, for example, individuals often don't seem to realize that their remarks about their supervisors may be copied by the system to a broader audience than they intend. In educational settings, some students use the anonymity that an electronic forum sometimes provides to redirect toward others their own self-dissatisfaction.

My own first experience with a flamer occurred about 13 years ago when I was typing a paper at a terminal on a university mini-computer. On that particular system, it was possible to send "mail" to someone through the system from one terminal to another. If the recipient was currently working "online," the message would suddenly appear embedded in the text that was already on the screen, even if that text was merely a word-processing document.

As I was working on my paper, a message suddenly appeared that invited, or rather directed me to perform a reflexive act that, while now falling perhaps under the generally understood rubric of safe sex, was nevertheless anatomically inconvenient, at best, if not altogether impossible. I was, of course, startled. Who could be angry enough with me to send a message like that? After a moment's reflection, I realized that the person had probably, for unknown reasons, asked the computer for a list of the account names for people who were currently "logged on" to the system. It happened that I was using the account of a person who was known on campus for generating a lot of ill-will. The "flaming" had been directed, not at little old me, but at the person the angry individual *thought* was there.

There is, thus, the possibility that you might not be communicating with the person you think is there (and the concept of "there" is intriguing in its own right, as suggested below). This state of affairs is what prompted my original discussion of the question, "Is this the party to whom I am speaking?" (Marcus 1989). It also leads us to one other unfortunate dark corner in the world of telecommunications.

Sexual Predators

A recent segment of a morning television show dealt with the proliferation of hard core sex discussions available through various electronic information services. The show's host was "going ballistic" over the content of some of these discussions and was trying, without much success, to articulate the situation for parents and to suggest that something should be done about it in order to protect their children. It didn't help that the two guest experts weren't suited to the nature or needs of the audience.

In point of fact, there *are* individuals who adopt a friendly *persona* in order to find lonely and unhappy kids. These individuals, usually adults, develop relationships with the children and often get them to reveal who they are and where they live. There is a dimension of "not speaking to strangers" that applies to electronic playgrounds, and savvy classroom teachers establish guidelines for telecommunications, including warning students not to give out home phone numbers or addresses. For whatever reasons, making even this obvious advice explicit didn't occur to the individuals on the show referred to above.

The issues of making yourself available and of presentation of self take on new twists in the electronic landscape. More elaborate—and healthier—versions of these phenomena exist in what are sometimes referred to as "virtual communities."

MUDs and MOOs

It will help broaden our notions of what's going on if we spend at least a little time reconsidering our notions of the medium. Don't think of telecommunication as a technology (computers, modems, electronic mail, bulletin board systems, etc.). And don't think of it as merely a method of communication. Instead, as suggested by computer visionary Brenda Laurel, you should think of telecommunication as a *destination*. That is, telecommunication is not simply a "conduit" for getting information from one place to another. Instead, it is itself *a place to go*.

What's been happening is the growth of discourse communities that exist only in what is sometimes referred to as "cyberspace," that is, the universe of information (more about this term, below). Groups of people sign on to a system through their computers, modems, and phone lines and join others who have sometimes assumed alternate identities and who have been carrying on conversations and playing games using only text as the mode of communication. These "multiple user dimensions" sometimes use "object oriented" programming languages—hence, MUDs and MOOs.

These electronic communities develop their own guidelines for appropriate behavior, for dealing with dissidents, and for setting identities, goals, and values. Individuals join the communities after having decided who they will be (or, in fact, what "form" they will take). There is, for example, a significant amount of gender-switching that takes place; people explore the differences they experience when they are "taken for" someone with a very different background.

As described by Linda Polin (1993), such a simulated environment is a "small, contained, but evolving world that has many analogs to daily reality. There are buildings, people, and things with which the user can interact.... There are other real people logged in to the same community at the same time as I am.... I can sit on the couch in the living room and chat with whoever has wandered in.... I can write and send mail to people I know, or send notes to appropriate authorities to ask for help or to discuss a community problem.... I write my own descriptions for my objects and for me. To talk, I write; to listen, I read the talk others have written. To hold, touch, or manipulate objects, I must write directives...."

These virtual communities require real writing for a real audience. Objects get created and events occur only by virtue of people's active participation. There is no there, there, unless you construct it.

There's Nöoplace Like Home

Teilhard de Chardin described an arena for consciousness and mind that J. S. Huxley, Marshall McCluhan, and others have discussed in terms of a "nöosphere," which McCluhan identified in *The Gutenburg Galaxy* as "the externalization of senses ... or technological brain for the world." This concept can be related to the notion of cyberspace, a term used to refer to the "place" where electronic information accumulates and exists, access to which is theoretically available to everyone.

Recall Postman's suggestion (noted above) that there are important consequences to changing the form of information, its quantity, speed, or direction. In cyberspace, "information wants to be free" (a rallying cry for many cybernauts), and everyone is contributing to its growth, shape, content, and nature.

The metaphor of the "information highway," is a workable concept; it's a good delivery-model for communicating a somewhat intimidating change in the way the world will accomplish its business—and the content of its business. But the highway metaphor actually obscures as much as it reveals. It suggests an electronic "pathway"; a means of getting something from one place to another. This is analogous to filling a new medium with an old content: like imagining that a word processor has you working with paper.

Cyberspace might more accurately, if more complicatedly, be identified with the nöosphere, the "place" where a collective consciousness is articulated by the collectively produced text, which itself is linked from system to system through a "network of networks" like the Internet. In this regard, the totality of the textual content available in cyberspace constitutes a single "text," existing in the nöosphere, of which all participants are co-authors. The manner in which it may be said to exist "in the world" depends on the level of abstraction at which the issue is discussed. In any event, the growing interest and active participation in cyberspace suggests that it evokes a kind of fascination even more engaging than that discussed above regarding simple databases. People seek it out and find an intriguing and complex kind of comfort there.

The ISTE On-ramp

Members of the ISTE community are leaders in developing the kinds of expertise in electronic communication—both for student writing and for teacher support and training—that will prove invaluable in years to come. They are helping enlarge and clarify the repertoire of resources, voices, and behaviors to which students and teachers have access. The choices made, and the consequences of those choices, are of significant concern in light of the organization's goals.

We have the skills and the mission to develop our own and our students' talents in this as in other ways we wish to become smart, sensible, and savvy users of technology. And to retain a useful metaphor, we have the responsibility to help ourselves, our colleagues, and our students acquire continuing "driver's education," to avoid the unpleasant consequences of speeding down the digital highway. ❧

References

Marcus, S. "Is This the Party to Whom I Am Speaking?" *The Writing Notebook* (April/May 1989).

Polin, L. "Global Village As Virtual Community." *The Writing Notebook* (November/December 1993).

*S*tephen Marcus is chair of the Committee on Future Technology for the International Society for Technology in Education. The discussion above is part of a series that discusses the impact of current and evolving technologies. In a previous issue of "The Computing Teacher," Marcus asked for reader contributions that made predictions about the effects of technology on classrooms. He is still collecting those contributions, and they will be featured in a later article in the series.

Stephen Marcus, University of California, Graduate School of Education, Santa Barbara, CA 93106–9490.

Technology and Schools

A Conversation with Chris Dede

John O'Neil

The graveyard of school reform is littered with technological innovations that failed to live up to their advance billing. Chris Dede, futurist and expert on educational technology, thinks he knows why. Too often, we've attempted to graft technological solutions onto antiquated structures and traditional approaches to learning. Dede says that emerging technologies can provide sustained support to teachers as they experiment with new ways of teaching and learning.

Some experts predict that technology will have an enormous impact on K–12 education. Do you agree?

Will the information superhighway revolutionize education? Chris Dede says that new technologies can help transform schools—but only if they are used to support new models of teaching and learning.

It depends on what models of teaching and learning we use. If technology is simply used to automate traditional models of teaching and learning, then it'll have very little impact on schools. If it's used to enable new models of teaching and learning, models that can't be implemented without technology, then I think it'll have a major impact on schools. And if it's used to enable models of teaching and learning that extend beyond the walls of the school into the community, into the workplace, into the family, then it will also have an enormous impact on education and learning.

Technology hasn't had a widespread, transformative impact on schools yet. Why not?

Schools are like other organizations. Our first instinct is to use technology to do the same things faster. I remember when my university first got word processors, we set up a dedicated area with special secretaries who did nothing but word processing. It was used as a faster kind of typewriter. Only later did people begin to realize that the computer and word processing enabled everyone to compose more effectively, and that having specialists who did nothing but keyboard wasn't the right approach. In schools, we've gone through this preliminary period, and now we're at a point where technology could really take off for us.

Some educators seem tired of the hype about new technologies. They wish they could get their hands on some old technologies—like a copier or a phone.

That's understandable. Teachers are often expected to do something different, but they don't have the resources or the training to do it very well. One of the mistakes that we made in implementing educational technology was focusing first on students rather than teachers, because when the computers on students' desks are mysterious devices to teachers, it's unreasonable to expect effective integration into the curriculum. Politically, however, it's easy to see why: school boards and parents don't want to be told that teachers will be using technology first and students will use it eventually.

People begin to use a technology when it is readily accessible and also when important information becomes available only through that technology.

For example, businesses can encourage the integration of technology by not sending around paper announcements anymore, relying instead on e-mail. That forces people to get into the e-mail world. In and of itself, that doesn't do anything, because reading paper announcements on the screen doesn't enhance value. But once employees are in the e-mail world, even if they're not there for the right reasons, then there's a much greater possibility of luring them into more productive parts of the technology.

We're being inundated with news stories about the information superhighway, the suggestion being that it's going to change our lives. What is the information superhighway, and does it really hold transformative potential for schools?

I prefer the term *information infrastructure*—a synthesis of high-performance computing and high-performance communications. The high-performance computing gives us the power of super computers on the desktop—but at personal computer prices. And high-performance communications let us link that power to other people's machines and to send across these channels not just data but video and voice.

At least three different groups are competing to become the backbone of the country's information infrastructures. The phone companies prefer their phone lines, the cable television providers would like their wires used, and the computer companies want to see the Internet as the dominant medium. Then you have secondary players, like the wireless technologies. In practice, I think all of them will play some role. In any particular local area, one or another group may dominate, but everything will interconnect. Eventually, we'll have devices that sometimes act like a telephone system, in the sense that you can do teleconferencing and video conferencing. Some of the time they'll act like a cable television system, in that you get digital video delivered to you on demand. And sometimes these tools will act like the Internet, which offers knowledge webs and different sorts of synthetic environments and discussion groups; things that begin to become virtual communities.

Some critics are calling it the "information hypeway," saying the benefits are being wildly oversold.

The vendors talk about things like video dialtone, which would allow you to order movies at home. That, to me, is absolutely uncompelling. I get much more excited about some of the innovations that we're seeing with the World Wide Web. Here, people are using "netcrawlers" like Netscape or Mosaic not only to reach data that wasn't at their fingertips before, but to reach interlinked information. In other words, when they find one piece, they're linked to other things they might want to know. I get excited about telepresence and virtual communities, where people who are not physically near one another can share ideas. And I'm excited about synthetic environments that allow people to step outside of the real world and into a virtual universe for a while, as a way of getting some insights on the real world. If we use information infrastructures for that kind of thing, we'll see where the true power is. If we just use it as a bigger pipe to shovel more data through—which is what the superhighway concept conveys—we won't see very much value added.

Access to information seems to be one of the big selling points of the information superhighway idea. You have some doubts about how useful this is to schools, though.

Classrooms right now are not information-poor environments. Many teachers feel overwhelmed by how much information they're already supposed to convey. If anything, the curriculum is too crowded now. We teach a wide array of things very superficially through presentation, which we then have to reteach a couple of years later because students don't remember it. If the purpose of the Internet is seen as adding more information, it will make current educational problems worse rather than better.

Again, the question of whether this access to information that technology affords us is a good thing depends on what model of teaching and learning we're striving for. One way of looking at it is to distinguish between inert knowledge—which is something that you know, but that doesn't make any difference in your life—and generative knowledge, which changes your mental model, your whole perspective on how you view the world.

How do people translate access to vast archives of information into personal knowledge in a generative way? We've found that learner investigation and collaboration and construction of knowledge are vital, and these things don't follow from teaching by telling and learning by listening. It isn't that assimilation of knowledge isn't a good place to start, because it's hard to investigate something unless you know a bit about it. But assimilation is a terrible place to stop. The excitement about the access to information is that it is the first step in access to expertise, to investigations, to knowledge construction. Only if access to data is seen as a first step—rather than an end in itself—will it be useful.

High-powered computing and access to all these resources within the classroom could create major challenges for teachers. Students might want to take more ownership of the curriculum and have more choice in what they study. And some of those topics might be things about which the teacher knows very little. What will this mean for teachers, who traditionally have planned the curriculum in advance, based on the content and skills they thought most important for students to learn?

To me the purpose of education is to make you more effective in life, and life doesn't come packaged in disciplines. In real life, you're not always in the same room with an expert who knows the right answer. The best way to educate is to start where people are. If a learner is interested in baseball, you start with baseball; if a learner is interested in rap music, you start with rap music. What we know about real-world situations, authentic phenomena, is that they contain all the disciplines swirled around within them. An effective teacher can involve students from many different disciplinary perspectives by beginning with something that learner is interested in, rather than some artificial problem.

What you're describing sounds like an incredible challenge for teachers.

Certainly, it's a more difficult kind of teaching, and it means that even an expert teacher will be in situations where the right answer is, "I don't know, but I know how to find out." And that answer is very valuable, because it models that not knowing is not a failure, that not

knowing is a typical condition. The important thing is having the skills to find out.

Look at how the world of work has changed. A lot of blue-collar and white-collar employees are not solving problems as they did a generation ago, when they would look at a problem, reflect on it until they understood it completely, and then apply some problem-solving technique they'd learned. In today's workplace, by the time you fully understand something, conditions have already changed. So what people are mastering in work is the ability to make decisions given incomplete information, inconsistent objectives, and uncertain consequences. And that's what we need to be teaching in education—not so much what we know and how we know it, but what to do when you don't know something, and how to act when you don't know exactly how to get to where you want to be.

And how can technology support this?

Many of the things that we've been talking about—collaborative learning, constructive learning, and apprenticeships—are not new concepts in learning. But they've never been sustainable. Teachers who try them usually burn out. Why? Because they didn't have an infrastructure that supported them. Technology can help establish a supportive infrastructure that makes it possible to use those powerful models without burning out.

If students were learning effectively from lectures and were excited about it, I would be the last person to say: "Stop! Wait a minute! You've got to do this using technology." But what we see too often is that many students aren't getting much from the current curriculum, and teachers don't have anything in their repertoire that's sustainable to involve those learners. So if beginning an e-mail relationship with a student in Japan is the right thing to use with a student, do it. If simulating being on the starship Enterprise gets kids involved, do it. Whatever works. And technology can expand the repertoire of what works.

We're experiencing two important trends right now. One is that many students, especially those in wealthier families, have access to computers at home. Many students may even have greater access at home than they do at school. The other trend is that the home market for educational software is exploding. What do these trends mean for the future of schools?

The issue is complex, in part because schools have three different functions: they are learning environments, they are socialization institutions, and they are custodial settings. Because of the custodial and socialization aspects, in particular, I don't think that schools will ever disappear. We may not call them schools, but there will be some place that students go to keep them safe and to enhance their socialization into our nation.

Some of the growth in home infrastructure is very positive, because during the last generation a lot of families have dumped all their educational responsibilities onto the school. We know that the biggest single impact that we could make in the lives of many children would be to involve their parents more deeply in their learning. So if technology creates the partnership between school and home, whether through homework hotlines or whatever, that's very exciting.

Teachers and Technology: Potential and Pitfalls

Schools are steadily increasing their access to new technologies, a comprehensive federal study finds. But an enormous gap exists between present practice and what technology enthusiasts envision.

Technophiles and skeptics alike can find plenty of ammunition for their views in a new report from the Office of Technology Assessment (OTA). *Teachers and Technology: Making the Connection* is a comprehensive study of the presence and impact of technology in U.S. schools.[1]

First, the good news. Schools' access to various technologies is rising at a steady clip. For example, OTA estimates that U.S. schools have about 5.8 million computers for instruction—about one for every nine students. That's an increase of about 700,000 computers per year for the past three years. Thirty-five percent of schools now have access to some kind of computer network, and nearly every school has TVs and VCRs. Almost 30 percent of schools now have CD-ROMs, a fourfold increase since 1991.

Better still, some schools are capitalizing upon this access by offering richer, more varied, and more engaging learning opportunities to students. OTA's report is bursting with examples of teachers and students' taking advantage of new technologies in exciting and productive ways. In scattered schools

1. OTA's report, *Teachers and Technology: Making the Connection*, is available for $19 from the U.S. Government Printing Office. Call (202) 512–1800 for more information.

around the nation, students are participating in international research projects via computer and modem, sending e-mail to scientists, preparing multimedia research papers, or videotaping one another for a class project. Teachers are communicating online with colleagues, scanning CD-ROM databases for lesson resources, or using software to effortlessly calculate grades. But such practices, OTA says, remain the exception, not the norm—at least for now.

Modest Applications

For a variety of reasons, most teachers today who use technologies use them in traditional ways. OTA found that

> the most common uses of technology today are the uses of video for presenting information, the use of computers for basic skills practice at the elementary and middle school levels, and the use of word processing and other generic programs for developing computer-specific skills in middle and high schools.
>
> Other uses of technologies—such as desktop publishing, developing mathematical and scientific reasoning with computer simulations, information-gathering from databases on CD-ROM or networks, or communicating by electronic mail—are much rarer in the classroom. Technologies are not used widely in traditional academic subjects in secondary schools.

→

But this also creates an equity challenge. Anytime a new medium comes along, initially it widens the gap between the haves and the have nots. Early in the development of the telephone, people who had telephones had a large advantage over people who didn't. Because it was new and expensive, gaps widened. However, when a medium is mature, it narrows gaps. From a policy point of view, the challenge is how do we minimize that early period and quickly move to the more mature stage?

What complicates the situation is that many people now are dissatisfied with public education. Along with the explosion in home computers and home software, we're seeing an explosion in independent schooling, pressure for vouchers and home schooling. These trends are interrelated. People who are going outside of the public schools are finding that these new infrastructures are an efficient and effective way of delivering services—curriculum across the wires, supervision across the wires, and certification across the wires. If public educators don't effectively use the technologies to enhance their services, a decade from now we could be in a situation where public schools are responsible for a smaller group of students who are, on balance, harder to educate—and the more privileged students would be served through other means. And a smaller proportion of taxpayers would care about whether public education succeeds or not. That would be a very grim situation.

You're doing some exciting research on new forms of technology. What's that about?

A lot of my own research right now is in the area of immersive distributed virtual environments.

That's a mouthful.

Here's a simpler way to describe it. Some of it is like virtual reality, where people are wearing computerized clothing, and their nervous systems are placed inside an artificial universe. Through their visual sense, through their auditory sense, through their haptic sense—touch and pressure—they experience something that's not possible to experience in the real world. A colleague of mine and I are building virtual "universes," where you can personally experience what it would be like to be a charge in an electromagnetic field, or a ball in a world without friction and gravity, or a molecule that's about to bond on the quantum level. We call these *immersive* environments.

How can this enhance learning?

Take science as an example. There are lots of things in science that we don't personally experience in the real world in a conscious way, like relativity or quantum mechanics, even though they're there. By putting ourselves into an immersive environment, we can experience such things, and we think these experiences will help people understand those concepts more fully.

And what are "distributed virtual environments"?

These allow people separated by distance and time to occupy a shared synthetic world, where they can collaborate to evolve common virtual experiences. One scenario I use frequently is learners tuning into a *Star Trek* channel. Their "avatar," their computer graphics figure in the virtual world, appears on the deck of the starship Enterprise with the avatars of everyone else who signed in at that time. This is a very compelling setting in which kids in Germany and kids in America can practice each other's language and work

In fact, only nine percent of secondary students report using computers for English class, six to seven percent for math class, and three percent for social studies. Why aren't more schools tapping into the power of new technologies to reshape curriculum and instruction? The list of barriers identified by OTA is long and disheartening.

Despite increases in access to new technologies, schools are not sufficiently stocked, powered, or wired. About one-half of the computers in schools are older 8-bit models incapable of supporting advanced applications, such as CD-ROM or network integration. Further, computers and peripherals often are located in a computer lab, where teachers don't have the access to them that would support their use as an everyday tool. About one-half of the computers used for instruction in 1992 were placed in computer labs, while about 35 percent were in teachers' classrooms, OTA found. About one-third of U.S. schools have access to the Internet, but only three percent of classrooms do.

Moreover, most teachers have not had adequate training in how to use various technologies in their classrooms. And the training they receive usually focuses on the mechanics of operating new machines, with less attention given to how technology can be helpful in studying specific subjects. The picture in preservice programs is not much brighter. "Overall, teacher education programs in the United States do not prepare graduates to use technology as a teaching tool," OTA found.

A third explanation for the somewhat disappointing status of technology use is an overall lack of vision and clarity of goals with regard to technology's role in the school. Technologies are changing rapidly, and so are the ways schools are expected to use them. Schools were first urged to teach students computer programming, for example; a few years later, they were prodded to focus on applications such as word processing and spreadsheets. Add in the fact that "getting the technology" sometimes overshadows the question of how teachers want to change their instruction, and what role technology can play in assisting that. "It is small wonder that teachers have become confused, and administrators frustrated, with many educators unclear where they should be headed in technology use," OTA says.

Perhaps the biggest barrier to technology use is time: time for training, time for teachers to try out technologies in their classrooms, time to talk to other teachers about technology. If teachers aren't given more time to explore the uses of various technologies, and if the help they need in terms of training and support isn't available, progress toward the vision held by proponents will be slow indeed.

on their skills in math, science, or communication. The motivation comes from trying to help the starship move forward or deal with a new galactic entity.

Are there examples of this in practice?

The military has had success with nonimmersive distributed simulation in dial-a-war systems for virtual battlefields. It's easy to see analogies to some of the same types of training-related things that schools do. Also, the text-based virtual worlds emerging on the Internet (MUSEs, MUDs, MOOs) are primitive types of distributed simulation.

How far along is your research?

We're a year into a project, funded by the National Science Foundation, which is designed to evaluate the potential of immersion through science education. We're seeing if there's something there that's worth exploring. The equipment that we're working with now is in the half-million dollar range, so there would be no point today in trying to build a curriculum out of what we've found.

But we believe that, because of advances that the entertainment industry is going to make, that same level of power will be under the Christmas tree within eight years. So if there is learning power in immersion, we think there should be alternatives to Super Mario in 3D or Mortal Kombat 45, or whatever will be the entertainment at that time. In the long run, depending on what we find in the research, we should be able to have an influence. In the short run, there won't be any direct impact.

Clifford Stoll is getting a lot of attention because of his book, Silicon Snake Oil. *He argues these virtual worlds have a dark side. People become immersed in virtual communities and ignore their real communities. Since educators today are so interested in creating classrooms as communities, do you think new technologies might be a threat to this goal?*

Technology is a double-edged sword. Even when a family watches television together in the same room, they can be isolated spectators rather than people who are sharing a common experience. The information infrastructures will have a somewhat better record, because at least they're interactive. But educators should be wary of placing too much emphasis on these virtual worlds. After all, the whole purpose of learning is to help you function more effectively in reality. It will require very careful design. The commercial incentive, with movies and television and so on, is to lure people into the virtual world. That's how they make money.

In education, we have to set up the incentive system the opposite way: by using these virtual worlds to teach, but always helping students apply what they're learning in a real-world context. The best role for technology is to make community-centered constructivist classrooms sustainable for the teacher. ❖

C hristopher Dede is Professor of Information Technology and Education at George Mason University, Fairfax, VA 22030– 4444 (e-mail: cdede@gmu.edu).

J ohn O'Neil is Senior Editor of Educational Leadership.

Four Days that Changed the World

And Other Amazing Internet Stories

Paul J. McCarty

I t is Monday, August 19, in Salt Lake City, Utah. Sixth-graders Corey, Shannon, and Jennifer are in tears. Their key pals in Russia haven't communicated with them in days. The 1991 counterrevolution attempt in Moscow has stopped all information leaving the country.

Excitement and wonder had filled the previous months as almost daily electronic mail messages had communicated stories of daily life in the students' homelands. For example, Jennifer's amazement that Tatyana liked pizza, Nintendo, and cute boys, too, opened her eyes to the fact that a child on the other side of the globe shared similar feelings. And then there was Jennifer's

A remarkable electronic mail network links Utah's students with pen pals in Russia and around the world.

and Corey's eagerness to plan with Sergei their goal to be the first astronaut/cosmonaut team to Mars—something their parents would have never thought possible.

But not all of the letters are lighthearted. Sometimes sharing a deep concern has made it easier to bear. For example, Shannon shared her fears with her friend Natasha about her dad's safety as an F-16 pilot in the Persian Gulf. Natasha, in turn, confided in Shannon her worries that her uncle might be wounded in Afghanistan.

Now the dialogue has been cut short. The dark days of the Soviet Union's crisis are their crisis, too. Suddenly the following e-mail message comes across their computer screen:

> Due to the militia revolution all the independent radio and TV stations are not working. I am not sure if this channel of information is disabled also.... We will send the details of the situation here as soon as we realize what happens. I am afraid that the time that comes will not be the best time in the history of our country.
>
> —Andrew Portnov
> the Soviet children's teacher

The children are elated! The message gives them hope. But what can they do to help? Jennifer suggests daily downloading of *KSL TeleText 5* electronic mail news services[1] and uploading to Moscow all the international events that pertain to the Soviet Union. This way, at least Andrew Portnov and his students can find out how the world is reacting—and maybe even communicate about what is happening inside Russia.

> Tuesday, August 20
> Moscow, Russia, U.S.S.R.
>
> Dear Children, Thank you. Thank you. We received your message with the news accounts. Please keep sending. We have translated the news into Russian, made copies, and passed them out to those in the streets supporting [Russian President Boris] Yeltsin against the KGB and the Army gener-

als. The situation is quite fuzzy. The Army generals took power but the resistance of the people is high. And Yeltsin asks people not to obey the "new order." I really hope the action of the KGB and Army will fail.... We have only one TV channel, and that is controlled by KGB.... It is a miracle that they forgot to cut our e-mail wires.

> —Andrew

> Wednesday, August 21
> Moscow, Russia, U.S.S.R.
>
> We are so grateful to your words of help and daily news reports. We are listening to the independent Echo of Moscow radio, and we learn the news.... This night about 10 people were killed. People that went to Russia Government [to defend Yeltsin] have stopped troops attack. Several tanks were burned....

> Thursday, August 22
> Moscow, Russia, U.S.S.R.
>
> Thanks to God the junta's time is over! Thank you so much for your caring, daily news and prayers! We are very grateful to you. Now we are proud to be Russian. We are proud to have America as our friends!

The events of these four days may have taken place four years ago, but the former sixth graders who participated in them believe to this day that they helped change the course of Russia's history.

---

1. The local CBS affiliate has an Internet address that updates current news around the world every few hours.

The World at the School Door

Utah has long been a leader in use of the Internet. In 1969, the University of Utah was one of the first four sites on the Internet. Our state is now a national focal point for high-tech companies, such as WordPerfect and Novell. Micron Technologies based its decision to locate a plant near Salt Lake City in part on the reputation of two highly advanced engineering schools, the Brigham Young University and the University of Utah.

Continued use of the Internet in our schools will accelerate the information flow and give Utah's schools the same opportunity to enjoy many of the resources available to our universities. This access is especially important for our children as they find themselves involved in international events, such as Salt Lake City's hosting of the 2002 Winter Olympics!

As principal of three elementary schools in Utah over the past eight years, I have seen the incredible learning that is possible through the Internet.[2] One amazing tool accessible through this network is *WorldClassroom*, a global electronic information service that has helped us bring the world to our schools.[3] In addition to the Russian example, our students have communicated with children in countries that include Argentina, Australia, Belgium, Canada, Denmark, France, Germany, Great Britain, Hungary, Iceland, Indonesia, Kenya, Lithuania, Mexico, Singapore, Taiwan, the Netherlands, and Zimbabwe.

When the war in the Persian Gulf began, students at Hillview Elementary in Salt Lake City were very frightened. Our school was near several military installations, where many of our students' parents, relatives, and close friends worked. As the children shared their concerns with their key pals around the globe, they received many questions about the war.

To help answer them, we received permission from the public affairs officer at Hill Air Force Base for our students to send questions from children around the world over the Air Force's telecommunication lines to Air Force Command headquarters in Saudi Arabia. Front line pilots and officers, in turn, transmitted answers through *WorldClassroom*. Although these transmission lines were closed to major news services, our school was fortunate to have direct access. All the news services had to wait for briefings from General Colin Powell!

When our fourth graders in the Granite School District began communicating via e-mail with the fourth graders of Warmbrook Elementary in Chapel-en-le-Frith, Derbyshire, England, they learned to think beyond their own expe-

---

2. A major concern of public and private educators is the issue of cybersex and unacceptable information on the Internet. Educators and Internet providers need to work together to screen unwanted material from children while maintaining adequate content. For example, Innovative Systems Design has successfully filtered such material *before* it comes into the classroom. For more information, contact the company at 2144 South 1100 East, Suite 150–272, Salt Lake City, UT 84106; (801) 583–8014.

3. *WorldClassroom* was created by Global Learning Corporation, P.O. Box 201361, Arlington, TX 76006; 800–866–4452.

rience. For example, the English students asked our children how old Salt Lake City is. Our fourth graders answered proudly, "Salt Lake City is *very* old. It was settled in 1847! How old is your town?" Back via satellite e-mail came the reply: "Chapel-en-le-Frith was settled by the Normans. The name means 'chapel in the forest.' The chapel our town was built around was constructed in 1225."

Our students were practically speechless. Elementary children, being egocentric and ethnocentric at this stage of their cognitive development, think the world revolves around them. As one child exclaimed in disbelief, "How can that be? The whole world didn't even begin until 1492!"

Then, when freighter ship Captain Gary Schmidt left port in San Francisco for Japan and Hong Kong, students at Hillview Elementary read his daily log uploaded to the electronic Information Superhighway. As they plotted the daily latitude and longitude of his journey, he communicated to them his thrilling accounts of whale migrations, the eerie glow of bioluminescence on the sea at night, and why true seamen never eat fish! (Seafarers, unlike people who fish the seas for profit, have a reverence for their finned friends.)

And in a project called "It's Not My Fault!" students around the world plotted the frequency of earthquakes globally. Imagine their amazement when our students and their peers in sister schools in the Bay area predicted the San Francisco earthquake within two weeks of its occurrence!

It Is a Small World after All

Of course, all of this does have a cost. Cost varies with the services provided and the speed of the connection. The simplest connection might provide service for one computer to a school for approximately the price of a phone line and $10 to $30 per month. The high end of access to the Internet might provide service to 50–100 users at a time for thousands of dollars in installation costs and up to $2,000 per month in operating fees.

The costs, however, need to be weighed against the benefits. Having access to the Internet dramatically changes teaching and learning. Here's an example of what students can accomplish in a day.

At Hillsdale Elementary, 10-year-olds Sara and Tamara and 12-year-old Jennifer were surfin' the Net. Tamara swept the mouse at dazzling speeds, as she and her friends clicked into pictures of the American History exhibit at the Smithsonian. Next, they communicated with astronauts on board the Space Shuttle on NASA's SpaceLink. Then they printed off copies of maps of Boston, Massachusetts, from the Internet's "Virtual Tourist" for Sara's social studies report. They finished the day by talking to their e-mail key pals in London and Phoenix *live* on the Internet phone. They did all this without leaving their desks and for the insignificant price of a local phone call. The only required equipment was a 386 (or above) computer, a modem, Windows software, and phone access to the Internet.

Postscript

Did the four days in 1991 during which our sixth graders communicated with a Russian class change the course of history? Are they in some small way responsible for keeping Boris Yeltsin in power? Incidentally, we later found out that Andrew Portnov, the Russian students' teacher, had published information transmitted by our students in an underground newspaper that supported Yeltsin. Who knows?

We *do* know that the episode dramatically changed the students' views of the world in which they live. And, every day in classrooms around the world, thanks to the wonderful world of technology, other students are participating in experiences that may not change the world but will, at the least, transform their own lives. ◈

P aul J. McCarty is Principal of Hillsdale Elementary Schools in the Granite School District, 3275 West 3100 South, West Valley City, UT 84119–1776 and a part-time professor at Brigham Young University in Provo, Utah (e-mail: paul@isdi.com).

chapter 8

Resources for Using Technology in Social Studies Education

The preceding chapters have described a number of software programs, including ones specifically designed for the social studies curriculum as well as applications and tool programs for use by any classroom teacher. It is virtually impossible to keep up with all the updates and new versions of software that are occurring because vendors are constantly working on product development. This chapter provides the necessary information to reach some of the vendors of products that were described in earlier chapters. Additionally, this chapter will identify journals, books, and other resources that social studies teachers can use to keep current with the latest developments in their field. An annotated bibliography of URLs of social studies sites on the WWW is also provided. It should be noted that these URLs may change, but a simple search should help you locate a particular page if it has moved to a different server. Technology is a field that is constantly changing, and these resources are important for keeping abreast of the latest information.

If there is any difficulty contacting a publisher listed below, or if you are looking for additional software/CD-ROM materials, you might contact the Social Studies School Service, a supplier of educational resources that searches out supplementary learning materials, including books, CD-ROMs, videos, laserdiscs, software, charts, and posters. You can contact the Social Studies School Service in any of the following ways:

email: **Access@SocialStudies.com**

phone: 800–421–4246 (U.S. and Canada); 310–839–2436 (international)

WWW site: **http://www.socialstudies.com**

Social Studies Software Producers/Distributors

Company	Address/Phone	Sample Products
Broderbund Software	500 Redwood Blvd. P.O. Box 6125 Novato, CA 94948-6125 800-474-8840 Fax: 415-382-4419	*Where in Time is Carmen San Diego?*
Claris Corp.	P.O. Box 3023 Salinas, CA 93912 408-987-7000	*Culture 2.0*
Davidson & Associates, Inc.	P.O. Box 2961 Torrance, CA 90509 800-545-7677	*KidCAD*
Didatech Software	4250 Dawson St., Ste. 200 Burnaby, BC V5C 4B1 800-665-0667	*Cross Country*
Learning Company	6160 Summit Dr. N. Minneapolis, MN 55430 800-825-0828 http://www.learningco.com	*African Trail*
Maxis Software	950 Mountain View Dr., Ste. 113 Lafayette, CA 94549 800-336-2947	*SimCity*
Scholastic Inc.	730 Broadway New York, NY 10003 212-505-3317	*Point of View*
Tom Snyder Productions	80 Coolidge Hill Rd. Watertown, MA 02172-2817 800-342-0236	*Decisions, Decisions; Timeliner; National Inspirer International Inspirer; Choices, Choices; Cultural Debates*
Sunburst Communications	101 Castleton St. Pleasantville, NY 10570 800-321-7511 http://www.nysunburst.com	*Voices of the 30s*
The World Game Institute	University City Science Center 3508 Market St. Philadelphia, PA 19104 215-387-0220 http://worldgame.org/~wgi	*Global Recall*

Applications- and Research-Related Software Producers/Distributors

Company	Address/Phone	Sample Products
Advanced Ideas	2902 San Pablo Ave. Berkeley, CA 94702 510-526-9100	*Game Show*
Broderbund Software	500 Redwood Blvd. P.O. Box 6125 Novato, CA 94948-6125 800-474-8840 Fax: 415-382-4419	*Printshop Deluxe;* *KidPix*
Castle Software	1228 Powell Ave. N. Merrick, NY 11566 800-345-7606	*TestWiz*
Gametek	2727 Tucker St. Extension Burlington, NC 27215 800-426-3835	*Jeopardy*
Learning Company	6493 Kaiser Dr. Fremont, CA 94555 800-852-2255	*Children's Writing and* *Publishing Center;* *Student Writing Center*
Logo Computer Systems, Inc.	330 W. 58th St., Ste. 5D New York, NY 10019 212-967-2447	*LogoWriter*
Minnesota Educational Computing Consortium (MECC)	6160 Summit Dr. N. Minneapolis, MN 55430-4003 800-685-6322	*Puzzles and Posters*
Scholastic Inc.	730 Broadway New York, NY 10003 212-505-3317	*Survey Taker*
Springboard	7807 Creekridge Circle Minneapolis, MN 55425 612-541-0383	*Newsroom*
Sunburst	101 Castleton St. Pleasantville, NY 10570 800-321-7511	*Ten Clues*
Teacher Support Software	P.O. Box 7125 Gainesville, FL 32605 352-332-6404	*Semantic Mapper*
Tom Snyder Productions	80 Coolidge Hill Rd. Watertown, MA 02172-2817 800-342-0236	*All Star Drill;* *Graph Club*

CD-ROM Producers/Distributors

Company	Address/Phone	Sample Products
Against All Odds	P.O. Box 1189 Sausalito, CA 94966-1189 800-558-3388	*Passage to Vietnam*
Applied Optical Media	1450 Boot Rd., Bldg. 400 Westchester, PA 19380 805-545-8515	*Mediasource: Historical Library*
Doris Kindersley Multimedia	95 Madison Ave. New York, NY 10016 800-356-6575	*Eyewitness History of the World*
Facts on File, Inc.	460 Park Ave. S. New York, NY 10016 800-322-8755, 212-683-2244	*News Digest (1980-1990)*
Fife & Drum Software	316 Soapstone Ln. Silver Spring, MD 20905 http://www.ils.unc.edu/fife/ fife.html	*The Revolutionary War; Powers of Persuasion*
Learning Company	6160 Summit Dr. N. Minneapolis, MN 55430 800-825-0828 http://www.learningco.com	*Explorers of the New World; Pathways through Jerusalem*
Grafica Multimedia	1777 Borel Place, Ste. 500 San Mateo, CA 94402 415-358-5555	*A House Divided: the Lincoln- Douglas Debates; CNN Faces of Conflict*
Grolier Electronic Publishing	Sherman Turnpike Danbury, CT 06816 800-356-5590, 203-797-3500	*New Grolier Electronic Encyclopedia*
Instructional Resources Corporation	1819 Bay Ridge Ave. Annapolis, MD 21403 800-922-1711	*The American History CD-ROM*
Microsoft	One Microsoft Way Redmond, WA 98052-6399 206-882-8080	*Encarta; Ancient Lands; 500 Nations: Stories of the North American Indian Experience*
Minnesota Educational Computing Consortium (MECC)	6160 Summit Dr. N. Minneapolis, MN 55430-4003 800-685-6322	*MayaQuest; Oregon Trail II*

CD-ROM Producers/Distributors (cont.)

Company	Address/Phone	Sample Products
National Geographic Society	1145 17th St. NW Washington, DC 20036 800-368-2728	*Picture Atlas of the World;* *The Presidents: A Picture History of* *Our Nation*
Pierian Springs Software	5200 SW Macadam, Ste. 570 Portland, OR 97201 503-222-2044	*Interactive Geography—Digital Chisel*
Central Intelligence Agency	http://www.odci.gov/cia /publications/nsolo/ wfb-all.htm	*USA Factbook;* *CIA World Factbook*
The Bureau of Electronic Publishing	805 Third Ave., 8th floor New York, NY 10022 212-832-7000	*Countries of the World;* *U.S. History on CD-ROM*
The Discovery Channel Multimedia	7700 Wisconsin Ave. Bethesda, MD 20814-3579 800-762-2189	*Nile: Passage to Egypt;* *Normandy: The Great Crusade*
The Voyager Company	514 Market Loop, Ste. 103 West Dundee, IL 60118 847-428-2184	*Exotic Japan;* *Who Built America?*
Videodiscovery	1700 Westlake Ave. N., #600 Seattle, WA 98109-3012 800-548-3472, 206-285-5400	*Small Blue Planet*
Ztek Company	P.O. Box 11768 Louisville, KY 40577-1768 800-247-1603, 502-584-8505 http://www.ztek.com	*European Monarchs;* *USA Wars: World War II;* *U.S. Atlas;* *World Atlas*

Videodisc Producers/Distributors

Company	Address/Phone	Sample Products
AIMS Multimedia	9710 DeSoto Ave. Chatsworth, CA 91311-4409 800-367-2467, 818-773-4300	*The Way of Life* series (Japan, Germany, Mexico, England)
Encyclopedia Britannica	310 S. Michigan Ave. Chicago, IL 60604 800-621-3900, 312-347-7000	*U.S. Regions* series; *American Foreign Policy* series; *Paths to Freedom* (w/CD-ROM)
Image Entertainment	933 Oso Ave. Chatsworth, CA 91311 800-473-3475, 818-407-9100	*America and the World since WW II* series
Instructional Resources Corporation	1819 Bay Ridge Ave. Annapolis, MD 21403 800-922-1711	*Western Civilization;* *World History* (non-European); *American History*
Optical Data Corporation	512 Main St., Ste. 100 Atlanta, GA 30318 800-524-2481, 908-668-0022	*The '88 Vote;* *In the Holy Land;* *Martin Luther King, Jr.;* *Communism and the Cold War;* *Powers of the President/Congress/Supreme Court;* *The Lessons of War* (ABC News Interactive); *GTV* (National Geographic)
Scholastic, Inc.	P.O. Box 7502 Jefferson City, MO 65102 800-541-5513	*History in Motion: Milestones of the 20th Century;* *Struggles for Justice*
Coronet Film & Video	Coronet Film & Video 108 Wilmot Rd. Deerfield, IL 60015 800-621-2131	*Investigating History: Treasures from the Deep*
The Voyager Company	514 Market Loop, Ste. 103 West Dundee, IL 60118 847-428-2184	*The Great Quake of '89* (ABC News Interactive)

Note: Many of these individual titles are also available from other distributors, like MECC (Minnesota Educational Computing Consortium) and Brøderbund.

Sample Digital Video Producers/Distributors

Company	Address/Phone	Sample Products/Format
Applied Optical Media	1450 Boot Rd., Bldg. 400 West Chester, PA 19380 805-545-8515	*World Vista Atlas* CDTV
Learning Company	6160 Summit Dr. N. Minneapolis, MN 55430 800-825-0828	*Time Magazine Multimedia Almanac* PhotoMotion & DVI
Decision Development Corporation	2680 Bishop Dr., Ste. 122 San Ramon, CA 94583 800-800-4332	*PilgrimQuest* PhotoMotion
Encyclopedia Britannica and Jostens, Inc.	310 S. Michigan Ave. Chicago, IL 60604 800-621-3900 and 9920 Pacific Heights Blvd. San Diego, CA 92121-4330 619-622-5096	*Compton's Multimedia Encyclopedia* QuickTime (Networked version from Jostens)
Grolier Electronic Publishing	Sherman Turnpike Danbury, CT 06816 800-356-5590, 203-797-3500	*New Grolier Multimedia Encyclopedia* QuickTime & PhotoMotion
National Geographic Society	Education Services Dept. 89 Washington, DC 20036 800-368-2728	*The Presidents: It All Started with George; National Geographic Picture Atlas of the World* PhotoMotion
The Voyager Company	514 Market Loop, Ste. 103 West Dundee, IL 60118 847-428-2184	*To New Horizons (1931-45); You Can't Get There from Here (1946-1960)* QuickTime
Xiphias	8758 Venice Blvd. Los Angeles, CA 90034 310-841-2790	*Time Table of History: Science and Innovation; American Heritage Illustrated Encyclopedic Dictionary* CDTV

Source: *Technology and Learning* (February 1991 and April 1992).

Resources

Books

Ellsworth, Jill H. *Education on the Internet: A Hands-on Book of Ideas, Resources, Projects, and Advice*. Indianapolis: Sam's Publishing, 1994.

Felix, Kathie, ed. *Only the Best: Annual Guide to the Highest Rated Educational Software and Multimedia*. Alexandria, VA: Association of Curriculum and Supervision Development, 1996.

Glassbrenner, Alfred. *Little Online Book: A Gentle Introduction to Modems, Online Services, Electronic Bulletin Boards, and the Internet*. Berkeley: Peachpit Press, 1994.

Johnson, Judi Mathis, ed. *The 1996 Educational Software Preview Guide*. Eugene, OR: International Society for Technology in Education, 1996.

Leshin, Cynthia B. *Internet Adventures: Step-by-Step Guide to Finding and Using Educational Resources, Version 1.2*. Boston: Allyn & Bacon, 1995.

Williams, David B., and Peter R. Webster. *Experiencing Music Technology*. New York: Schirmer Books, 1996. (See Viewpoints I, VIII, and IX for elaborations on elements of using instructional technology for networking and multimedia including the Internet, as well as guidelines for using operating systems and system software efficiently. A CD-ROM of tutorial and demonstration software is also available.)

Online Services

America Online	800–827–6364 or Web page: **http://www.aol.com**
Prodigy	Web page: **http://www.prodigy.com**
CompuServe	Web page: **http://world.compuserve.com**

Journals

The National Council for the Social Studies produces two journals that have sections in each issue that provide resources on instructional technology. Look at the "Media Corner" section in *Social Studies and the Young Learner*, a journal intended for elementary school teachers. The "Instructional Technology" section of *Social Education* includes not only reviews of software and articles on using technology, but a monthly feature on the Internet as an instructional tool.

Social Education and *Social Studies and the Young Learner*
National Council for the Social Studies
3501 Newark St. NW
Washington, D.C. 20016–3167
202–966–7840

Learning and Leading with Technology: The ISTE Journal of Educational Technology and Practice and Policy, which has a special section on social studies.
International Society for Technology in Education
1787 Agate St.
Eugene, OR 97403–1923
541–346–4414, 800–336–5191
        Or contact Tony Foy, the Director of Marketing Services, through e-mail:
Tony_Foy@ccmail.uoregon.edu

NetGuide: The Guide to the Internet and Online Services
P.O. Box 420355
Palm Coast, FL 32142–9371

Electronic Learning
Scholastic, Inc.
555 Broadway
New York, NY 10012
212–505–4900

Phi Delta Kappan: "Power Tools" is a column that provides a brief but informative look at the latest in technology and education.
Phi Delta Kappan
P.O. Box 789
Bloomington, IN 47402–0789
812–339–1156

An electronic journal called *Computers and Social Studies Journal* can be found at **http://www.cssjournal.com/journal/welcome.html**

Other Resources

HyperCard Stacks

"Alternate Models for Treating Value Conflicts in the Classroom: A Hypermedia Unit" (1996).
Junior high–college level
Professor Timothy H. Little
Michigan State University
452 Erickson Hall
East Lansing, MI 48824
517–355–4501
e-mail: timlittl@pilot.msu.edu

"Cool Moves: Teaching Geography and History with a *HyperCard* Stack" (1995).
Junior high–college level
Richard Adams
Pleasant Hill High School
Pleasant Hill, OR 97455
541–747–4541
radams@lane.k12.or.us

Newsletters

Children's Software is a newsletter for parents or teachers; it includes software reviews and articles about using technology. Write to:

Children's Software
Diane Kendall, Editor
720 Kuhlman
Houston, TX 77024
713–467–8686

CUE Newsletter
Computer-Using Educators
4655 Old Ironsides Dr.
Santa Clara, CA 95054
408–496–2955

Workshops

Some vendors (such as Tom Snyder Productions and Pierian Springs) offer workshops that focus on using their products proficiently. Contact the vendor directly for additional information about upcoming training opportunities.

Conferences

NCSS has a technology lab at its annual national conference in November where the latest software is available and workshops and clinics are held for using technology more effectively. Regional conferences are usually held in the spring and often have a technology lab as part of the program. There is also a special interest group (CASE-SIG) within the NCSS devoted to computer technology. You can contact the NCSS through its Web site (see the "Internet Sites" section below for the URL) or by contacting the national office. (Look under the "Journals" section in this chapter for information regarding this organization.)

ISTE is an excellent source of information and resources for teachers. It sponsors an annual National Educational Computing conference every June, and it publishes a number of useful books and journals, including *Learning and Leading with Technology*. (See the "Journals" section in this chapter for information regarding this organization.)

▬ Internet Sites ▬▬▬▬▬▬▬▬▬▬▬▬▬▬▬▬▬▬▬▬▬▬▬

One of the authors maintains a Web site that is used as part of an elementary social studies methods course. It includes strategies for content area readings with coalmining as the theme. The URL is **http://coe.ilstu.edu/jabraun/socialstudies/coalmining/ welcome.html**.

Two professors at Illinois State, Larry McBride and Fred Drake, together with John Craig from the Illinois State Department of Education Office of Assessment, helped produce a particularly useful site for alternative assessment (Illinois Department of Education Office of Assessment, 1996). It should be noted that this site is considered in progress; i.e., the developers are seeking additional examples of student multimedia products for assessment. All examples of student products were done with pencil and paper, and while they provide good nontechnical examples of student responses and teacher evaluation, they do not reflect the type of work students are doing with multimedia and hypertext environments. This site contains links for e-mail addresses so teachers can contribute multimedia examples and increase the information base for this site. The URL is **http://www.coe.ilstu.edu/jabraun/socialstudies/assessment**.

Favorite Sites for History	
American History Archives Project	**http://www.ilt.columbia.edu/k12/history/demo.html**
American Memory Collection	**http://rs6.loc.gov/amhome.html**
Ancient Cultures	**http://eawc.evansville.edu/index.htm**
Holocaust Museum	**http://www.ushmm.org**
Immigrations	**http://www.bergen.org/AAST/Projects/Immigration/index.html**
The Middle Ages	**http://www.burbank.k12.ca.us/%7Eluther/midages/beginhere.html**
Seven Wonders of the World	**http://pharos.bu.edu/Egypt/Wonders**
Web Chronologies and Timelines	**http://humanitas.ucsb.edu/projects/pack/rom-chrono/others.htm**

Favorite Sites for Geography	
FishNet	**http://fishnet.org**
GeoGame Project	**http://www.tapr.org/%7Eird/Nordick/Standards.html**
The GlobaLearn Classroom	**http://www.globalearn.org/expeditions/brazil/classroom/index.html**
The Mining Company	**http://geography.miningco.com**
Trike Trek Virtual Adventure	**http://www.bitech.com/triketrek/index.html**
USA CityLink	**http://www.usacitylink.com/default.html**

Favorite Sites for Law and Government	
Character above All: An Exploration of Presidential Leadership	**http://www.pbs.org/newshour/character/index.html**
Civics at Work	**http://206.106.95.11:80/groups/civics/links.htm**
Democracy and the National Debt	**http://www.kn.pacbell.com/wired/democracy/debtquest.html**
Kids Voting USA	**http://www.kidsvotingusa.org**
Thomas Legislative Information on the Internet	**http://thomas.loc.gov**
Washington State Courts Page	**http://www.wa.gov/courts/educate/lessons/lpmiddle.htm**

Social Studies Councils Maintaining Web Sites	
Illinois Council for the Social Studies	http://www.wiu.edu/users/mficss/icss.htm
National Council for the Social Studies	http://www.ari.net/online
Ohio Council for the Social Studies	http://www.iac.net/~pfilio
Southeast Regional Council for the Social Studies	http://Class%20D2/Public%20Folder
Washington Council for the Social Studies	http://www.learningspace.org/socialstudies

References

Grolier's Encyclopedia is the online *Academic American Encyclopedia*. It is the equivalent of a 20-volume printed encyclopedia. Telnet to: **victor.umd.edu**.

Login: **pac**. Select **5** (VT100) as your terminal type. Then go to **4** to access categories of other libraries in the state of Maryland; go to **94** to access the Baltimore County Public Library; go to **4** to access information databases; go to **48** to access *Grolier's Encyclopedia*.

Other Internet Links for Social Studies

NCSS Online is the homepage for the NCSS. It contains information about the organization as well upcoming events, special publications, and links to other Web sites. The URL for this site is **http://www.ari.net/online**.

Resources for Teaching K–12 Social Studies is a homepage maintained by one of the authors. Of particular note is a link to a great Web site on alternative assessment produced by the Illinois State Department of Education. The URL is **http://coe.ilstu.edu/jabraun/braun/professional/sslinks.html**.

Social Studies Sources includes a wide variety of categorized sites that are useful to all social studies teachers—a good first step into Internet resources for teachers. The page covers these topics: classroom-based Internet projects, cultural diversity, general good starting points, general history, geography/culture, government/politics, new sites on the Internet, news sources, peace/conflict, professional development, social studies listservs, U.S. history, and world history. The URL is **http://education.indiana.edu/~socialst**.

ERIC/ChESS is the Clearinghouse for Social Studies Education. It provides a comprehensive collection of resources and research reports related to social studies education. A valuable source for information about a variety of topics and issues. The URL is **http://www.indiana.edu/~ssdc/eric-chess.html**.

Social Studies Resources is a site started a number of years ago in Washington by Howard Levin and now maintained at Indiana University by Fred Risinger, a former president of NCSS. This site has been an award-winning repository for a number of years. The URL is **http://education.indiana.edu/~socialst/**.

History/Social Studies Web Site for K–12 attempts to make the Internet accessible for busy social studies teachers and encourages the use of the Web as a tool for learning and teaching. The documents, links, and text files listed in the various categories provide help for classroom teachers (especially at the middle and secondary level) in locating and using Internet resources in the classroom. The URL is **http://www.execpc.com/~dboals**.

Social Science Resources Homepage includes the official definition for social studies and a listing of the 10 themes in the K–12 social studies framework. Each theme has links to supporting resources and lesson plans. The URL is **http://www.nde.state.ne.us/SS/ ss.html**.

Galaxy—Social Sciences covers the following topics: academic organizations, anthropology, collections, communication, directories, documents, education, geography, history, library and information science, nonprofit organizations, political science, psychology, social science—listservs, and sociology. The URL is **http://doradus.einet.net/ galaxy/Social-Sciences.html**.

Northwest Territories Social Studies Links include the following links: AskERIC, DeweyWeb, Educom, environmental education, history/social studies Web page for teachers, K–12 education, NASA Aerospace Education Services Program, National Space Simulations Project, SchoolNet, Telecomputing Network's Academy One Program for Schools, The Commonwealth of Learning Homepage, and using technology in education. The URL is **http://www.learnnet.nt.ca/SocStudies/main.html**.

World Wide Web Resources—Social Studies provides links for the following topics: ACLU, African-American resources, aged/aging, American Civil Liberties Union, Ancient World Web, anthropology, Appalachian resources, broadcasting and media, business, child development, communications, countries, ecology, economics, education, ethnography, Europe, family studies, finance, general social sciences, geography, Hispanic resources, history, human environmental sciences, journalism, kinesiology, library science, maps, political science, psychology, public administration, research engines for the social sciences from the Universal Codex for the Social Sciences, resources, Social Sciences Data Collection, Social Sciences Information Gateway, Social Sciences Virtual Library, social work, sociology, sports medicine, telecommunication, The Action Coalition, U.S. Government, women's studies, and the University of California. The URL is **http:// www.uky.edu/Subject/social-sciences.html**.

WebEc—Social Sciences provides links to Collections, Data, Social Sciences Guides, and Other Social Science Services. The URL is **http://www.helsinki.fi/WebEc/webeczs.html**.

Eastchester Middle School provides links to American History (American Civil War Homepage, Civil War Page, National Museum of the American Indian, and United States historic documents), current events and today's news (ABC TV's Behind the News, B/CS Presidential Campaign Tour and Opinion Page, BosniaLINK, CNN Interactive, Countdown '96 Homepage, Election '96, Election '96 Homepage, Internet CNN Newsroom, NBC News, National Public Radio Online, Public Broadcasting System Online, *Time* World Wide Web Homepage, USA Today, Sole Site of the 1996 Presidential Campaign, Yahoo: 1996 United States Elections: Presidential Election, 1996 Presidential Election Material, 1996 Presidential Candidates), maps and flags (City.Net, flags, maps, maps of the United States, United States of America and state flags, Virtual Tourist World Map, world flags, and World Map Viewer), museums and libraries (Federal Bureau of Investigation, historic United States documents, how to write your members of Congress, Library of Congress World Wide Web Homepage, The Smithsonian Institution Homepage, the United States Senate, THOMAS: Legislative Information on the Internet, United States Federal Government Central Intelligence Agency Homepage, United States Constitution, United States Holocaust Memorial Museum, United States House of Representatives Homepage, White House, and Yahoo: Presidential Libraries), world history (1492: An Ongoing Voyage, Ancient Egyptian Digital Mummies, archaeology and adventure, United Nations, World War II: 50 Years Ago, and World War II: The World Remembers). The URL is **http://www.westnet.com/~rickd/Kids.html**.

Educational Newsgroups includes social studies and history curricula for grades K–12. The URL is **gopher://news:k12.ed.soc-studies**.

Educational Listservs

The e-mail address where you send a subscription for a listserv generally contains a name different from the actual name of the list. To subscribe, leave the subject line blank and enter only the following in the body of the message: **SUBSCRIBE <name of the listserv> your name**.

To join the listserv for the National Council for the Social Studies, send e-mail to **listproc@bgu.edu** with **SUBSCRIBE NCSS-L your name** in the body of the message.

There is a Web site that provides a database of different listservs. The URL is **http://www.indiana.edu/~eric_rec/comat/lstsrvs.html**.

― Links for Teaching Materials ―――――――――

Busy Teachers' Web Site: The URL is **http://www.ceismc.gatech.edu/BusyT/TOC.html**.

Cisco Educational Archives: The URL is **http://sunsite.unc.edu:80/cisco/web-arch.html**.

New Media Classroom: The URL is **http://chnm.gmu.edu/chnm/nmc**.

American Memory—The Library of Congress: The URL is **http://rs6.loc.gov**.

ASCII

The standard for digitizing text that allows the same files to be read on DOS, Macintosh, or UNIX machines.

BTW

An e-mail abbreviation that stands for "by the way."

bandwidth

The quantity of data that can be transmitted in a given amount of time. A T1 line can transmit about 1.544 megabits per second (Mbps); the phone line in your house can transmit about 1/10 of that amount of data. Bandwidths are like pipelines through which bits of information are transmitted.

binary files

Files in a form readable only by a program, as opposed to simple text files. These files are often executable or program files, but they can also be data files in a particular format.

browser

Software, such as Netscape Navigator or Microsoft Internet Explorer, that allows one to view the World Wide Web.

CGI scripts

The Common Gateway Interface provides a way for Web servers to run applications as requested by Web clients, i.e., browsers. CGI scripts (short programs) allow for the processing of forms that can send e-mail, search pages, and perform a variety of other tasks.

client

A computer program that is capable of accessing information from another computer (server) on the Internet.

cyberspace

A concept that embodies the collapse of time and space as irrelevant dimensions when telecommunicating by computer.

download

To transfer files from a remote computer to your own desktop for printing, viewing, or accomplishing other tasks with them.

emoticon

Small graphical rendering composed of ASCII characters, which substitute for facial expressions and body language. Common examples are a smiley face :) and an unhappy face : (and a smug expression : > and sealed lips :X.

FAQ

Frequently asked questions; a file that provides new users with general questions and answers about a specific topic.

FTP

File transfer protocol; a method for moving text, audio, or graphic image files from one computer to another. FTP is a useful and necessary tool for transferring information available on the Internet to your own computer.

flame

A sharp retort or criticism (even insult) that is sent among newsgroup readers as a rejoinder to a posting that is deemed stupid. Flaming can also be inspired by a breach of netiquette.

GIF

Graphic Interchange Format; an image format designed to make files as small as possible for transmitting over modem connections. It is popular on bulletin board services (BBSs), and on the Web it is most often used for inline images. This format uses lossless compression, i.e., there is no loss of image quality during compression and decompression. (JPEG is another format for compressing graphic images.)

GUI

Graphical user interface; the screen representation of programs and commands as icons. Graphical representations (icons), pull-down menus, and windows replaced text commands and function keys, making computers easier to use.

Gopher

A client/server that was created at the University of Minnesota. Until the onset of the WWW, it was one of the most popular ways to surf the Internet. Thousands of Gopher sites are available on different servers throughout the world, and the client/software uses a menu system for providing access.

helpers (viewers)

Most browsers use helper applications, sometimes called "viewers," to display full-size graphics and play sound and video clips. These are separate applications that the browser initiates after it has downloaded the image or clip. These applications generally need to be acquired separately. The most complete collection of these applications is at **ftp.ncsa.uiuc.edu** in the /Web/Mosaic/ Mac/Helpers, /Web/Mosaic/UNIX/ viewers, and /Web/Mosaic/Windows/ viewers directories.

hosts file

Trumpet Winsock uses a simple text file called "hosts" (no extension) that resides in the Winsock directory. This file is used to resolve IP addresses and is more efficient than looking up a name with a DNS on the Internet. Since the name is resolved on your computer, it minimizes the drain on network resources. You should determine the numeric IP address of any addresses you use frequently and enter them into this file.

HTML

Hypertext Markup Language; the formatting language of the World Wide Web. It consists of a variety of codes, or tags, that are inserted into text files so that WWW browsers can display documents properly after they have been transferred.

HTTP

Hypertext Transfer Protocol; the method used to transfer hypertext documents over the World Wide Web.

IMHO

An e-mail abbreviation that stands for "in my humble opinion."

IP address

Internet Protocol address; the unique address assigned to a networked computer. Usually, it is represented in dotted decimal notation, which is the syntactic representation for a 32-bit integer that consists of four 8-bit numbers written in base 10 with periods separating them. The IP address is important when trying to establish a telecommunications link from a home modem to a server.

Java

A sophisticated programming language that increases interactivity between the Internet user and a Web page.

MPEG

Moving Picture Expert Group; a file format for digitized video clips created by this group within the International Standards Organization (ISO). This format consists of a set of complex algorithms that provide varying degrees of compression.

NCSA

National Center for Supercomputing Applications; the home of the first Mosaic client for browsing the WWW. The URL for NCSA is **http://www.ncsa.uiuc.edu**.

NNTP

Network News Transfer Protocol; the protocol used by newsreaders (Usenet clients) to retrieve messages from Usenet servers.

netiquette

Originally coined by users of Usenet, this term describes expectations for decorous behavior while using the Internet. Having a signature for your e-mail of no more than four lines is an example of proper netiquette. A complete guide can be found at **news.announce.newusers**.

newbie

A slightly derogatory term used to describe an Internet user who has not bothered to learn netiquette.

OTFL

An e-mail abbreviation that stands for "on the floor laughing."

POP

Post Office Protocol; the protocol used by mail clients to retrieve messages from a mail server.

private room

Real-time chat room where only invited users can communicate.

public room

Real-time chat room where anyone can participate.

ROTFL

An e-mail abbreviation that stands for "rolling on the floor laughing."

real-time chat

A conversation between Internet users in which e-mail messages are encoded and received simultaneously. Like a phone call that uses text instead of voice, the exchange has somewhat of a lag time.

server

A computer that provides stored data and files to client workstations in a network.

shareware

Independently written, copyrighted software that is distributed on a try-now, pay-later basis that works on the principle of honesty. The author shares his or her work with you but asks you to send them some monetary compensation if you want to keep using their software. A common way for software to be downloaded from the Internet.

TCP/IP

Transmission Control Protocol/Internet Protocol; a suite of protocols that computers on the Internet and many smaller networks use for communication, error correction, and retransmission of data. It was originally developed by the United States government's Advanced Research Projects Agency (ARPA).

UNIX

An operating system that runs on various computers and is popular with high-end computer users, academics, and the research community. Many servers are UNIX machines. The syntax of UNIX is similar to MS-DOS—a tree-structured file system that is not very user-friendly.

URL

Uniform resource locater; the address used to access a page on the WWW. The general syntax for a URL is **scheme:// host/path/filename**.

WYSIWYG

What you see is what you get; an interface that allows authors to see what their printed documents will look like while they are editing them on the computer screen. Different Web browsers will display the same HTML document in different formats; thus WYSIWYG doesn't always hold true.